Paul Broca and the Origins of Language in the Brain

BROCA

Paul Broca and the Origins of Language in the Brain

Leonard L. LaPointe, PhD

PLURAL
PUBLISHING
INC.

SAN DIEGO
OXFORD
MELBOURNE

PLURAL PUBLISHING
INC.

5521 Ruffin Road
San Diego, CA 92123

e-mail: info@pluralpublishing.com
Web site: http://www.pluralpublishing.com

49 Bath Street
Abingdon, Oxfordshire OX14 1EA
United Kingdom

Library of Congress Cataloging-in-Publication Data

LaPointe, Leonard L.
  Paul Broca and the origins of language in the brain / Leonard L. LaPointe.
— 1st ed.
      p. ; cm.
  Includes bibliographical references and index.
  ISBN-13: 978-1-59756-478-6 (alk. paper)
  ISBN-10: 1-59756-478-8 (alk. paper)
  I. Title.
  [DNLM: 1. Broca, Paul, 1824-1880. 2. Neurology—France—Biography.
3. History, 19th Century—France. 4. Neurology—history—France.
5. Neurosciences—history—France. WZ 100]
  LC Classification not assigned
  616.80092—dc23
  [B]
                                        2012022840

Contents

Preface   *ix*
Acknowledgments   *xiii*

Chapter 1. Précis   1

Chapter 2. Early Times: Deep Sulci of History   9
  Descartes: Reason and the Scientific Method   14

Chapter 3. Phrenology and Serendipitous Bumps   25
  Franz Joseph Gall   25
    Time Line of Phrenology   27
  Phrenology's Principles   35
  Faculties and Head Bumps   36
  Terms Used to Differentiate the Sizes of Organs   45
      According to George Combe (1853)
  Spurzheim's Tour   46
  Flourens   47
  Sex and Amativeness   52
  The American Tour   54
  The Combe Brothers   57

Chapter 4. Relics of Aphasia: The Artifacts of Lost Words   67
  Liepmann and Apraxia   72
  Time for Lichtheim   74
  Strange Words Recalled in Literature   77
  Larrey: An Unlikely Aphasiologist   78
  Lordat: *Alalia* and Early Accounts of Aphasia   83
  Bateman, Leeches, and Other Novel Descriptions   86
      of Aphasia

Chapter 5. Turmoil, Revolt, and Enlightenment: 101
Historical Context for Advances in Brain Science
  A Wondrous and Dreadful Machine   103
    Dr. Guillotin: Severer of French Heads   103
    A Look of Astonishment   105
  French Turbulence: Kings and Revolutions   107
  Napoleon and the 19th Century   111

Chapter 6. Cortical Localization of Function   115
  Jean-Baptiste Bouillaud: The Anterior Lobes   116
  Bouillaud's Alleged Folly   123
  Simon Alexandre Ernest Aubertin and the   127
      Catalytic Spatula Case
  Gratiolet: Adversary of Aubertin and Broca   129
  British Expansions on Cortical Localization of Function   131
  Stendhal's Shrunken Testicles and Transient Aphasia   134
  Finger and the Debates   135
  1861: A Year Laden with Historical Episodes   137
  Prodigious Debates: The Brain and Its Doings   140
  Broca Listens   142

Chapter 7. Broca's Nascent Years   145
  The Caves   145
  The Brocas and Huguenot Persecution   146
  Broca's Village   148
  Broca's Historians   149
  Broca's Lineage   151
  Happy Birthday to Paul   152
  Samuel-Jean Pozzi, Eulogist, Biographer, and Rake   154
  Paul Prodigy   158
  Broca Leaves Home   160
  A Carriage Ride and a Thinker   160
  Savants Move to Paris: Again, the Brain and Art   161

Chapter 8. Medical Student and Developing Dissident   165
  On the Rues Where He Lived   170
  Carl Sagan   170
  History   172
  Clinical Education   173
  Fetid Tonsils and Insurrection   176

Chapter 9. A Massive Thesis and Graduation   181
  Culmination of Medical Studies   181
  Finally and Efficiently, A Doctor   182
  Freethinkers Society   185
  Life in Paris   186
  Paris Makeover   188
  Wife in Paris   191
  Art, Violin, and Iodine   193
  Mme. Augustine Broca   194

Chapter 10. Landmark Cases: M. Leborgne and M. Lelong   197
  The Legendary French Brains   205
  Leborgne   207
  Conclusions After Examining "Tan" Leborgne's Brain   212
  Lelong   218
  Pictures at an Exhibition   220
  Broca on Language, Articulated Speech, and Aphemia   225
  Precedence and the Pair a Dax   237
  Much Earlier Precedence on Hemispheric Specialization   239
    and Localization

Chapter 11. Broca's Auxiliary Contributions   243
  Priority and Precedence with a Modicum of   244
    Appreciation
  Limbic System   244
  Cancer   246
  Broca and Handedness   248
  Anthropology   248
  The French Anthropology Society: A Venue for   250
    Pioneering Presentations and Debate
  School of Anthropology   252
  Cornflowers and Hybrids   253
  Genetic Interruption   255
  Anthropometry and Cephalametrics   260
  Controversy and Racism   262
    The Full Moon, Interpretation, and Refutability   267
  Neuroimaging and Broca's Thermometric Crown   269
  Trepanation and Surgery   271
  The French Senate   275

Chapter 12. Broca's Legacy   281
  Broca's Death   281
  Eulogies and Biographies   282

Appendix A. Green Translation of Broca's 1861 Paper   *289*
on the Faculty of Articulated Language

Appendix B. Broca Time Line (2012)   *319*

Appendix C. Editorial—Broca's Brain: Brother,   *321*
Wherefore Art Thou?

Appendix D. Permission to Access the Collections of the   327
Musee de l'Homme, Paris

References   329

Index   345

Preface

The days flow ever on
The weeks pass by in vain
Time never will return
Nor our loves burn again
Below the Pont Mirabeau
Slow flows the Seine

As sung by The Pogues on their album *Pogue Mahone;*
based on the poem *Pont Mirabeau*
by French poet Guillaume Apollinaire

The Seine indeed flows on and with it time. But we have ways of retrieving the past and time can truly return if we do not neglect the threads of our childhood and of history. We may learn and be inspired by the giants of the past, upon whose shoulders we stand and upon whose work our contemporary bridges are built. Pierre Paul Broca, the 19th century giant of brain science, surgery, and anthropology, never tired of discovering and presenting, in exquisite detail, noteworthy and curious case reports. At the end of his brilliant career and barely four months before his death in 1880, he was unearthing fanciful and intriguing cases of people whose behaviors boggled the minds of contemporaries. Witness his own words from a lecture to his colleagues, an audience of esteemed physicians and professors, at the meeting of a learned society in Paris on March 4, 1880. This presentation was entitled "On the Illiterate Child, Named Jacques Arnodi, Gifted with the Faculty of Performing Very Complicated Calculations."

Messiers: . . . As you see, this [11-year-old] child, named Jacques Arnodi, is also with us here today. He was born in Coni (Piedmont), but has mainly lived in the south of France. He accompanies his father, a street organ player, asking for coins. For the last few months he's been living with his older brother who is a waiter at a cafe in Marseille. The habitués of the cafe learned that this boy knows how to do calculations in his head. They amuse themselves by posing questions to him, making him do large multiplications or having him extract square roots and cube roots; and whenever he astonishes them, they give him a reward. (Broca, 1880)

Broca proceeded to speculate on how this remarkable skill was accomplished by the mind of this illiterate boy, who gathered coins in a cup to his father's organ grinding not unlike the task usually assigned to a monkey. But this remarkable coin-collecting 11-year-old sheltered unexplored and unexplained secrets of brain and mind. Broca could not explain it then, but he suspected someday, someone would. Even today we have only rudimentary understanding of what is happening in the minds of savants, those extraordinary persons who display implausible mental feats. The savant studied the savant. Once again, Broca appeared to be way ahead of his time and of the wave crest of contemporary understanding of brain and mind issues.

But this was not to be the only or the most famous case presentation of Paul Broca. As will be elucidated in these pages, Broca truly was a savant in the sense of the French use of the word. He was a gifted and prodigious contributor to many aspects of brain, medical, and behavioral science. He was a philosopher and a great and free thinker who plied his trade amid social and political storms and turmoil, a context that makes his contributions even more remarkable. Few realize that amid his over 500 published scientific contributions, he reported and speculated about the rare condition in which people with "developmental delays" of the brain (notably on the autism spectrum), or those who suffer rare and selected types of brain injury, demonstrate profound and prodigious capacities and abilities far in excess of those considered normal. Few realize that Broca was an inveterate inventor and pioneered the development of cephalometric gadgets or of the thermometric crown, which made use of measures of scalp temperature for the early diagnosis of brain lesions. Few realize that Broca was a prodigious contributor to the study of arterial aneurysms and to the genetics of cancer. Few realize that Broca played the horn and almost had it confiscated when it arrived at his Paris flat and he, overjoyed, exuberantly blew it into the night until finally being silenced by a gendarme.

By far the most recognized and perhaps important contribution of Pierre Paul Broca would be his famous case reports of 1861, where he for the first time linked clinicopathological evidence from his patients Leborgne and Lelong on the relationship between speech, language, and a relatively circumscribed area of the brain. This is what he is most known for, and this is the contribution that led to a selected area of the left hemisphere of the cerebral cortex to be named "Broca's Area." It must be quite a distinction to have a star or astronomical body named after an explorer or scientist. Perhaps it is even more of an honor to have one's name attached to an area of the brain, that seat of everything that is human. Broca's methods were unique and indeed a milestone in neural science, but the idea that localization of functions and even speech preceded him. The work of Descartes, Gall, Larrey, and especially Broca's French contemporaries Bouillaud and Aubertin all have their place in the history of advances in the understanding of brain and cortical localization of human functions. But Broca's work was distinctive. His work championed new and revolutionary methods and served as a wellspring for future advances of interpretation of brain-behavior riddles.

Mapping the human brain, especially for complex and higher level functions such as elements of cognition and language, is a prickly task. No doubt advances in brain imaging and other exciting futuristic methods will reveal these complexities and pitfalls. The future is now, and we appear to be on the threshold of amazing discoveries in this vast murk of what has been for so many centuries terra incognita. Progress in technology, including functional imaging, electrophysiologic studies, perfusion imaging, diffusion tensor imaging, and the wonderful world of magnets and transcranial magnetic stimulation, have led to novel visions about the relationships between language and the brain. This unfolding understanding, not unlike the furled convolutions of the brain itself, along with ever more sophisticated mathematical and computational models of language processes, will no doubt converge on the view that a given language task must rely on a complex set of cognitive processes and representations carried out by an intricate network of neural regions working together; and that restitution of fractured language can call into play previously veiled principles of neural plasticity, including synaptogenesis and changes in neural architecture. This is our future. But future neurocognitive scientists and all those who have fought the upstream current of brain damage and language loss will be forever beholden to 1861 and the remarkable work of that French savant whose name is emblazoned on the Eiffel Tower, Broca.

REFERENCES

Broca, P. (1880). "On the Illiterate Child, Named Jacques Arnodi, Gifted with the Faculty of Performing Very Complicated Calculations." Transcript of the March 4, 1880, Meeting of the Anthropological Society of Paris. Retrieved May 9, 2012, from http://www.archive.org/details/ReminiscencesOfAFrequenterToThe1878-1881MettingsOfThe AnthropologySocietyofParis

Acknowledgments

I am indebted to Philippe Mennecier, Charge de Conservation des collections d'anthropologie biologuique, Musée national d'histoire naturelle, Musée de l'Homme, Paris. I am indebted to the Museum of Natural History, Paris, for permission to access the collections from the former Broca Museum and the collections of materials on Broca, Gall, and others scientists important to the history of localization of brain and language. To examine the skulls of Rene Descartes and Franz Josef Gall and the artifacts of facial masks and casts important to anthropological milestones was exhilarating. I am grateful to the Museum of Natural History for permission to reprint images from their impressive collections. Most of the images in this book are the result of my personal photography in Paris, but images reproduced from the Museum of Natural History collection are specifically indicated.

I met Dr. Mennecier, a noted anthropological linguist, on our first visit to the Musée de l'Homme in 2009. Dr. Mennecier facilitated approval from French authorities for my visit and access to relevant collections in the museum. He and his staff met with me on many occasions during my two-month visit in the summer of 2011. I am deeply grateful to his staff (especially Aurélie Fort and Véronique LaBord) and to Dr. Mennecier for orienting and escorting me through the collections.

I am grateful as well to Patrick Conan, Assistant Curator of the Dupuytren Museum, for his help during many visits to this special holding place of the brains of M. Leborgne and M. Lelong, Broca's extraordinary patients.

Finally, I would like to thank the very gracious and helpful Yamile and Stephane, from whom we rented the lovely Paris Sweet 36 flat, perfectly positioned to allow ready access to the museums, the wonderful open air markets of Rue Mouffetard and Place Monge, and the ghosts of Hemingway and his cohorts on Place Contrescarpe.

This book is dedicated to my beloved nephew Kyle Stewart LaPointe (1981–2011) and to his parents, Thomas and Kathryn LaPointe, who gave him the most enriched and noble life possible. All kids with physical challenges should be so lucky.

May all those who have central nervous system disorders endure them with as much perseverance, good humor, word play, and grace as Kyle did.

He will be forever missed but never forgotten.

Chapter 1

Précis

Impressionism, one of the most dominant developments in French painting in the 19th century, was a reaction against academic tradition, romanticism, and the startling influences of the technological invention of the camera. No longer were careful realistic painters the only ones who could render precise reflections of reality. The camera provided true-to-life portraits, landscapes, and documentation of events with efficiency and economy of effort. The term *impressionism* was derived from a painting by Claude Monet — *Impression: Sunrise* (1872, Musée Marmottan, Paris; Figure 1–1), a view of the port of Le Havre in the mist — and was coined for this group of artists by the less than friendly critic Louis Leroy. Monet probably intended his title for the remarkable Le Havre sunrise to refer to the sketchy, unfinished look of the work, similar to receiving an impression of something on the basis of an exposure that is partially obscured and incomplete in its detail. The term, however, was quickly taken up by compassionate critics, who used it in an alternative sense to mean the impression stamped on the senses by a visual experience that is rapid and transitory, associated with a particular moment in time, not unlike the fleeting, immediate sensory memory we get from our filtered and rapid perceptions of the world. Monet, Renoir, Pissarro, and Sisley were incredibly talented artists who perfected this sense impression style of art. Beginning in the later 1860s and culminating in 1872 to 1875,

Figure 1–1. *Claude Monet,* Impression: Sunrise *(1872), Musee Marmottan, Paris. A view of the port of Le Havre in the mist.*

they chose to paint outdoors (*en plein air*), recording the rapidly changing conditions of light and atmosphere as well as their individual sensations of nature. They used brilliant colors and a variety of brushstrokes, which allowed them to be responsive both to the material character and texture of the object in nature and to the impact of light on its surfaces (Rosenblum, 1989).

Other French brains were beginning to make their mark as well. Not on art, but on the then mystical world of neuroscience; and the enchanted universe of human language and the communication of ideas. It would be generations before this science evolved and benefited from the remarkable camera technology that allowed the actions and functions of the brain to be recorded in realtime, noninvasive ways. But other French brains were at work, questioning, observing, and developing early empirical observation techniques that allowed us to better understand ourselves. One of these remarkable scientists, who curiously labored during the same general 19th century time frame as the impressionist painters, was Pierre Paul Broca, a child prodigy who fulfilled his promise by becoming a brilliant neurologist, surgeon, anthropologist, and more. He was surrounded temporally and in proximity by a number of other philosophers, thinkers, and scientists who would handle, examine, and interpret brains from their patients. The artists and scientists of this era had another shared characteristic. The context in which they labored was tumultuous. Political and social unrest was rife in France for most of the 19th century. Many historians have noted these difficult times and it is remarkable how much was accomplished in the arts and in science against the backdrop of this grueling turbulence. This bewildering era was characterized by seesaw-like periods of stability, uprisings, monarchies, empires, republics, abject poverty of the masses, and opulent wealth by the nobles and the aristocracy. Despite these troubled waters, French brains managed to fashion useful sailcloth. Those who steered and pulled the oars of the ferryboats of progress coped well and persevered. Magnificent headway was cataloged in French culture and in intellectual development. The intellectual fleet of French brains was prolific in the middle and late 1800s, and art and science would never be the same.

My personal visits to the museums of Paris in the summer of 2011 have crystalized my admiration of these French brains. The startling impressions of Monet's lilies in the *Musée d'Orsay* and the delicate convolutions, floating still in formalin, of Leborgne's brain in the *Musée Dupuytren* at the University of Paris School of Medicine have created this synapse of French thought and art, both of which would have profound influences on everything thereafter.

This convergence of developments in impressionistic art and the science of the brain was shared and discussed with my colleague and good friend in the Program in Neuroscience and College of Medicine at Florida State University in this summer of 2011. Dr. Charles Ouimet, a noted researcher on brain function, has an abiding interest in the history of neuroscience as well. His laboratory, amid the azaleas and cardinals of the new medical school in Tallahassee, conducts research on recovery of function after brain damage from Alzheimer's disease, stroke, or trauma. His lab works on growing dendritic spines, small protrusions from dendritic shafts on which synaptic contacts are made with other neurons. This work has important implications for issues of neuroplasticity and changes in neural architecture and connectivity as a result of experience or treatment. We relished some shared time, along with our Francophile wives, Janice and Corinne, at the Musée Dupuytren, the Musée d' Orsay, and Bouillon Racine art nouveau restaurant this summer in Paris and enjoyed our discussions of the historic overlap of developments and radical departures on the topic of brain and water lilies. Ouimet (2011) commented as follows:

> It is interesting that the development of both Monet's (et al.) and Broca's work required a sharp break with tradition. And it also fascinates me that both Monet and Broca spoke to us about brain function. To me, Broca's larger contribution (broader than the discovery that a specific lump of brain was needed for the production of speech) was the very discovery of functional neuroanatomy. Monet's insight was that the visual brain was capable of constructing (startlingly beautiful) images, seemingly concrete and whole, from daubs of paint on canvass that when viewed up close were meaningless.
>
> This stands as a metaphor for the brain's amazing ability to make mass synaptic activity sensible in the face of the meaninglessness of the individual daubs of electrical activity bursting at each synaptic connection.

Broca fulfilled his promise and his potential was pollinated and nurtured by others. Broca and his work were conducted and vetted during a firestorm of intellectual and scientific debates on the relationship between head size, brain weight, and intelligence; and on the whereabouts of human reasoning, thought, and higher cerebral functions in the brain. Perhaps, Broca's most lasting contribution to neuroscience was his proposal that the third frontal convolution of the left cerebral hemisphere of the brain is the seat of that most human attribute, the production of articulate speech and language. This notion was advanced by detailing the autopsy findings, with quite evident lesions, in the brains of his two now famous cases, M. Leborgne (known as "Tan," for that is all he could say) and M. Lelong. These case presentations were made at the Society of Anthropology in Paris in 1861 amid the milieu of enduring fuming debate on cerebral localization of functions versus a more holistic approach to the brain. As Broca (1861) wrote of his patient Leborgne, the poor, aphasic laborer who had been hospitalized for over 20 years and was to become the sine qua non in this clash of ideas:

> He could no longer produce but a single syllable, which he usually repeated twice in succession; regardless of the question asked him, he always responded: *tan, tan*, combined with varied expressive gestures. This is why, throughout the hospital, he is known only by the name *Tan* . . . [at autopsy it was found that] most of the other frontal convolutions were entirely destroyed. The result of this destruction of the cerebral substance was a large cavity, capable of holding a chicken egg, and filled with serous fluid. (Broca, 1861a, p. 335)

Broca's presentations were milestones in the history of the neuroscience of language and the brain, but they were only more defined echoes of ideas that had preceded him. Faint impressions of localization of functions in the brain were in the wind for a long time preceding Broca, just as in the French art world vague evocative impressionism stirred debate, outright revolt, and further experimentation. French brains were in a state of mutability and flux and echoes of the enlightenment were felt in philosophy, the arts and science. Franz Josef Gall, residing in Paris, advanced ideas on specific brain areas associated with "faculties" or character traits and passed his hands over skulls to interpret head bumps. The French physicians Jean-Baptiste Bouillaud and his son-in-law Ernest Aubertin had previously advanced notions of the primacy of the anterior lobe of the cerebral hemisphere and its role in human speech. In fact, Broca's curiosity was piqued by an earlier presentation by Aubertin to the Society of Anthropology that described the cessation of speech in a conscious patient whose brain was exposed. Aubertin repeatedly placed and removed a medical instrument not unlike a tiny spatula and observed that his patient's speech was interrupted. This primitive spatula experiment set the stage for Broca who listened to Aubertin's presentation at the Society meeting.

Who are these French scientists and pioneers who contributed so much to what we know about the brain's considerable role in speech and language? Broca's significant being has been rhapsodized in biography and historical articles, but what else captivated his interest? What were his views as a member of the French Senate and did they coincide with his life as a scientist? What of Broca, the man, aside from his prodigious published offerings? What other avenues of interest did Broca pursue and what led him to the exploration of second and third frontal convolutions of the left cerebral hemisphere that would subsequently be named "Broca's area?" Who were Bouillaud and his son-in-law Aubertin? How did they intersect and relate to Broca? How did the quasiscience and eventual fad of phrenology contribute to our understanding of localization of functions in the brain? Were there other French "brains" who have been historically neglected in our understanding of these milestone developments? What of M. Leborgne and M. Lelong, whose brains now reside preserved in formalin in the Dupuytren Museum in Paris? Who were they and what were the circumstances that brought them to become encased in preservative, as everlasting testaments to brain and disrupted language?

These are the questions I would like to pursue and formulate into a cohesive history of the "French Brains" that created these pioneering neuroscience impressions. The events in Paris in the 1860s and before form a backdrop of a roiling and tumultuous political canvas and constituted a turning point in the history of ideas regarding brain function. Some of the controversies that peaked during that era are unresolved today, but they surely advanced our thinking about them. Many of them gave convergence and exactitude to brilliant advances that would strengthen our understanding of mind, brain, and the incredibly human attributes of thought, language, and communication. Human communication is one of those precious gifts that is taken for granted until it is unavailable or lost. I have had more than one person with aphasia relate to me with varying degrees of fractured language, "I didn't realize. I took it for granted. I never missed the water till the words went dry."

Communication is the bedrock of all learning, living, and loving and its loss compromises each of these all-encompassing aspects of life. Without language and communication life is a void, a vacuum, a living death. With it, in all its creativity, grandeur, and even tedium, life is marvelous and vivid. Language is life. Language is identity.

This book portrays some of the influential early understanding on human communication and its loss and how the events of early tragedies are rooted to an extraordinary epoch. French brains in both a metaphoric and literal sense played an important role in contemporary neuroscience and in our understanding of the vagaries and tragedy of aphasia and language loss. This work returns to that era with its people, ideas, debates, discoveries, and brains suspended even today in bottles of preservative. France and particularly Paris in the 19th century were at a rendezvous of intellectual discovery and reflection, even while they struggled with social and political puberty. Wars, revolution, uprisings, emergence of republican ideas, anarchy, and periods of relative restiveness and prosperity would color the milieu. The medical arts would be introduced to clinical-pathological methods of empirical research and the rewards of defining the functions of the most mysterious of all organs. Witchcraft, superstition, and black magic were fading into the deep recesses of dubious medical intervention. The brain would begin to emerge from its historic conception of an amorphous mass of undifferentiated gruel, with convolutions that were more analogous to intestines than the seat of human creativity and reasoning. Speech, language, memory, and the vast array of higher cortical human functions would become targets of consternation and analysis. This era would influence the development of research approaches and techniques and would propel the future of all clinical neuroscience. Return with us now to the thrilling days of yesteryear.

Chapter 2

Early Times:
Deep Sulci of History

The 19th century was a time of immense transformation and discovery in art, science, and philosophy. The great debate about mind and brain occupied the thoughts of philosophers, physicians, anthropologists, and physiologists. In another astonishing example of activity of the only organ capable of studying itself, the brains and minds of thinkers focused on itself. Where was the mind? Where was the "soul?" Were the mind and brain separate? Were they codependent? Were functions localized in the brain or was it some holistic organ? Was it like a bubble so that if it were pricked it would destroy its entirety? What functions were localized in the brain?

In a diffuse and vague way, the idea of functional localization had been touched upon since antiquity. A notion of "soul" as it might be related to the brain, for example, can be found in the work of Pythagoras, Hippocrates, Plato, and Galen, among others. During the 5th century BC, Democritus, Diogenes, Diabetes, and Theophrastus also indicated the brain as the seat of the body's activities. Also among the Greeks, Herophilus (335–280 BC) dissected and wrote about the skull and its contents, being the first one to describe its cavities, the cerebral ventricles, which importantly, he associated with mental functions. This notion, as

we shall see, would become very important in the "neurophysiology" of the forthcoming centuries.

The father of medicine, Hippocrates (460–400 BC; Figure 2–1),
wrote prolifically and with precious insight about brain diseases.
He stated that "Men ought to know that from the brain and from

Figure 2–1. Bust of Hippocrates, father of medicine. Wikimedia Commons, public domain.

the brain only arise our pleasures, joys, laughter and jests, as well as our sorrows, pains, grieves and tears." (Finger, 1994). Hippocrates had a far-reaching understanding of the human body and in particular the brain. He supposed that the body must be treated as a whole and not just a jumbled collection of parts. He was the first observer to assert that thoughts, ideas, and feelings come from the brain and not the heart as others of his time believed. Musicians and poets have rhapsodized about the heart since antiquity, but the brain gets less attention in song and poem, with the notable exception of the Ray Bolger's Scarecrow in the *Wizard of Oz*. Hippocrates attempted to change some of that. Refuting the idea that epilepsy as a curse or a prophetic power, as was previously believed, Hippocrates stated that this "sacred disorder" is indeed a brain malady. "It is thus with regard to the disease called Sacred: it appears to me to be nowise more divine nor more sacred than other diseases, but has a natural cause like other affections." He documented that the brain was involved in sensation, emotions, and was the epicenter of intelligence (Cantor, 2002).

The pneumatic physiologists of the middle ages thought that mental capacities were housed in air or fluid of the ventricles. Humankind has been linking mind to the brain for a long time, despite the efforts of Descartes and philosophy of dualism of brain and mind. Human skulls with holes deliberately made in them were found in sites more than 10,000 years old (Figure 2–2). Probably, those holes were made to grant a way out for the bad spirits that should be tormenting those brains (Poynter, 1958).

The link between brain and mental functions perhaps was natural, because primitive people in all ages could easily observe that strong blows to the skull resulted in loss of consciousness and of memory, and even "fits" or convulsions, which often led to significant alterations of perception and behavior. When Korg dropped a boulder on the head of Mog from a ledge or when a saber-toothed tiger clamped and penetrated the skull of Walnut Nose, the consequences were obvious, even to those whose language consisted primarily of grunts and wheezes.

The most important documental proof about this knowledge comes from the famous Surgical Papyrus, discovered by archeologist Edwin Smith which was written around 1600 BC in Egypt

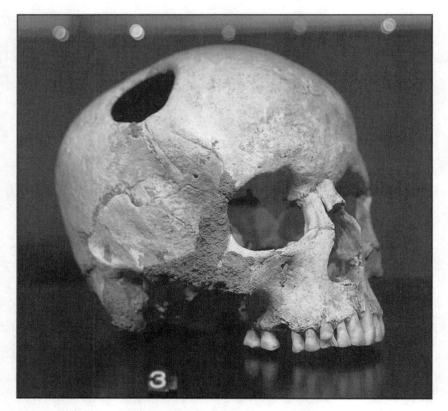

Figure 2–2. *Trephinated skull. Wikimedia Commons, public domain.*

(Minagar, Ragheb, & Kelley, 2003; Wilkins, 1964). This monumental work contains the first known use of the word "brain" and rather vivid descriptions of cranial sutures, the external brain surface, and brain "liquor" (cerebrospinal fluid). The vaunted author of the Surgical Papyrus describes 30 clinical cases of head and spine trauma, making poignant notes how several of these brain injuries were associated with dramatic changes in the function of other parts of the body, especially in the lower limbs. Conditions were described and associated with brain damage such as hemiplegic contractures, paralysis, and problems with urination, ejaculation and priapism, due to trauma inflicted to the spinal cord or perhaps the brainstem (Finger, 1994).

The Surgical Papyrus opens by addressing injuries to the head, and continues with treatments for injuries to neck, arms, and torso. The title of each vivid case details the nature of trauma, such as, "Practices for a gaping wound in his head, which has penetrated to the bone and split the skull" (Allen, 2005). The treatments are interesting and in keeping with availability of items in the local pharmacy at the time. These include closing wounds with sutures (for wounds of the lip, throat, and shoulder), preventing and curing infection with honey, and stopping bleeding with raw meat (Allen, 2005). This last treatment is not that unlike the not too distant past practice of slapping a steak on a black eye.

Edwin Smith purchased this landmark document in Luxor, Egypt, in 1862; coincidentally, about the time study of the brain was heating up in Paris, from an Egyptian dealer named Mustafa Agha. The papyrus was in the possession of Smith until his death, when his daughter donated the papyrus to New York Historical Society. In 1948, the New York Historical Society and the Brooklyn Museum presented the papyrus to the New York Academy of Medicine, where it remains today (Allen, 2005). Figure 2–3 is the Egyptian hieroglyphic name for the word "brain" ironically reproduced on a modern day iPhone skin.

As belief in animal spirits faded, however, so too did credence in the long-held ventricular hypothesis and the notion that the brain was filled with four or more spirits (Selby, 1993). Perhaps the air-pockets view of vital animal spirits might be better translated as life-carrying fluids or vital liquids. Foxes in little

Figure 2–3. *Hieroglyphic word for "brain."*

boxes? Animal essence coursing through our bodies? In English, the word "spirit" can mean anything from the Holy Ghost to a glass of Bombay Blue Sapphire gin. In fact, such ambiguity exists across French and the other romance languages as well, deriving from the Latin *spiritus animales*. The linguistic root is common with respire and expire (*spiro* meaning "I breathe") *spiritus* originally meant breath, then breath of life, but also temperament, courage, and even phantasm. Likewise the meanings of *anima* range from breath to vital principle and rational soul (Sutton & Sutton, 2007). John Locke thought of the pneumohydrolic model as "fluid and subtle Matter, passing through the Conduits of the Nerves." The nerves were thought to transmit information among sense organs, brain, and muscles.

René Descartes is often maligned for alienating our minds from our bodies with his concept of dualism or separation of brain and mind. But a Cartesian view of memory entails the dynamic interaction of mind, body and the external world. Processing and ruminating about feelings, thoughts, and memories is not always tranquil. Jonathan Swift satirically painted the spirits as "a crowd of little animals, but with teeth and claws extremely sharp." Besides proving painful, the spirits may be untrustworthy. Vogli described how "especially in dreams and imaginings the same nervous fluid may indeed produce confused phantasms, but nonetheless fabricated from those objects which at one time we saw or in some way sensed" (Sutton & Sutton, 2007).

DESCARTES: REASON AND THE SCIENTIFIC METHOD

Dualism and Cartesian philosophy were steeped in separation of the brain and mind. Damasio (1994) wrote an insightful critique of Descartes (Figure 2–4) and the propensity of scientists and laymen to view separation of mind and body. This is an intriguing philosophical issue and it has occupied the discussion and debate of cognitive scientists throughout history. One can only imagine the countless parties and social gatherings either at the Parisian cafes of Le Flore or the Deux Magots over wine or café crème or at a Tallahassee neuroscience job talk–social get-together over Pringles and mullet dip, of the intriguing discus-

Figure 2–4. *René Descartes, advocate of reason and the scientific method.* Wikimedia Commons, public domain.

sions and persistence of thinking about dualism and separation
of mind and body. Descartes immortalized it, with his *cogito*
summary of "I think, therefore I am." Some of us believe (or
in Damasio's perspective "feel," that the famous saying should
be amended to, "I think, therefore I am not sure."). Damasio
speaks of Descartes' "error" and urges the importance of emotion
and feeling as a weighty contributor to rationality and reason.
Descartes argued for reason and perhaps formed many of the
vertebrae in the backbone of the scientific method, but Damasio

contends he was in error in discounting the role of subjectivity and emotion in our everyday decision-making. The French brains of Descartes and Pascal weighed in on these issues and contributed mightily to the dry ingredients of our philosophical *gateaux*. If emotion is inherently part of human reasoning, what becomes of scientific objectivity? Blaise Pascal once said, "The heart has its reasons of which reason knows nothing." If Damasio is correct, then Pascal preceded him is invoking emotions and the wonderful world of the limbic system in our decision making.

Descartes may not have been as much in "error" as he was a victim of the evolution of scientific thought, just as he was injudicious when he concluded the pineal body in the brain was the seat of the soul. There is little doubt that Cartesian thinking was a clear split with history and his *Discourse on the Method* (Descartes, 1637) was a vibrant signal that science could not be conducted at the whim of theological doctrine but must seek the path of objectivity. For that contribution alone, Descartes assumes his place on the starting team of the world's great thinkers and philosophers. Descartes' precepts on method are as much a guide for careful science today as they were in the 1600s. They should be learned and adhered to by every scientist, graduate student, and tenure-seeking assistant professor.

> I thought that the four following precepts would suffice, provided that I could make a firm, steadfast resolution not to violate them even once.
>
> The first was to never accept anything as true which I could not accept as obviously true; that is to say, to carefully avoid impulsiveness and prejudice, and to include nothing in my conclusions but whatever was so clearly presented to my mind that I could have no reason to doubt it.
>
> The second was to divide each of the problems I was examining in as many parts as I could, as many as should be necessary to solve them.
>
> The third, to develop my thoughts in order, beginning with the simplest and easiest to understand matters, in order to reach by degrees, little by little, to the most complex knowledge, assuming an orderliness among them which did not at all naturally seem to follow one from the other.
>
> And the last resolution was to make my enumerations so complete and my reviews so general that I could be assured that I had not omitted anything. (Descartes, 1637, p.16)

René Descartes was born on March 31, 1596 in a village in Touraine, France, which is now called La Haye-Descartes or just Descartes. His mother died shortly after he was born (when young René was only 13 or 14 months old, historical reports differ). About 1606, René entered the Jesuit college of La Fleche, during which a relative of his, Father Charlet, would serve as in loco parentis for him. Because of his delicate health, Descartes was allowed to spend mornings in bed, meditating, reading, and writing, a habit he maintained for most of his life (Gorst-Williams, 1977).

In about 1648, Queen Christina of Sweden invited him to come to her court to instruct her in philosophy. Despite his reported reluctance, Descartes accepted her invitation. She sent an admiral with a warship to carry him to Sweden, and Descartes left for Stockholm in September of 1649. Some have called this the dearest mistake of his life. He reached Stockholm with no trouble, but when he arrived the Queen wanted him to instruct her in mathematics, philosophy, and the ways of the world at 5 AM. Today's students complain about 8:00 classes. The Queen was an early riser; he was a slug-a-bed where he did much of his meditating. Incidentally, Descartes also was an early advocate of meditation and in his letters can be found advice to sit as one would in the forest with the mind occupying no particular theme or thought. This focus on the healing powers of meditation can be seen in his correspondences with Princess Elisabeth (eventually a widowed Queen) of Bohemia and in other sources (Gorst-Williams, 1977). His extensive and regular correspondence with Princess Elisabeth is rich in detail and today perhaps would be cast in the realm of twitter-flirting. His brilliance was recognized widely and he served great counsel to royalty.

Descartes and his dogma also have been criticized by domesticated pet lovers and those who think that he promulgated ideas about cruelty to animals. Not so, according to the distinguished medical historian Stanley Finger (2000). Finger recalls that all of his students knew that the great philosopher René Descartes wrote about animals being "beast machines" without souls. Their fascination with the work and ideas of Descartes grew when Finger told them that the man who denied higher thought and conscious feelings to animals had a housebroken and sentient pet dog of his own. The dog was suitably named *Monsieur Grat* ("Mr. Scratch"), and Descartes revered his pet and treated him with great affection (Finger, 2000). The vision of an exalted intellect like Descartes playfully scratching an itchy dog is ironically delicious.

In Sweden, Descartes was still used to sleeping in, and continued his lifelong habit of remaining in bed to study and to contemplate whatever subjects he ruminated about. This combined with the cold weather, may have caused him to contract pneumonia. Some speculations surfaced about the real cause of his death, and rumors emerged that perhaps he was poisoned. According to Theodor Ebert (2009) an academic at the University of Erlangen, Descartes died not through natural causes but from an arsenic-laced communion wafer given to him by a Catholic priest. Ebert's book, *The Mysterious Death of René Descartes,* was published in 2009 and presents the case that there may have been theological motivations by the hierarchy of the Catholic Church for wanting Descartes' influence obliterated. Many historians remain unconvinced however and the consensus conclusion is that the great philosopher likely died of Swedish-winter induced pneumonia. He died on February 11, 1650. As Descartes was a Catholic, and Sweden a Protestant country, he was buried in a cemetery reserved for un-baptized children. It turns out that the story of the journeys of Descartes body is as interesting as his life and death. Russell Shorto traces these journeys in his book, *Descartes' Bones* (2009). Shorto presents us with a one-way ticket for this trip by weaving a tale that involves three different burials, events in six countries, and haunting questions, some resolved and some still enigmatic, about the authenticity of Descartes' corpse, and its scattered parts. One finger went missing and his skull was separated from the rest of his skeleton at an early date.

Philippe Mennecier, my collaborator and the *Charge de Conservation des collections d'anthropologie biologuique, Musée national d'histoire naturelle* in its temporary quarters at the *Jardin des Plantes* in Paris, retrieved the skull from a wooden box, tucked away in a cabinet on June 15, 2011, and we examined it, Yorik-like, from all conceivable angles, including a careful look inside this shell where for 53 years existed one of the greatest French brains in the history of the world. In 1667, Descartes' remains were taken to Paris and buried in the Church of St. Genevieve-du-Mont which later became the Pantheon, a mausoleum and tribute to the great brains of France. It is a great irony that the philosopher, who posited the separation of mind and body, indeed has had his body disjointed. Since his death René Descartes's corpse has been picked apart by foragers who stole his fingers for posterity, some of his bones for jewelry, and his head for academic preservation. During the French Revolution, the secularization of some churches (bell towers were destroyed; holy relics were removed; heads were whacked off statues, so to speak) was the impetus for the Pantheon to become a mausoleum. Some uncertainty still exists about the separated remains of Descartes but perhaps at least a fraction of the remains of Descartes were transferred to this classic monument to be placed among the great French thinkers (Figure 2–5). A memorial marker

Figure 2–5. *Descartes memorial in Église St. Germaine des Prés, Paris.*

exists as well in a quiet side-chapel in one of the oldest churches in Paris, at St. Germaine des Prés (Figure 2–6).

We live now, in this summer of 2011, in the shadow of the Pantheon, in the ancient Mouffetard Village of the Latin Quarter

Figure 2–6. *Descartes bust and commemorative plaque, St. Germaine des Pres, Paris.*

of Paris that drew its name from the language spoken on the streets by its unrelenting history of scholars. We have made many visits through the majestic Corinthian columns of the Pantheon as well as the St. Germaine des Pris church to visit the places of final honor for Descartes and other noble French brains (Figures 2–7 through 2–9).

After his death the church added his works to the Index of Forbidden Books, in 1663, and to this day controversy surrounds the great issues that Descartes amplified, including the enigma of the coexistence of faith and reason (Gaukroger, 1995). The skull of Descartes is still kept in the anthropology collection of the Paris Museum of Natural History. An image of that skull, which housed the synapses of one of the greatest, though mortal minds of history, is presented in Figures 2–10 and 2–11.

Figure 2–7. *The majestic Pantheon, resting place of national heroes, 5th Arrondisement, Paris.*

Figure 2–8. *Columns of the Pantheon.*

Figure 2–9. *In the crypt of the Pantheon.*

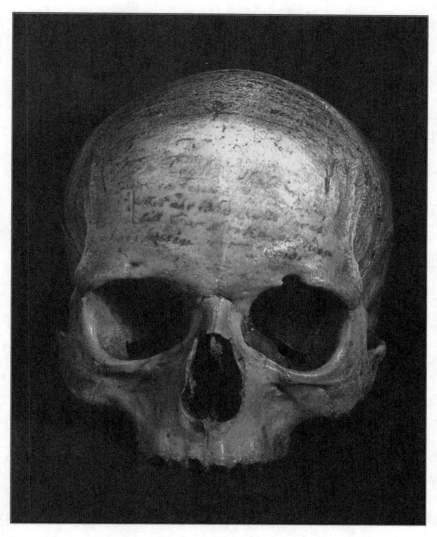

Figure 2–10. Descartes skull. Photo used with permission of Philippe Mennecier, Charge de Conservation des collections d'anthropologie biologuique, Musée national d'histoire naturelle.

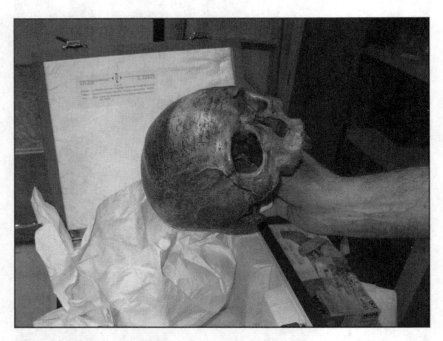

Figure 2–11. Holding Descartes' skull. Photo used with permission of Philippe Mennecier, Charge de Conservation des collections d'anthropologie biologuique, Musée national d'histoire naturelle..

Chapter 3

Phrenology and Serendipitous Bumps

FRANZ JOSEPH GALL

As Selby (1993) has speculated, the concept of cerebral localization may be directly traceable to the concepts of the Viennese physician, Franz Josef Gall. The "science" of phrenology, as with fads and novel "breakthroughs" was embroidered with personal bias, lack of empirical evidence, anecdote, and not so lightly tainted by financial incentive. Gall and his protégé's were not immune to the potential and temptations for profiteering from the phrenology craze. The debates about localization of function in the brain were to generate heat and light in the halls of scientific discussions.

In the early days of phrenology, the gentle scholars, anxious for association with the new craze of belonging to scientific societies, often met weekly or biweekly at their local phrenological chapter. Here they would hear a lecture, drink tea or perhaps brandy, and marvel over new authorizations of phrenology. They often kept small libraries of phrenological works and museums of phrenological busts, skulls, and casts of the heads of the famous and infamous or examples of different "races" of humans (Van Wyhe, 2011). One can see that in this new "science" there was perhaps motivation for endorsement of racial or class superiority and ascendency. This use of science to endorse preconceived or elevated self-beliefs would continue through the era of skull and head measurement and conclusions regarding deceitful correlates of head size and brain size.

During phrenology's early heyday in the 1820s to 1840s, many employers could demand a character reference from a local phrenologist to ensure that a prospective employee was honest and hard-working. Polygraphs and unreliable lie-detector measurements today are echoes of the potential employer head bump detectors of the past. This confidence that the protuberances on the skull provided an accurate index of talents and abilities was urged by many to be applied to education and criminal reform. Phrenologists, not unlike those who in today's Sunday newspaper supplements believe in strong demarcations in "left-" or "right-brains," thought they could determine the most suitable career for the young and match prospective mates with greater accuracy than "old-fashioned love." Visiting a phrenologist was akin to seeking the advice of so-called psychics, clairvoyants, or astrologers today. A phrenologist was someone who claimed to have access to special knowledge about people. Just as today's lottery and house-biased gambling odds are seemingly a tax on the mathematically naïve, the ignorant and gullible were particularly susceptible to the charades of phrenologists. Pretension, authority, and junk science are alive and well and line the pockets of the unwary every day.

The concept of functional localization in the brain—the impression that specific mental processes are correlated with discrete regions of the brain—and the efforts to establish localization by means of empirical observation were fundamentally 19th-century achievements. Some of these observations may have been misguided, though it is easy to find folly in the evolution of thought and science. There is little doubt, however, that of the early thinking about functional organization of the brain laid the groundwork for refinement of thinking about where in the brain certain functional regions are placed. The pioneering essential steps toward those ends can be traced to the work of Franz Josef Gall (1758–1828). Gall's birth occurred in temporal proximity to the first sighting of Halley's Comet and in the same year as that of Maximillien Robespierre, the eventual force in the French Revolution. I am indebted to the meticulous scholarship and documentation of historian John van Van Wyhe (2011) for his superlative collection on the Internet. This is perhaps the most prodigious and complete overview and history of phrenology that exists and I am grateful to him for permission to use some of his scholarship. John van Van Wyhe (B.A., M.A., Ph.D.) is a historian of science and Senior Lecturer in the Departments of Biological Sciences and History at the National University of Singapore. Van Wyhe provides a valuable timeline of the important dates in the history of phrenology and it is reproduced with permission below.

Time Line of Phrenology[1]

1790s *Franz Joseph Gall creates his system of organology and brain anatomy in Vienna.*

1796 *Gall begins to offer lectures in his home in Vienna on his system.*

1798 *December, the first account of the system in Gall's own words published in the Neue Teutsche Merkur.*

1800 *J. G. Spurzheim begins to attend Gall's lectures*

1801 *December, emperor Francis II issues decree that forbids Gall's lectures and bans him from publishing the same.*

1804 *Spurzheim becomes Gall's paid dissectionist and assistant.*

1805–1807 *Gall undertakes successful lecture tour throughout Europe, accompanied by Spurzheim as paid assistant.*

1807 *Oct., Gall arrives in Paris, where he remains.*

1808 *March, Gall and Spurzheim submit a Mémoire to the Institut de France outlining (for the first time) "their" anatomical and physiological claims.*

1810 *Gall and Spurzheim begin publication of* Anatomie et physiologie du système nerveux en général, et du cer-

---

[1]Reproduced with permission, Van Wyhe, 2011.

veau en particulier, Avec des observations sur las possibilité de reconnoître plusieurs dispositions intellectuelles et
morales de l'homme et des animaux, par la configuration
de leurs têtes. *4 vols., Paris, 1810–1819 (first two vols. only
with Spurzheim).*

1813   *Gall and Spurzheim part company forever.*

1814   *March, Spurzheim arrives in Britain to lecture on
"his" and Gall's system.*

1815   *Spurzheim begins to publish on the new system,
starting with The Physiognomical System of Drs. Gall and
Spurzheim; founded on an Anatomical and Physiological
Examination of the Nervous System in general, and of the
Brain in Particular; and indicating the Dispositions and
Manifestations of the Mind.*

   ◆ *scathing articles in the Edinburgh Review and Quar-
      terly Review lambast Spurzheim, simultaneously giving
      him nationwide exposure.*
   ◆ *the name **phrenology** given to the system by Dr. Thomas
      I. M. Forster.*

1816–1817   *Spurzheim faces down his critics, especially
John Gordon, in Edinburgh and makes devout converts for
the science.*

1817   *George Combe begins to publish articles about
phrenology.*

1819   *George Combe's first book on phrenology published:
Essays on Phrenology.*

   ◆ *Sir George Steuart Mackenzie's, Illustrations of
      Phrenology.*

1820   *Edinburgh Phrenological Society, established by
George and Andrew Combe, David Welsh, James Brownlee,
William Waddell, and Lindsey Mackersey.*

1821   *Transactions of the [Edinburgh] Phrenological Society published.*

1822   *George Combe begins to lecture on phrenology in
Edinburgh.*

◆ *Philadelphia Phrenological Society, established (the first in USA)*

1823   *Gall lectures briefly in London.*

◆ *London Phrenological Society, established by John Elliotson, B. Donkin, J. DeVille.*

◆ *December, Phrenological Journal (of Edinburgh) founded (the first phrenological journal).*

1824   *George Combe's Elements of Phrenology.*

1825   *Wakefield Phrenological Society, established by William Ellis.*

1826   *Francis Jeffrey's attack on phrenology in the Edinburgh Review.*

1826–1827   *Sir William Hamilton engages in controversy with Combe and Spurzheim.*

1827–1828   *schism in the Edinburgh Phrenological Society between evangelicals and Combeans over Combe's doctrine of the natural laws.*

1828   *George Combe publishes Constitution of Man.*

◆ *Gall dies near Paris.*

1830   *Manchester Phrenological Society, established.*

◆ *Dublin Phrenological Society established.(?)*

1831   *Paris Phrenological Society, established.*

◆ *Spurzheim last lectures in Britain.*

1832   *Spurzheim dies in Boston Massachusetts while on lecture tour.*

◆ *Boston Phrenological Society, established.*

1833   *The Fowlers begin their phrenological lecturing concerns in New York.*

1836   *Aberdeen Phrenological Society, established.*

1838   *[British] Phrenological Association first meets in Newcastle (formed as an alternative to the British Association for the Advancement of Science which had spurned the phrenologists).*

- *American Phrenological Journal founded in Philadelphia*
- *Birmingham Phrenological Society, established*

1839 *Phrenological Association meets in Birmingham.*

1840s *George Combe, Robert Noel, and Dr. Gustav Scheve lecture on phrenology in Germany.*

1840 *Phrenological Association meets in Glasgow.*
- *Exeter Phrenological Society, established.*
- *Hewett Watson, one of the foremost phrenologists, abandons the science.*

1841 *Phrenological Association meets in London.*
- *Dumfries Phrenological Society established.*

1842 *another great schism created at meeting of the Phrenological Association in London when W. Engeldue declares phrenology proves materialism to be true.*
- *Sheffield Phrenological Society, established.*
- *[London] Christian Phrenological Society, established by John Epps and J. Hawkins.*

1843 *Lancaster Phrenological Society, established.*
- *Zeitschrift für Phrenologie (1843–1845) founded in Heidelberg by Dr. E Hirschfeld and Gustav von Struve.*

1844 *Robert Chambers's Vestiges of the Natural History of Creation published, joining phrenological naturalism with transmutation.*

1845 *Gustav von Struve, Handbuch der Phrenologie.*

1850s *phrenological societies mostly defunct, few publications on the subject—the early advocates are either aged or dead. The science is largely discredited and moribund in Britain.*

1858 *George Combe dies at Dr. Lane's hydropathic establishment at Moor Park where Charles Darwin's daughter Etty is also being treated.*

1860s *"Phrenological Fowlers" come to Britain from USA and bring about a revival of phrenology.*

1863   *Fowler Institute, London, established by L. N. Fowler*

1870   *last meeting of Edinburgh Phrenological Society*

1881   *British Phrenological Society established.*

1911   *American Phrenological Journal ceased publication (began in 1838)*

1967   *British Phrenological Society disbanded.*

Franz Joseph Gall (Figure 3–1) was born in the vicinity of the healing baths of Baden and studied medicine at Strasbourg and Vienna, where he received his degree in 1785. Impressed as a child by apparent correlations between unusual talents in his friends and striking variations in facial or cranial appearance, Gall set out to evolve a new "let me feel your skull bumps" method of localizing mental faculties. His first public lectures on cranioscopy date from around 1796. Apparently he discovered as well that people were willing to pay good money to have their inner character read. No doubt, just as with today's hope from visits to astrologers or psychics, we have a need to have our "future" unraveled and hear some authority pontificate about our wondrous qualities. Fortune telling and the psychic industry of even today is a multimillion dollar business preying on people's needs to hear what they want to hear. Gall's lectures almost immediately aroused skepticism and opposition on the grounds of his presumed materialism, and in 1805, he left Vienna. After two years of travel, he arrived in Paris accompanied by his colleague, Johann Gaspar Spurzheim (1776–1832). (Van Wyhe, 2011). In 1810, Gall and Spurzheim published the first volume of their *Anatomie et physiologie du système nerveux en général*, followed by an 1811 publication roughly translated from the French as "The innate provisions of the soul and the spirit: Materialism, fatalism and moral freedom, with reflections on education and on the criminal legislation" (Gall & Spurzheim, 1811). These publications formed the foundation of the Phrenological Movement and contained Gall and Spurzheim's fundamental important contributions to neuroanatomy and their major statements on the science of "cranioscopy" and skull reading.

The essence of Gall's method of localization lay in correlating variations in character with variations in external craniologi-

Figure 3–1. *Franz Josef Gall, pioneer of cortical localization; advocate of phrenology. Wikimedia Commons, public domain.*

cal signs (Figure 3–2). The validity of this approach depended on three critical assumptions: that the size and shape of the cranium reflected the size and shape of the underlying portions of the cerebrum, that mental abilities were innate and fixed, and that the relative level of development of an innate ability was a reflection of the inherited size of its cerebral organ. On these

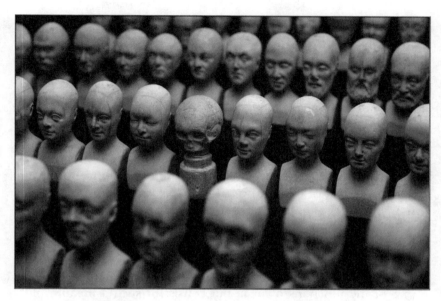

Figure 3–2. *Head casts used to study differences in skull configurations. Wikimedia Commons, public domain.*

assumptions, an observed correlation between a particularly well-developed ability and a particularly prominent area of the cranium could be interpreted as evidence of the functional localization of that ability in the correlative portion of the cerebrum.

The migration of Gall and colleagues to practice and live in Paris took place in 1807. After receiving his diploma he practiced medicine in Vienna in 1785, but his energies were mainly devoted to the scientific investigation of problems which had occupied his attention from boyhood. Several sources on the life of Gall and the birth of phrenology (originally called "cranioscopy" by Gall and changed to "phrenology" by his cohort, Spurzheim) report that he formed the notion that in humans verbal agility and a powerful memory were associated with prominent eyes (Selby, 1993). Big eyes equaled big words and strong recall. One aspect of cerebral localization involved Gall's placement of centers for verbal expression in the cerebral regions just posterior to the orbits of the eyes. Allegedly, Gall had formulated a hypothesis about the eyes and speech from an early age. He is reported to have commented that many of his early classmates who were particularly adept at speech and were verbally agile seemed to have slightly bulging eyes. Apparently the highly developed cortical regions just behind the orbits caused the eyes to protrude and gave the appearance of excellent debaters with exophthalmos or bulging eyes. As indicated in Gall and Spurzheim (1810 and relayed by Pearce (2009): "The competence to skillfully learn words and names by heart and to save them in memory is seated in the posterior part of the eye socket."

Not everyone agreed with this placement of speech and language behind the eyes, nor of the tenets of phrenology in general. A storm of contemporary criticism is catalogued on van Van Wyhe's excellent site on the history of phrenology (Van Wyhe, 2011). A few examples follow:

> The writings of Drs. Gall and Spurzheim have not added one fact to the stock of our knowledge, respecting either the structure or the functions of man; but consist of such a mixture of gross errors extravagant absurdities, downright mis-statements, and unmeaning quotations from Scripture, as can leave no doubt, we apprehend, in the minds of honest and intelligent men, as to the real ignorance, the real hypocrisy, and the real empiricism of the authors.

> We look upon the whole doctrines taught by these two modern peripatetics, (Drs. Gall and Spurzheim), anatomical, physiological, and physiognomical, as a piece of thorough quackery from beginning to end.

> Such is the trash, the despicable trumpery, which two men, calling themselves scientific inquirers, have the impudence gravely to present to the physiologists of the nineteenth century, as specimens of reasoning and induction.

Further observations enabled Gall and his colleagues to define the external characteristics indicative of special talents for painting, music, amativeness (making love) and the mechanical arts. After these observations began to crystalize, so did strong convictions, not only that the talents and dispositions of men are dependent upon the functions of the brain, but also that these talents, dispositions, and "faculties" maybe inferred with perfect exactness and precision from the external surface appearances of the skull (Gall, NNDB People, 2011). Gall's expertise as an anatomist was challenged by few. But the evolution of his hypotheses about skull and character were to come under much criticism. One of these important critics was Gordon (1815) who apparently threw team Gall and Spurzheim into a defensive stance. Several detailed theses and dissertations have been written about the phrenological movement, not the least of which are those of Spoerl (1934) and Walsh (1974).

Gall's conclusions and generalizations metastasized into unsupported premises. That one could discriminate the relative strengths, weaknesses, penchants, inclinations, and abilities of an individual's behavior from measurement of the contours of one's head did not appear to be bothered by the psychometric measurement principles of reliability or validity. They rested on authority and so-called expertise. An important underlying premise was that these character traits were believed to be indicative of underlying cerebral contours. Physiognomy has a very long history in medicine, the arts, and literature, but Gall focused his attention upon the detailed configuration of the human head (Selby, 1993).

PHRENOLOGY'S PRINCIPLES

Spurzheim was not only a true believer and protégé but augmented the principles of phrenology. He believed that there were 21 emotional faculties (the term for abilities or attributes) and 14 intellectual faculties (Tartakovsky, 2011).

Phrenology had five main principles, which Spurzheim laid out in *Outlines of Phrenology* (Goodwin, 1999):

1. "The brain is the organ of the mind."
2. The mind consists of about three dozen faculties, which are either intellectual or emotional.
3. Each faculty has its own brain location.
4. People have different amounts of these faculties. A person that has more of a certain faculty will have more brain tissue at that location.
5. Because the shape of the skull is similar to the shape of your brain, it's possible to measure the skull to assess these faculties (known as the "doctrine of the skull").

In this text, Spurzheim featured highly detailed descriptions of the faculties and their locations (Goodwin, 1995; Greenblatt, 1999).

FACULTIES AND HEAD BUMPS

Originally, Gall proposed 27 faculties or characteristics that could be discerned from irregularities and bumps on the skull of humans (Figures 3–3 through 3–7). This list of 27 underwent some change as the years and heads rolled by. Spurzheim translated these characteristics into English and George Combe, who became a rabid convert to the causes of phrenology, wrote extensively about it and provided a list of amended faculties. Van Wyhe (2011) provides a list of Combe's characteristics that are amended but much in keeping with Gall's original 27 traits along with moralistic implications of their abuse.

Order I. FEELINGS.

Genus I. PROPENSITIES—*Common to Man with the Lower Animals*.

THE LOVE OF LIFE—Organ not indicated on the bust.

1. AMATIVENESS—Produces sexual love.
2. PHILOPROGENITIVENESS—*Uses:* Affection for young and tender beings. *Abuses:* Pampering and spoiling children.
3. CONCENTRATIVENESS—*Uses:* It concentrates and renders permanent emotions and ideas in the mind. *Abuses:* Morbid dwelling on internal emotions and ideas, to the neglect of external impressions.
   3a. INHABITIVENESS—*Uses:* It produces the desire of permanence in place. *Abuses:* Aversion to move abroad.
4. ADHESIVENESS—*Uses:* Attachment friendship and society result from it. *Abuses:* Clanship for improper objects, attachment to worthless individuals. It is generally strong in women.

Figure 3–3. Early cast of phrenology head from the Gall collection. Photo used with permission of Philippe Mennecier, Charge de Conservation des collections d'anthropologie biologuique, Musée national d'histoire naturelle.

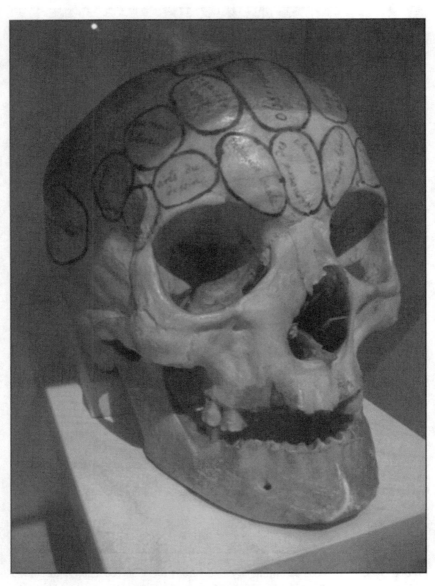

Figure 3–4. *Human skull with phrenological faculties superimposed. Public domain.*

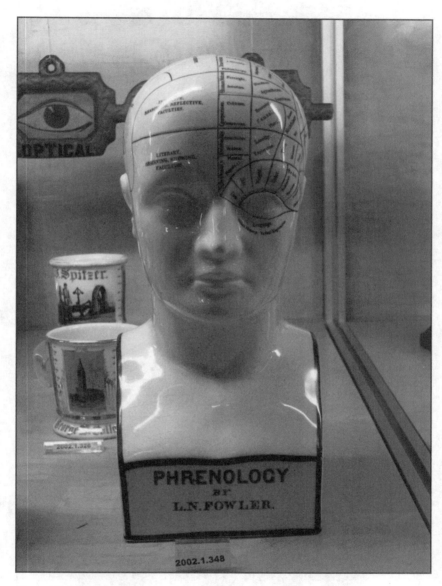

Figure 3–5. *Fowler's popular interpretation of a phrenological bust.*

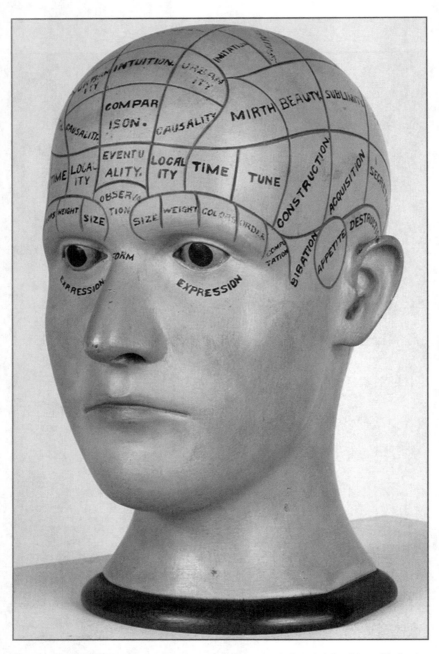

Figure 3–6. Realistic phrenology bust with characteristics and faculties of behavior.

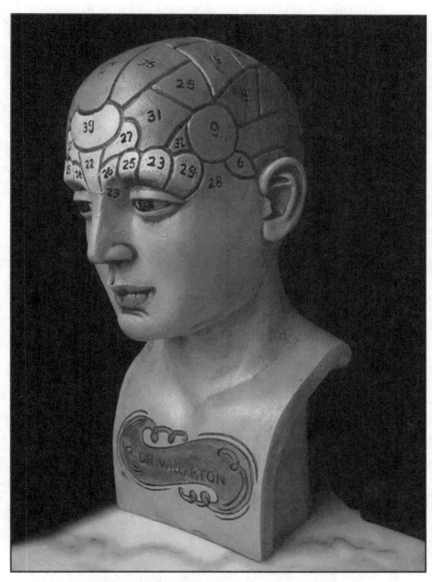

Figure 3–7. *Wistful phrenology bust.*

5. COMBATIVENESS — *Uses:* Courage to meet danger and overcome difficulties, tendency to defend, to oppose and attack, and to resist unjust encroachments. *Abuses:* Love of contention, and tendency to provoke and assault. This feeling obviously adapts man to a world in which danger and difficulty abound.

6. DESTRUCTIVENESS — *Uses:* Desire to destroy noxious objects, animate and inanimate, and to use for food animals in which life has been destroyed. *Abuses:* Cruelty, murder, desire to torment, tendency to passion, rage, and harshness and severity in speech and writing. This feeling places man in harmony with death and destruction, which are woven into the system of sublunary creation.

6a. APPETITE FOR FOOD — *Uses:* Nutrition. *Abuses:* Gluttony and drunkenness.

7. SECRETIVENESS — *Uses:* Tendency to restrain-with-in the mind the various emotions and ideas that involuntarily present themselves, until the judgment has approved of giving them utterance; it is simply the propensity to conceal, and is an ingredient in prudence. *Abuses:* Cunning, deceit, duplicity, and lying.

8. ACQUISITIVENESS — *Uses:* Desire to possess and tendency to accumulate; the sense of property springs from it. *Abuses:* Inordinate desire of property, selfishness, avarice, theft.

9. CONSTRUCTIVENESS — *Uses:* Desire to build and construct works of art. *Abuses:* Construction of engines to injure or destroy, and fabrication of objects to deceive mankind.

Genus II. SENTIMENTS. I. *Sentiments common to Man with some of the Lower Animals*

10. SELF-ESTEEM — *Uses:* Self-respect, self-interest, love of independence, personal dignity. *Abuses:* Pride, disdain, overweening conceit, excessive selfishness, love of dominion.

11. LOVE OF APPROBATION — *Uses:* Desire of the esteem of others, love of praise, desire of fame or glory. *Abuses:*

Vanity, ambition, thirst for praise independently of praiseworthiness.

12. CAUTIOUSNESS — *Uses:* It gives origin to the sentiment of fear, the desire to shun danger, and circumspection; and it is an ingredient in prudence. The sense of security springs from its gratification. *Abuses:* Excessive timidity, poltroonery (*Author note: great word; synonyms are cowardliness, cravenness, dastardliness, gutlessness, cowardice, pusillanimity, spinelessness*), unfounded apprehensions, despondency, melancholy.

13. BENEVOLENCE — *Uses:* Desire of the happiness of others, compassion for the distressed, universal charity, mildness of disposition, and a lively sympathy with the enjoyment of all animated beings. *Abuses:* Profusion, injurious indulgence of the appetites and fancies of others, prodigality, facility of temper.

Genus II. SENTIMENTS — *Proper to Man.*

14. VENERATION — *Uses:* Tendency to venerate or respect whatever is great and good; it gives origin to religious emotion. *Abuses:* Senseless respect for unworthy objects consecrated by time or situation, love of antiquated customs, abject subserviency to persons in authority, superstitious awe. To these Mr Scott adds, "undue deference to the opinions and reasonings of men who are fallible like ourselves; the worship of false gods, polytheism, paganism, idolatry.

15. FIRMNESS — *Uses:* Determination, perseverance, steadiness of purpose. *Abuses:* Stubbornness, infatuation, tenacity in evil.

16. CONSCIENTIOUSNESS — *Uses:* It gives origin to the sentiment of justice, a respect for rights, openness to conviction, the love of truth. *Abuses:* Scrupulous adherence to noxious principles when ignorantly embraced, excessive refinement in the views of duty and obligation, excess in remorse, or self-condemnation.

17. HOPE — *Uses:* Tendency to expect future good it cherishes faith. *Abuses:* Credulity with respect to the

attainment of what is desired, absurd expectations of felicity not founded on reason.

18. WONDER—*Uses:* The desire of novelty; admiration of the new, the unexpected, the grand, the wonderful, and extraordinary. *Abuses:* Love of the marvelous and occult; senseless astonishment; belief in false miracles, in prodigies, magic, ghosts, and other supernatural absurdities. *Note.* Veneration, Hope, and Wonder, combined, give origin to religion; their abuses produce superstition.

19. IDEALITY—*Uses:* Love of the beautiful, desire of excellence, poetic feeling. *Abuses:* Extravagant and absurd enthusiasm, preference of the showy and glaring to the solid and useful, a tendency to dwell in the regions of fancy and to neglect the duties of life.

   19a. Unascertained, supposed to be connected with the sentiment of the Sublime.

20. WIT—Gives the feeling of the ludicrous, and disposes to mirth.

21. IMITATION—Copies the manners, gestures, and actions of others, and appearances in nature generally.

Order II. INTELLECTUAL FACULTIES.

Genus I. EXTERNAL SENSES

Uses: To bring man into communication with external objects, and to enable him to enjoy them. *Abuses:* Excessive indulgence in the pleasures arising from the senses, to the extent of impairing bodily health, and debilitating or deteriorating the mind.

FEELING or TOUCH. TASTE. SMELL. HEARING. SIGHT.

Genus II. KNOWING FACULTIES THAT PERCEIVE THE EXISTENCE AND QUALITIES OF EXTERNAL OBJECTS

22. INDIVIDUALITY—Takes cognizance of existence and simple facts.

23. FORM—Renders man observant of form.

24. SIZE—Gives the idea of space, and enables us to appreciate dimension and distance.

25. WEIGHT—Communicates the perception of momentum, weight, and resistance; and aids equilibrium.
26. COLORING—Gives perception of colors, their harmonies and discords.

Genus III. KNOWING FACULTIES THAT PERCEIVE THE RELATIONS OF EXTERNAL OBJECTS

27. LOCALITY—Gives the idea of relative position.
28. NUMBER—Gives the talent for calculation.
29. ORDER—Communicates the love of physical arrangement.
30. EVENTUALITY—Takes cognizance of occurrences or events.
31. TIME—Gives rise to time perception of duration.
32. TUNE.—The sense of Melody and Harmony arises from it.
33. LANGUAGE—Gives facility in acquiring knowledge of arbitrary signs to express thoughts, readiness in the use of them, and the power of inventing and recollecting them.

Genus IV. REFLECTING FACULTIES, THAT COMPARE, JUDGE, AND DISCRIMINATE
34. COMPARISON—Gives the power of discovering analogies, resemblances, and differences.
35. CAUSALITY—Traces the dependences of phenomena, and the relation of cause and effect.

Combe elaborates on the principles necessary to appreciate the elements of skull differentiation. He presents the following suggestions on determination of head-size differences.

TERMS USED TO DIFFERENTIATE THE SIZES OF ORGANS ACCORDING TO GEORGE COMBE (1853)

"The observer should learn, by inspecting a skull, to distinguish the mastoid process behind the ear, and several bony prominences which occur in every head, from elevations produced by development of brain; as also to discriminate bony excrescences sometimes formed by the sutures, when such occur. The terms used to denote the gradations of size in the different organs, in an increasing ration, are "Very small, Small, Rather small, Moderate, Rather full, Full, Rather large, Large, Very large" (Combe, 1853, p. 35). No evidence is presented on the intra- or inter-examiner reliability of these perceptions or measurements.

SPURZHEIM'S TOUR

Gall's younger colleague Spurzheim traveled abroad to evangelize and elaborate upon Gall's concepts in both the United States and Britain. Though the lectures of Gall and Spurzheim grew in popularity and drew a considerable fashionable following, the premises upon which they were based did not go unchallenged by the professional community. In a telling commentary after a Spurzheim lecture at an academic society in Edinburgh, Anderson commented at some length not only about the more magnanimous issue of brain and mind, but also on the ignored psychometric principles of the phrenologists:

> In soliciting your attention, even at this distance of time, to the subject of Dr Johann Gaspar Spurzheim's Lectures, I feel myself under no necessity to apologize for intrusion; and, I am not ashamed to confess, I entertain the hope of experiencing something more satisfactory than your compassionate forbearance. The avowal of your belief in the substantial truth of the science of Phrenology, conveyed in the very fact of your being members of this Society, is ample warrant, for any individual of your number, respectfully to offer to your notice such matter and communications as have proved efficacious in enlightening and confirming his own mind, in regard to the system, or seem to him in any degree calculated to promote among others an interest in its cultivation and advancement. I have only to add, in the way of preface, that the Spurzheim Lectures of which I propose to give a view, were delivered in the Hall where the meetings of our Society are now held. The object of the science of phrenology is not what it has often been asserted to be. No investigation into the nature of mind is even so much as attempted in it. We know no more of mind, as it is in itself, than we know of matter; and,

accordingly, we must content ourselves with observations on the properties of the one, and the manifestations of the other, as presented through the medium of our bodily organs. No argument, it is evident, is thence to be drawn as to the materiality of the mind. Such a question is never once agitated in the system; far less does the system afford anything like an approach to the affirmative, as has sometimes, most erroneously, been imagined. The object of the system, then, is the manifestations of the human mind, as dependent on, or connected with, organization. Here Dr Spurzheim thought it necessary to explain away the notion which had been entertained respecting the system, namely, that it undertook, from the organization, to conclude as to the actions of mankind. Nothing can be farther from the truth. An important question presents itself for discussion. What part of the animal frame is allotted as the organ of the mind, that by which it manifests itself, or operates on the rest of the system? Various considerations, and what we may call the method of exhaustion, besides the concurrent testimony of most philosophers, direct our attention to the brain, that mass of curiously wrought and singularly diversified matter, which occupies the interior of the bones of the skull. The first proposition to be stated in respect to this organ, is, that without it no manifestation of mind has ever yet been known. The second proposition, founded also on observation, is, that a certain quantity of brain is required for the manifestation of mind. In the third place, it may be remarked, that, other circumstances being alike, the manifestations of the mind bear a proportion to the size of the brain. The chapter closes with discussions on: (1) specifying the modes in which Spurzheim and Dr. Franz Joseph Gall proceeded with a view on determining the nature of differences between and similarities within faculties and propensities; (2) Phraseology employed to denote the faculties; and (3) It is not affirmed that all the organs which have been enumerated are equally demonstrable, or have been with equal certainty determined. (Van Wyhe, 2004)

FLOURENS

Opinions unreceptive to phrenology were cropping up everywhere. In Paris, Flourens took a daring stance (Wozniac, 1995). Flourens was a pre-eminent Parisian physiologist, and a follower of the general ideas of René Descartes (Figure 3–8). Flourens

Figure 3–8. *Jean-Pierre Flourens. Used with permission of Gallica, Banque of Images, Bibiotique Nationale Francais.*

vigorously confronted and attempted to refute the claims of phrenology (Selby, 1993). He had primitive tools and no sophisticated imaging devices to conduct his experiments upon the brain, but he took Gall to task on several testy issues. But even as Gall's most persistent opponent, Marie-Jean-Pierre Flourens (1794–1867) was willing to admit that it was Gall who, by virtue of marshaling detailed evidence of correlation between variation in function and presumed variation in the brain, *first* fully established the view that brain serves as the organ of mind (Finger, 1994).

In almost all other respects, however, Flourens was highly critical of Gall. Something of a child *wunderkind*, Flourens enrolled at the famed Faculté de Médecine at Montpellier when he was only 15 years old and received his medical degree before he had turned 20. Shortly thereafter, while Gall was at the height of his career in Paris, Flourens himself moved to the capital. On the basis of his 1824 *Recherches expérimentales sur les propriétés et les fonctions du système nerveux,* he was elected to membership and eventually to the office of Perpetual Secretary of the *Académie des Sciences,* rising to become one of France's most dominant scientific figures (Flourens, 1824).

In *Recherches expérimentales,* Flourens provided the first experimental demonstration of localization of function in the brain. Although previous investigators had lesioned the brain through a trephined aperture that made it difficult to localize damage, Flourens completely uncovered and isolated that portion of the brain to be removed (Wozniak, 1995).

Flourens was cautious. As he stated about his method (Flourens, 1842),

> My method consisted in first uncovering the entire brain, and second, looking in this way at the limits of each part, guiding the hand always by the eye, and never making lesions which would cut across the proper limits of each distinct part. In a word, in examining, testing, interrogating one part after another, and always apart from the others.

Taking some care to minimize operative trauma and postoperative complications, as much as could be accomplished without cautery and modern techniques, he employed ablation to cut out and localize a motor center in the medulla oblongata. He also provided the first experimental evidence that stability and motor coordination was associated with selected damage to the cerebellum. Flourens conducted a series of experiments (1814–1822) to determine physiological changes in pigeons after removal of certain portions of their brains. In seeming retribution, Paris is awash with pigeons to this day that decorate the statues of the great French brains in their version of the impressionistic painters who work primarily in pigeonic excrement.

In a profound conclusion that separated the functions of old brain from more recently evolved brain, Florens began to clarify the functions of the cerebrum. He found that removal of the cerebral hemispheres, at the front of the brain, destroys will, judgment, and the senses of perception; that removal of the cerebellum, at the base of the brain, destroys the animal's muscular coordination and its sense of equilibrium; and that removal of the medulla oblongata, at the back of the brain, results in death. These experiments led him to conclude that the cerebral hemispheres are responsible for higher cortical and intellectual abilities, that the cerebellum regulates movements, and that the medulla controls vital functions, especially respiration. Flourens also was the first to recognize a role of the semicircular canals of the inner ear in maintaining body equilibrium and coordination, paving the way for treatment by my colleague Dr. Gerald Maitland and all neuroclinicians who deal every day with balance disorders. In 1822 Flourens began to study the effects of extirpation and disabling of successive layers of the cerebellum. He found that at an intermediate point of his process a loss of stability and motor skill appears, as if the animal, although still able to walk, run, fly, or swim, has lost its "balance wheel." This was the original discovery of the function of coordination (Flourens, 1842).

Although his treatment of sensation was still rather unclear in 1824, by the time the second edition of the *Recherches expérimentales* (1842) appeared, Flourens had articulated a clear distinction between sensation and perception (treating perception as the appreciation of the meaning of a sensation).

With respect to the cerebrum, however, the results were quite different. A successive slicing through the hemispheres produced diffuse damage to all of the higher mental functions—

to perception, intellect, and will—with the amount of damage varying only with the extent and not the location of the lesion. Today we struggle as well with determination of the differential effects of degree versus location of lesion. Small lesions in critical locations can cause devastating effects. Larger lesions if occurring in so-called "nonelegant" cortex can create less havoc. If adequate tissue remained, function might be restored; but total ablation led to a permanent loss of function. From these results, Flourens concluded that whereas sensorimotor functions are differentiated and localized subcortically, higher mental functions such as perception, volition, and intellect are spread throughout the cerebrum, operating together as a single factor with the entire cerebrum functioning in a unitary fashion as their "exclusive seat."

Flourens' most productive period was in the 1820s with his experiments on reptiles, birds, and mammals; he rarely made distinctions between the brains of these animals. The brain of a zebra finch and the brain of a gecko were much the same to Flourens. He arrived at some remarkable conclusions based on his experiments of ablation (Finger, 1994). His principal conclusions were: "1. Despite the diversity of action of each of its parts, the whole nervous system is still a particular system; 2. Independently of the proper action of each part, each part has a common action with all the others, as have all the others with it." (Flourens, 1842)

Thus, Flourens viewed the brain as having some degree of localized function, but that it acted as a unit. One of his great discoveries was that the control of respiration resided in the medulla oblongata. Another incredible implication for its day was that Flourens demonstrated that there is considerable plasticity in the cerebral cortex because deficits in behavior caused by cortical lesions could recover. As it was known that brain tissue did not regenerate, this was taken to be evidence that the same functions can be controlled by different parts of the brain. This element of recognition relating to brain plasticity forms the foundation for one of the most exciting elements of neuroscience in the 21st century.

As Doidge (2007) and others have noted, the notion of brain plasticity, that is, changes in neural architecture and neural connectivity based on treatment, therapy, or programmed relevant experience, is one of the most promising avenues in contemporary neuroscience and neurorehabilitation. These implications, rooted in the work of Flourens and eventually Paul Broca have an enormity of potential not only for individuals with neurologic disease and brains gone bad, but for all human beings, not to mention human culture, human learning and human history. The implications of neuroplasticity are immense.

SEX AND AMATIVENESS

One of the faculties or character traits that aroused a good deal of attention at the lectures and readings on phrenology was that of "Amativeness." Just as "romance" novels have captivated the contemporary publishing industry and smutty sites acount for most current hits on the internet, naughtiness commanded popularity in the 1800s. Some things never change. Gall had asserted that "Amativeness" is apparent by the degree of prominence of the occipital bone, and reasoned that sexual proficiency or heightened interest must be localized within the cerebellar hemispheres. The correlation of a large occipital protuberance with sexuality apparently gave rise to interest in other protuberances.

George Combe, a British advocate of Gall who published extensively on the teachings of phrenology explains the origins of the faculty of Amativeness (Combe, 1853).

Dr Gall was led to the discovery of the function of this organ in the following manner. He was physician to a widow of irreproachable character, who was seized with nervous affections, to which succeeded severe nymphomania. In the violence of a paroxsym, he supported her head, and was struck with the great size and heat of the neck. She stated, that heat and tension of these parts always preceded a paroxysm. He followed out, by numerous observations, the idea, suggested by this occurrence, of connexion between the amative propensity and the cerebellum, and he soon established the point to his own satisfaction.

This faculty gives rise to the sexual feeling. In newly born children, the cerebellum is the least developed of all the cerebral parts. At this period, the upper and posterior part of the neck, corresponding to the cerebellum, appears attached almost to the middle of the base of the skull. The weight of the cerebellum is then to that of the brain as one to thirteen, fifteen, or twenty. In adults, it is as one to six, seven, or eight. The cerebellum enlarges much at puberty, and attains its full size between the ages of eighteen and twenty-six. The neck then appears greatly more expanded behind. In general, the cerebellum is less in females than in males. In old age it frequently diminishes.

A mental faculty related to amativeness is "philoprogenitiveness," the characteristic that nurtures the creativity of powerful love poems, and apparently flourishes in cold climates. In the words of George Combe:

PHILOPROGENITIVENESS.

This faculty also inspires the poet and dramatist in compositions on the passion of love; and it exerts a very powerful influence over human conduct. Dr Spurzheim observes, that individuals in whom the organ is very large, ought not to be dedicated to the profession of religion, in countries where chastity for life is required of the clergy.

The organ is more prone to activity in warm than in cold climates. When very large, however, its function is powerfully manifested even in the frozen regions. The Greenlanders and other tribes of Esquimaux, for example, are remarkable for the strength of the feeling; and their skulls, of which the Phrenological Society possesses twenty-one specimens, indicate a large development of the cerebellum.

As Woody Allen and others have noted, the brain is only the second favorite organ of many and apparently amativeness, philoprogenitiveness and the wonderful world of sexuality to the phrenologists was hanging in and around the region of the cerebellum. That conclusion would be taken to task by several future scientists and authorities.

Flourens' research noted no sexual behavior changes following removal of the corresponding structures from experimental animals. He concluded that there was essentially no localization of brain functions, in keeping with the traditions of Descartes, and published a small volume vehemently attacking phrenology (Selby, 1993).

The public argument was rather heated. Some academics and physicians were skeptical and some were swayed by Flourens; other, usually younger doctors, felt that there might be merit to at least some of Gall's and Spurzheim's ideas (Selby, 1993). In Great Britain, Spurzheim met with similar reaction, but gained a rather wide following among many educated people. A phrenology movement arose there and particularly in Scotland where an organized Phrenological Society was founded.

THE AMERICAN TOUR

All was not to remain calm among the proponents of phrenology. The paths of Spurzheim and Gall deviated and they began to develop different ideas and philosophies on how the subject should be developed. Spurzheim, it seemed, was more aware of the admiration of phrenology with the popular press. He apparently decided to capitalize on this by scheduling an extensive European and American lecture tour.

Spurzheim ventured to Boston to conduct orations on phrenology, the first such lecture of his intended American tour (Figure 3–9). He was, in general, well received though a few prominent Boston physicians had reservations about the scientific validity of the concept and the popularization of phrenology. Unfortunately, he became quite ill; some reported his illness as "he took a chill," but others say his demise was possibly from typhoid. The eminent advocate of phrenology died shortly after his arrival in Boston during the kickoff of his great American tour. An archive of the *Boston Medical and Surgical Journal* of November 14, 1832 reports these details (Boston Medical and Surgical Journal, 1832):

> It is our melancholy duty to record the death of a great and good man. Dr. Spurzheim, so well known in Europe and America as the companion of Dr. Gall—as a deep thinker and close observer of human nature—as an interesting teacher of moral and intellectual philosophy, and the author of several works on the anatomy and physiology of the brain and nervous system,—so highly esteemed for his eminent social virtues and moral worth, and so

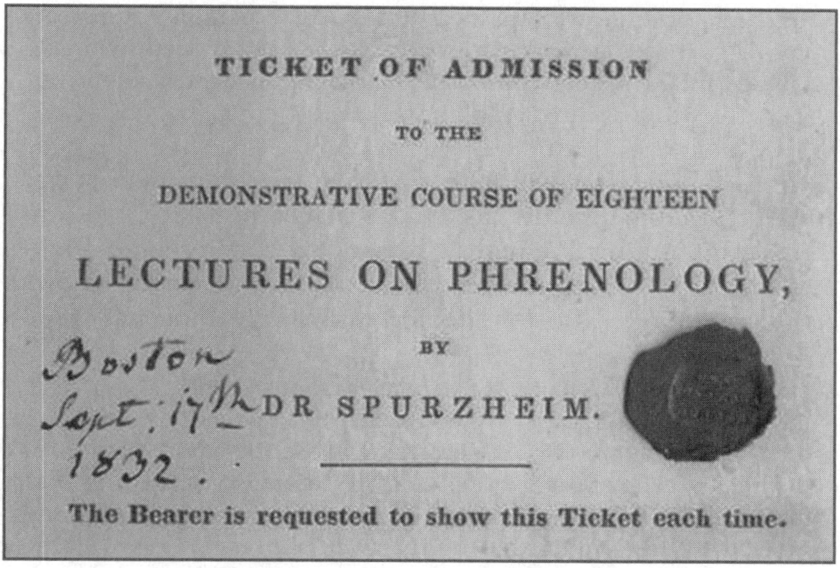

TICKET OF ADMISSION

TO THE

DEMONSTRATIVE COURSE OF EIGHTEEN

LECTURES ON PHRENOLOGY,

BY

DR SPURZHEIM.

The Bearer is requested to show this Ticket each time.

Figure 3–9. Ticket to a Boston lecture by Spurzheim on phrenology.

much beloved by all who shared his friendship, has been prematurely removed from this new scene of his contemplated labors. He died on Saturday evening, at his residence in Pearl Street, after an illness of about four weeks, deeply lamented by the friends he had made during his short residence in this city; his decease will also be a source of sorrow and disappointment to the inhabitants generally, not only of Boston, but also of other cities in other States, where his visits have been solicited, and anticipated with unusual interest.

Dr. S. was born near Treves, in Germany, in 1776. He arrived in this country in September last. Just three weeks ago this day he delivered his last lecture. He was then evidently laboring under serious indisposition, contracted by occasional exposure to the cold night air after being much heated at his lectures. The greater part of Wednesday night he was disturbed by rigors and restlessness; and although too ill to leave his apartments the next day, he was unwilling to submit himself to active medical treatment. This unwillingness was not removed until his disease, which was a typhous fever, had so far advanced that his medical attendants deemed it too late to expect benefit from medication. His brain was chiefly implicated, his reason departed, and he died without

apparent suffering. He was anxious to live to accomplish the great
moral purposes he had in view, but looked upon death without
dread, and with that composure and serenity which might be
expected from a Christian philosopher.

His funeral was well attended. Services were held at Park
Street Church, where his casket was placed in its crypt because
the Mount Auburn cemetery was not yet completed (Selby,
1993). First, however, his heart, brain, and skull were removed.
As recorded in the Boston Medical and Surgical Journal (1832):

> After the bust was taken of this celebrated stranger, and a cast
> made of his brain, the body was properly embalmed and depos-
> ited in a leaden coffin, which was enclosed in another of rich
> mahogany. The abdominal viscera, the thoracic viscera, and the
> brain, were severally preserved in separate cases. The brain was
> unusually large, and weighed fifty seven ounces.

Spurzheim left his heart and brain in Boston, and his skull is
on display at the Warren Museum of Harvard Medical School.
Although there is a grave for Spurzheim (Figure 3–10) at Mount
Auburn, there is no record that his remains were ever moved
there (Selby, 1993; Walsh, 1974). The archive of the *Boston Medical and Surgical Journal* (1832) also contains a resolution to
promulgate Spurzheim's views. At a meeting of the society the
members of the Boston Medical Society passed the motion:

> Resolved, That we recommend to our fellow-citizens the opinions
> of the deceased, on the improvement of our systems of educa-
> tion; and especially what relates to the developement [sic] of the
> physical powers and moral dispositions; and as they can no more
> expect to hear them, from the lips of our lamented friend, that
> they lose no time in making a practical application of them, to the
> existing state of our institutions, for the culture of the human mind.

The Henderson Trust, the inheritors of the museum collection of the Phrenological Society of Edinburgh, possesses a
considerable number of items that relate to Dr. Johann Gaspar
Spurzheim (1776–1832), the disciple of, and from 1804 co-worker
with Franz Joseph Gall, the founder of phrenology (Kaufman &
Basden, 1996).

Figure 3–10. Johann Spurzheim, deciple of Gall. Retrieved April 2, 2012, from https://www.countway.harvard.edu/chm/ rarebooks/exhibits/talking_heads/scans/spurzheimport.jpg.

THE COMBE BROTHERS

Spurzheim visited Edinburgh in 1816 where he defended his system of phrenology against Dr. John Gordon and other of his principal detractors in Scotland. George Combe, one of his audience, was immediately convinced of the rightness of phrenology, and became a most enthusiastic and voluble advocate for the subject, publishing over the years numerous articles and books in its defense. In 1820, with his brother Andrew and a small group of like-minded friends, George Combe founded the Phrenological Society of Edinburgh (Kaufman & Basden, 1996; Figure 3–11). He developed a close relationship with Spurzheim

A

B

Figure 3–11. George (**A**)
and Andrew Combe (**B**),
Scottish advocates of
phrenology. Wikimedia
Commons, public domain.

and in 1828, during one of the latter's visits to Britain, Spurzheim and his wife were the guests of the Society. Combe became a revitalizing force for phrenology in the UK and published several treatises on phrenology (Van Wyhe, 2002).

Both Spurzheim and his ideas flowered in the United States. Phrenology became rather widely accepted and practiced, once again with varying degrees of acceptance by the medical community. Following the U.S. Civil War, the school of phrenology received further and enthusiastic support and usage by two rather remarkable families, the Fowlers and the Wells, and by a good many other phrenology disciples and practitioners in other cities and states.

Phrenology parlors began springing up in the larger cities of Philadelphia, Boston, and New York and, much like psychics and astrologers became popular with people who wanted to hear good things about themselves for a price. Head analyses were relatively expensive. Following each analysis, the summary of findings would be inscribed, often in a small book, which explained the principles of phrenology and the particular qualities of an individual associated with prominence or lack of it of the many areas of the head. The person's strengths, relative weaknesses, and other attributes were noted, sometimes with advice for correction or improvement. It was not uncommon for young couples to present themselves prior to marriage to learn if they were compatible. Perhaps, some people were helped psychologically by the analysis.

American notables became fans of phrenology and attributed some of their success to the insights gained from having their heads examined. Clara Barton, the American nurse, humanitarian, and founder of the Red Cross attributed her successful career to the phrenological analysis made of her when she was quite young, shy, and uncertain about herself. Clarissa Harlowe Barton was born on Christmas day, 1821, in Oxford, Massachusetts, to Stephen and Sarah Barton. She was the youngest of five children. Clara's father was a farmer and horse breeder, while her mother Sarah managed the household of little Bartons. When Clara was eleven, her brother David became her first patient after he fell from a rafter in their unfinished barn. Clara stayed at his side for three years and learned to administer all his medicines, including the "great, loathsome crawling leeches" (Ross, 1956).

For a time, Walt Whitman worked for the Fowlers in New York. Phrenology was "the science of mind" in the United States during the nineteenth century. It was serious business and artists who wished to express their scientific side adopted and endorsed it. Politicians and writers were followers and phrenology was the fad of a great number of people. Walt Whitman was one of those people. Fowler and Wells established a money-making industry of the phrenological trade and Whitman and others frequented their Phrenological Cabinet in New York. In the 1855 preface to *Leaves of Grass,* Whitman includes the phrenologist among those he describes as "the lawgivers of poets" (Mackey, 1997).

Likewise, several major writers assumed a much more skeptical stance toward phrenology than did Whitman. Edgar Allan Poe, though he favorably reviewed phrenological journals early on and used phrenological categories in some of the characterizations in his fiction, went on to write parodies of it (Poe, 2011).

Mark Twain, the great American author and humorist dealt skeptically with it as well. Stone (2003) in a historical vignette about Twain and phrenology presents excerpts of the great one's commentary on this new fad science of the 19th century. This skepticism about phrenology is apparent in the collections of the Mark Twain Museum in Hannibal, Missouri as well and a personal visit in the summer of 2010 triggered my interest in Twain's parody of head reading. Mark Twain (Samuel L. Clemens) (1835–1910) is often described as the foremost American author and humorist of the 19th century. Twain had an interest in psychology and was examined by several phrenologists. (Stone, 2003). The following excerpt was taken from *The Autobiography of Mark Twain*, Vol. 1 (2010) and is reproduced with permission:

> I lately received a letter from England from a gentleman whose belief in phrenology is strong and who wonders why phrenology has apparently never interested me enough to move me to write about it. I have explained as follows:
>
> Dear Sir:
>
> I never did profoundly study phrenology; therefore I am neither qualified to express an opinion about it nor entitled to do so. In London, 33 or 34 years ago, I made a small test of phrenology for

my better information. I went to Fowler under an assumed name and he examined my elevations and depressions and gave me a chart which I carried home to the Langham Hotel and studied with great interest and amusement-the same interest and amusement which I should have found in the chart of an impostor who had been passing himself off for me and who did not resemble me in a single sharply defined detail. I waited 3 months and went to Mr. Fowler again, heralding my arrival with a card bearing both my name and my *nom de guerre*. Again, I carried away an elaborate chart. It contained several sharply defined details of my character, but it bore no recognizable resemblance to the earlier chart. These experiences gave me a prejudice against phrenology which has lasted until now. I am aware that the prejudice should have been against Fowler, instead of against the art; but I am human and that is not the way that prejudices act.

In America, 40 or 50 years ago, Fowler and Wells stood at the head of the phrenological industry, and the firm's name was familiar in all ears. Their publications had a wide currency and were read and studied and discussed by truth-seekers and by converts all over the land. One of the most frequent arrivals in our village of Hannibal was the peripatetic phrenologist and he was popular and always welcome. He gathered the people together and gave them a gratis lecture on the marvels of phrenology, then felt their bumps and made an estimate of the result, at twenty-five cents per head. I think the people were almost always satisfied with these translations of their characters—if one may properly use that word in this connection; and indeed the word is right enough, for the estimates really were translations, since they conveyed seeming facts out of apparent simplicities into unsimple technical forms of expressions, although as a rule their meanings got left behind on the journey. Phrenology found many a bump on a man's head and it labeled each bump with a formidable and outlandish name of its own. The phrenologist took delight in mouthing these great names; they gurgled from his lips in an easy and unembarrassed stream, and this exhibition of cultivated facility compelled the envy and admiration of everybody. By and by the people became familiar with these strange names and addicted to the use of them and they batted them back and forth in conversation with deep satisfaction-a satisfaction which could hardly have been more contenting if they had known for certain what the words meant.

It is not at all likely, I think, that the traveling expert ever got any villager's character quite right, but it is a safe guess that he was always wise enough to furnish his clients character-charts that would compare favorably with George Washington's. It was a long time ago and yet I think I still remember that no phrenologist ever came across a skull in our town that fell much short of the Washington standard. This general and close approach to perfection ought to have roused suspicion, perhaps, but I do not remember that it did. It is my impression that the people admired phrenology and believed in it and that the voice of the doubter was not heard in the land.

I was reared in this atmosphere of faith and belief and trust, and I think its influence was still upon me, so many years afterward, when I encountered Fowler's advertisements in London. I was glad to see his name and glad of an opportunity to personally test his art. The fact that I went to him under a fictitious name is an indication that not the whole bulk of the faith of my boyhood was still with me; it looks like circumstantial evidence that in some way my faith had suffered impairment in the course of the years. I found Fowler on duty in the midst of the impressive symbols of his trade. On brackets, on tables, on shelves, all about the room, stood marble-white busts, hairless, every inch of the skull occupied by a shallow bump, and every bump labeled with its imposing name, in black letters.

Fowler received me with indifference, fingered my head in an uninterested way, and named and estimated my qualities in a bored and monotonous voice. He said I possessed amazing courage, an abnormal spirit of daring, a pluck, a stern will, and a fearlessness that were without limit. I was astonished at this, and gratified, too; I had not suspected it before; but then he foraged over on the other side of my skull and found a hump there which he called caution. This hump was so tall, so mountainous, that it reduced my courage-bump to a mere hillock by comparison, although the courage-bump had been so prominent up to that time-according to his description of it-that it ought to have been a capable thing to hang my hat on; but it amounted to nothing, now, in the presence of that Matterhorn which he called my Caution. He explained that if that Matterhorn had been left out of my scheme of character I would have been one of the bravest men that ever lived—possibly the bravest—but that my cautiousness was so prodigiously superior to it that it abolished my courage and made me almost spectacularly timid. He continued his discoveries, with the result that I came out safe and sound, at the end, with a hundred great and shining qualities; but which lost their value and amounted to nothing because each of the hundred was coupled up with an opposing defect which took the effectiveness all out of it.

However, he found a cavity, in one place; a cavity where the bump would have been in anybody else's skull. That cavity, he said, was all alone, all by itself, occupying a solitude, and had no opposing bump, however slight in elevation, to modify and ame-liorate its perfect completeness and isolation. He startled me by saying that that cavity represented the total absence of the sense of humor! He now became almost interested. Some of his indif-ference disappeared. He almost grew eloquent over this American which he had discovered. He said he often found bumps of humor which were so small that they were hardly noticeable, but that in his long experience this was the first time he had ever come across a cavity where that bump ought to be.

I was hurt, humiliated, resentful, but I kept these feeling to myself; at bottom, I believed his diagnosis was wrong, but I was not certain. In order to make sure, I thought I would wait until he should have forgotten my face and the peculiarities of my skull, and then come back and try again and see if he had really known what he had been talking about, or had only been guessing. After three months I went to him again, but under my own name this time. Once more he made a striking discovery—the cavity was gone, and in its place was a Mount Everest—figuratively speak-ing—31,000 feet high, the loftiest bump of humor he had ever encountered in his life-long experience! I went from his presence prejudiced against phrenology, but it may be, as I have said to the English gentleman, that I ought to have conferred the prejudice upon Fowler and not upon the art which he was exploiting [Feb. 10, 1907; the English gentleman was not really a gentleman: he sold my private letter to a newspaper].

Eleven years ago on board a ship bound for Europe, William T. Stead made a photograph of my right hand, and afterwards, in London, sent replicas of it to twelve palmists, concealing from them my name and asking them to make and send to him esti-mates of the character of the owner of the hand. The estimates were furnished and Stead published six or seven of them in his magazine. By those estimates, I found that my make-up was about like anybody else's; I did not seem to differ much from other people; certainly in no prominent and striking way—except in a single detail. In none of the estimates was the word humor mentioned-if my memory is not mistreating me-except in one; in that one the palmist said that the possessor of that hand was totally destitute of the sense of humor. (Twain, 2010)

Other prominent authors have come under the spell of phrenology also, and Melville, in *Moby Dick,* has Ishmael attempt to phrenologize the whale only to conclude that it can't be done (Mackey, 1997). Some heads are too big to rub.

Slowly, enthusiasm waned for phrenology as increasing skepticism and loss of acceptance by physicians and other occurred, and by the 1920s it was largely denounced as medical quackery.

Phrenology might otherwise be a sociological curiosity except that it stirred the thoughts of a few doctors, primarily in France that some localization of cerebral functions might exist. The most notable initial observation was that of Jean-Baptiste Bouillaud who was an avid phrenologist. Eventually Aubertin and Paul Broca became involved in the debates about localization of functions in the brain and this was the impetus for Broca's remarkable initiation of clinic-pathological research that led to his landmark 1861 pronouncements about the seat of language in the brain.

Despite subsequent misgivings, the overstated and over-generalized pseudoscience of phrenology contributed to the initial discoveries and concepts of cerebral localization. The latter eventually reached rather extreme parcellation of both cortical functions and anatomy, which have undergone significant modifications in understanding. Yet the development of the initial ideas of localization allowed the preoperative diagnosis of the location of the first successful surgery for brain tumor, thus making possible important contributions to clinical neurologic exams (Finger, 1994; Selby, 1993; Van Wyhe, 2011).

Gall died in Paris, on August 22, 1828 when Pierre Paul Broca was four years old and still romping around the fields and vineyards of Ste. Foy-La-Grande. In 1819 Gall became a naturalized French subject, but his efforts two years afterward to obtain admission to the Academy of Sciences, although supported by E. Geoffroy Saint-Hilaire, the eminent French naturalist, were unsuccessful.

I walk along the street named after Saint-Hilaire on my way to the Broca collection in the temporary location of the Musée de l'Homme near the Jardin des Plantes these weeks in June and July of 2011. Connections to French brains are everywhere in this locale of French thought and learning. The rue names are reminders to those who notice or remember that the French respected and honored their scientists.

In 1823 Gall visited London with the intention of giving a series of phrenological lectures, but his reception was not what he had anticipated, and he abandoned his plans. He continued to lecture and practice in Paris until the beginning of 1828, when he was disabled by an "apoplectic" seizure. Apoplexy was the old term for a cerebrovascular accident or stroke. Irony, indeed, for both Gall and several of his predecessors who would be cut down by the pathologies they studied or implied. His death took place at Montrouge near Paris (Gall, 2011). Gall's phrenological theories and practices were best accepted in England, where the ruling class were accused of using it to justify the "inferiority" of its colonial subjects, including the Irish, and then in America, where it became very popular from 1820 to 1850. The misuse of Gall's ideas and work to justify discrimination were deliberately furthered by his associates, including Spurzheim. However, the basic premise of phrenology proved too simplistic and fell victim to overgeneralization, that great trapdoor of critical and scientific reasoning. Gall believed that since psychological functions were localized in the brain, the personality and talents of a person would be identifiable by the shape of their skull. Later work, however, revealed that the surface of the skull does not reflect the topography of the brain, invalidating his idea.

Overgeneralization and less than meticulous critical thinking struck again. However, Gall's contributions to neurological science were significant. He popularized that emotions were not located in the *heart* but in the *brain*, just as Hippocrates had recognized, and that certain parts of the brain controlled particular emotions and actions. At the time these were revolutionary ideas (Gall, New World Encyclopedia, 2011), and led, as we shall see to paths of clinical experimentation that would further our knowledge the steppingstones of understanding about brain and behavior.

Gall's attention to skulls and his contributions to the localization of functions in the brain paved the way for Broca and others to move on and establish detail to the principles of what we know about brain and human behavior. Ironically, Gall's own skull now rests forever in the collection of anthropology in the *Musée de l'Homme's* temporary quarters in the *Jardin des*

Plantes in the 5th arrondisement of Paris. On a rainy June day in 2011, Philippe Mennecier escorted me on one of my many visits through the 87 cabinets and holdings on Broca and Gall and revealed for me the skull of Franz Josef Gall (Figure 3–12). I was able to rub my hand lightly across this famous skull of all skull readers, but I felt no remarkable bumps.

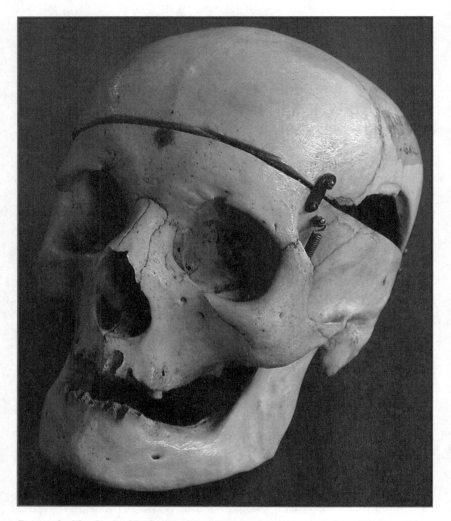

Figure 3–12. *Skull of Franz Josef Gall. Photo used with permission of Philippe Mennecier, Charge de Conservation des collections d'anthropologie biologuique, Musée national d'histoire naturelle.*

Chapter 4

Relics of Aphasia: The Artifacts of Lost Words

Problems with speech and language, and specifically aphasia, have been recorded for centuries. Descriptions and characteristics of aphasia have been around since the time of the ancient Egyptians who wrote with little hieroglyphic icons on papyrus. Aphasia no doubt existed in the dank recesses of pre-history or at least as long as humans have had language. The earliest reports of aphasia harken back to the Surgical Papers of the Egyptians (Minagar, Ragheb, & Kelley, 2003), as indicated previously. Benton and Joynt (1960) trace the history of so-called "exhumed" early descriptions of aphasia that surfaced after the attention to the disorder drawn by Paul Broca in the 1860s. As these authors indicate, one of the features of the spirited and prolonged discussion that followed Broca's famous pathological demonstrations before the Académie de Médecine of Paris in 1861 was the "exhumation" of ancient and long-forgotten descriptions of aphasia. Thus, Falret, in his analysis of the clinical forms of aphasia, mentioned case reports by Johann Gesner (1770) and Alexander Crichton (1798) as being among the earliest in the field. Trousseau, who argued with Broca about what to label the disorder (and whose suggestion ultimately prevailed) went farther back into the recesses of history, citing the anecdotes of Pliny the Elder as evidence that aphasia was known as early as the first century AD. Pliny the Elder, was a Roman author, naturalist, and philosopher, as well as a naval and army commander of the early Roman Empire. Although there is historical evidence of the existence of the works of Pliny the Elder and Pliny the Younger, there is no evidence, to my knowledge, of Pliny the Thinner or Pliny the Plump.

The 1800s proved to be the seminal century for speculations on where in the brain the regulator of language was housed. Forms and signs and symptoms of language loss are scattered throughout early times, though few commentaries offer explanations of its nature. A number of thorough examinations of the history of aphasia are available, though many of them smack of either a nationalistic or philosophical perspective. Schools of thought and divisive debate have characterized study of the phenomenon since early times. Debaters at societies and in published form have not hesitated to attach labels and name-calling to those who held differing opinions. "Diagram-makers" and other labels characterize particularly the holistic versus localizationist arguments from early on. The history of aphasia is well-seasoned with "forgotten history," "memory-holes," and "collective amnesia." Just as today, selective history and emphasis has served particular stances, viewpoints, and schools of thought. This even has extended regionally in the United States as witnessed by the fertile history of the "Mayo Clinic" or "Minnesota" approach to aphasia versus the "Boston school." Disciplinary emphasis on particular approaches to the perspective of aphasia also is abundantly evident.

The literature archive of the Clinical Aphasiology Conference is a good example of unawarness or benign neglect of a significant archive of literature on aphasia. This archive of over 40 years of conference presentations and publications on aphasia now has participation increasingly from international aphasiologists, although it started in the basement of a Veterans Administration Hospital in Albuquerque, New Mexico by Dr. Bruce Porch. This four decade archive of writings and observations about aphasia is largely absent from many contemporaneous reviews of aphasia. Through the impetus of Malcolm McNeil and the auspices of the University of Pittsburgh, the entire archive of accessible abstracts and proceedings since 1971 is available from the Clinical Aphasiology Conference Web site as well as at the Clinical Aphasiology University of Pittsburgh archive at http://aphasiology.pitt.edu/

Contemporary programs at international meetings or at the Academy of Aphasia or Clinical Aphasiology Conference meetings in the United States are at the mercy of the winds and tides of the current program committees, and grumblings are heard about overemphasis or neglect of topics in neurolinguistics, rehabilitation, diagnostics, or fascination with the mesmerizing topic of the *condition* of aphasia as opposed to its debilitating effects on *persons* with aphasia. Perhaps this is to be expected. It certainly sets up echoes in the great canyon of aphasia and scientific history. It contributes to phenomenological myopia though, and perhaps fosters the waxing and waning of disciplinary representation in academies and societies. Nothing much has changed. We are at the mercy of human nature, perhaps, and bias is sanctified with ubiquity. Aphasiologists and scientists in general are and have viewed and colored topics from the limited viewpoint of their discipline; how they were trained and who trained them; who they like and dislike; and what they have to gain from embracing a school or approach to a topic. although this is a tension and a struggle, it also is remarkably illustrated by attempts to instill a semblance of the noble tenets of balance, good science, and objectivity, though the information explosion has destined us to run the risk of overlooking important erstwhile views. The history of aphasia is a testament to this imperfect fabric of debate, neglect, and intermittent balance.

Several contemporary treatments of the history of aphasia and brain-based speech loss are noteworthy exemplars. Tesak and Code have written an authoritative work on the topic entitled *Milestones in the History of Aphasia* (2008). This book takes a predominantly "through-the-ages" approach starting with an examination of the earliest medical documents and medieval attempts to understand aphasia, across the critical events of the 19th and 20th centuries. It traces the development of theory about and understanding of aphasia, and the reflections and role of significant individuals in this history of lost words. This book is indeed a notable milestone in its own right on the main events and personalities in the fertile history of aphasia. Tesak is a German aphasiologist and Chris Code is a British professional bass guitar player who studies aphasia and is well-tuned to the chord progressions of history.

Eling (1994) has edited a reader in aphasia history that includes translations of many of the seminal works on the topic. This collection brings together original publications by 19th- and 20th-century scientists concerned with the relationship between language and the brain. In selecting texts the emphasis was on those that deal explicitly with the opinion of an author on language processes as revealed by aphasic phenomena. All texts in Eling's collection are presented in English (many of them translated for the first time), and supplemented by in-depth introductions by present-day specialists in the field. This collection is representative, but certainly not exhaustive, of some of the critical early publications by historic figures. Original texts of notable articles include those by *Franz Joseph Gall* (1758–1828); *Paul Broca* (1824–1880); *Carl Wernicke* (1848–1905); *Henry Charlton Bastian* (1837–1915); *John Hughlings Jackson* (1835–1911); *Sigmund Freud* (1856–1939); *Jules Dejerine* (1849–1917); *Pierre Marie* (1853–1940); *Arnold Pick* (1851–1924); *Henry Head* (1861–1940); *Kurt Goldstein* (1878–1965); and *Norman Geschwind* (1926–1984).

Another celebrated publication, in the form of a *festschrift* after his death, is a collection of articles on the work of Frederic L. Darley (Duffy & Wertz, 2001), an American aphasiologist. Frederic Darley contributed mightily to our contemporary understanding of aphasia and motor speech disorders including critical works on the dysarthrias and apraxia of speech. He also provided important insights on the psychosocial issues in aphasia and speech loss (LaPointe, 2001). Both Darley and Harold Goodglass (Goodglass, 2011) are perhaps two of the most recognized American aphasiologists of recent times. Important captures of the history and relevance of acquired speech and language disorders are also sprinkled throughout a work by Murdoch (2010), an influential contributor to the science of acquired speech and language disorders from Wivenhoe Pocket in Australia. Murdoch is a scientist who abandoned a promising career in speed boat racing to study the art of artificial insemination of rabbits and eventually carve out his extensive vocation in neurogenic disorders of communication.

Others have noted the history of Paul Broca and the documentation of aspects of aphasic language. These records were noted by Lee (1981) in another tribute to the impact of this noted French pioneer.

Not all aphasia history centered in France. Though this book is on the French brains who molded current understanding of cortical localization of language and aphasia, our cultural myopic view is sometimes a bit skewed. Zago and Berkovic (2006) remind us that contributions from Italy have been plentiful as well. While the debate about cerebral localization of articulate speech was raging in France in the 1860s with Paul Broca as a leading celebrity, there were some Italians who made important contributions to the subject. Among those was the physician Antonio Berti, who in 1865 furnished interesting observations on the association of aphasia with the frontal lobe. Zago and Berkovic (2006) document a somewhat forgotten episode that represents one of the early Italian observations on the issue of cortical localization of speech.

Luminaries such as Carl Wernicke, who met a tragic death after falling off his bicycle and being run over by an ox cart in the mountains; and Hugo Liepmann, a reticent German neurologist, made monumental marks on acquired brain disorders. In 1873, Wernicke studied a patient who had suffered a stroke. Although the man was able to speak and his hearing was unimpaired, he could barely understand what was said to him. Interestingly, Wernicke's patient also could not comprehend written communication and is another example of acquired dyslexia. After the patient died, Wernicke reported a lesion in the posterior parietal/temporal region of the patient's left cerebral hemisphere. Wernicke concluded that this region, which is proximal to the primary auditory reception area of the brain, was involved in speech comprehension. Wernicke christened the syndrome sensory aphasia, although now it is typically called Wernicke's aphasia (Bynum, 1970). This area of the brain, posterior to the Rolandic fissure in the temporal lobe, has come to be known as Wernicke's area, an area of the brain that is not consistently or specifically defined.

LIEPMANN AND APRAXIA

Hugo Liepmann, who first described the nature and characteristics of apraxia and volitional movement disorders, and other German scientists contributed to the prominent efforts to advance behavioral neuroscience and these efforts in Germany continue to this day in Germany at Aachen and elsewhere. Scandinavia also has a rich history of research in aphasia and other parts of Europe, Asia, South America, and particularly Canada in North America have their own sweet histories, by and large neglected by many contemporary writers in neurological disorders. Hugo Karl Liepmann (April 9, 1863, to May 6, 1925) was a German neurologist and psychiatrist who was a native of Berlin. From 1895 to 1899 he was an assistant to the now eminent Carl Wernicke in Breslau (Goldenberg, 2003). Beginning in 1900, he began extensive work with a disorder he called apraxia. Apraxia is the inability to act or move different parts of the body in a purposeful manner, even though the physical capability of movement is normal. Liepmann reported that damage in the parietal lobe prevented activation of learned sequences of actions that are necessary to produce desired results on command. As a result of his studies, he divided apraxia into three types:

◆ Ideational: object blindness, where the patient is incapable of making appropriate use of familiar objects upon command.
◆ Ideomotor: the inability to follow verbal commands or mimic an action, such as saluting or waving goodbye.
◆ Kinetic: clumsiness in performing a precision act that is not due to paralysis, muscle weakness, or sensory loss.

Hugo Liepmann acquired both MD and PhD degrees and was fascinated with philosophy, though he is characterized by his daughters as "a typical absent minded professor" who was plagued by self-doubt and suffered from stage fright and was genuinely uneasy with public lecturing (Goldenberg, 2003). His landmark contributions to the nature of apraxia and disorders of volitional movement include detailed descriptions of the nature of faulty movements, both of omission and commission and his early detailed descriptions served as the basis for generalization to the disorder of apraxia of speech in the first comprehensive book on the disorder by Wertz, LaPointe, and Rosenbek (1984).

Ogar et al. (2005) have provided an update and overview of apraxia of speech with attention to Liepmann's early contributions. The review by Ogar et al. (2005) details the history and confusion of the early terminological maze surrounding the disorder apraxia of speech and particularly its relationship to Broca's original description of *aphemia* and aphasia. The distinctions among these disorders are still unclear and continue to plague clinicians, diagnosticians, and historical writers.

Liepmann introduced the general term "apraxia" and defined it as an inability to perform voluntary acts despite preserved muscle strength (Liepmann, 1908). Liepmann's notation of "apraxia of the glosso-labio-pharyngeal structures" was refined by Darley, who first coined the term "apraxia of speech" in the 1960s (Darley, 1969).

The conception of a disorder of articulate or "articulated" speech in the presence of preserved language skills and unimpaired muscular function was originally introduced a century earlier by Paul Broca (Broca, 1861a). He called the disorder *aphemia* and observed that:

> There are cases in which the general faculty for language remains unaltered; where the auditory apparatus is intact; where all muscles—including those of speech and articulation—are under voluntary control; and where nevertheless, a cerebral lesion abolishes articulated language.

Even though Broca distinguished between speech and language disorders early on, it is unclear if his aphemia is synonymous with today's apraxia of speech, particularly because Broca's original patient Monsieur Leborgne only produced recurrent utterances and not enough spontaneous speech to discern specific characteristics of apraxia of speech (Ogar et al., 2005). M. Leborgne is reported to be able only to utter the syllable "Tan" repeatedly, hence the origin of his rather demeaning nickname that persists in the literature today.

The cloud of confusion surrounding the relationship between linguistic, phonologic, and motoric elements of disrupted articulate speech and language has persisted to this day, despite attempts to object to it, clarify it, re-define it, and separate it and measure it with contemporary instrumentation of speech science (Hillis et al., 2004; McNeil, Pratt, & Fossett, 2004).

The border zone of linguistic, phonologic, and motoric disruption is so plagued by complex interactions among the elements, that attempts to separate them are much like trying to define precisely and with consensus when it is dark as we experience dusk; or straining to discern the dry ingredients of a cake (*gateau*) batter once they have been irretrievably intermixed. Liepmann apparently recognized this and his careful attempts to precisely describe the nature of the planning and programming disorders of apraxia and disrupted volitional movement go largely neglected today.

TIME FOR LICHTHEIM

With his manifesto for disconnectionist modeling, first published in German and then in English in the journal *Brain*, Ludwig Lichtheim (1845–1928) added a third classic 19th century account of aphasiology to those already written by Paul Broca and Karl Wernicke. Lichtheim attempted to settle controversies relating to aphasia by observing and then explaining the "experiments of nature" or specific cases of aphasia. With foresight Lichtheim (1885) predicted that his day's clinical curiosity would become some of the future laws of aphasiology. He remarked on the contributions of both Broca and Wernicke by suggesting that Broca, after many mistakes had been made historically, brought into sharp relief aphasia in its narrower sense and Wernicke made the distinction between "motor and sensorial aphasia" and a third type designated as the commissural aphasia called *Leitungsaphasie* (Lichtheim, 1885). Of course, the dust has not settled on the great debates about aphasia classification and types.

The debate on classification of aphasia was only to heat up. In 1906, Marie published a paper with the provocative title; *The Third Left Frontal Convolution Plays No Special Role in the Function of Language*. Brais, (1992) captures the spirit of Marie's argument in his review of Marie's rather firmly planted stance. In it, Marie asserted that language contains both sensorimotor and psychological elements and that it is a faculty rather than a sen-

sorimotor function. He supported this with a series of pathological studies in which patients with lesions in Broca's area lacked
any aphasia. He claimed that the *faculty* view of neurological
function meant that persons with aphasia invariably have mental symptoms as well as physical ones. His article touched off
a spectacular public fight with Dejerine, who dismissed Marie's
claims out of hand. In an exchange of articles, each man criticized the other's ideas and character. Marie and Dejerine did
not get along, and from all accounts their interactions were a
titanic clash of personalities. Marie's style was direct, to say the
least. His bluntly titled article and his continuing debate with
Dejerine heated up. His article was so offensive that it provoked
Dejerine to challenge Marie to a duel on the fields of the Bois de
Boulogne park in Paris (Feinberg & Farah, 1997). Marie believed
that there was just one basic form of aphasia ("aphasia is one"),
a posterior aphasia, which was a type of general intellectual
loss not specific to language per se. He held that the speech
problems of anterior lesions in so-called aphasia were motoric in
nature. Some of the most explicit of historic quarrels on aphasia
occurred during three meetings of the French Society of Neurology in 1908, when, in one corner Joseph Jules Dejerine and in
the other corner, Pierre Marie crossed swords, almost literally.

Andre Roch Lecours, a professor of neurology in Montreal
has traced a rich history of these historical debates and squabbles
over the topic of aphasia (Roch Lecours, 1999). Good fights have
been well chronicled in brain science history including grap-
pling by Lordat versus Gall; Dax versus Bouillaud; Broca versus
Dax; Gratiolet versus Aubertin; Trousseau versus Broca; Lordat
versus Trousseau; Geschwind versus Darley; and McNeil versus LaPointe, Wertz, Rosenbek, Duffy, Pratt, et al. Roch Lecours
(1999) and his colleague, my imaginary cousin, Yves Joanette,
have done much to illustrate the tumultuous and glorious history
of aphasia in their writings.

York (2005) and Roch Lecours (1999) have captured interesting recapitulations of these great aphasia debates (not that the linguistic spitting has withered much in some places) and adds a bit
of enlightened spice to the history of aphasia. In some arrondise-
ments, the rapiers and tongues are still pointed and sharp.

From Pierre Marie's statement "aphasia is one," to modern
day arm wrestling about the necessity, validity, and futility of

classification systems of aphasic phenomena, the murkiness of aphasia taxonomy continues. Pierre Marie's extensive study of aphasia and brain-based language disorders sharply contrasted with the generally accepted views of Paul Broca. See McNeil and Copland (2011) for another perspective on aphasia classification. One is reminded of the quotation attributed to another French brain, Jean-Baptiste Karr, "*plus ça change, plus c'est la même chose*" usually translated as "the more things change, the more they stay the same."

The demand for care of brain-injured soldiers after the First World War resulted in more intensive study of aphasia. Kleist in Germany and Head in England based much of their case material on war injuries. Wepman and Schuell in the United States worked primarily with brain-injured veterans and eventually the Veterans Administration (now called the Department of Veterans Affairs) attracted many American aphasiologists to do research and rehabilitate American war veterans. It was the Second World War, however, that initiated the burst of new interest in aphasiology that continues to grow in many clinical and academic centers throughout the world. In the United States, three National Veterans Aphasia Centers were established immediately after World War II, one in Long Beach, California, one in Minneapolis, Minnesota, and one in Framingham, Massachusetts. The Framingham center moved into the Boston VA Hospital in 1952 and became the clinical base for the development of the respected Goodglass Aphasia Research Center which contributed mightily to advancing interest and research in aphasia. Many contemporary aphasiologists in the United States honed their chops working with surviving head-injured veterans. My clinical experience in brain-based disorders was largely grounded on assessment and treatment of head-injured survivors of the Vietnam War and countless hours were logged at the Fitzsimons Army Hospital and the Veterans Administration Medical Centers of Denver and Gainesville, Florida trying to understand and facilitate recovery from the amalgam of cognitive and communication puzzles that presented themselves in our clinics every day. The article by Marshall, Golper, Boysen, and Katz (2009) lists no fewer than 34 books on brain-based communication disorders published by clinician-researchers based at Veterans Medical Centers in the United States.

STRANGE WORDS RECALLED IN LITERATURE

Fancher (1996) in a book entitled *Pioneers of Psychology* remarks on the unusual aphasia of Jonathan Swift (1667–1745) the famous British author of *Gulliver's Travels*. Following a stroke the year before he died, Swift became unable to speak with his former adeptness of language, but instead was nearly speechless. When he became irritated or under highly emotional circumstances, his language arose from its vault, and certain exclamations were uttered with complete intelligibility. He is reported to have angrily shouted at a servant who was attempting to break up a chunk of coal, "That is a stone, you blockhead!" On another occasion when he was upset with himself he exclaimed, "I am a fool!" In circumstances requiring ordinary conversation, however, he is reported to have remained nearly mute (Fancher, 1996).

A similar case is reported by Fancher involving a priest with aphasic socially inappropriate language. In 1843 this man of the cloth suffered a stroke and was left only with the ability to produce "the most forceful oath beginning with an 'f,' and which our dictionaries have never been able to print."

Some of the early accounts of aphasia were by great writers, among them Samuel Johnson (who described the frustrations of his own aphasia) as cited by Critchley (1962), and Goethe (probably of his maternal grandfather)as reported by Riese (1947).

Critchley (1962) reports Samuel Johnson's letters regarding his own aphasia (though apparently Johnson retained writing ability).

Letter 1. First Day of Illness

Dear Sir, It hath pleased almighty God this morning to deprive me of the powers of speech; and, as I do not know but that it may be his farther good pleasure to deprive me soon of my senses, I request you will, on the receipt of this note, come to me, and act for me, as the exigencies of my case may require.

Critchley (1962) also reports a dubious notion by Johnson of what might reverse his speechlessness.

Dear Sir,

I think that by a speedy application of stimulants much may be done. I question if a vomit vigorous and rough would not rouse

the organs of speech to action . . . I sometimes alleviate a painful, or more properly, an oppressive constriction of my chest, by
opiates, and have lately taken opium frequently but the last, or
two last times in smaller quantities . . .

Jellinek (2002) reports that the Swedish botanist and physician Linnaeus wrote of the condition in a fellow academic at
Uppsala. Pinel, the Paris liberator of psychiatric patients, gave a
classic description in 1809 of a notary who could not speak, read,
or write after a stroke and whose words were unfathomable.

LARREY: AN UNLIKELY APHASIOLOGIST

Jellinek (2002) has uncovered a previously unrecognized aphasiologist in Dr. D. J. Larrey, who served as Napoleon's wartime
surgeon. The vast literature of aphasia is rich in improbabilities
and veiled references to speech or language disorders that may
or may not be aphasia. Two pioneers have become eponyms
(Broca and Wernicke), and many are famous or notorious, such
as Gall, Bouillaud, Trousseau, and Pierre Marie in France, Liepmann in Germany, and Hughlings Jackson and Bastian in England for their association with aphasia in the literature. Larrey
too deserves reputation, according to Jellinek's historic sleuthing, but was rarely cited by his contemporaries. The writings of
Larrey contain no fewer than twelve cases of aphasia, two with
some rather gruesome illustrations. This military surgeon started
his long career in the navy of the Bourbon royalty in 1787 and
recorded his experiences in twenty-six bloody Napoleonic campaigns, and their aftermath, in multivolume works (Larrey, 1817).
    According to Jellinek (2002), Larrey's prize example of apha-
sia is also a very early account of compensation for the disorder. Larrey's subject was a soldier named Louis Manez. This
corporal in Napoleon's horse guards was struck at long range
by a British musket ball in the left eyebrow at Waterloo on
June 18, 1815. He lost consciousness and lay on the battlefield
for two nights. He was then tended by a citizen of Brussels for
some months while his right hemiplegia improved. He became
mobile, and at the end of 1815 came under the care of Dr. Larrey

at the Guards Hospital in Paris. Despite a messy wound with half the projectile still impacted, he improved to the extent that he returned to duty in the royal foot guards, and was promoted to sergeant instructor. In a remarkable example of return to work and compensatory strategies for aphasia, Jellinek reports that the returning soldier compensated for his inability to name his pupil soldiers, or the parts of the weapons, by reading from lists and instruction booklets. He died of pulmonary tuberculosis 12 years after Waterloo. His skull vault had multiple small depressed fractures deep to the bullet remnant, overlying the lateral surface of the frontal lobe and the course of the left middle cerebral artery. Larrey deposited the skull vault specimen in the museum of the Paris Jardin des Plantes, where I labored regularly amid the collections of Gall and Broca and others in 2011. I had newly discovered respect for the small street that I wandered down (Rue Larrey) on my way to the anthropological collections at the Jardin des Plantes.

Jellinek (2002) reports that five others of his aphasia cases were battle casualties: one, a sailor (case 6), had been wounded and captured by the British in the West Indies, and had been trephined in England while a prisoner of war. Larrey himself taught conservative management of head injuries, except when bone splinters or other matter had penetrated the brain through the meninges. Figure 4–1 depicts the illustration of his patient with aphasia from a gunshot wound that accompanied Larrey's original description.

Larrey, like other battlefield surgeons of the time, worked without gloves, wearing only an apron to stop blood from splashing onto his fine cornflower blue uniform (Nestor, 2003; Richardson, 1974). He is reported to have held a bloodied scalpel between his teeth as he tied off severed blood vessels with his bare hands. Few drugs were available to assist with pain relief during surgery, except for the old standby John Barleycorn or alcohol, which was used to induce intoxication prior to "going under the knife." This method was not entirely successful during surgery, as most patients were still conscious and had to be physically restrained. A padded stick to bite on was less than satisfactory means of comfort in helping patients cope with the pain (Nestor, 2003).

Figure 4–1. *Larrey's Napoleonic war victim with head wound and aphasia. Reproduced from E. H. Jellinek, "An Unlikely Aphasiologist: D. J. Larrey (1766–1842)," Jour-*nal of the Royal Society of Medicine, 95(7), 368–370.

Adding to the trauma was the ambience of the operating room or theater. Theater is indeed a good word for it since high drama was played out, many times with the patient having the best seat in the house. A grizzly pile of amputated limbs decorated the operating room, which increased as patients were brought in by the horse-drawn ambulances. It was a nightmarish scene with patients screaming, moaning and sobbing, surgeons shouting orders, inability to muffle the terrible sound of the bone saw at work, and all this with the pandemonium of battle nearby. The floors were awash with blood and discarded human tissue, and in the warmer months flies swarmed everywhere. Instead of intravenous drips, soup, made from horsemeat carved from the carcasses littering the battlefield, was boiled in the breastplates of dead cavalry troopers and fed to the patients after surgery, in a dumbfounding effort to replace body fluids. This is the all too ghoulish scene painted by historians of battlefield trauma medicine and Nestor (2003) re-creates this tawdry portrait for current readers of history.

Larrey was able to perform most amputations in less than 2 minutes, providing the bone was already shattered and didn't require sawing or if he could amputate cleanly through the joint. It is amazing that he was able to preserve his impressions of the battlefield wounded to become one of the first writers to record details of aphasia in 12 of his patients. After the turmoil of the Napoleonic era in France's political cauldron, Larrey was later appointed by the new King Louis as medical director of a large veterans' hospital called the Hotel des Invalides, where he devoted the remainder of his life to the long-term care of wounded veterans (Nestor, 2003). Larrey is reported to have wanted to be buried among the veterans at the Invalides gardens, but again politics intervened. His heart was placed in an urn in the Chapel of the Val de Grace and his remains were buried in a Paris cemetery among regular folks. In 1992 on the 150th anniversary of his death, Larrey's remains were exhumed and reburied in the grounds of the Invalides with full military honors (Nestor, 2003; Richardson, 1974).

This summer of 2011 while viewing the magnificent works of art in the Rodin Museum, the gold *Dôme des Invalides* monument that houses the remains of Napoleon I, the Emperor, is magnificently visible and casts its shadow across the final resting place of Dr. Dominique Jean Larrey, a true battlefield surgical hero, and one of the least recognized of the early describers of aphasia (Figure 4–2).

Figure 4–2. *Dôme des Invalides.*

LORDAT: *ALALIA* AND EARLY ACCOUNTS OF APHASIA

In 1825, in another ironic stroke of historic coincidence with the publication of Bouillaud's publication on language localization in the brain, Jacques Lordat, a professor in Montpellier, France suffered a stroke. His condition is chronicled by Long (2004) in an insightful discussion of the experience of aphasia and the beginnings of incorporation of reports from those who actually experience the disorder into a clearer and more relevant understanding of it. In the summer of 1825 a professor of anatomy and physiology at Montpellier in France, Jacques Lordat, experienced a long illness. Long (2004) has commented on the fascinating account of Lordat in the captivating book, *Lost Words: Narratives of Language and the Brain, 1825–1926* (Jacyna, 2000). Jacyna has pieced together an astonishing piece of scholarship on the early narratives of language and language loss and its value is appreciated by Long (2004) and perhaps anyone who reads this intriguing work. As Jacyna reports, Lordat observed a certain "heaviness" in his head and "became conscious that when I wished to speak I did not find the expressions I required." When he received a visitor after a bit of recovery, he found that he couldn't respond to the visitor's inquiry about his health. He is reported to have thought to himself, "So it is true that I can no longer speak." His language returned at a later time, and he often spoke of this experience, using the word *alalia* (Greek for "without speech") to describe his former condition. After his recovery, Lordat presented his experiences and opinions on his loss of speech in an article in the *Journal of the Society of Medical Practice of Montpellier* (Lordat, 1843). The cover and title of this historic article is reproduced in Figure 4–3 from *La Bibliothèque nationale de France* (BnF), a wondrous source of everything ever printed in the French language, and a great repository of the works of French brains, that I have been grateful to access this summer of 2011.

Lordat's story of his own aphasia marks another notable marker in the history of understanding aphasia and that is the peculiar and important insight to be gained from listening to those who have experienced it. As Long (2004) notes ever so correctly, narrative in aphasia refers not just to the documents and

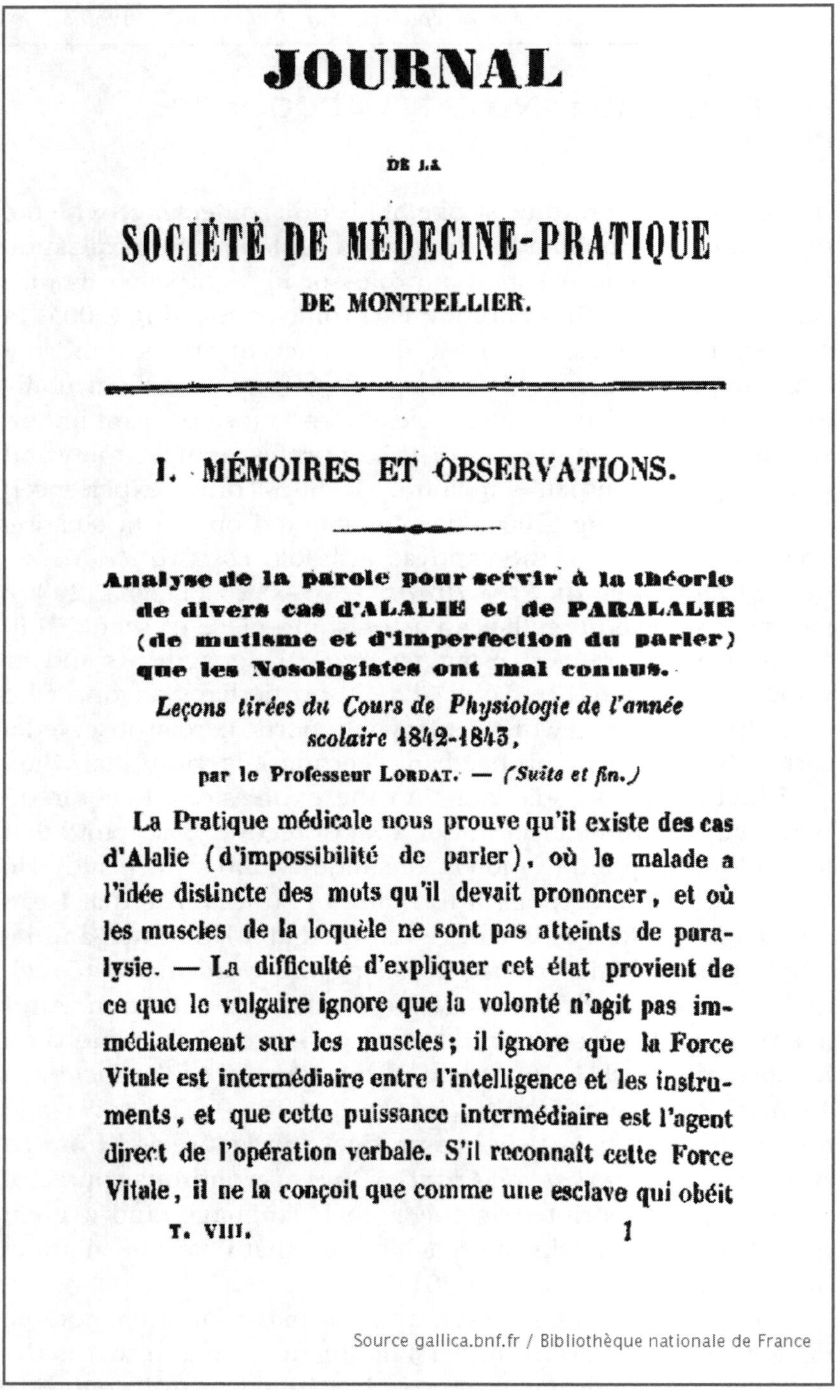

JOURNAL

DE LA

SOCIÉTÉ DE MÉDECINE-PRATIQUE

DE MONTPELLIER.

I. MÉMOIRES ET OBSERVATIONS.

Analyse de la parole pour servir à la théorie de divers cas d'ALALIE et de PARALALIE (de mutisme et d'imperfection du parler) que les Nosologistes ont mal connus.

Leçons tirées du Cours de Physiologie de l'année scolaire 1842-1843,

par le Professeur LORDAT. — *(Suite et fin.)*

La Pratique médicale nous prouve qu'il existe des cas d'Alalie (d'impossibilité de parler), où le malade a l'idée distincte des mots qu'il devait prononcer, et où les muscles de la loquèle ne sont pas atteints de paralysie. — La difficulté d'expliquer cet état provient de ce que le vulgaire ignore que la volonté n'agit pas immédiatement sur les muscles ; il ignore que la Force Vitale est intermédiaire entre l'intelligence et les instruments, et que cette puissance intermédiaire est l'agent direct de l'opération verbale. S'il reconnaît cette Force Vitale, il ne la conçoit que comme une esclave qui obéit

Figure 4–3. Lordat's 1843 article on his own aphasia.

stories told by physician and scholars, but just as legitimately to the stories told by the *sufferers* of this condition. These narratives were rarely brought out, as Long (2004) notes, until the 1990s, perhaps an indication that even our academic culture, for all its commitment since the 1960s to letting the "little person" tell his or her story, didn't really hear the inarticulate or language-impaired cries of people with aphasia until just a few years ago. Yet, when those narratives are painted by Jacyna (2000), he reveals the dark side of the disorder and people who were terrified, embarrassed, frightened, infantilized, and dehumanized by this loss of speech. This dehumanization and loss of individuality is not an unusual aspect of the experience of illness when one is swept into the morass of health care systems. Reports by the noted and gifted storyteller Oliver Sacks (1984) and by LaPointe (1996, 2010) have noted issues surrounding loss of identity when thrust onto the conveyer belt of bureaucratic health care.

Long (2004) argues that one sees the need not simply to study the narratives of physicians and medical professionals as well as those of sufferers, but to compare and contrast these narratives. Clinical case studies are the most basic elements, the fundaments of knowledge on which the dominating network of modern medical science is built. Long (2004) and Jacyna (2000) imply that if one really wanted to be a rebel in the medical community one would suggest another *literary* strategy to deal with patients. Those who know the daily routine of physicians and healthcare professionals know that most of their time is *not spent* in the lab or the operating room. Most of their time is spent talking with patients, providing understanding, comfort, or insight into perceived symptoms. Skilled and thoughtful medical professionals know that their primarily utility is in their words and not their hands. This point is poignantly reiterated in a touching novel of medicine and coming of age in Ethiopia entitled *Cutting for Stone* by Abraham Verghese (2009), and commented upon in an essay entitled "Pathography of Love" (LaPointe, 2011). The recurring zenlike question in this novel is, "What is the only medical treatment delivered by ear?" and the answer is, "Words of comfort."

Lordat's influence on the narrative of aphasia sets the tone for future incorporation of the view from within: the vista that can only be wholly appreciated by one who has experienced it. As Long (2004) optimistically forecasts, (perhaps) the future of the history of medicine, itself a young discipline, will be to discover the individuality of the patient and, in so discovering that individuality, revolutionize the study of medicine and health care. One can only hope.

BATEMAN, LEECHES, AND OTHER NOVEL DESCRIPTIONS OF APHASIA

In the remarkably rewarding labor of prospecting through the mother lode of archival medical history, one occasionally stumbles across a nugget or vein that stands out with the striking iridescence of glimmering opal in the depths of a dusty mine in Coober Pedy. Such is the preserved work of Sir Frederic Bateman, listed as a Fellow in the Royal College of Physicians; Fellow Laureate of the Academy of Medicine in Paris; Senior Physician at the Norfolk and Norwich Hospital; and Consulting Physician at the Eastern Counties Asylum for Idiots. This remarkable document, available on an Internet historical archive (Bateman, 2011) presents a voluminous overview of aphasia, debates on cerebral localization of language and other functions, and preservation of the content of early learned society debate and primary materials on aphasia. This monumental work by Bateman was apparently presented in Paris as the Alvarenga Prize Essay of the Academy of Medicine of Paris for the year 1890. It does a great service to the early history of aphasia. In the Preface to the Second Edition of this capacious work, Bateman states:

> Perhaps there is no subject in the whole range of neuro-pathology that has engrossed so large a share of the attention, not only of the medical profession, but of scientific men generally, in all parts of the world, as the Localisation of Speech, and the causes which interfere with the outward manifestation of that faculty.
>
> My first edition, published just twenty years ago, was one of the earliest, if not the very first treatise on Aphasia that appeared in this country; and the favourable reception accorded to it both at home and abroad, might justly have encouraged me to issue a second edition long ago. I was deterred, however, from a hasty

reproduction of the work, by the great diversity of opinion prevalent upon the points at issue, and I have preferred to wait till the horizon of scientific controversy was somewhat cleared, and the tangled skein of medical psychology partly unravelled. (Bateman, 1890, p. 1.)

Among the ample details of Bateman's two editions are remarkable details on the characteristics of aphasia by authors writing in obscure journals in Europe and America. Bateman states that he has had the occasion to research various British and foreign authors and noticed "a number of curious observations" that illustrate various theories in connection with loss or lesion of the faculty of speech. He adds as well that he will provide examples from his own personal experience on the clinical history of cases "with a considerable amount of detail."

One of the remarkable case descriptions in Bateman's treatise appears to be an early description of epileptiform aphasia with a novel treatment intervention.

Bateman reports:

A few minutes before the attack he felt tingling and convulsive twitchings in the right hand, and, as he was driving, the reins fell from his hand. Being alarmed, he quickly returned home, but was unable to tell his wife what had happened. He then made a sign that he wished to write, but when pen, ink, and paper were brought to him, he found himself as incapable of expressing his thoughts by writing as by articulate speech. After several fruitless attempts, he succeeded in pronouncing the word " blood." This was understood by the bystanders that he wished to be bled, and twenty leeches were applied to the anus. He then lost consciousness, and was seized with epileptiform convulsions, followed by a state of coma which lasted several hours. On recovering consciousness he could say a few words; the speech gradually improved, and forty-eight hours after the commencement of the seizure, he spoke as well as ever, and there remained no trace whatever of this singular attack. About a month afterwards this gentleman had a recurrence of the above symptoms, the aphasia, however, lasting only twenty minutes. During the next three years he had twenty-nine similar attacks, varying in duration from ten minutes to several hours, and on two occasions lasting over twenty-four hours. In almost every instance there was more or less tingling and convulsive movement of the right arm. During the interval between these attacks the patient enjoyed excellent health, with the exception of occasional headaches, to which he had been subject nearly all his life. (Bateman, 1890, p. 239)

Treatment of aphasia by the application of 20 leeches to the anus is certainly an intervention that has fallen out of favor, particularly in the mode of group therapy (Figure 4–4).

Aphasia cases from traumatic etiology, not unlike the cases presented by the Napoleonic surgeon of the Imperial Army, D. J. Larrey, are reported in Bateman's work as well.

Another case of traumatic aphasia has recently occurred in the practice of Dr. Castagnon, the subject of it being a young girl, aged 20, who was shot in the head, the accident resulting in a comminuted fracture of the antero-superior portion of the left parietal . . .

There was a comatose condition for six days, dextral paralysis and complete loss of speech for a month, at the end of which time she could speak, her vocabulary, however, being limited to four phrases, "Mon Dieu! Jesus! monprema mere." At the expiration of a year, the paralysis had subsided and the patient resumed her occupation, but although the intelligence was as perfect as before the accident, the young girl spoke but very little, and with great difficulty. (Bateman, 1890 p. 29)

The puzzle surrounding aphasia in bilingual or polylingual speakers is also the topic of case reports presented by Bateman. He states that Professor Behier, in one of his clinical lectures delivered at the Hotel Dieu, mentioned the case of a woman who was admitted into one of his wards with right hemiplegia, the result of cerebral hemorrhage, and in whom one of the first symptoms was aphasia. The aphasia in this woman took a very exceptional form. She was born in Italy, and had resided both in Spain and in France. She was fluent in three languages but after her cerebral damage had completely "forgotten" Italian and Spanish, and had only retained a most limited use of French. Her communication in French consisted of only repeated words as an echo to the words pronounced in her presence. She used no language, beyond this echolalia that had any apparent meaning to it (Bateman, 1890).

Figure 4–4. Leech jar. London Science Museum. Reproduced with permission.

In another case reported in the European literature by Romberg, a German neurologist, Bateman again includes an interesting note on treatment by leeches. Romberg reported the case of a sailor, who, on being struck on the left side of the head by a loose rope, fell into a state of "insensibility." After a quarter of an hour the sailor recovered consciousness, but was found to have lost the use of the right half of the body, and became speechless. Three weeks afterwards, the mobility of the extremities was restored, and the tongue could be moved in every direction without difficulty, but the faculty of speech was arrested; and although perfectly conscious, it was only with the greatest effort that the sailor was able to utter a few inarticulate sounds. Some blood was taken locally on several occasions by leeches applied behind the left ear. In this case, it seems the placement of leeches for treatment was a bit more localized to the site of damage. In addition, a combination of sulphate of magnesia and tartar emetic was administered. There seems to be a confound in the design of this particular intervention study and the positive result is difficult to attribute to time, leech, or emetics, but at any rate, in three weeks from the commencement of this treatment the speech of the sailor returned, and he was completely restored (Bateman, 1890, p. 45).

Cases presented by German physicians were enumerated in some detail by Bateman and he also presents an approving nod to the work of Kussmaul, the physician who commented on his own mentor Lordat's aphasia and acquired dyslexia. Kussmaul opined that the loss of the ability to read was Lordat's greatest perceived loss and that the material of the world's libraries had been closed to him "as if with seven seals." Of Kussmaul, Bateman asserts, that by far the most important German work is that of Professor Kussmaul of Strasburg, whose elaborate and exhaustive treatise "I have had frequent occasion to consult, and to which I shall again refer in subsequent chapters; it is a work quite encyclopedic in character, full of valuable information, and should be in the hands of all who desire to possess a compendium of all that is at present known of the pathology, diagnosis, and treatment of disturbances of the faculty of speech" (Bateman, 1890, p. 51).

The British physician Crichton provided several interesting examples of the jumbled words of aphasia and particularly difficulty with word retrieval, naming, and even on the torque in identity that can accompany aphasia. This effect on identity can be an unrecognized and devastating aspect of aphasia and has been commented on by a few (LaPointe, 2011; LaPointe, Murdoch, & Stierwalt, 2010). Crichton's cases illustrate several of these conditions and adjuncts of aphasia.

Bateman selects several of Crichton's cases that are reported in the language appropriate to the day but not necessarily appropriate to contemporary case reporting:

An attorney, in his seventieth year, having indulged in great venereal excesses, was suddenly seized with great prostration of strength, giddiness, insensibility to all the concerns of life, and every symptom of approaching fatuity. When he wished to ask for anything, he constantly made use of some inappropriate term; instead of asking for a piece of bread he would probably ask for his boots, and if these were brought he knew they did not correspond to the idea he had of the things he wanted, and therefore he became angry, yet he would still demand some of his boots or shoes, meaning bread. If he wanted a tumbler, he would ask for a chamber utensil; and if it happened to be the said chamber utensil he wanted, he would ask for a tumbler, or a dish. He evidently was conscious that he used wrong words, for when the proper expression was employed by another person, and he was asked if it was such a thing that he wanted, he always seemed aware of the mistake, and corrected himself by adopting the appropriate expression. This gentleman was cured of his complaint by large doses of valerian [an herb promoted as a mild sedative] and other proper remedies.

A man, aged 70, was seized with a kind of cramp in the muscles of the mouth, accompanied with a sense of tickling all over the surface of the body, as if ants were creeping on it. A few weeks later, after having experienced an attack of giddiness and confusion of ideas, a remarkable alteration in his speech was observed to have taken place. He articulated easily and fluently, but made use of strange words which nobody understood, and he himself was conscious that he spoke nonsense. What he wrote was equally faulty with what he spoke.

Crichton also mentions instances of persons who suddenly found that they could not remember their own names, the most striking being that of an ambassador at St. Petersburg.

This ambassador, who, on calling at a house where he was not known by the servants, and wishing to give his name, could not at that moment remember it, and turning round to his companion said, with much earnestness, "For God's sake tell me who I am." (Bateman, 1890, p. 53)

John Hughlings Jackson was an eminent British physician and a contemporary of Paul Broca and they engaged in dialogues and shared the podium at presentations at learned societies in both London and Paris. Bateman (1890) gives much credit to the opinions of Hughlings Jackson on the localization of language in the brain. In his opus on the topic, Bateman cites Jackson's exceptional work on description and demographics of case presentations of patients with speech loss. In Jackson's work are the seeds of future epidemiology of aphasia. Of interest as well is the foreshadow of future pronouncements on differences between propositional and nonpropositional speech to be suggested by Jon Eisenson in the United States. The sometimes associated problem of impairment of taste and smell was also noticed by Jackson. Says Bateman:

Beyond all doubt the observer who has done the most in this country to elucidate the subject of cerebral loss of speech is Dr. Hughlings Jackson, who, in the London Hospital Reports for 1864, has given the details of thirty-four cases of hemiplegia with loss of speech. Of these cases, the paralysis was observed thirty-one times on the right side and three times on the left; the heart was more or less affected in twenty instances (valvular disease existing in thirteen cases); in four cases there was loss or defect of smell. I much regret that want of space will not allow me to dwell on this most interesting communication; there are, however, two cases in this collection to which I must briefly allude. One is a case of aphasia with left hemiplegia occurring suddenly in a gentleman 64 years of age, who fourteen years before had received a very severe blow in the right occipital region, which had left him ever afterwards deprived of the power of smell and taste. In the other case the patient, although continuing aphasic, had recovered the power to swear, which Dr. Jackson explains on the principle that ejaculatory expressions are prompted by the emotions and not by the will; he also considers that oaths and similar interjectional expressions are not parts of speech in the broad sense in which the words that form them are, when used to convey intellectual propositions. (Bateman, 1890, p. 65)

Several other interesting and instructive examples of specific aphasic impairment are documented throughout Bateman's imposing volume. He relates the case report and description of the patient of an Irish physician that presents perhaps some of the earliest detail about the use of simple augmentative-alternative strategies to facilitate word retrieval.

In the *Dublin Quarterly Journal* for February, 1851, Graves has recorded a most singular instance of amnesic aphasia, limited to substantives and proper names. The subject of it was a Wicklow farmer, fifty years of age, who, after an attack of hemiplegia, was affected with an incapacity to employ nouns and proper names, he being able in other respects to express himself well. This defect was accompanied by the following singular peculiarity: that he perfectly recollected the initial letter of every substantive or proper name for which he had occasion in his conversation, though he could not recall to his memory the word itself. He consequently made for himself a little pocket dictionary of the words in most general use, including the proper names of his children, servants, and acquaintances, and during a conversation he would look in his dictionary till he found the word he wanted, keeping his finger and eye fixed on the word until he had finished the sentence, but the moment the book was closed, the word passed out of his memory and could not be recalled, although he recollected its initial, and could refer to it again in his dictionary when necessary. (Bateman, 1890, p. 80)

Ireland provided another unique description of how words go awry in aphasia. This case involved some unusual paraphasias or use of non-intended words. This case seems to support the ideas of Broca on the seat of articulate language, but not all of the cases presented by Bateman completely support Broca's suppositions. Several examples of negative cases, with well documented aphasia and subsequently no autopsy evidence for damage to the 2nd or 3rd frontal convolutions being apparent are presented. This case, from County Cork, however, reinforces Broca's notions on the area of the brain that is associated with aphasia.

Dr. Popham, of Cork, in a very elaborate paper in the *Dublin Quarterly Journal*, mentions the following case, which he says bears on M. Broca's views. Mary Murphy, aged sixty, was admitted to the Union Hospital with right hemiplegia and impaired speech. The memory of words was very defective, and the articulation confused; for "Thank you, sir," she said "Fancy sell," and being asked what her husband, a peddler, sold, she replied "procties and pudding pans," which Dr. Popham found out meant "brooches and bosom pins." She eventually died of pneumonia, when the following appearances were observed at the post-mortem examination: The heart was covered with fat, the mitral orifice was narrow, its margins ossified, and there were some vegetations on the auricular surface. There was considerable effusion under the arachnoid membrane. On careful examination of the left hemisphere, the convolution of Broca was softer in consistence than the neighbouring parts, and the remains of an apoplectic cyst, of the size of an almond, and empty, was situated close to the anterior third of the corpus striatum, and running parallel to its course. (Bateman, 1890, p. 82)

Case descriptions and interesting cataloging of specific disruptions of language were not limited to Europe during this era. Bateman (1890) cites several cases of "our American cousins." In the following case description, there is yet another allusion to treatment by removal of blood. In this case it is not by leeches, but apparently by the direct needle and syringe method.

I now arrive at the consideration of the labours of our American cousins, beginning with Dr. S. Jackson, of Pennsylvania, who records the following curious case.

The Rev. Mr. , [name] 48, endowed with intellectual powers of a high order, of a sanguine temperament, with latterly a strong tendency to obesity, having exposed himself to the influence of the night air, received a check to the cutaneous perspiration. The next morning he awoke with a headache, and when a friend went into his room to inquire after his health, he was surprised to find Mr. R could not answer his questions. Dr. Jackson having been summoned, found the patient in full possession of his senses, but incapable of uttering a word; the tongue was not paralysed, but could be moved in every direction; all questions were perfectly comprehended and answered by signs, and it could be plainly seen by the smile on the countenance, after many ineffectual attempts to express his ideas, that he was himself surprised, and somewhat amused at his peculiar situation. The face was flushed, the pulse full and somewhat slow, and to the inquiries if he suffered pain in the head, he pointed to his forehead as its seat. When, furnished with pen and paper, he attempted to convey his meaning, but he could not recall words, and only wrote an unintelligible phrase, "Didoes doe the doe." Forty ounces of blood were drawn from the arm and before the operation was completed speech was restored, though a difficulty continued as to the names of things, which could not be recalled. The loss of speech appearing to recur in fifteen minutes, ten ounces more blood were abstracted, and sinapisms supplied to the arms and thighs alternately. These means were speedily effectual, and no further return of the affection took place. Dr. Jackson, in analysing this case, calls attention to the following facts. Firstly, sudden suppression of the cutaneous transpiration, succeeded by cerebral irritation and determination of blood to the brain: secondly, frontal pain immediately over the eye: thirdly, perfect integrity of the sensations and voluntary movements: fourthly, the general operations of the intellect undisturbed; ideas formed, combined, and compared; those of events, of time, recalled without difficulty: fifthly, loss of language or of the faculty of conveying ideas by words though not by signs; this defect not being confined to spoken language, but extending to written language also. (Bateman, 1890, p. 84)

Another interesting case is presented with exquisite description by an American physician. Again, we see the precursor of alternative communication strategies to facilitate language retrieval. With this particular "blacksmith" case, we also are treated to the astute speculations of Dr. Hun on theoretic wonderings on the underlying mechanisms that may explain his patient's symptomatology. Given the early date of this case presentation (1829), prior to the publications of either Bouillaud or Broca in Paris, we can see another prescient precursor to those who received the most recognition on speculations about the seat of articulate speech in the brain.

Dr. Hun, of Albany, mentions the case of a blacksmith, [age] 35, who, before the present attack, could read and write with facility, but who had been labouring for several years under a disease of the heart. After a long walk in the sun, he was seized in the

evening with symptoms of cerebral congestion, remaining in a
state of stupor for several days. [This report is cited by Bateman
(1890) to have been published in the *American Journal of Medical Sciences*, February, 1829, p. 272.]

After a few days he began to recover from this condition,
and understood what was said, but it was observed that he had
great difficulty in expressing himself in words, and for the most
part could only make his wants known by signs. There was no
paralysis of the tongue, which he could move in all directions.
He knew the meaning of words spoken before him, but could not
recall those needed to express himself, nor could he repeat words
when he heard them pronounced; he was conscious of the difficulty under which he was labouring, and seemed surprised and
distressed at it. If Dr. Hun pronounced the word he needed, he
seemed pleased, and would say, " Yes, that is it," but was unable
to repeat the words after him. After fruitless attempts to repeat a
word, if Dr. Hun wrote it for him, he then would begin to spell
it letter by letter, and, after a few trials, was able to pronounce
it; if the writing were now taken from him, he could no longer
pronounce the word; but after long study of the written word,
and frequent repetition, he would learn it so as to retain it and
afterwards use it. He kept a slate, on which the words he required
most were written, and to this he referred when he wished to
express himself. He gradually learned these words and extended
his vocabulary, so that after a time he was able to dispense with
his slate. He could read tolerably well from a printed book, but
hesitated about some words; when he was unable to pronounce a
word, he was also unable to write it until he had seen it written;
and then he could learn to write as he learned to pronounce, by
repeated trials. At the end of six months, by continually learning new words, he could make himself understood pretty well;
often, however, employing circumlocution when he could not
recall the proper word, somewhat as if he were speaking a foreign language, imperfectly learned. Dr. Hun infers, from what
precedes, that there is a portion of the brain connected with
language or the memory of words, as distinct from the memory
of things and events; and that there is another portion on which
depends the co-ordination of the movements of articulation. It
will be observed that in the above case, the impression made on
the acoustic nerve was not sufficient for rendering the articulation
of the word possible, but that it was necessary that an impression
should be made upon the optic nerve. Dr. Hun asks whether this
can be explained by the supposition of a more intimate con-

nection between vision and articulation, or by the fact that the impression on the acoustic nerve is transient, whilst that on the optic is more permanent.

Bateman then startlingly describes another case of an American physician. In a rather brief and off-handed manner, Bateman alludes in passing to one of the most classic and celebrated cases in neuroscience. It is apparent after reading the details of this case that it is no other than the landmark case of Phineas Gage, the railroad construction foreman who suffered extensive frontal lobe damage and who was reported to have survived with no significant speech or language difficulties but exhibited remarkable changes in personality and behavior. Gage is a fixture in the publications and syllabi of neuroscience, psychology, psychiatry, speech-language pathology, and related disciplines, and is frequently mentioned as a milestone in understanding personality and the frontal lobes in books and academic papers. A large iron railroad tamping rod was driven completely through his head producing effects so profound that friends reported he was "no longer Gage."

There is no question Gage displayed changes in personality and behavior after his accident, but Gage has traversed into the wonderful world of popular culture and books and articles usually describe his changes in terms well beyond anything given by the reports of his physician Dr. Harlow or others who had contact with Gage (Macmillan & Lena, 2010). Psychologist Malcolm Macmillan (1986) and in his book, *An Odd Kind of Fame: Stories of Phineas Gage* (2000), surveys scores of accounts of the case (both scientific and popular), finding that they are varying and rather inconsistent, typically poorly supported by the evidence, and often in direct contradiction. Nevertheless, Phineas Gage has been converted into a celebrity and milestone in neuropsychology and Bateman's incredible inclusion of him as one of Harlow's patients in America foreshadowed his remarkable fame-to-be. Harlow, Bigelow, and Bateman were there first in the astonishing case of Phineas Gage, even though Bateman didn't have his occupation right.

Professor Bigelow, of Boston, has reported a remarkable case which occurred in the practice of Dr. Harlow of Vermont, of very extensive injury to the brain, without loss of the power of articulate language.

On September 13th, 1848, the foreman of a mine, a young and healthy man, was engaged, with a tamping iron in his hand, in ramming down a charge of powder in a rock to be blasted. The tamping-iron was an iron bar, pointed at one end, three feet seven inches in length, one and a quarter inches in diameter, and weighing thirteen pounds four ounces. Thinking that the blast had been properly covered with sand, he struck it a blow with the round end of the bar, when a spark flying from the rock ignited the uncovered powder, producing an explosion which drove the tamping-iron completely through his skull. The pointed extremity entered in at the angle of the lower jaw, on the left side, passing upward and a little inward, emerging in the neighbourhood of the anterior fontanelle junction, thus passing quite through his head. In a few minutes he recovered consciousness, was put into a cart and conveyed to his residence, conversing on his way home; he then was able to walk into his house. During the progress of the case the patient retained full command of speech, and though at times drowsy, was always rational. Recovery was perfect in about eleven weeks, but the sight of the left eye was lost. It is stated that he became very profane, never having been so before the accident. He lived twelve years and a half after this formidable injury, when, after having had several convulsions, he died.

Bateman also relates some interesting historical speculations on causes of aphasia. In addition to the obvious and recognized etiologies, he relates a case of speechlessness in a young boy who consumed some poisonous plants from a field he mistakenly thought were carrots. He also suggests that certain repeated use phenomena might induce aphasia. Hence this report of "Hammer Palsy."

Loss or disturbance of speech may also be caused by cerebral vibration without visible lesion, by simple molecular disturbance of the brain cells, as exemplified in a form of cerebral disturbance described by Dr. Franks-Smith under the name of Hephsestic Hemiplegia, or Hammer Palsy, as it occurs amongst the artisans of Sheffield. In many of these observations, aphasia was a prominent symptom, and the patients were exposed to none of the causes of cerebral lesion with the exception of the continual use of the seven-pound single-handed hammer. In every instance complete or partial recovery followed the use of phosphorus, iron, strychnia, and cod-liver oil, with absolute rest and prolonged absence from the forge.

Bateman (1890) also catalogs reports of sudden emergence from speechlessness. One such case is reported under the heading of "Rousing the Dormant Faculty of Language."

> Again, Wiedermeister relates the history of a female who became speechless as she left her wedding breakfast to start on her bridal trip with her husband, and who remained so until she happened to see a church burning, when she cried out, "Fire!" and at once regained the power of speech. (Bateman, 1890, p. 295.)

Although many forms and symptoms of aphasia were described and a small number of theoretical explanations of its nature were advanced prior 1800 (Benton & Joynt, 1960; Prins & Bastiaanase, 2006); significant hypotheses about the localization of aphasia were not formulated until the golden years of 1800 to 1860. Gall was a leader in advancing concepts of cerebral localization, despite his seduction and embellishment. Gall (Gall & Stuart, 1806) was the first to position language in the frontal cortex. This speculation was then tested and rudimentary neuropathological evidence and further speculation was advanced by Bouillaud (1825) who not only suggested that the home of language was in the frontal lobes, but also made the fundamental distinction between "a general faculty of language" and "the faculty of articulated speech," thus preparing the ground for Broca's famous discovery in 1861 (Hecaen & Dubois, 1969; Prins & Bastiaanase, 2006; Schiller, 1979). The historical context of Paris in the 18th century and details on the influences of these luminaries in the scrutiny of the cerebral localization of language are covered in some detail subsequently.

Chapter 5

Turmoil, Revolt, and Enlightenment: Historical Context for Advances in Brain Science

Paul Broca lived through the trials and tribulations of extraordinary social unrest in France, in an era where as much as one third of the million inhabitants of Paris were dependent on charity and the generosity of the state or of others. This surely colored his beliefs and values and approach to science and society. He was not alone. It influenced his father, village mates, and his Huguenot ancestors as well. The historical context of the fruitful scientific days of the 1800s provided a turbulent milieu for advances in thought and art. The great French revolution of 1789 and the wars, unrest, changes in government, and ostentatious displays of monarchs that both preceded and followed it were extraordinary. One wonders how continuity of effort could not have been disrupted or influenced by civil unrest and unstable rule. Conceivably it was. In some cases, the presiding and dominant moral, ecclesiastic, and frightful censorship of thought and science retarded or prevented publications of ideas. Just as in contemporary life, academic freedom and the free flow of ideas ought not be hindered by axe-bearing fad or mindset, but in fact it was and is. Academic freedom and responsibility have long been topics for public concern and debate and it certainly was cause for distress in France of the 17th, 18th, and 19th centuries.

Academic freedom to explore significant and controversial questions is an essential prerequisite to fulfill the academy's mission of educating students and advancing knowledge. Academic responsibility requires professors and researchers to submit their knowledge and claims to rigorous and public review by peers who are experts in the subject matter under consideration; to ground their arguments in the best available evidence; and to work collectively to foster the education of students. The free flow and discussion of controversial thought is less possible if policy makers and controllers of the purse-strings are allowed to let their personal moralistic convictions dictate what can or cannot be studied, discussed, or published. Academic freedom is the life blood of the modern university just as it was in the great academies of the past. It is the right to teach, learn, study, and publish free of orthodoxy or threat of reprisal and inequity. Politicians and policy makers who are certain they have received wisdom and must then impose their views on the academic system are a great historical impediment to the progression of knowledge.

Are the threats to academic freedom real or imagined? When scholars attempt to teach or communicate ideas or facts that are troublesome to external political groups or to authorities, they may find themselves targeted for public vilification, job loss, imprisonment, or even death. For example, in North Africa, a professor of public health discovered and communicated that his country's infant mortality rate was higher than government figures indicated. He lost his job and was imprisoned (Fuchs, 1969). The history of academics is littered with such cases, particularly during unpopular wars or flare-ups of controversial social policy or religious beliefs. Today's hot buttons of potential academic freedom suppression include evolution versus creationism; abortion; sexual orientation; deism versus atheism; patriotism; environmentalism; foreign policy and invasion of small countries; liberal versus conservative economic thought; militarism; and religious freedom for rabbits. In France, the topics revolved around the power of the monarchy; republicanism; influence of the church on science; and freedom of religion. History is a great governess but sometimes her words fall on deaf ears. As the influential quotation above the portals of the University of Colorado Norlin Library reminds us, "Who knows only his own generation remains always a child."

A WONDROUS AND DREADFUL MACHINE

In France, the early days of the 1800s would turn out to be not nearly as chaotic as the days of the revolution in 1789 and beyond. Scientists and scholars then and in subsequent decades found their research and studies scrutinized and censored. The 18th century in France was the epitome of social unrest, but did not take a holiday in Broca's era. During the 1700s, executions in France were public events where entire towns gathered to watch. A common execution method for a poor and under-privileged criminal was quartering. With this technique, which required considerable inconvenience and the collaboration of four bovines, the prisoner's limbs were tied to four oxen. The animals were then driven in four different directions with great hoo-hah resulting in the condemned person being ripped apart. Imagine a French family at one of these public spectacles packing baguettes, camembert, and strawberries along with a good *vin rouge* and enjoying their picnic while witnessing this exceptional event. These happenings, coupled with man's amygdaloid-driven genetic nature, perhaps account for a slice of the apparent proliferation of contemporary preoccupation with the violence of television, film, and video games. The oxen did not pull all. Upper-class criminals could buy their way into a less painful death by hanging or beheading. (Bellis, 2011; Caryle, 1839).

Dr. Guillotin: Severer of French Heads

Enter a ray of "humanity," Dr. Joseph Ignace Guillotin (Figure 5–1). Dr. Guillotin belonged to a small political reform movement that held as a premise the banishment of the death penalty completely. Guillotin made a case for a painless and private capital punishment method equal for all the classes, as an interim step towards total proscription of the death penalty.

Figure 5–1. *Dr. Joseph Ignace Guillotin. Public domain.*

Beheading devices had already been used in Germany, Italy, Scotland, and Persia and elsewhere, though perhaps not in Antarctica, for blue-blooded criminals. However, never had such a device been adopted on a large institutional scale. Dr. Guillotin advanced his case. He supported the humane nature of his beheading device with the following support (Caryle, 1839).

> My machine will take off a head in a twinkling, and the victim will feel nothing but a refreshing coolness. We cannot make too much haste, gentlemen, to allow the nation to enjoy this advantage.

The French named the *guillotin* after him and the extra "e" at the end of the word was added by an unknown English poet who found guillotine easier to rhyme (Bellis, 2011; Farrell & Sutherland, 1986).

Doctor Guillotin together with German engineer and harpsichord maker Tobias Schmidt, built the prototype for an idyllic guillotine machine. Schmidt suggested using a diagonal blade instead of a round blade and that is the design that was incorporated into the death machine (Caryle, 1839). In a scientific effort to determine if any consciousness remained following decapitation by the guillotine, three French doctors attended the execution of Monsieur Theotime Prunier (the unfortunate linguistic pun in "Prunier" is not lost) in 1879, and in a precursor to today's Institutional Review Board (IRB) obtained his prior consent to be the subject of their experimentation.

A Look of Astonishment

Immediately after the blade fell on the pruned Prunier, the trio retrieved his head and attempted to elicit some sign of intelligent response by "shouting in his face, sticking in pins, applying ammonia under his nose, silver nitrate, and candle flames to his eyeballs." In response, they could record only that M. Prunier's face "bore a look of astonishment" (Bellis, 2011).

The arguments surrounding consciousness after beheading have persisted to this day, and my friend and colleague Robert Olen Butler (2006) has cleverly crafted a collection of stories based on the thoughts of the beheaded immediately after the incident. *Severance* (Butler, 2006) depicts the final thoughts of people as they are losing their heads. This collection of stories on the topic of beheadings has been celebrated by critics as "glorious" (*Los Angeles Times*) and a revelation of "the limitless will of the author's imagination" (*New York Times*). Butler creates the imagined ultimate words of famous and invented figures — Medusa, Sir Walter Raleigh, Anne Boleyn, Jayne Mansfield, and a chicken, beheaded for Sunday dinner.

Anatomists and other scientists in several countries have tried to perform more definitive experiments on severed human heads as recently as 1956. Inevitably, the evidence is only anecdotal. What appears to be a head responding to the sound of its name, or to the pain of a pinprick, may be only random muscle twitching or automatic reflex action, with no awareness involved. At worst, it seems that the massive drop in cerebral blood pressure would cause a victim to lose consciousness in a few seconds. That evidence does not detract from the fertile imaginings of Robert Olen Butler (Figure 5–2), nor from the stark terror that characterized the backdrop of French history that would be

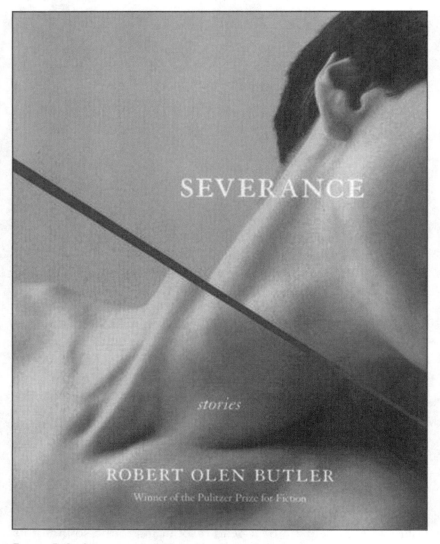

Figure 5–2. Severence *by Robert Olen Butler. Reprinted with permission.*

woven into the tapestry of science and art in the 19th century. This history fueled the imaginations and work of French brains like Flourens, Bouillaud, Aubertin, and Broca.

The period from June 1793 to July 1794 in France is known as the Reign of Terror or simply "the Terror." It is a deep and dark part of French history and even today is spoken of at the cafés of Place Contrescarpe with subdued and hushed tones by those who recall the oral history relayed and passed down by ancestors of the years of horror. The upheaval following the overthrow of the monarchy, and the beheading of the Louis XVI and Marie Antoinette were to last decades and influence science, medicine, and the arts. Invasion by foreign monarchist powers and the Revolt in the Vendée combined to throw the nation into chaos and the government into frenzied paranoia (Farrell & Sutherland, 1986). Most of the democratic reforms of the revolution were suspended and far-reaching executions by guillotine began. Vendors would sell programs listing the names of those scheduled to die. Many people would come day after day and vie for the best locations from which to observe the proceedings; knitting female citizens *(tricoteuses)* formed a cadre of hardcore regulars, inciting the crowd as kind of antediluvian cheerleaders. Parents would bring their children. By the end of the Terror, the crowds had thinned drastically. Excessive repetition had made even this most gruesome of entertainment a bit stale and audiences grew bored (Bellis, 2011). During the "Terror" years of 1792–1794 estimates vary, but from 17,000 to some reports of 40,000 people were subjected to the "national razor" or "Madame Guillotine" (Figure 5–3).

Contrary to legend, Dr. Joseph Ignace Guillotin was not executed by his own machine; he lived until 1814, and died of biological causes, suggested by some from the unlikely etiology of a carbuncle in his shoulder (Bellis, 2011).

FRENCH TURBULENCE: KINGS AND REVOLUTIONS

After the Renaissance and religious wars of the previous two centuries, France settled into the absolute monarchy of Louis XIV, the *Roi Soleil* or Sun King. This supreme monarch solidified his

Figure 5–3. *The trimming instrument of Dr. Guillotin. Public domain.*

power, neutered the nobility, and revoked the Edict of Nantes. The Edict of Nantes, issued on April 13, 1598, by Henry IV of France, granted the Calvinist Protestants of France (also known as Huguenots) substantial rights in a nation still considered essentially Catholic. In the Edict the good king Henry aimed primarily to promote civil unity. The Edict separated civil from religious unity, treated some Protestants for the first time as more than mere schismatics and heretics, and opened a path for secularism and tolerance that was unprecedented in France (Horne, 2004). Freedom of religion was now a part of French law. Although the foreboding clouds of the Revolution and decades of mayhem separated many good French brains from the rest of their bodies, at the time, the Nantes capitulation was important for the families of French Huguenots who were to come, including one family Broca in the Bordeaux region of southern France.

The Sun King, known as such because of the splendor of Versailles, which he created, became king at the age of four, but the country was ruled by a cleric, Cardinal Mazarin, in the King's name until the death of the red hat and Louis XIV's assumption of power at age 23 (Figure 5–4). Louis XIV believed he was an absolute ruler. He professed that his authority was inherited and derived from God. He was not accountable to anyone but his

Figure 5–4. The Sun King, Louis XIV. Wikimedia Commons, public domain.

own conscience and set the standard for monarchs and emperors who were still unborn (Horne, 2004).

Louis developed a large, well-trained army that wore dazzling uniforms. He administered the country through "intendants." He displayed his wealth and power by building his resplendent palace at Versailles. He transformed the formerly independent nobility who had commanded armies and ruled their own provinces into the courtiers and lap dogs of the king. In the arts and science, enlightenment sowed the seeds of democracy. This was the resplendent and ostentatious age of France, but with revocation of the Edict of Nantes and the growing chasm between the rich and the poor, dark clouds were on the horizon. War was considered the "sport of kings" and invasions to conquer new lands and expand current holdings were regular and tragic (Horne, 2004).

Louis XIV saw his sun and splendor begin to fade considerably. Discontent and poisonings of members of the royal court, a huge freeze that killed many of the great vines even as far south as Provence, and starvation and protest among the poor heralded a decline that would create restlessness and instability. Personal tragedy visited the Sun King as well. He is reported to have felt a stabbing pain in his left leg, and 10 days later, despite prescriptions of massive doses of asses' milk, it turned black. Gangrene had caught the resplendent Sun King and he died four days short of his 77th birthday (Horne, 2004). Although the great century or *grand siècle* was truly over; the bills would be presented for payment in the coming years and no amount of asses' milk would afford a cure.

The Sun King's absolutist system of government functioned under his two successors, almost on autopilot, until the outbreak of the French Revolution in 1789 (Horne, 2004). The successors of Louis XIV were to preside over a gradual decline of the country, further realization of the gap between the monarchy and nobles and the hungry working class, and indifference and intolerance in royal leadership.

With the decadence and subsequent great revolution of 1789, thousands lost their heads to the Dr. Guillotin's razor and France underwent periods of great instability of republic, terror, reversals to absolute power and monarchy, and more revolutions. This would affect the ancestors of Paul Broca, contribute to their persecution, and perhaps mold his republican and anti-monarchy ideas. It was not an easy time for the ancestors of those who would later contribute to our understanding of language in the brain.

NAPOLEON AND THE 19TH CENTURY

After a series of military successes, a charismatic commoner who was born in Corsica rose from amid the now everyday chaos of France. Napoleon Bonaparte (Figure 5–5) promised stability and soon was to be self-crowned Emperor of France. He was quoted as believing that a constitution should be obscure and short. Historians characterize him as one of the greatest military commanders of all time (despite his crushing defeat at Waterloo); a risk-taking gambler; a workaholic genius; an impatient short-term planner; a vicious cynic; and a misogynist who could enthrall men but defile women (Johnson, 2002). Napoleon's excesses as a little tyrant (he is reported to have been five feet two inches tall) are thoroughly recorded by historians.

Johnson (2002) links Napoleon the flawed person to Napoleon the abhorrent ruler. He reports Napoleon's rapacious use of women; his unsatisfying experience with an Ottoman leader's gift of an eleven-year-old virgin and a pre-adolescent boy; his customary cheating at cards; and his habitual lying and deceitfulness. Johnson's description of Napoleon's autopsy is vivid and unnerving:

> The teeth were healthy but stained black by the chewing of licorice. The left kidney was one-third larger than the right. The urinary bladder was small and it contained gravel; the mucosa was thickened with numerous red patches. Had the urethra been sectioned (or so runs the theory) it would probably have demonstrated a small circular scar, too tight to allow the passing of even small stones. That would have been the key to the slow decline in health and performance that started when Bonaparte was in his late thirties. The body was what doctors call "feminized"—that is, covered by a deep layer of fat, with scarcely any hair and well-developed breasts and mons veneris. The shoulders

Figure 5–5. *The little tyrant, Napoleon Bonaparte. Wikimedia Commons, public domain.*

were narrow, hips broad, and genitals small. We can all make up our minds about these findings, their significance and reliability. (Johnson, 2002).

Whatever Napoleon's "size matters" issues (Hall, 2006), before he was eventually banned to his prison island, he presided over many grandiose projects in Paris (Figure 5–6). The *Arc*

Figure 5–6. *Paris panorama today, from Montparnasse Tower.*

de Triomphe, rebuilding throughout the city, renovation around the Louvre, and the plans for the magnificent Opera Garnier, resulted in what has been referred to as "the most beautiful city that could ever exist" (Horne, 2004).

But France and Paris would continue its upheaval and turmoil that formed the setting for the great scientific discoveries and artistic innovations of the 1800s. The Second French Republic with Napoleon's nephew, Napoleon III as its leader, was a colonial empire in slow decline, and a disastrous Prussian siege of Paris during the Franco-Prussian War of 1870 formed the scenery for French intellectuals that would continue to advance French culture and a remarkable torrent of activity in French medicine and science. France's political clout was fading, but Paris remained the world's cultural center during the belle époque or beautiful age.

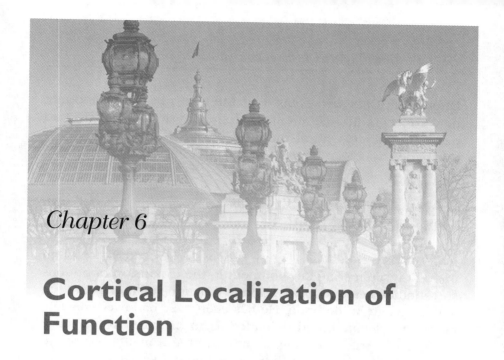

Chapter 6

Cortical Localization of Function

As an illustration of how the political and social backdrop of an era can influence science and the healing arts, the Napoleonic era (1795–1815) introduced another period of great social, economic, political, and scientific change. The spirit of medical science was inspired by reasoned logical diagnosis and meticulous autopsy control (Silverman, 1996). During the first half of the nineteenth century there was a transformation in the treatment of disease and the development of a fresh school of medicine and clinical science. Patients had been cupped, bled, blistered, purged, leeched, and vomited. They snorted, ingested, and had their orifices inserted with strange mixtures of polypharmacy. They were dressed in donkey skins and their heads were rubbed with the grease from a fat fox to cure baldness and headaches. Frequent doses of mercury, antimony (a chemical element that causes many of the same poisoning effects as arsenic), cocaine, and other compounds were regularly prescribed without a full appreciation of their side effects. However, during this age, there was the growth of a noteworthy skeptical spirit; and the arrival of a new school of physicians and scholars who sought to study rationally and scientifically. France, though suffering its consistent political turmoil, was becoming the Medical Center of the world. Physicians and scientists such as Bichat, Portal,

Dupuytren, Corvisart, Louis, and Laennec advanced important new concepts in anatomy, pathology, physical diagnosis, and pathophysiology. One of the most distinguished physicians of this period was Jean-Baptiste Bouillaud (Silverman, 1996).

JEAN-BAPTISTE BOUILLAUD: THE ANTERIOR LOBES

Jean-Baptiste Bouillaud (Figure 6–1) was the centerpiece of an important pioneering development in the expansion of notions surrounding cerebral localization of function and human speech and language in the brain. He has been overshadowed, reviled, neglected, debated, and defended as to his role. He played a fundamental role in calling attention to the frontal lobes of the cerebral hemispheres of the brain as being associated with language use (although it was unclear if he really specified the *left* frontal lobe).

Bouillaud was a commanding and eminent figure in Parisian scientific circles, and in fact was a student of Gall and founding member of the *Société Phrénologique* (Stookey, 1963). Jean Baptiste Bouillaud was born on September 16, 1796, at Bragette, a hamlet near Angoulême, where his parents owned a tile works. He received his early education at the Angoulême lycée, where he was awarded the prix d'excellence, or first prize in the school, as well as a prize for Latin verse. Bouillaud as with many students with a hard-knock life, had a harsh battle with poverty and lack of finances for his education, and was an inmate of the boarding house immortalized by Balzac in *Le Pere Goriot* under the name of the Pension Vauquer, Bouillaud himself, was the model for Horace Bianchon, who figures in many of Balzac's novels. Apparently Bouillaud relished in relating this story or legend that Balzac immortalized him (Rolleston, 1937).

Bouillaud's medical education was interrupted when he joined Napoleon's army during the Hundred Days (1815), but he returned to study in Paris after Waterloo. His rise to prominence was rapid. He married in 1824, and found his wife a useful assistant in his experiments on animals in connection with cerebral localization, to which he had been attracted by the study of Gall's work. This union would bear him a daughter who would end

Figure 6–1. *Bust of Jean-Baptiste Bouillaud. Public domain.*

up marrying Simon Alexandre Aubertin who became a colleague as well as family member and advocate of Bouillaud's views on language and the anterior lobes of the brain.

Bouillaud became a professor of clinical medicine at the Charité in Paris in 1831, publishing an important book about the diseases of the heart four years later and another about rheumatism and the heart the following year. The first accurate methods of weighing and measuring the heart are the result of Bouillaud's studies. He is credited with creating the topographical anatomy of the heart (Silverman, 1996). He was the first to accurately describe endocardium and endocarditis and introduced these terms for them into medicine. Bouillaud was a pupil of Dupuytren and attended him in his last illness. It is remarkable to note the interconnections and "small world" phenomena that laced together Bouillaud, Dupuytren, Aubertin, and Broca. Bouillaud was instructed by his eminent professor to perform the autopsy of his mentor, Dupuytren (Silverman, 1996). As early as 1825, Bouillaud published a paper that employed clinical evidence to support Gall's view that the faculty of articulate language resides in the anterior lobes of the brain. His classic paper on language and the anterior lobes was published in the *Archives generales de medecine* 1825, VIII, 25, and was entitled *"Recherches cliniques propres d' demontrer que la perte de la parole correspond d la lésion des lobules anterieurs dit cerveau, et á confirmer l'opinion de M. Gall sur le siegede l'orga'ne du langage articulé."* This was an early and pioneering position on the location of language in the brain and would inspire a few others, as well as draw fire in the future (Rolleston, 1937).

For almost 40 years, in the face of considerable opposition, Bouillaud had succeeded in keeping the cerebral localization hypothesis alive (Luzzati & Whitaker, 2001; Wozniak, 1995).

Bouillaud was deeply inspired by the phrenology of Franz Joseph Gall, and the waxing and waning of the debate over localization of intellectual and specific functions in the brain perhaps caught Bouillaud in mid-career. After phrenology was out of favor, and despite the contributions of Gall and his cohorts to several solid principles of cerebral localization, Bouillaud may have been viewed as an inflexible retainer of now unfashionable phrenological principles. Bouillaud's work also has been associated with the suggestion of the principle of double dissociation, a concept that was to become one of the pillars of theoretical neuropsychology of 19th and 20th centuries and would attract ample debate in its own right (Bouillaud, 2011; Stookey, 1963). As Prins and Bastiaanase (2006) in an excellent review of the history of aphasia offer, although many forms and symptoms of aphasia have been described through the years and a handful of theoretical explanations of its nature of aphasia was offered before 1800, significant hypotheses about the localization of aphasia were not formulated until the period 1800 to 1860. Based on his phrenological ideas, Gall may well have been the first to localize language in the frontal cortex, though his placement of this seat of language and verbal agility just posterior to the orbits of the eyes were a little off. Prins and Bastiaanase (2006) give credit to Bouillaud for testing this hypothesis and correlating it with his prodigious neuropathological data.

In 1848 Bouillaud succeeded Orfila, the celebrated and fiery toxicologist and administrator as Dean of the Paris Faculty of Medicine. Broca's letters to his parents in the 1840s are smattered with unfriendly references to Orfila. In 1862 Bouillaud was elected president of the Académie de Médecine, and in 1867 became president of the prestigious first international congress of medicine which was held in Paris. In 1868 he was made a Commander of the Legion of Honor and a member of the Institut de France in the section of medicine of the Académie des Sciences (Rolleston, 1937).

Buckingham (1981) an eminent scholar of aphasia history also presents finite details about the pre-Broca era of language localization in the brain, including particulars on the infamous wagers of Bouillaud and his son-in-law Aubertin, both inveterate gamblers apparently. Bouillaud offered 500 francs if anyone could produce a person with aphasia who did not present with damage to the anterior or frontal lobes and later Aubertin was to follow in his father-in-law's footsteps by proposing an equally startling dare that he would *renounce* his views on the anterior lobes and language if anyone could produce a patient that countered his claim.

Negative cases (those with language loss and no damage to the proposed areas or those with no language loss and confirmed damage to the proposed areas) would become a double dissociation conundrum for years to come. Buckingham (1981) has an enlightening discussion of what the revelation of these negative cases does or do not prove. As subsequent research has shown, one cannot become too wedded to double dissociation or a logical divorce might be in the offing.

Bouillaud (1825, 1830, 1864–1865) not only localized language in the frontal lobes, but also made the fundamental distinction between "a general faculty of language" and "the faculty of articulated speech," thus preparing the ground for Broca's famous discovery and attempt at clarification in 1861.

Bouillaud's reasoning, which influenced subsequent followers who were to venture heavily on the principle of double dissociation, was that if language is located in the frontal lobes of the brain, then two conclusions can be drawn: lesions in the frontal lobes of the brain should create impairments in language; and language should be spared with lesions in other lobes of the brain. Time, and evolving sophistication of specific methods for precisely localizing lesions, would show that this conclusion was a bit oversimplified.

Bouillaud did yeoman's work by systematically analyzing the data reported by a neurologist colleague, Claude-Francois Lallemand (Stookey, 1963). From this labor, he concluded clinical-pathological confirmation of this hypothesis about the role of the frontal lobes in language. Bouillaud contributed other suggestions about language that may be no less important (Bouillaud, 2011). He discussed that the loss of language could exist in two forms that result either from a failure to understand, store and generate words, or an inability to produce language.

Bouillaud was way ahead of his time in postulating the character and types of language disorder that could accompany lesions to the "anterior" lobes. Bouillaud proposed two varieties of impaired communication:

> It is quite necessary to distinguish in the act of speaking 2 different phenomena, namely, the faculty of creating words as signs of our ideas, to preserve their memory, and to articulate these same words. There is, so to speak, an internal speech and an external speech: the latter being only the expression of the former . . . The loss of speech depends sometimes on that of the memory of the words, and at other times on that of the muscular movements which constitute the words, or which is perhaps the same thing, sometimes on the lesion of the grey matter, and at other times on that of the white matter of the anterior lobes. (Bouillaud, 1825, p. 35)

This idea precluded both Broca's descriptions of aphemia and Wernicke's subsequent clarification of an important second form of aphasia. Much to the chagrin of those who gag slightly at the idea of aphasia classification types (McNeil & Copland, 2011), both of these forms would be subsequently designated by the labels Broca's aphasia and Wernicke's aphasia.

Bouillaud's 1825 paper, read before the Académie de Médecine was to stand as an overshadowed milestone on the localization of speech in the "anterior lobes." (Bouillaud, 1825). In this paper he described cases from his own experience and that of others, showing that patients who during life had suffered from loss of speech, on postmortem examination showed lesions of the anterior lobes, whereas those with no disturbance of speech showed lesions in the middle and posterior lobes, while the anterior lobes remained intact. The analysis of these cases, drawn from previously published casebooks and his personal caseload, were to come under question. His primary conclusions in this 1825 paper were as follows:

- ◆ The brain in man plays an essential part in the mechanism of a great number of movements.
- ◆ The movements of the organs of speech, in particular, are governed by a special, distinct, and independent cerebral center, situated in the anterior lobes.
- ◆ Loss of speech does not necessarily involve loss of the movements of the tongue considered as an organ of prehension, mastication or deglutition of food, or of the sense of taste. (Rolleston, 1937)

By 1848 Bouillaud still was vigorously defending his point and declared "Herewith I offer 500 francs to anyone who will provide me with an example of a deep lesion of the anterior lobules of the brain without a lesion of speech" (Schiller, 1992).

However, for the next thirteen years the major debate in the *Société d'Anthropologie* concerned the importance of cerebral volume in relation to intellect. This debate on cerebral volume, intellect, and "inferior versus superior" classes of people were to consume discussions, including the time and efforts of Bouillaud and Broca and were to have serious implications on the scholarship and scientific findings of this era.

Bouillaud's views on the anterior lobes and the location of speech were also incorporated in his work on encephalitis published later in 1825, and these views were maintained by him with vigor and persistency throughout his long and active career, particularly in discussions at the *Académie de Medecine* in 1839, 1848, 1864, and 1877, as well as the *Académie des Sciences*, in spite of opposition from his colleagues. Andral (1837) in particular stated that out of 37 cases observed by himself or others, with various lesions of the anterior lobes, there had been preservation of speech in 16, whereas in another 14 cases there had been abolition of speech without any changes being found in the anterior lobes post-mortem. These negative cases will be found to plague future claims as well on the localization of language in the brain. Broca will have to fend off claims of negative cases that appear to negate the claim that certain areas are invariably found to be damaged with subsequent aphasia and that certain cases are found to have damage to these tagged areas that had no apparent disorder of language.

Rolleston (1937) poses some interesting sidelights to the debates that followed Bouillaud and subsequently that marked the meetings of the medical societies in Paris in the 1850s and 1860s. Rolleston states "Some of my audience may remember the sensation caused a quarter of a century ago by Pierre Marie's contention that the third left frontal convolution does not play any special role in the function of speech, but the excitement caused by the discussions at the *Académie de Médecine* and elsewhere on cerebral localization was far greater in the middle of the nineteenth century, when, according to Marie, even political passions were involved, and belief in cerebral localization almost formed part of the republican creed in France." "Republican," it should be noted, has a very different and almost opposite meaning in French history and politics than it does in contemporary American political ideology.

The interweaving of political agendas and political philosophies continues to color belief systems and encroach ugly heads on neutrality and objectivity of science, just as they did in France. The United States and other countries that have broadly demarcated populist versus capitalist interests, and fund their democracy and elections by special interests and "Super Pacs" have foul histories of social and political philosophy tainting the funding and reporting of science (Mooney, 2005). When an environmental scientist starts putting forward fact or opinion on certain controversial matters that ideologues want kept off the table, he or she may find a blockage by censors and redactors. Immigration, evolution, population growth, abortion, environmental degradation, and other social issues can steer funding and reporting of science and compromise the potential to advance scholarship. These issues, as they did in France in the 18th and 19th centuries may influence the objective advancement of science and strident debate and negative campaign advertising and oversimplified, fear-based "sound bites" can drown out reason and caution, just as it has for generations. This historical given is as important to understand in the debates that surrounded Darwin, Bouillaud, and Broca as it is in contemporary politics. Sometimes the objectivity of science suffers.

During these academic debates, colored as they were with political implications, Broca appears to have been at first dubious of the value of Bouillaud's researches. Although at first Bouillaud accepted Broca's support in a somewhat hesitant spirit, styling him "the St. Paul of the new doctrine" and alluding to him as one of the "organizers, subinventors, augmenters, revisers and correctors" of Gall's work, eventually he appeared to value Broca's discovery (Rolleston, 1937).

One of the criticisms of Bouillaud was that he had a high and exaggerated reverence for Gall, ranking him with Copernicus, Kepler, and Newton. Bouillaud, however, was not entirely blind to the embroideries of Gall and Spurzheim and as early as 1827 published two papers, in which he brought forward experimental and clinical evidence refuting the phrenologists' opinions about brain functions. Bouillaud did not accept the cerebellum as an organ of the instinct for sexuality, love-making, propagation and all things wild and amatory. Instead, Bouillaud just as had Flourens, agreed that the cerebellum was the organ of equilibrium, station, and gait (Rolleston, 1937).

BOUILLAUD'S ALLEGED FOLLY

In the detailed analysis of Bouillaud's contributions by Luzzati and Whitaker (2001) these authors consider and deflower in exquisite detail the observations made by Bouillaud in his most important contribution on localization of language in the anterior lobes. In a remarkable example of re-meta analysis, they report:

> In 1825, Jean-Baptiste Bouillaud read a paper at the Royal Academy of Medicine in Paris supporting Franz Gall's theory of a relation between speech and the frontal lobes. Bouillaud argued that if the frontal lobes are crucial to speech, two conditions must be satisfied: when the frontal lobes are affected, speech must also be affected; conversely, when the frontal lobes are spared, speech is also spared. Following these principles, he tested and argued in support of Gall's theory by analyzing the data from 2 neuropathological casebooks (Lallemand, 1820–1823; Rostan, 1820 and 1823). We now know that Bouillaud was wrong, since the crucial dichotomy is between the left and right hemispheres and not between the anterior and posterior areas. What is interesting is that the actual data refute Bouillaud's conclusion. We replicated his experiment by reanalyzing the 147 clinical cases described by Lallemand. There were, of course, some cases with frontal lesions and speech disorders; other cases, however, had speech disorders with lesions outside the frontal lobes, and still others had frontal lesions without speech disorders. Although Bouillaud did not notice it, as we expected, almost all patients with speech disorders had a left hemisphere lesion. (Luzzati & Whitaker, 2001, p. 1157)

Luzzati and Whitaker go so far as to accuse Bouillaud of scientific deceit. They state, "in this event his paper constitutes an early example of scientific fraud" (p. 1161).

Bouillaud died in his 88th year in 1881, a year after the death of Paul Broca, and a statue was erected in his honor four years later. He was regarded as an outstanding clinician (with some misgivings on his persistent use of discredited practices); a thoughtful researcher; a striking scholar with prodigious publications; a respected teacher; and a trailblazer in neuroscience. Despite his voluminous contributions, Bouillaud was criticized and almost forgotten after his death and his reputation has been resurrected and tainted with the aura of scientific swindle (Luzzati & Whitaker, 2001).

Bouillaud's fall from grace with his peers may have been the result of his resistance to accept change, especially his insistence on bleeding or blood-letting as a treatment. Heavy and repeated bleeding was characteristic of his practice long after it had been widely discredited (Rolleston, 1937). Bleeding bowls were used to collect blood during bloodletting, a practice once carried out to treat a broad range of maladies and medical ailments (Figure 6–2). Bloodletting was used as cure for many fevers, diseases that were believed to be caused by a logjam of blood. The bowl pictured is made from pewter and has a scale marked in fluid ounces engraved on the inside to allow precise monitoring of the quantity of blood being removed. Bouillaud held onto his bleeding bowl long after it had gone out of fashion. The London Science Museum has an impressive collection of objects and images of historic medical treatment, including the bleeding bowl in the following illustration. This striking collection can be retrieved from: http://www.sciencemuseum.org.uk/broughttolife/objects/display.aspx?id=5042

Bouillaud apparently was not the most even-tempered or affable creature. Rolleston (1937) relates comments of colleagues who did not hesitate to speak of Bouillaud's "combative disposition . . . determined and arrogant advocacy of doctrines which the advance of science was fast leaving in the background."

Schiller (1992) extracts some chilling perceptions of Bouillaud's character in his scholarly text on Broca. The attributes of

Figure 6–2. Bleeding bowl. London Science Museum. Reprinted with permission.

Bouillaud include "dignity in bearing," a facile diction, a habitual ability to generalize, and an independent character. He cites as well that Bouillaud had too much awareness of his own merit; was quick to anger at the slightest show of opposition and seemed to be in an eternal state of discontent and excitement. A day with Bouillaud may not have been a day at the beach, as many of his associates and minions soon discovered.

Though he may have been an irrasible character, Bouillaud played a monumental role in advancement of the idea of the localization of speech and language in the "anterior" lobes of the brain. He described patients who, though unable to speak, were able to write, attesting that their intelligence was unimpaired; and he observed that other patients expressed themselves by signs, conveying their ideas with their hands, their eyes, and their facial expression. He was, perhaps, one of the early observers of the importance of coverbal and nonverbal communication. It would take many years for these aspects of language in aphasia to be studied systematically (Katz, LaPointe, & Markel, 2005; Katz, LaPointe, Markel, & Silkes, 2005). Without his 30 years of research, countless case studies, and persistent advocacy, the stage for Broca may never have been set. The many contributions of Bouillaud are summarized with exquisite detail by Rolleston (1937). This synopsis of the research and ideas of this prodigious scholar from southwest France are presented not only with acclaim but also with the warts that marred his thinking and ideas. Perhaps we all have a few warts. Bouillaud, however, cannot be denied as a dominant researcher and thinker on the critical topic of brain and language. Bouillaud's ideas failed to receive broad acceptance among the scientific community until they were resurrected in 1861. This may have been in part due to the negative response to the concept of cerebral localization as a backlash against the disgraced doctrine of phrenology.

But now the year was 1861 and the arena was becoming primed for a tsunamic revival of curiosity about localization of speech and language in the brain. The debates at the *Société de Anthropologie* were heating up; fueled by controversial issues introduced by Darwin, old religious-secular taunts of soul and mind, and now by the fresh issue of the location of language in the brain. Could it possibly be that mind was merely a part of the organ of the brain, and not of the ethereal soul? The Church had a few opinions and these beliefs were to impose themselves on the free-thinkers in the *Société d'Anthropologie*. The *carte du jour* was becoming set. And it would be set not only with the sweetness of *tarte aux fraises* but also with the astringency of sour cabbage.

Jean-Baptiste Bouillaud was to discover a like-minded doctor and colleague, who embraced not only his ideas and philosophies but also his daughter. Simon Alexandre Ernest Aubertin was a young prodigy who was to become a physician, serve as a catalyst for Broca's monumental evidence-based clinical-pathological pronouncement, and marry Bouillaud's daughter.

SIMON ALEXANDRE ERNEST AUBERTIN AND THE CATALYTIC SPATULA CASE

In April of 1861 a new French newspaper made its appearance. *Le Temps* was born and lived for nearly 100 years. Its inaugural edition reached the streets filled with local and national news and included ads for metal coins and a review of a play about a woman in white ("La Femme en Blanc" (Le Temps, 1861). One can imagine Bouillaud, Aubertin, Broca, and other members of French society comparing this upstart publication *Le Temps* with the established paper *Le Figaro* and debating the merits of this newcomer over café or at lunch. But other, more vitriolic debates were to extend to other venues that day.

Disputes continued to flare in the halls of the academic and medical societies of Paris. Scientific and academic debate had and has a long history in the halls of societies and organizations (La Berge, 2004). Argumentation and the laying out of logical reasoning was viewed as a key scientific practice among the medical elite in 19th century Paris, and extensions of these refining arguments were recorded in the scientific/medical press. As an example, La Berge (2004) uses debate over the use of the microscope, which Paul Broca would champion, that took place in the Paris Academy of Medicine in 1854 to 1855 and concurrently in the medical press. Debate led to refinements in thinking and solidified conclusions and interpretations of scientific practice and research. Medical journalists used the debate in the Academy to raise larger questions about the nature of science and medicine and to authenticate medical practice. La Berge (2004) has taken the stance that debate was an essential scientific practice in 19th century Paris, in harmony with a long-standing belief that truth emerges through disputation. This practice of spirited and sometimes aggressive debate may have been related as well to the shared masculine culture of bellicosity and honor of the times. Some of the arguments appeared to fall just short of the chest pounding and stomping of some of our primate cousins. Some debates grew beyond the halls of academia and extended to the meadows of Paris where duels were held. The famous debates between Pierre Marie and Dejerine would result in the heated duel challenge, mentioned earlier though this particular duel was eventually aborted and the tumescence of testosterone-driven debate eventually drooped. This is splendidly reported in their chronicle of aphasia milestones by Tesak and Code (2008). The great debate between revisionism in aphasia would extend through the years, and as reported by Tesak and Code (2008), Liepmann would characterize Marie's attack on classic doctrine in aphasia as being quite excessive, as much argumentation is wont to be. Liepmann lambasted Marie for being a revisionist without appreciating the lucidity and scholarship that had preceded him. This is an argument that hangs around even today. Liepmann (1909) rails against Marie's view of "one classic doctrine" in aphasiology that was not classic at all but seemed to be Marie's fantasy even by one who had neglected or overlooked the collective work of many scientists in many nations. Liepmann accused Marie of rigid dogma and perpetrating the "booming wake-up call" of "on to revision!" And we thought "wake-up call" was a contemporaneous phrase.

Then, in the landmark year of 1861 the doctors and scientists of Paris reconsidered localism with a more open mind (Feinberg & Farah, 1997). The taint of phrenology had weakened. That year the Société d'Anthropologie in Paris held a series of debates between Pierre Gratiolet, arguing in favor of holism or equipotentiality, and Simon Alexandre Ernest Aubertin, the son-in-law of Bouillaud, arguing in favor of localism. Aubertin reported his clinical observations of a patient whose frontal bone was removed following a suicide attempt. He reported that when the blade of a spatula was applied to the "anterior lobes," there was complete cessation of speech without loss of consciousness. According to his report this was a patient

> who had shot himself in the head with a pistol and presented a large gash over the frontal lobes . . . curious to know what effect it would have on speech if the brain were compressed, we applied to the exposed part a large spatula pressing from above downwards and a little from front to back. With moderate pressure speech seemed to die on his lips; pressing harder and more sharply, speech not only failed but a few words were cut off suddenly. (Aubertin, 1861, p. 210)

Aubertin went on to describe a patient of Bouillaud's who had a speech disturbance and was near death. This would be the classic case of M. Leborgne. Before Broca met Leborgne, these debates played out at the society meetings. Broca had participated and in fact took minutes of the proceedings of several meetings of the *"Société d'Anthropologie"* in Paris. His signature is affixed beneath the meeting minutes of many of the reports of the Society in the French National Bibliotque, as he served as Recording Secretary as well as being the founder of it. The great debate between Aubertin (1825–1893) and Pierre Gratiolet (1815–1865) arose on the controversy over localization of functions in the brain (Amunts, 2007). These debates ranged from the general idea of localization of mental and higher cortical functions in the brain to the specifics of an area for language and speech in the frontal lobe. Like Gall and like Bouillaud, Aubertin was a staunch advocate of a place in the brain for speech and language. Aubertin declared that he would renounce the idea of cerebral localization if a single case could be demonstrated in which the loss of the faculty of articulate language is found without a lesion in the anterior lobes.

GRATIOLET: ADVERSARY OF AUBERTIN AND BROCA

Louis Pierre Gratiolet proved to be a creditable debater and his arguments resonated through the halls of the Paris academic societies with his bones of contention and worthy opposition to

Aubertin and later Broca. Once again we are indebted to remark-able historical scholarship of J. M. S. Pearce of the United King-dom for his rich tracing of neurological history (Pearce, 2006). Louis Pierre Gratiolet was born in 1815 at Ste-Foy-La-Grande. In another bit of historical small world coincidence and curios-ity, this was also the birthplace and home of Pierre Paul Broca and though they shared a common village near the banks of the Dordogne River in a region known for fine Bordeaux wines and quiet country life, these two minds of neuroscience did not share common opinions about many issues in brain science. In this quaint village that produced more than its share of scientists and physicians, Boulevard Gratiolet now opens onto Place Broca as present-day commemoratives to these forefathers who illumi-nated important aspects of our understanding of the structure and function of the innards of the cranium.

Gratiolet studied medicine in Paris and probably traveled by bumpy coach from this little village to the bustle and confusion of the City of Light somewhat before his other famous village-mate as he was nine years older than Broca. Gratiolet studied under Henri de Blainville (1777–1850). He no doubt was strongly influenced by Blainville, the prominent French zoologist and anatomist who served as professor at the Museum d'Histoire Naturelle, Paris. Blainville's paleontological work added valuable evidence for his theory of a chain of creation. Rue Blainville is a tiny street with a notable restaurant (La Truffiére) that commem-orates the anatomist just off the bustling Place de Contrescarpe, the former hangout of Hemingway and his posse of literary ex patriots. Fittingly, this excellent eatery specializes in the white truffles and foie gras that exemplify the home region around Sainte-Foy-la-Grande. Both Gratiolet and Broca would have recognized the smells of La Truffiére. Blainville has a memor-able quotation that is attributed to him that is ever so true and ever so sobering: "Life is the twofold internal movement of com-position and decomposition, at once general and continuous" (Blainville, 1858).

Pierre Gratiolet was employed at the *Musée de d'Histoire Naturelle* in Paris in 1842 to 1853, where he became a labora-tory assistant, as many of us must. He lectured on anatomy from 1844 to 1850, and was appointed director of anatomical studies (1853–1862) and deputy to the professor of zoology, Faculty of

Science, University of Paris (1862–1863). Though Gratiolet and some of his colleagues mapped the folds and fissures of the cerebral cortex, it was Gratiolet who demarcated and named them, and identified 'secondary folds' within each lobe. He was reluctant to ascribe function to the structures he had demarcated and retained his holistic view of brain function regarding intellect and higher cortical processes:

> In a general manner I agree with M. Flourens that the intelligence is one, that the brain is one, that it acts above all as a whole; but this does not exclude the idea that certain faculties of the mind stand in special relation, although not exclusively, with certain cerebral regions (Head, 1926, p. 16).

Gratiolet engaged in heated debates with Aubertin and took the stance of an avid anti-localizationist, and also engaged Broca in debate on intelligence and brain size. Pearce (2007) recorded it as carnival-like. He relates an "amusing sideshow" took place in a prolonged battle in the Anthropological Society of Paris between Gratiolet and Broca on intelligence and brain dimensions. This debate with Gratiolet would place Broca in the camp of believers of a correlative relationship between brain size and intelligence and lay him open to criticism even in modern times (Gould, 1980). Gratiolet's research agenda was diverse, to say the least, and included important discoveries about cortical ophthalmic pathways. The diversity of his interests can be found in his study of comparative anatomy of facial expressions in animals as well as in the comparative anatomy of the hippopotamus (Leuret & Gratiolet, 1839). His subjects were diverse, huge, and had big teeth.

BRITISH EXPANSIONS ON CORTICAL LOCALIZATION OF FUNCTION

While French brains were active in developing concepts of localization of specific functions of the nervous system, British brains were not idle. Wozniak (1995) has traced the contributions of these events. One such contributor was Alexander Bain (1818–1903) who was born, educated, and died in Aberdeen, Scotland.

Bain wrote about essential associations between motoric and sensory activity and further defined the higher cortical functions of plans, intent, and the independence of reliance on strictly sensory experiences to initiate and govern movements. Bain conceptualized spontaneous movements as being a feature of nervous activity prior to and independent of sensations. As Bain suggested in some of his influential writings, the acquired associations of spontaneous movements with the pleasure and pains following them, appear to inform the person so that its formerly random movements are tailored or adjusted to ends or purposes. This notion of cortical associations between movement intent and actual movement instigated a new role for the cerebrum, and, as we would learn, for the frontal lobes and higher intellectual functions in particular. This was an early indicator of the importance of motor plans or motor programming that would color the writings of Broca subsequently.

Another British scientist and philosopher, Herbert Spencer, also wrote about and influenced thinking on the role of the cerebrum and the localization of complex intellectual functions. Spencer was born in Derby, England and was largely self-taught. At the age of 17, he took up railway engineering but left that occupation in 1848 to work first as an editor and then as a freelance writer and reviewer. In his autobiography, as relayed by Wozniak (1995), Spencer tells us that, at age 11 or 12, he attended lectures by Spurzheim that for many years made him a believer in phrenology. As late as 1846, before his growing skepticism regarding phrenology led him to forsake the project, Spencer had designed a cephalograph for the purpose of achieving more reliable cranial measurements. This was to foreshadow mechanical inventiveness of Broca who also designed many instruments for more precise facial and cranial measurement. Spencer's major contributions were related to the role of the cerebrum in governing higher cortical processes and its relationships to subcortical structures. Prior to and highlighted by Descartes, the mind/body separation for two centuries had supported the impression that the cerebrum, functioning as the seat of higher mental processes, must function according to principles fundamentally different from those descriptive of subcerebral nervous function. Mind and soul were intertwined for centuries. The brain, and particularly the cerebrum, must have nothing to do with the ephemeral concept of "mind." This idea of cerebral localization of mind functions would have to be drastically modified according to Spencer. The ghostly and unmeasureable concept of "soul" was and remains a point of departure for many between science and theosophy.

As Wozniak (1995) points out in his trenchant work on mind and body through the ages, the implications of these evolutionary conceptions for the hypothesis of cortical localization of function are strong. The brain is the most highly developed physical system we know and the cortex is the most developed level of the brain. As such, it must be heterogeneous, differentiated, and complex. Furthermore, if the cortex is a continuous elaboration from subcortical structures, the sensory-motor principles that govern subcortical localization must hold in the cortex as well. Finally, if higher mental processes are the end product of a continuous process of development from the simplest irritation through reflexes and instincts, there is no justification for drawing a sharp distinction between mind and body. The notion of dualism of mind and body was called into question by the thoughts of Herbert Spencer. Perhaps the brain was indispensible for the concept of mind. Perhaps the soul was the mind. Perhaps the idea of soul was generated by the mind. Experiments led by scientists who split the corpus collosom has revealed that each of the separated hemispheres appears to have its own private sensations, perceptions, thoughts, feelings, and memories; in short, that they constitute two separate minds, two separate spheres of consciousness. These issues of the relationship between brain and mind and consciousness continue to baffle us today just as they baffled Descartes, Spencer, and other deep thinkers.

According to Wozniak (1995), Spencer's ideas were to be worked out and more fully developed by the noted British neurologist John Hughlings Jackson. As Wozniak (1995) implies, it was quite clear that even in 1855 Spencer was well aware of the implications of his concepts of continuity and development for cerebral localization. Herbert Spencer's *Principles of Psychology* (1855) was regarded by his contemporaries, including William James and John Dewey, as a major contribution to what was then a very new discipline. In this work, he wrote that, "no physiologist who calmly considers the question in connection with the general truths of his science can long resist the conviction that different parts of the cerebrum subserve different kinds of mental action" (p. 607).

With the ground prepared by the sensory-motor associationism of Bain and the psychophysiology of Spencer, and the insistence of Aubertin and Bouillaud, all that was needed in order to overcome the last impediment to the localization of language and other higher intellectual functions to the cortex was the momentum provided by striking research findings and new experimental techniques. These techniques and observations would be provided by Broca in 1861 and later by Fritz and Hitzig (1870). These experiments would provide the capstone to the classical doctrine of cortical localization. Wozniak, (1995) has done a remarkable service in tracing these developments on cortical localization and concepts of mind and brain. The work of Finger (1994, 2000, 2009) also has contributed greatly to our understanding of the evolution of ideas about cortical localization of functions and their implied or demonstrated relationships between brain and human consciousness.

STENDHAL'S SHRUNKEN TESTICLES AND TRANSIENT APHASIA

But even as the soon-to-be giant pioneers of cortical localization advocacy were taking their warm-up swings, one can find shards and remnants of allusion to speech and the brain in scattered earlier references. In March 1841, the year before he died of acute stroke, Stendhal, one of the most famous French novelists of the 19th century, developed a series of short-lived speech impairments which he precisely reported in his correspondence. Bogousslavsky and Assal (2010) have done some historical sleuthing and unearthed documentation of transient speech disruption in Stendhal.

Marie-Henri Beyle (January 23, 1783–March 23, 1842), was better known by his pen name, Stendhal. This remarkable French writer and *bon vivant* is known for his acute analysis of his characters' psychology, and he is considered one of the earliest and leading practitioners of realism as exemplified in his two novels *Le Rouge et le Noir* (The Red and the Black, 1830) and *La Char-*

treuse de Parme (The Charterhouse of Parma, 1839). Stendahl's "Charterhouse" is described by a few reviewers as an incredibly romantic novel containing a battle, a duel, a knife fight, various disguises for the hero, a poetry-writing revolutionary highwayman, and the most romantic setting for a love-affair possible, a passionate encounter between an unjustly imprisoned young nobleman and the beautiful daughter of the prison warden, soon to be married to a rich man she despises. It was made into a 1948 French film whose intriguing trailer can be found on YouTube at http://www.youtube.com/watch?v=qNrfDsYHrcg

Stendhal was a dandy and wit about town in Paris, as well as an inveterate womanizer who was obsessed with his sexual conquests, according to some reports (Jefferson, 1988). Stendhal suffered miserable physical disabilities in his final years as he continued to produce some of his superlative work. As he noted in his meticulous journals, he was taking iodide of potassium and quicksilver to treat his syphilis, resulting in swollen armpits, difficulty swallowing, pains in his shrunken testicles, sleeplessness, giddiness, roaring in the ears, racing pulse, and tremors so bad he could scarcely hold a fork or a pen. Indeed, he dictated *Charterhouse* in this sorry state (Jefferson, 1988).

Amid the horror of giddiness, tinnitus, and shrunken testicles, reports suggest that Stendhal also exhibited "spells" that were aphasic transient ischemic attacks (TIAs). The accuracy and precision of Stendhal's description of his spells in his journals, exactly 20 years before Broca's presentation at the *Société d'Anthropologie,* is remarkable as it occurred at a time when TIAs had not been studied in the medical literature and aphasia was still in its infancy. Stendhal's TIAs a few months before his fatal stroke constitute the first historical report of the warning nature of TIAs, which would be emphasized only over 100 years later (Bogousslavsky & Assal, 2010).

FINGER AND THE DEBATES

As Finger (2009) summarized, the theory of cortical localization of function presumes that different cerebral cortical territories serve different functions, such as vision and language.

This theory began to be entertained in the mid-1700s, but it had no impact until Gall made it central to his thinking in the early 1800s. Gall's phrenology, with its emphasis on cranial bumps and "phrenology parlors" where these head bumps would be read and interpreted . . . for a fee, soon fell into discredit, but in the decades that followed new proponents of modified versions of cortical localization were to emerge as Bouillaud, Aubertin, and Broca advanced the concept by revealing and documenting clinical-pathological cases of speech loss. In 1870 Fritsch and Hitzig demonstrated the validity of specific localization of specific functions by studying movements and motor functions with animals. As Finger (2009) highlights, the theory of cortical localization of function served as a guiding factor in changing the practice of neurology, as clinicians and researchers gathered and accumulated fresh material supportive of the doctrine. Surgical neurology, anatomy, neuropsychology, speech-language pathology, and physiology have benefited and incorporated this evolved way of thinking, contributing to a sounder understanding of the functional organization of the cerebral cortex, to neuroscience in general, and to all of the disciplines that deal with brain-based disorders.

The 1861 debates in the *Société de Anthropologie* is known for the arguments and presentations of Gratiolet and Aubertin and for the participation of members of the audience on an array of issues related to localization of functions in the brain and particularly on the home or associations of cortex with speech and language. It is best known, however, for the eventual participation of the society's founder and secretary, Paul Broca. By this stage of the game, Bouillaud, who had argued localization for decades now, was relatively silent and perhaps stewing in his own seething juices. He was to be somewhat placated by the arguments of his son-in-law Aubertin and the foreshadow of affirmation by Broca.

According to Pearce (2007) Gratiolet's research efforts were devoted to the structure of the brain, but his work was undervalued and he lived in poverty and hardship. He died in 1865 in Paris, the publication year of Broca's great synthesis and interpretation of his clinical-pathological findings of the past four years (Broca, 1865).

This belief of Gratiolet, of a more holistic conception of higher cortical function, formed the basis for the debate that would provoke Aubertin and inspire Broca. As well documented in the excellent histories of cognitive science and aphasia by Stookey (1963), Schiller (1992), Feinberg and Farah (1997), Finger (1994), as well as Nadeau, Gonzalez Rothi, and Crosson (2000), and Tesak and Code (2008) that landmark year, 1861, became a noted milestone in neuroscience.

1861: A YEAR LADEN WITH HISTORICAL EPISODES

In history, some years ascend to prominence and memory and others seem to be relegated to the detritus of passing events. The year 1861 was to become the temporal crossroads of numerous historical events in many parts of the world. In the United States the tragic Civil War was splitting the nation. In 1861, Cornelia Phillips Spencer wrote of a "*strange*, sad spring" that brought into bloom "a *strange,* enormous and terrible flower, the blood-red flower of war, which grows amid the thunders." (Spencer, 1861). In the month of April, that would witness the concurrent milestone presentations in the *Société d'Anthropologie* in Paris, American hostilities were breaking out and on April 12, 1861, barely a week after Auburtin's presentation to the Society and five days before Broca's classic paper, Confederate forces attacked a U.S. military installation at Fort Sumter in South Carolina. President Abraham Lincoln responded by calling for a volunteer army from each state to recapture federal property. This led to declarations of secession by four more slave states and to the increasing maelstrom that ripped the United States asunder for four years. It ended with the Emancipation Proclamation that freed the slaves; and the last shot was fired with the subsequent surrender of General Robert E. Lee on April 9, 1865.

The year 1861 was marked by significant inventions as well. The pencil was invented. Otis patented the steam elevator; and the flush toilet (with separate water tank and a pull chain) was invented and patented by Mr. Thomas Crapper. In yet another bit of ironic eponymous trivia London's first tramcars, designed by Mr. Train of New York, began operating. The telegraph brought the Pony Express to an abrupt end in the United States. A series of political and military events resulted in a unified kingdom of Italy in 1861. In Australia, the explorers Robert O'Hara Burke and William John Wills explored the length of the country from South to North but lost their lives on the return trip, perhaps from Vegemite poisoning. A comet that was visible to the naked eye for approximately three months appeared in this year and was called the Great Comet of 1861. The end of the First Taranaki War between Maori and the New Zealand government occurred, and in Russia the serfs were set free. The 1861 Battle of Shanghai was one of many confrontations of the Taiping Rebellion which was a widespread civil war in southern China from 1850 to 1864. About 20 *million* people died during this war, mainly civilians, in one of the deadliest military conflicts in history. In the United States Henry Wadsworth Longfellow penned "Paul Revere's Ride," and the haunting song "Aura Lea," was written by W. W. Fosdick and George R. Poulton to be immortalized much later during the Happy Days of the 1950s as the melody for Elvis Presley's "Love Me Tender" (History, 1861).

In France uproar ruled politics as well as culture. Wagner's opera Tannhauser was met with disorder. The audience interrupted the performance with hooting, whistles, and cat-calls. At the third performance on March 24, 1861, this uproar caused several stoppages of up to 15 minutes at a time. Wagner was not pleased and withdrew his opera from Paris after three performances (Warrick & West, 1979).

Musicians were playing Die Lorelei and Liszt, who had lived in Paris in the 1820s and 1830s, was a darling of Parisian culture. In fact, in sorting through the archives and artifacts of the National Museum, Dr. Philippe Mennecier displayed two of the masks made of Liszt that are still held in the museum, next to artifacts of Broca's work (Figure 6–3).

In Great Britain, *Great Expectations* by Charles Dickens was announced and published. Perhaps this was to set the tone for expectations in the world of science and discovery, for it was the dawning of crystallization of discoveries of operations of the human brain. France again was the venue and French brains engaged the podium and the laboratories of neural science (History, 1861).

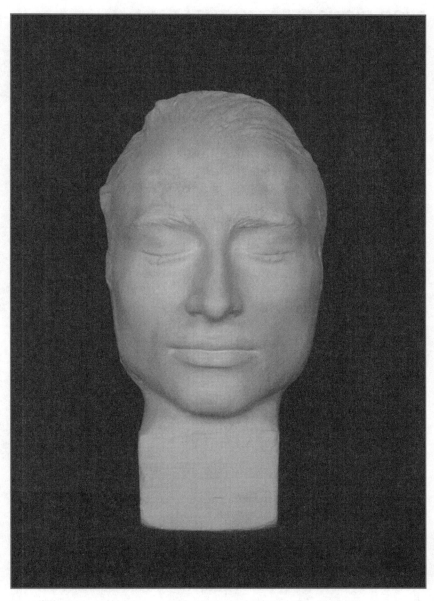

Figure 6–3. *Mask of Franz Liszt. Photo used with permission of Philippe Mennecier, Charge de Conservation des collections d'anthropologie biologuique, Musée national d'histoire naturelle.*

PRODIGIOUS DEBATES: THE BRAIN
AND ITS DOINGS

This extraordinary year began with the resurrection and fanning of debate on localization of functions in the brain. The *Société d'Anthropologie* in Paris organized this series of debates, perhaps each session with a bit of a break for madeleines and café. As mentioned above, in one corner was the verbally agile Pierre Gratiolet, arguing in favor of holism or equipotentiality, and in the other corner was Ernest Aubertin, young, brash, and embracing the nepotistic views of his father-in-law Bouillaud.

Aubertin argued in favor of localism and presenting evidence from his and his father-in-law's caseloads of people with speech and language loss and confirmed lesions to the anterior lobes. Gratiolet proved to be a worthy advocate of the holistic approach to the localization issue. In addition to the now broad prejudice against localization in the wake of Gall, there was a conviction, ever since Descartes, that the mind was a unity and the mind was related to the soul, so that even if the mind was associated with the brain, it was not broken into different faculties localized in different brain areas. These doubts were buttressed by empirical evidence of negative cases. Some audience members spoke clinically of their patients with frontal damage that did not show speech deficits and others offered patients with speech deficits but no frontal lobe damage. Lacking even a reliable pattern, prior to Broca's work, claims to the localization of language ability were generally dismissed (Bechtel, 2001). So the fencing expanded.

On April 4, 1864 Aubertin presented his views and his classic "spatula case" to the *Société d' Anthropologie*. He described an articulatory organ and a coordinating center that resided in the frontal lobe. Aubertin reiterated his position that localized in the frontal lobes "the faculty of coordinating the movements peculiar to language," based entirely on clinical observations. However, precise localization remained vague (Pearce, 2009).

The opening of Aubertin's presentation on April 4, 1861 was a beginning as well as a continuation of presentations that were heated but civil, and full of formalities and deference. But the inherent challenges and steadfastness of the positions were clear. Figure 6–4 presents Aubertin's opening gambit, from his

AUBURTIN. — SUR LA FORME ET LE VOLUME DU CERVEAU. 209

Reprise de la discussion sur la forme et le volume du cerveau.

M. Auburtin. J'ai déjà pris la parole dans une précédente séance pour demander à M. Gratiolet des éclaircissements sur quelques propositions qu'il avait émises et qui me paraissaient beaucoup trop exclusives. Les explications qu'il a bien voulu nous donner alors n'ont pas réussi à me convaincre. Je me propose aujourd'hui de présenter avec plus de développement les faits que je lui ai déjà opposés, et d'examiner la valeur de ses arguments. Le discours que M. Broca a prononcé dans la dernière séance me permettra de glisser rapidement sur plusieurs questions qu'il a étudiées très-complétement : mais j'aurai à insister sur quelques autres.

M. Gratiolet nous a dit que la masse cérébrale, c'est-à-dire le *volume du cerveau*, considéré par rapport à l'intelligence, n'est rien, ou presque rien, et que la *forme* est tout ; à l'appui de cette opinion, il a dit qu'on peut être très-médiocre avec un très-gros cerveau, et très-éminent avec un cerveau très-médiocre.

La première assertion est vraie, mais ne peut être acceptée sans commentaire. Oui, il y a des hommes peu intelligents qui ont un cerveau très-gros ou très-lourd, mais ces cas sont pathologiques. L'hydrocéphalie, l'encéphalite peuvent augmenter le volume et le poids du cerveau, et cet organe s'hypertrophie notablement dans certaines formes d'aliénation mentale. C'est ce qui résulte du tableau de M. Wagner ; mais M. Broca nous a déjà montré qu'un pareil relevé, où les hydrocéphales, les idiots, les aliénés, les épileptiques, les paralytiques, sont confondus pêle-mêle avec les individus sains, ne peut servir de base à des conclusions sérieuses, à

T. II. 14

Figure 6–4. *Aubertin's opening gambit, from the original debate at the* Société d'Anthropologie.

original article now preserved in the Bibliothèque Nationale de France. Aubertin opens his presentation by stating:

> I have already made a speech in a previous meeting to request Monsieur Gratiolet for clarification on a few proposals that he issued and which appeared to me to be much too exclusive. The explanations that he has kindly given us do not convince me. (Aubertin, 1861)

Figure 6–5 presents the preserved translations of some of the debate by members of the *Société d'Anthropologie* and an extract of Gratiolet's comments (Aubertin, 1861).

Gratiolet, in rejoinder, comments, rightly so, on the ambiguity of the definitions of the lesions in the cases presented to support the location of language in the brain. He even uses the metaphor of "brain soup" or "frappe" to characterize some of the lesions. As we will see, this criticism of ambiguity and extensiveness of lesions will continue to haunt those who are making a case for precise seats of intellectual faculties, especially speech and language. The advances in imaging that will allow reanalysis of the lesions in Broca's famous cases will confirm that the lesions were more extensive than was immediately concluded. Those revelations, however, do not detract much from the milestone advances that were to follow in 1861 on the adaptation of clinical pathological methods to interpret brain and behavioral functions.

BROCA LISTENS

Broca listened as Aubertin forcefully presented his stance. At the Société, Aubertin lay down the dare to Broca: he stated that if Broca, or anyone else were to find an aphasic patient without a lesion in the frontal cortex, he would repudiate his views. Broca, who had until then seemed somewhat luke warm to the debate on localization of function, took a renewed interest (Neurophilosophy, 2011). The debate and the challenge had apparently spurred him on to look further for clinicopathological evidence of his growing views on language in the brain. Paul Broca, as the secretary of the *Société d'Anthropologie* dutifully recorded that the session ended at 5:45 o'clock. Perhaps he returned home and

GRATIOLET. — SUR LE POIDS ET LA FORME DU CERVEAU. 263

la physiologie du système nerveux. La phrénologie de Gall, fondée sur une méthode essentiellement empirique, est matériellement incertaine. Gall est bien plus guidé par une sorte d'instinct physiognomonique que par une intuition claire et vraiment philosophique des grandes questions qu'il ose aborder; aussi Spix et Huschke lui ont-ils adressé le reproche plus ou moins fondé de s'être borné à traduire Lavater et Engel, et ce qui reste aujourd'hui de son système dans la crânioscopie de Carus diffère peu, quant à la méthode, de celle qu'Avicenne avait autrefois imaginée, et qui eut cours pendant tout le moyen âge parmi les scolastiques.

Mais je dois reconnaître que ni M. Auburtin, ni M. Broca, ni M. Perier lui-même, ne m'ont opposé la doctrine phrénologique, sinon d'une manière très-générale. Ils pensent que les facultés principales de l'esprit ont des siéges distincts dans le cerveau, et M. Auburtin, invoquant l'expérience et les observations pathologiques, considère comme absolument démontrée cette proposition, que la faculté du langage, par exemple, réside dans les lobes antérieurs du cerveau.

Loin de moi la pensée de mettre en doute un seul instant la parfaite exactitude des faits invoqués par M. Auburtin; tous ces faits sont vrais, et il en résulte que, dans un grand nombre de cas, une lésion des lobes antérieurs du cerveau peut entraîner la perte du langage; mais cette conséquence de la lésion des lobes antérieurs est-elle nécessaire? inévitable? c'est ce que nous allons examiner.

Citons seulement quelques faits bien constatés.

Un homme, c'est M. Chassaignac qui le rapporte, est frappé au front par un éclat de canon. Le frontal subit une destruction énorme; il sort immédiatement par la blessure une cuillerée à soupe de substance cérébrale,

Figure 6–5. Société d'Anthropologie *debate. Extract of Gratiolet's comments on Aubertin's presentation.*

read the newspaper *Le Figaro* for April 4, 1861. In it he would have found and perused the column of theater reviews called Petite Chronique des Theatres and read the letter from M. Souche that praised the performance of a Paris actress called "Fanny." An advertisement in the same paper may have also caught his eye. It listed a remedy for *Eau des Melisse des Carmes* for the treatment of apoplexy, paralysis, sea-sickness, or vapors. (Le Figaro, April 4, 1861). More likely, Paul Broca, a man who would be characterized in today's vernacular as a workaholic, returned to his work and conspired to generate some clinical-pathological evidence that would change how the world thought about the localization of special faculties in the brain. Broca founded the Society, dutifully took notes and published them in the Bulletins, and was shortly to mark the Society with one of its most germane presentations.

Pierre Paul Broca was already a revered scientist and physician, but events of this historic year of 1861 and the years to follow would mark his place in the annals of neuroscience history. This month of April 1861 would be painted as one that could not be ignored by serious scholars of brain science.

Figure 1–1. *Claude Monet,* Impression: Sunrise *(1872), Musee Marmottan, Paris. A view of the port of Le Havre in the mist.*

Figure 2–1. *Bust of Hippocrates, father of medicine. Wikimedia Commons, public domain.*

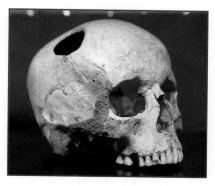

Figure 2–2. *Trephinated skull. Wikimedia Commons, public domain.*

Figure 2–3. *Hieroglyphic word for "brain."*

Figure 2–4. *René Descartes, advocate of reason and the scientific method. Wikimedia Commons, public domain.*

Figure 2–5. *Descartes memorial in Église St. Germaine des Prés, Paris.*

Figure 2–6. Descartes bust and commemorative plaque, St. Germaine des Pres, Paris.

Figure 2–7. The majestic Pantheon, resting place of national heroes, 5th Arrondisement, Paris.

Figure 2–8. Columns of the Pantheon.

Figure 2–9. In the crypt of the Pantheon.

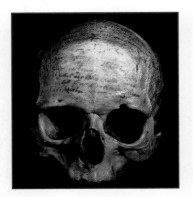

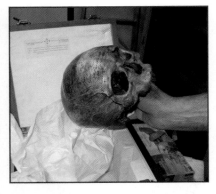

Figure 2–10. Descartes skull. Photo used with permission of Philippe Mennecier, Charge de Conservation des collections d'anthropologie biologuique, Musée national d'histoire naturelle.

Figure 2–11. Holding Descartes' skull. Photo used with permission of Philippe Mennecier, Charge de Conservation des collections d'anthropologie biologuique, Musée national d'histoire naturelle.

Figure 3–1. Franz Josef Gall, pioneer of cortical localization; advocate of phrenology. Wikimedia Commons, public domain.

Figure 3–2. Head casts used to study differences in skull configurations. Wikimedia Commons, public domain.

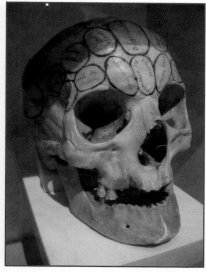

Figure 3–3. Early cast of phrenology head from the Gall collection. Photo used with permission of Philippe Mennecier, Charge de Conservation des collections d'anthropologie biologuique, Musée national d'histoire naturelle.

Figure 3–4. Human skull with phrenological faculties superimposed. Public domain.

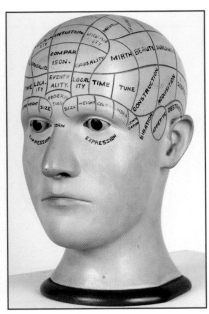

Figure 3–5. Fowler's popular interpretation of a phrenological bust.

Figure 3–6. Realistic phrenology bust with characteristics and faculties of behavior.

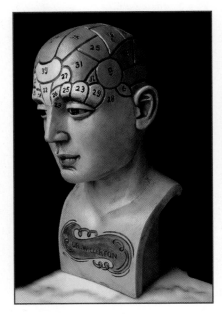

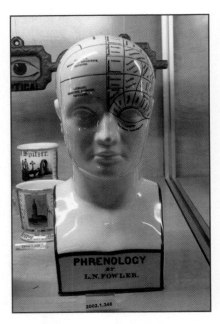

Figure 3–7. Wistful phrenology bust.

Figure 3–8. Jean-Pierre Flourens. Used with permission of Gallica, Banque of Images, Bibiotique Nationale Francais.

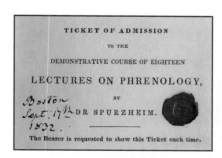

Figure 3–9. Ticket to a Boston lecture by Spurzheim on phrenology.

Figure 3–10. Johann Spurzheim, disciple of Gall. Retrieved April 2, 2012, from https://www.countway.harvard.edu/chm/rarebooks/exhibits/talking_heads/scans/spurzheimport.jpg.

A

B

Figure 3–11. George (**A**) and Andrew Combe (**B**), Scottish advocates of phrenology. Wikimedia Commons, public domain.

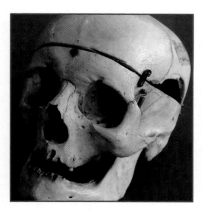

Figure 3–12. Skull of Franz Josef Gall. Photo used with permission of Philippe Mennecier, Charge de Conservation des collections d'anthropologie biologuique, Musée national d'histoire naturelle.

Figure 4–1. Larrey's Napoleonic war victim with head wound and aphasia. Reproduced from E. H. Jellinek, "An Unlikely Aphasiologist: D. J. Larrey (1766–1842)," Journal of the Royal Society of Medicine, 95(7), 368–370.

Figure 4–2. Dôme des Invalides.

Figure 4–3. Lordat's 1843 article on his own aphasia.

Figure 4–4. Leech jar. London Science Museum. Reproduced with permission.

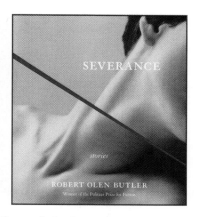

Figure 5–1. Dr. Joseph Ignace Guillotin. Public domain.

Figure 5–2. Severence by Robert Olen Butler. Reprinted with permission.

Figure 5–3. The trimming instrument of Dr. Guillotin. Public domain.

Figure 5–4. The Sun King, Louis XIV. Wikimedia Commons, public domain.

Figure 5–5. The little tyrant, Napoleon Bonaparte. Wikimedia Commons, public domain.

Figure 5–6. Paris panorama today, from Montparnasse Tower.

Figure 6–1. Bust of Jean-Baptiste Bouillaud. Public domain.

Figure 6–2. Bleeding bowl. London Science Museum. Reprinted with permission.

Figure 6–3. Mask of Franz Liszt. Photo used with permission of Philippe Mennecier, Charge de Conservation des collections d'anthropologie biologuique, Musée national d'histoire naturelle.

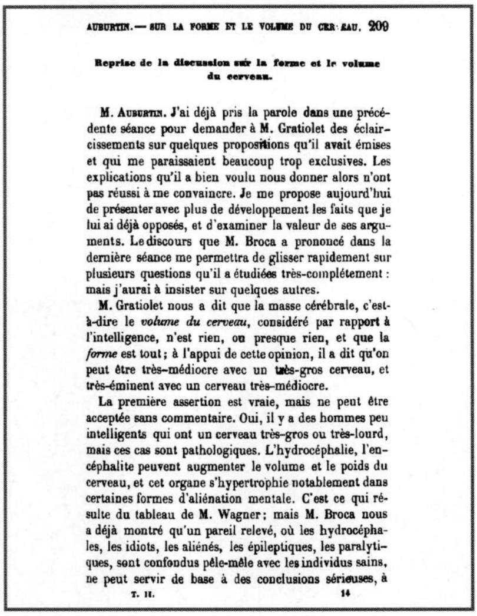

AUBURTIN.— SUR LA FORME ET LE VOLUME DU CERVEAU. 209

Reprise de la discussion sur la forme et le volume du cerveau.

M. Auburtin. J'ai déjà pris la parole dans une précédente séance pour demander à M. Gratiolet des éclaircissements sur quelques propositions qu'il avait émises et qui me paraissaient beaucoup trop exclusives. Les explications qu'il a bien voulu nous donner alors n'ont pas réussi à me convaincre. Je me propose aujourd'hui de présenter avec plus de développements les faits que je lui ai déjà opposés, et d'examiner la valeur de ses arguments. Le discours que M. Broca a prononcé dans la dernière séance me permettra de glisser rapidement sur plusieurs questions qu'il a étudiées très-complétement : mais j'aurai à insister sur quelques autres.

M. Gratiolet nous a dit que la masse cérébrale, c'est-à-dire le *volume du cerveau*, considéré par rapport à l'intelligence, n'est rien, ou presque rien, et que la *forme* est tout ; à l'appui de cette opinion, il a dit qu'on peut être très-médiocre avec un très-gros cerveau, et très-éminent avec un cerveau très-médiocre.

La première assertion est vraie, mais ne peut être acceptée sans commentaire. Oui, il y a des hommes peu intelligents qui ont un cerveau très-gros ou très-lourd, mais ces cas sont pathologiques. L'hydrocéphalie, l'encéphalite peuvent augmenter le volume et le poids du cerveau, et cet organe s'hypertrophie notablement dans certaines formes d'aliénation mentale. C'est ce qui résulte du tableau de M. Wagner ; mais M. Broca nous a déjà montré qu'un pareil relevé, où les hydrocéphales, les idiots, les aliénés, les épileptiques, les paralytiques, sont confondus pêle-mêle avec les individus sains, ne peut servir de base à des conclusions sérieuses, à

T. II.   14

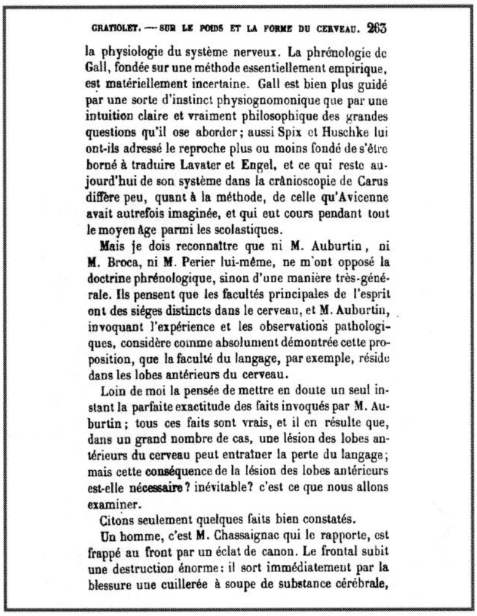

GRATIOLET. — SUR LE POIDS ET LA FORME DU CERVEAU. 263

la physiologie du système nerveux. La phrénologie de Gall, fondée sur une méthode essentiellement empirique, est matériellement incertaine. Gall est bien plus guidé par une sorte d'instinct physiognomonique que par une intuition claire et vraiment philosophique des grandes questions qu'il ose aborder ; aussi Spix et Huschke lui ont-ils adressé le reproche plus ou moins fondé de s'être borné à traduire Lavater et Engel, et ce qui reste aujourd'hui de son système dans la crânioscopie de Carus diffère peu, quant à la méthode, de celle qu'Avicenne avait autrefois imaginée, et qui eut cours pendant tout le moyen âge parmi les scolastiques.

Mais je dois reconnaître que ni M. Auburtin, ni M. Broca, ni M. Perier lui-même, ne m'ont opposé la doctrine phrénologique, sinon d'une manière très-générale. Ils pensent que les facultés principales de l'esprit ont des sièges distincts dans le cerveau, et M. Auburtin, invoquant l'expérience et les observations pathologiques, considère comme absolument démontrée cette proposition, que la faculté du langage, par exemple, réside dans les lobes antérieurs du cerveau.

Loin de moi la pensée de mettre en doute un seul instant la parfaite exactitude des faits invoqués par M. Auburtin ; tous ces faits sont vrais, et il en résulte que, dans un grand nombre de cas, une lésion des lobes antérieurs du cerveau peut entraîner la perte du langage ; mais cette conséquence de la lésion des lobes antérieurs est-elle nécessaire ? inévitable ? c'est ce que nous allons examiner.

Citons seulement quelques faits bien constatés.

Un homme, c'est M. Chassaignac qui le rapporte, est frappé au front par un éclat de canon. Le frontal subit une destruction énorme ; il sort immédiatement par la blessure une cuillerée à soupe de substance cérébrale,

Figure 6–4. Auburtin's opening gambit, from the original debate at the Société d'Anthropologie.

Figure 6–5. Société d'Anthropologie debate. Extract of Gratiolet's comments on Aubertin's presentation.

Figure 7–1. *Cave drawings from the Dordogne. Wikimedia Commons, public domain.*

Figure 7–2. *Salle de Broca, Sainte-Foy-La-Grande. From village website.*

Figure 7–3. *Jean-Samuel Pozzi, Broca friend and biographer. Portrait by John Singer Sargent Wikimedia Commons, public domain.*

Figure 7–4. *Cathedral Hands, Auguste Rodin.*

Figure 7–5. *Le Penseur, Auguste Rodin.*

Figure 8–1. Collège Sainte-Barbe.

Figure 8–2. 20 Rue Serpente, Broca's first apartment of his own.

Figure 8–3. 20 Rue Serpente, Broca's first apartment of his own.

Figure 8–4. 18 Rue Cujas. Another Broca apartment during medical school.

Figure 8–5. Bicetre Hospital.

Figure 8–6. Outside Broca's windows. Prisoners from the "Days of June" 1848. Wikimedia Commons, public domain.

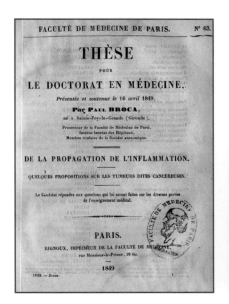

Figure 9–1. Title page of Broca's thesis. Reprinted with permission from Gallica, Bibliotique Nationale France.

Figure 9–2. Opera Garnier, Paris.

Figure 9–3. Caricature of Marguerite Belenger: Mistress of the Emperor. Wikimedia Commons, public domain.

Figure 9–4. Adele-Augustine Lugol Broca. From Schiller, 1992.

Figure 10–1. Dupuytren Museum courtyard.

Figure 10–2. Statuary at the Dupuytren Museum.

Figure 10–3. Cordeliers Convent.

Figure 10–4. Bust of Broca with medal at entrance to Dupuytren Museum.

Figure 10–5. Collections in the Dupuytren Museum.

Figure 10–6. Medical anomalies of the Dupuytren Museum.

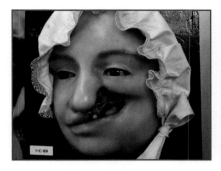

Figure 10–7. *Wax figure with craniofacial anomaly.*

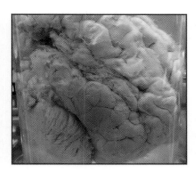

Figure 10–8. *Leborgne's preserved brain, 2011. Dupuytren Museum.*

Figure 10–9. *Lelong's brain. Dupuytren Museum.*

Figure 10–11. *Civil war photography. Wikimedia Commons, public domain. http://www.radio1.si/strani/Oddaje. aspx?ID=10174&LNK=3*

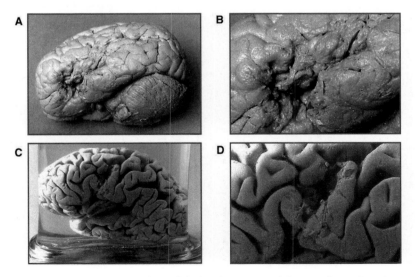

Figure 10–10. *Leborgne's and Lelong's preserved brains. From Dronkers (2007). Used with permission.*

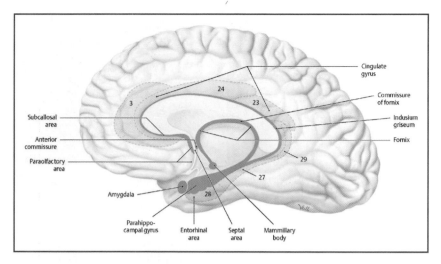

Figure 11–1. *Limbic system. Reprinted with permission. Thieme Medical Publishers. LaPointe, L. L. (2011).* Atlas of Neuroanatomy for Communication Science and Disorders.

Figure 11–3. *Philippe Mennecier, Director of Collections of National Museum of Natural History, displays a relief plaque of Paul Broca.*

Figure 11–2. *Statue honoring Gabirel Mortillet at Arénes de Lutéce, Paris.*

Figure 11–4. *Jardin des Plantes and Mosque Café.*

Figure 11–5. Jardin des Plantes and Mosque Café.

Figure 11–6. Cephalametric instruments of Broca. Wikimedia Commons, public domain.

Figure 11–7. Cephalametric instruments of Broca. Wikimedia Commons, public domain.

Figure 11–8. Cabinets in the Broca, Gall, and Spurzheim Collection Musee de l'Homme, Paris.

Figure 11–9. Poster of old Broca Mussee assembled by staff of National Natural History Museum.

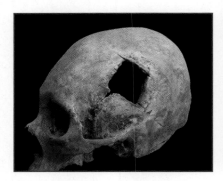

Figure 11–10. *Trepanated skull. Wikimedia Commons, public domain.*

Figure 11–11. The Extraction of the Stone of Madness *by Hieronymus Bosch. Wikimedia Commons, public domain.*

Figure 11–12. *Hôpital Broca.*

Figure 11–13. *Bronze bust of Broca with one of his biographers in lobby of Hôpital Broca.*

Figure 12–1. *Montparnasse Cemetery —Broca's final resting place.*

Chapter 7

Broca's Nascent Years

The literal, as opposed to the neuroanatomic, Broca's area is on the banks of the Dordogne River in southwest France. Dordogne, also called by its older name Perigord, is located in the northeastern Département of the Aquitaine region of France. The Dordogne is noted for its prehistoric caves, its castles and its cuisine. As some of the contemporary travel sites indicate, the Dordogne is beautiful throughout the year, but it is most picturesque in the spring, when the many fruit orchards are in bloom, and the fall, when the light is rich and the countryside alive with color.

THE CAVES

The Dordogne is abundant in history as well, with layer upon layer of antiquity personifying the region. More than 150 prehistoric sites have been discovered in the area, the best known being Lascaux II, famous for its Paleolithic cave paintings. These paintings are estimated to be 17,300 years old (Curtis, 2006). The most well-known section of the cave is The Great Hall of the Bulls where bulls, equines, and stags are depicted. The four black bulls are the dominant figures among the 36 animals represented here. One of the bulls is 17 feet (5.2 m) long: the largest animal discovered so far in cave art. The bulls appear to be running and some historians have attributed the artistic attributes of perspective and motion to these very early prehistoric artists (Curtis, 2006). Figure 7–1 depicts images of some of these rich prehistoric cave drawings in Lascaux II in the Dordogne region.

The cave was discovered on September 12, 1940 by four teenagers, Marcel Ravidat, Jacques Marsal, Georges Agnel, and Simon Coencas, as well as Marcel's dog, Robot. The Dordogne is rich in prehistoric history and this home region of Paul Broca would prove to be a fertile area for exploration of some of his later toil in anthropology. Although Lascaux II was not discovered until World War II, the region is full of caves and opportunities for the broods of the Dordogne to explore and develop interests in fossils, relics, and the study of the remnants of early man. This may well be how Broca's early interest in anthropology and the science of man was cultivated.

THE BROCAS AND HUGUENOT PERSECUTION

Southwest France and the boroughs around the Dordogne were speckled with the history of the religious reformation movement as well and became an area settled by people subscribing to the

Figure 7–1. *Cave drawings from the Dordogne. Wikimedia Commons, public domain.*

reformed religions of the various varieties of Protestantism. The impact of the Protestant Reformation was felt throughout Europe in the early 16th century. Its most important protagonists were the German Martin Luther and the Frenchman Jean Calvin. In France, Calvinism permeated all ranks of society, especially those of the literate craftsmen in the towns (Benedict, 2002).

Eight civil wars raged in France between 1562 and 1598: the Wars of Religion. In 1589 the Protestant Henri de Bourbon, King of Navarre, inherited the French throne after the deaths of his three cousins, sons of Catherine De Medici. Civil war continued, so in 1593, in the spirit of the then popular slogan, "Paris is worth a Mass," Henri converted to Catholicism. Five years later the bloody civil wars ended and King Henri issued the Edict of Nantes which gave the Huguenots, his former co-religionists and comrades in arms, considerable privileges, including extensive religious liberty. Over time Huguenots became loyal subjects of the French crown. However, their position became increasingly insecure as the Sun King, Louis XIV, grandson of Henri IV, listened more and more to those who advised him that the existence of this considerable religious minority was a threat to the absolute authority of the monarch (Huguenot Society, 2011). Gradually the Huguenots' privileges were eroded. When the revocation of the Edict of Nantes annulled religious toleration, Louis XIV instituted legal persecution with the additional ghastly policy of terrorizing noncompliant Huguenots. Those who refused to convert to Catholicism were dealt with by the Sun King by billeting dragoons in their homes and instructing the soldiers to harass and intimidate the occupants to persuade them to either convert to the state religion or to emigrate. As mounted infantry, some of the 14 regiments of dragoons in the French Army of the period were an effective and terrible instrument for persecuting the Huguenots.

Protestants, especially in the enclaves of southwest France, were bullied and coerced by this policy of quartering of unruly troops in their homes ("the Dragonnades"). Stories that survive the Dragonnades era suggest that the troops not only enjoyed the fromage and bread of the Huguenot households, but also the confections found in the bedrooms. With the 1685 revocation of the Edict of Nantes, all Protestant pastors were exiled and the laity were prohibited from leaving France. To the considerable surprise of the government many did leave, often at great risk to themselves. Many Huguenot men were imprisoned, murdered, or sent as galley slaves to the great wooden ships of the French fleet in the Mediterranean. Women were imprisoned and their children sent to convents (Huguenot Society, 2011).

About 200,000 Huguenots left France, and settled in non-Catholic Europe—the Netherlands, Germany, Prussia, Switzerland, Scandinavia, and even as far as Russia, where Huguenot craftsmen could find patrons at the court of the Czars. The Dutch East India Company sent a few hundred to the Cape to develop the vineyards in southern Africa. About 50,000 emigrated to England, perhaps about 10,000 relocating on to Ireland. So there are many inhabitants of Great Britain who have Huguenot blood in their veins, whether or not they still bear one of the hundreds of French names of those who took "refuge," thus bringing the word *refugee* into the English language (Huguenot Society, 2011).

On January 17, 1686, Louis XIV claimed the Protestant population of 800,000 to 900,000, had been reduced to 1,000 to 1,500 in France. This is a magnitude of diaspora that has been repeated far to frequently in history, but the Huguenot dispersion is not nearly as realized as other great migrations. Ironically, the campaign turned out to be detrimental to France's economy because the Huguenots who chose to flee possessed skills such as silk weaving, clock-making, and optometry, and became a valuable addition to the economy of the countries to which they fled (Chadwick, 1977).

BROCA'S VILLAGE

Sainte-Foy-la-Grande is a small community of approximately 2,500 souls and is proud of its heritage of education and the production of internationally-recognized scholars. The current mayor of the community, Robert Provain, exalts the features of this proud village. He characterizes it in this manner on the village Web site: http://www.saintefoylagrande.net/pages/Le_Mot_du_Maire-1068773.html

   ◆ Home of the land of the Reformation where humanism flourished at the intersection of ideas and freedoms.

◆ Our city thrives on its many artisans, traders, merchants, and today is the center of a pool of life. Since its origins, its Saturday market, one of the most beautiful in France, runs happily.

◆ Early on, our city has, both for girls and for boys, fostered many outstanding educational institutions, furthering the emergence of scholars and writers whose influence has crossed our borders: Pierre Gratiolet, Paul Broca, Reclus (the famous French geographer and anarchist), and Elie Faure (art historiean), to name only the most famous.

◆ For a taste of "the dusk of evening on the Dordogne," dear to Cyrano de Bergerac, one must stroll along the docks after a hot summer day and enjoy "the beautiful lazy" (Provain, 2011).

In the present day Paul Broca, one of its distinguished sons, is commemorated by streets and schools. The Lycée Paul Broca de Sainte-Foy-la-Grande is a high school dedicated to educating the young people of the community. In another cross-fertilization of aspects of art and science, just as the Impressionists ripened in close temporal proximity to Broca's events in brain science, a room in his home community is a gallery and presents the work of current artists (Figure 7–2).

BROCA'S HISTORIANS

Just a few historic biographies of Broca trace his early days. Pozzi (1880a, 1880b), his student and one of his eulogists, and Munod-Broca (2005), a French surgeon and great-grandson of Broca, have lovingly depicted some details of his life. Perhaps the most complete detailed biography, and one that is scholarly, well-documented, and incorporates precious details from the prodigious collection of personal letters that Paul Broca generated, is that written by the eminent scholar Francis Schiller. I am deeply indebted to Schiller for his remarkable portrait of the life of Broca and for pointing me to many of the precious primary sources of information on Broca. Schiller's work, entitled *Paul Broca: Explorer of the Brain* (1992) although it was first published in the late 1970s and then in paperback in 1992, is classic

Figure 7–2. Salle de Broca, Sainte-Foy-La-Grande. From village website.

scholarship on the life of Broca. Schiller died in 2003 at the age of 94 and his work on Broca will be long remembered. As was listed in his eulogy in one of his professional journals, "our dear Francis departed from us on July 16, 2003." Francis Schiller was born in Prague, Czechoslovakia, and spent most of his life as a neurologist in California. Schiller was at Kaiser Permanente medical center for 30 years and was head of the Neurology Department until he retired in 1978. He also served at the Veterans Administration Medical Center in San Francisco. He was a great medical historian and all of us who have attempted to paint a portrait of Pierre Paul Broca and the issues and discoveries of his times are deeply beholden to Schiller.

BROCA'S LINEAGE

As early as 1569, during the Wars of Religion, a Huguenot pastor named Gilles de Broca arrived at Sainte-Foy-la-Grande. He may have been an ancestor of the 1860's Broca family and had once been arrested for his beliefs and sentenced to whipping and banishment. He lived and died in Sainte-Foy-la-Grande and Schiller (1992) reports that he was instrumental in the building of the first Protestant church in the town. The Brocas were a family replete with nonconformists. Paul Broca's paternal grandfather Jean was a volunteer and died fighting the counter revolution in 1793. Paul's maternal grandfather, Pierre Thomas, has "Victim of the Terror" engraved on his tombstone in the family plot outside of Sainte-Foy-la-Grande (Schiller, 1992). The Broca lineage has a razor-sharp history of nonconformity and persecution on both sides of the family, not unlike many of the ancestors of these quaint southwestern Huguenot villages.

About 1817, Pierre Thomas, the "Victim of the Terror," gave away the hand of his daughter Annette to the local town physician, Dr. Jean Pierre Broca. This Broca physician was called Benjamin, not unlike several in the family who went by either their middle names or names not on their christening documentation. Benjamin and Annette lived on the arcaded main square in Sainte-Foy-la-Grande, in a nice two story house along with the doctor's two unmarried sisters, whose store on the ground floor contributed to the family's income. Fresh food products then, as now, were displayed and peddled at the bustling local markets, but the revered maiden aunts supplemented the Broca family income perhaps by selling buttons, sugar, syrup, salt, tea, coffee, tobacco, spices, dried fruit, colorful cloth, and other household items. These aunts were to have a special place in Broca's correspondence when he was away and one of them became the butt of some of young Paul's jibes and mild parody in his letters to his mother.

HAPPY BIRTHDAY TO PAUL

Pierre Paul Broca was born in Sainte-Foy-la-Grande on June 28, 1824 in a small corner house on the junction of the presently named Rue Louis Pasteur and Rue J. L. Faure. In Broca's day these streets were known as Rue de l'Union and Rue Sainte Foy. Some confusion has existed and is perpetuated in some of Paul Broca's biographic summaries on his actual birthday and death day. His birth was registered on June 29, 1824 in the Register of Births in the Canton and Commune of Sainte-Foy-la-Grande, Arrondissement of Libourne, Département Gironde, but importantly, the registration contains the notation "born yesterday." That certifies that mother Annette labored and Paul's birth occurred on June 28th, another remarkable bit of startling coincidence for that is the birthday of this writer, 115 years later.

The year 1824 was auspicious for many reasons, not just for the birth of one of the most brilliant scientists in the history of the brain. Beethoven's 9th (Chorale) Symphony premiered in Vienna; the first steam locomotive was introduced, paving the way for improved commerce and transportation and the eventual brief bloom of the little railroad town of Channing, in Michigan's Upper Peninsula. Women were quick to take their laundry indoors when the sooty steam engines of Channing huffed, gurgled, and switched cars of iron ore and pulpwood up until the 1950s when diesel replaced the more colorful steam and life changed and began its economic downturn for steam-engine dependent villages everywhere.

In more auspicious locales, a huge fire at a Cairo ammunitions dump killed 4,000 horses; and J. W. Goodrich introduced rubber galoshes to the public (History, 1824). In France, things were heating up again after the significant events of the French Revolution and the birth of the Republic. In 1824 Charles X of the now restored monarchy became king only to be followed in the chaotic years to come by being overthrown during the July Revolution of 1830, the election of Louis Napoleon Bonaparte, a nephew of the Emperor Napoleon, in 1851, and eventually the seizing of complete power in 1852 with Louis Napoleon Bonaparte declaring himself Emperor Napoleon III. This historic seesaw of monarchy and republic along with his family's vivid knowledge of the persecution of the Huguenots was to become imbued in the life and values of the Brocas and opulently color the politics of Pierre Paul Broca.

Paul's father, Benjamin Broca, became known as the doctor of the poor in Sainte-Foy-la-Grande. He had served as a surgeon in the little tyrant Napoleon's Imperial Army and, before returning to the relative peace of his little village, had generated experiences and stories surrounding Napoleon's campaigns including the Battle of Waterloo. Schiller (1992) reported that Dr. Benjamin Broca had an impressive mutilated index finger "eternally covered by a tight sheet of black silk" that was the result of his attending to a wounded man. Measure twice and cut once was no doubt an important axiom that may have been important even in the days of Waterloo. Schiller (1992) suggests that from his pleasant and other-oriented father, Paul may have either learned or inherited his kind and cheerful though somewhat restless disposition; his appreciation and love of nature and good companionship; and the admiration of healing and the rudiments of natural history as an important part of treatment and understanding.

Annette, Paul's mother, is reported by several biographers to have a more serious and intellectual strain. This Huguenot pastor's daughter was moralistic, and seemed to be concerned more about the right things in life rather than in the materialistic entities of life. Her righteousness and solid belief in truthfulness was paired with humility and tolerance. She attended faithfully to the home, the office of Dr. Benjamin, and their little vineyard. To this day the wines from the chateaux in Broca's area, around Bordeaux and especially St. Emilion are products of a number of notably fine small vineyards. St-Emilion, Medoc, and Pomerol produce rich, warm wines that win over those of us who are beginning to appreciate the Broca's area juice of Bordeaux and vicinity. Many of these regional wines have a high concentration of the Merlot grape. This creates a fruity and often more alcoholic wine (sometimes 1% stronger than Medoc wines). The limestone and gravel hills of the region has produced superb products for generations and Annette Broca no doubt tilled and nurtured her small vineyard diligently so Dr. Benjamin could enjoy a fruity repast after a hard day of extracting spleens and lancing boils.

As Schiller (1992) infers, Annette Broca, the mother with whom Broca would keep up a regular letter correspondence for years, was a perfectionist, perhaps with a tinge of depression that colored her life. She badgered absent members of the family to keep up their letter-writing and exhibited a certain amount of "querulousness" which may have been transmitted to her son, Paul, along with all of her qualities of diligence, perseverance, and loyalty. The young vines of the Broca plot matured to the *vieilles vignes* that were destined to yield worthy fruit.

SAMUEL-JEAN POZZI, EULOGIST, BIOGRAPHER, AND RAKE

Sainte-Foy-la-Grande was the home of a rather famous Calvinist school for boys and included an impressive number of native sons who studied there. One of these was Samuel-Jean Pozzi (Figure 7–3), who would eventually become a world-renowned gynecologist after serving an internship with Broca. He shared neural interest and apparently revered Broca, and although another organ was destined to consume his attention, as with many of us, his focus would be distracted by structures other than the brain. Samuel Pozzi was a major figure in the early development of modern gynecological surgery. His textbook, *A Treatise on Gynaecology,* published in French in 1890 and translated into five other languages, was the first internationally acclaimed text and in later editions remained a standard reference up to the 1930s. He was the author of more than 400 papers on gynecological and general abdominal surgery and his technical expertise drew surgeons from all over the world to his theatre in the Hospital Broca, in one of the poorer parts of Paris (DeCosta & Miller, 2007).

Figure 7–3. *Jean-Samuel Pozzi, Broca friend and biographer. Portrait by John Singer Sargent, Wikimedia Commons, public domain.*

The Pozzis, too, were Huguenots, as were so many families in the region, who migrated from Italy via Switzerland to southwestern France in the eighteenth century. Samuel was born in 1846 in Bergerac, another lovely town on the River Dordogne. Pozzi established a lucrative gynecological practice in Paris and apparently was a physician to the stars and the elite. Pozzi met the famous actress Sarah Bernhardt, who became an international celebrity and Paris resident in 1869. The handsome Pozzi was a medical student in the Latin Quarter and she was playing at the adjacent Odéon Theatre. According to DeCosta and Miller (2007), they began an affair that lasted until Pozzi's marriage in 1879, and had a close friendship that continued until his death. He became her medical adviser and personal physician and she called him *Docteur Dieu*, (Doctor God), and his pet name for her was the "Divine Sarah."

Pozzi became a genuine patron of the arts and counted among his friends a rich hodgepodge of authors, poets, painters and actors. He was a friend as well of the medical-artistic Proust family, and he corresponded regularly with Marcel Proust until his own death. The famous "Proustian Moment" of Marcel (dipping the madeleine into mint tea and smelling it to generate a flood of memories) would contribute to his epic work, *Remembrance of Things Past*. The Proust family was steeped in medical affiliation and perhaps Marcel was aware of the rich connections between smell and memory and the proximity of the entorhinal cortex to the memory headquarters of the paired hippocampus in the brain. Marcel's brother, Robert, also a surgeon, served for ten years as Pozzi's first assistant at the Broca Hospital. Pozzi believed stanchly that attractive surroundings in a hospital encouraged the healing process, and he commissioned several artists to paint murals and pictures for the walls of his hospital, the most notable being Georges Clairin, whose painting, *Health Restored to the Sick,* featured Pozzi's former lover Sarah Bernhardt as the radiant portrayal of Health. This interesting painting can still be seen in the *Musée d' Assistance-Publique* in Paris (DeCosta & Miller, 2007).

Pozzi (1880b) was to become Paul Broca's biographer and assembled the extraordinary bibliography of all of Broca's published works that would be reproduced later by several other writers. The Huguenot Protestants who grew up along the banks of the Dordogne at Sainte-Foy-la-Grande formed a solid attachment and those who became notable persons seemed to be bonded by their mutual histories and affection for their roots as well as their professional alliances.

Pozzi was elected member of the Academy of Medicine in 1896, and in 1898 he was elected a senator from his native district, following in the footsteps of his teacher Broca. Pozzi had a wide-reaching reputation as an educator, and he was reported to be a striking figure on rounds, dressed in white overalls and wearing a black Florentine cap, as befitted his family's Swiss-Italian heritage. He also traveled to America after the turn of the century and visited the Mayo Clinic in Rochester, Minnesota and became friends with William Mayo who later visited Paris and enjoyed the hospitality of Pozzi (De Costa & Miller, 2010). He also played a role in the famous Dreyfus affair, sided with Emile Zola in professing the innocence of Dreyfus, and came to the aid of Dreyfus when he was shot in the arm in the courtroom. When the journalist Gregori shot at Dreyfus and wounded him, Pozzi rushed to his aid. In 1879, Pozzi married Therese Loth-Cazalis, heiress of a railroad magnate, and had three children: Catherine, Jean, and Jacques. Pozzi apparently was not grateful for the fact that his wife wanted her mother to live with them, an experience that made for a very unhappy marriage. Pozzi logged a number of romances, so to speak, including those with the opera singer Georgette Leblanc, the actress Rejane, the widow of Georges Bizet, of course his divine Sarah Bernhardt, and Emma Sedelmeyer Fischof, the beautiful daughter of an art dealer and wife of a horse breeder (DeCosta and Miller, 2006). Pozzi led an active professional and extracurricular life and selected elite beauties as his consorts. His charm and strikingly handsome bearing apparently contributed to his magnetism that actresses, singers, and wealthy beauties of France could not resist. Thankfully, he reserved some of his efforts to generate an important biography and eulogy of Paul Broca, his cherished friend.

It is fortunate that the gifted Pozzi was able to commemorate his mentor Paul Broca, for he was to come to a tragic end. On June 13, 1918, Maurice Machu, a former patient from two years earlier, approached Pozzi in his consulting room. Pozzi had had to amputate his leg and his patient Machu had become impotent. Machu asked him to operate again. When Pozzi refused because he could not remedy the situation, Machu shot him four times in the stomach. Pozzi was taken on his own demand to a hospital where he had toiled many years in Paris. His laparotomy, a deep incision in the abdominal wall revealed 12 perforations of the abdomen and a laceration of one of his kidneys. His wounds were fatal and he died shortly afterward. Pozzi was a dashing and decorated war hero who cut quite swathe through French history.

PAUL PRODIGY

Young Paul Broca was remembered as an excellent student in Sainte-Foy-la-Grande and something of a prodigy. Schiller (1992) quotes a classmate who remembers Paul as a scholar at the age of eleven. He was reported to be good at classical and modern languages and was gifted in mathematics. He showed an artistic as well as a scientific bent and his drawings were regarded as "perfect." He also played the horn "quite agreeably" which he returned to later in life to accompany his daughter on the piano. Creative writing was one of his strong points as well as can be seen in his prodigious letter writing as well as his preserved examples of poetry. Schiller (1992) says that most of his creative writing and poetry was to "let off steam" and was satirical and pithy. He generated a few love poems between the ages of 17 and 29, the age of course of hormonal driven limbic interests. The "limbic lobe," ironically would be another of his consuming scientific interests and its role in emotions and location would be studied in detail in his medical years. As much as he was interested in the organic aspects of emotion, he would never be characterized as sentimental but rather always as a skeptical rationalist who would interpret and conclude within the guiding principles of reason rather than emotion. This perhaps guided much of his criticism of church, government, authority, and dogmatism that seemed to infiltrate his freethinking philosophy which would be keenly developed, and get him in trouble, in his later years. Paul's poking around the caves in the region whetted his appetite for prehistory and anthropology and his shadowing of his father when he ministered to patients honed his abiding interest in medicine, though his first inclination upon leaving the banks of the Dordogne was to study mathematics in Paris.

Young Broca was strikingly impressed with the idealism of the principles of civil and religious liberty. His Huguenot upbringing and impressions of the history of the Wars of Religion firmly established that against the backdrop of a Catholic country governed and dictated by the dogma of the majority church. He and many of his village-mates were clearly in the minority. At six years of age, he and the other children of France were witness to political turmoil when rioters forced a change of government and the "Three Glorious Days" of July, 1830 forced another change in the monarchy of France. These political disturbances would mark much of Broca's life and also would tint his values. In 1832 Broca entered the Communal College of Sainte-Foy, an institution which was then patronized by many of the Protestant youth of France, and at which most of the distinguished men of the Reformed Churches were educated. Broca's father wished him to study medicine. He, having a taste for mathematics, preferred the Polytechnic School. He obtained a baccalaureate in science, and earned the degree of Bachelor in Letters, first in rank, in 1840, when only 16 years old. He then gained permission from his father to be examined for the bachelor's degree in mathematical sciences. Having gained this, he began to prepare himself for the prestigious École Polytechnique, teaching in the day-time in the college where he had been a student, studying differential calculus at night. Broca apparently had his heart set on studying at the elite École Polytechnique in Paris with its history of dashingly uniformed students who formed the backbone of France's military and civil engineers. The École Polytechnique, nicknamed the "X," is a university of higher learning that still is one of the most esteemed schools in the world. But young Paul Broca's plans were to change.

His plans were suddenly altered by the premature death of his older sister, Léotine. Schiller (1992) suggests that an acute appendicitis attack may have killed her. Paul was now an only child, and had deep doubts about embracing a profession in engineering that might call him to practice far away from his parents. With some initial trepidation, he finally resolved to study medicine, and share his father's practice at Sainte-Foy.

BROCA LEAVES HOME

Broca lived in the house in Sainte-Foy-la-Grande until 1841 when he would leave home and travel to Paris to press on with his education. The clairvoyants of the day would have been hard pressed to foresee that this young village boy would become recognized as one of the world's historic and compelling figures in neuroscience. He left his home after just turning 17 years of age. He had been regarded as a wunderkind by his teachers and village-mates and now was to travel to the daunting city of Paris and be plunged into the river of brisk maturity.

A CARRIAGE RIDE AND A THINKER

Broca must have thought about his lodgings and how he would get along during his long carriage ride from the Dordogne region to the great city. The Brocas were not wealthy. His doctor father was frequently paid in chickens and produce, and money was an object.

As with others who have been plunged into the transition of a village to the complexities and noise of a chaotic city, this adventure must have seemed like a galaxy compared to his village. The family had Huguenot friends in Paris, including a cousin Elie who was 10 years older and a teacher. Cousin Elie made arrangements for him to live in rather monastic conditions at the Collège of Sainte-Barbe and for his lodging would receive a small amount of money as *pion* or tutor to the younger students at the school. So he would become a pion as well as a *carabin* or medic, named after the surgeon's mates and apprentices in the French armies of the Napoleonic Wars in the distant past (Schiller, 1992). His ride might have been bumpy and perhaps filled with the identity crisis angst that accompanies all young people leaving home for the first time and wondering if they will fly or come crashing down onto the jagged rocks of spoiled plans and a new reality.

SAVANTS MOVE TO PARIS: AGAIN, THE BRAIN AND ART

Just one year earlier and once again with remarkable juxtaposition of players who were to become compelling players in their chosen professions, another French savant was born. In Limoges, France not far from the route of the carriage that would carry young Broca to Paris in 1841, François-Auguste-René Rodin was the second child of Jean-Baptiste Rodin and Marie Cheffer (though some sources say he was born in Paris). Renoir, too, would move to Paris, the City of Light, and eventually fraternize with the likes of Degas, Monet, and Sisley. Interestingly, Rodin would eventually toil in proximity to Broca 20 years later in the École de Medicine and the Dupuytren Museum (Larson, 2009). Rodin gained familiarity with newly emerging medical concepts of the body when he took classes in mycology, neurology, and osteology at the École de Medicine. He also sketched physical deformities at the nearby Musée Dupuytren, the medical museum of human anatomy and pathology that was used as a teaching tool of the École de Medicine. The confluence of neurology and art are quite evident in much of Rodin's work. Some medical experts, who have examined Rodin's many individual hand sculptures (Figure 7–4), have suggested that a number of them are deformed by nerve disorders. Rodin's *Large Clenched Left Hand*, some suggest is an example of paralysis of the median nerve of the wrist referred to by some as "median claw hand" or "Benedictine hand" (Larson, 2009). At the peak of his career Rodin was regarded as the greatest sculptor since Michelangelo. He challenged the established styles of his day and thereby revolutionized sculpture. After his first venture into sculpture, Rodin saw a new light and refused to idealize his subjects as in the tradition of Classical sculpture. This was not Rome or Athens. This was Paris. He chose to show his subjects as they were, even if they were deformed. He drew as much inspiration from the old and wrinkled as he did from the young who like his student and long-time mistress Camille Claudel, wreaked sensuality. He believed everything in nature was beautiful and any artist who tried to improve upon nature by adding "green to the springtime, rose to the sunrise, carmine to the young lips . . . creates ugliness because he lies" (Rodin, 2009, p. 86).

Figure 7–4. *Cathedral Hands, Auguste Rodin.*

Rodin's sculptures are rooted in contemporary scientific experiments that mapped neurological activity and areas that established corresponding relationships between the body and the brain. Rodin was an artist who annoyed contemporaries with his distressingly unfinished monuments; a sensualist who shocked even the people of France with his scandalous relationships; and a colleague and friend to the most gifted writers and artists of his day. He was to usher in the days of modern sculpture and is regarded as a radical and innovative influence in art. Rodin was to tread some of the same trails as Broca.

In the 1860s the École de Medicine, where Rodin sketched in the Museum and attended classes, was distinguished by a faculty considered controversial. For its pursuit of secular explanations of human behavior some faculty members were subject to scrutiny and suppression. Among the prominent scientists was Paul Broca, whose work and views on mental and intellectual functions in the brain and not the "soul" was still creating excitement and storm when Rodin was there (Larson, 2009).

Some 20 years after the carriage ride of Broca and the birth of Rodin, the concepts of impressionistic art would emerge from the boys of the countryside who spent time together in the cafes of Paris. The clinical evidence about cerebral localization of language was ripening and would begin to emerge from the clinics and laboratories of French hospitals, just as the blurred images would defy the times and begin to appear on the gallery walls of Paris. This year of 1841 was a big year for both movements. Pierre Paul and Pierre-Auguste were to become key players.

Once again the French Brains who forged new streams in impressionism, sculpture, and neuroscience converged to transform their respective fields. The river of thought and creativity would flow into and with the Seine (Figure 7–5). The imaginings of the creative would rupture into new directions. The diligence of the ants would not cease. Paul Broca was about to experience the diligence.

Figure 7–5. Le Penseur, *Auguste Rodin.*

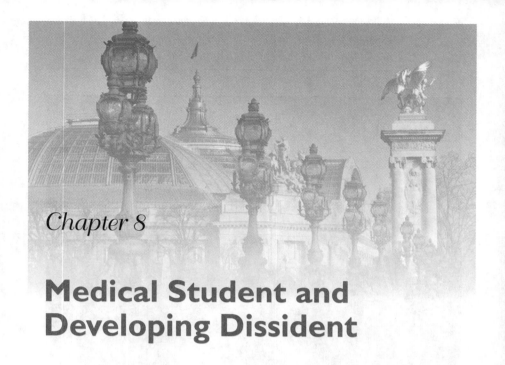

Chapter 8

Medical Student and Developing Dissident

Paris in November is gentle and contemplative. As the days grow shorter and the mercury starts to drop, tourist numbers dwindle. High season has evaporated away. The locals begin to abandon the sidewalk cafes and move inside to peer at the bustle from behind steamed windows. Scarves are now double-looped. The autumnal shades of trees lining the boulevards add a new dimension to the city's beauty and the Jardin des Plantes, Luxembourg, and Tuileries are resplendent in shades of mauve and purple with many of the plane trees and horse-chestnuts beginning to expose their skeletons. The London plane tree or *"platane à feuille d'érable"* as it is known in France has been regarded by some as the "King of the Urban Forest" and it graces in precise straight lines the aisles and colonnades of the great gardens of Paris (Plane Trees, 2011). The sculptors, decorative stonemasons, street accordionists, fish mongers, boulangers, and illiterate daughters of master wigmakers went about their business in 1841 and paid little attention to the young man from Sainte-Foy-la-Grande who was moving into his "dorm," the humble quarters of the Collège de Sainte-Barbe (Figure 8–1).

Broca settled in. As Schiller (1992) relates, some of his mother's admonitions to visit Protestants influential in medicine were courteously rebuffed. According to the brilliant and prodigious

Figure 8–1. *Collège Sainte-Barbe.*

volumes of Broca's charming letters to his mother and his family, he resisted his mother's nagging about visiting a Professor Marjolin. As young Paul wrote, "He was infinitely more occupied with his little dog than with me." (Broca, 1886, 12/25/41, p. 26) He wrote this on Christmas Day, 1841, his first Christmas away from home and understandably appeared a bit petulant. As with most who travel out of their belt of the accustomed, his friends and acquaintances were primarily from his comfort zone of familiarity; and this meant his initial small circle was from the regions along the banks and plains of the Dordogne River. They met Sunday nights for tea and cake and engaged in a bit of weekend relaxation by playing chess, whist, and piquet. But as young Paul assured in his letters so as not to be thought a squanderer, these games were played not for money but for love. Piquet is a trick-taking card game that dates back to the 16th century in France. It is played with a 32-card deck normally referred to as a *piquet deck*. The deck is composed all of the 7s through to 10s, the face cards, and the aces in each suit, and can be assembled by removing all 2 to 6 values from a 52-card poker deck, if one were to want to recreate a Parisian Sunday evening. A Gateau Breton with hints of hazelnuts, cinnamon, lemon peel, and vanilla would be a suitable accompaniment or perhaps a simple Proustian madeleine to dip in the mint tea and trigger childhood memories.

Young Paul Broca worked hard, with a prodigious school schedule including Anatomy, Medical Chemistry, Legal Medicine, Surgical Pathology, Internal Medicine, Therapeutics, Operations and Instruments, Hospital Rounds at Hôtel-Dieu and La Pitié, and Physics and Chemistry at the Sorbonne (Schiller, 1992). In addition he did his tutoring at the Collège Sainte-Barbe, a task he found less than rewarding. He understood the necessity of taking on this additional responsibility as *pion* or tutor but found the students less than diligent and his job more of a caretaker of the recalcitrant. He writes, "I have no more illusions about my work at Sainte-Barbe. I am not an assistant . . . I am the executioner, the hangman. My job is to administer punishment and to watch the pupils who are kept after school . . . " (Broca, 1886 10/22/41, p. 5).

Apparently the young *carabin* Paul had some difficulty with the messy but necessary parts of learning anatomy and pathology. He relates early on going twice to the dissecting room. He startles his correspondents at home, perhaps with the exception of his father, by relating in particular detail seeing students in their blue smocks bent over corpses, cutting, snipping, clipping, and probing the human flesh, " . . . plunging their hands into it and withdrawing them all covered with blood and pus! All this is too much to think about, and as I entered I expected promptly to have to get out again. At present the main point is cleared up, the great obstacle lifted, and I can become a physician without inconvenience" (Broca, 1886, 10/25/41, p. 8).

This was Paul Broca's first of 15 trimesters that included five major examinations, one for each of his five years, and a final doctor's dissertation. He settled into it. Indeed, he settled into excellence but not without the seeds of some dissent and an encounter or two with authority. In his second year in Paris his beloved horn was sent via a friend to Paris. He reported, "Yes, I did enjoy getting my horn. Locked with it in my tiny room, I started to laugh and jump around like a madman." Apparently he failed to appraise the effect his ode to horn joy would have on the neighbors. His bleating was not as soothing to others.

Paul wrote, "A police commissar came this morning to impose silence on me in the name of the King (between 9 PM and 6 AM). You are lucky he said, that we do not confiscate it" (Broca, 1886, 5/4/42, p. 80).

Broca's six months at Sainte-Barbe was Dickensian. His quarters were spartan. Tiny, cramped, and not adequately warmed; he suffered and wrote home about some of his colds and winter illnesses. Finally his parents approved of his moving from the despicable job and quarters at Sainte-Barbe and he was able to find his first of many apartments in Paris. As he wrote to his parents, he was now able to give his own private address. He was still near school and hospitals and had a bit more privacy and some upgrade of accommodations. He was now at number 20 Rue Serpente, half a minute from school (Figures 8–2 and 8–3). He relished in the independence. He wrote, ". . . launched on my life as a bachelor, *in my own room*, for the first time in my life, sitting in front of my own fire, my writing accompanied by the sound of boiling water from my own kettle, making myself a tisane for my cold . . . " (Broca, 1886, 4/13/42, pp 62–63).

Figure 8–2. *20 Rue Serpente, Broca's first apartment of his own.*

Figure 8–3. *20 Rue Serpente, Broca's first apartment of his own.*

A tisane is an infusion of herbs and tea used for medicinal purposes. It soothes the stomach, warms the soul, clears the sinuses, and sends mucus on its merry way. As another French brain, Honore de Balzac, one of Rodin's recurrent subjects once remarked, "Great love affairs start with champagne and end with tisane."

ON THE RUES WHERE HE LIVED

I tracked down some of the apartments of Broca during this summer of 2011 in Paris and found some of them remarkably as they had been described, some with a few modern and ugly touches. To a historian there is an eerie feeling when one frequents the pathways and abodes of figures of yesterday. Standing and picturing the places of Broca gave me pause. Broca's first apartment at 20 Rue Serpente is close to the lovely cafés of the Boulevard St. Michel and the Place Sorbonne. Later, as his medical studies progressed, Broca occupied an apartment at 18 Rue Cujas (Figure 8–4). This is on the street that runs alongside the Pantheon which holds the bones of so many remarkable contributors to civilization. Voltaire and Braille and Zola and Hugo (*"Un pour tous, tous pour un"*) and more recently Marie and Pierre Curie now rest in this grand place of history. Now, 18 Rue Cujas houses apartments and rooms on the upper floors and a Chinese Restaurant and the small Hotel Cujas on the ground level. At 20 Rue Serpente, where Broca waxed lyrical over his first ever address of his own, one can in the summer of 2011 find a video games store (GAMES WORKSHOP!) on the lower level. Broca without doubt never stayed up all night playing video games, but he most certainly lost some sleep in that little room with the boiling kettle studying anatomy of the nervous system. The names of the convolutions of the cerebrum would come in handy later.

These little rooms and apartments along Rue Serpente and Rue Cujas housed the necessary and the mundane in the 1840s, but they were destined to play their part as well in unforeseen historical events.

CARL SAGAN

Boiling your own tea in your own room with your own fire in the fireplace warmed Broca; and I could not help but loiter and

Figure 8–4. *18 Rue Cujas. Another Broca apartment during medical school.*

reflect as did Carl Sagan when he wrote of *Broca's Brain* generations later (Sagan, 1979). Contemplating Broca's brain (which now is nowhere to be found but still may be hiding in the deep recesses of one of the Paris Museums. See Appendix C.). Sagan posed some of the profound and perhaps unfathomable questions. How much of Broca is still in that formalin of his preserved brain? The irony of staring at Broca's area of the cerebral cortex in the very brain of Broca was not lost on Sagan. He mulled the deep-rooted questions. Might it be possible at some future time, when neuroscience has advanced sufficiently, to reconstruct the memories of someone long dead? Would bits and pieces of DNA or other molecular matter make it possible to resurrect memory and knowledge and identity that had long ago washed downstream? The ethics of this were not lost on Carl Sagan. He wondered, would that be a good thing? It would be the ultimate

HIPPA violation and breach of privacy. The bioethics of cloning were not specifically addressed in Sagan's *Broca's Brain,* but he was not far away in his wondering and ethical diffidence. Cloning is an asexual reproductive mode, which opponents say could distort generation lines and family relationships, and limit genetic distinction and differentiation, which now ensures that human life is distinctive. Cloning also can infer an instrumental attitude toward humans, which risks turning them into synthetic, factory-made objects, and interferes with evolution, the implications of which we lack the insight or prescience to predict. These are the topics of innumerable Orwellian science-fiction musings. Where would it all end? Where could it all end? What is life? What is genuine and what is contrived and unreal? What effect would all of this have on those wedded to an authoritative, if less than evidence-based, religious belief system? Anecdotes, even anecdotes that have been passed down and soaked in minds for centuries, do not a science make. These are the questions that Sagan mulled while staring at the brain of the man who lived at 20 Rue Serpente and then 18 Rue Cujas. As we are to learn, the brain in the bottle, Pierre Paul Broca, had wrestled with these thoughts as well as he developed his philosophy of free-thinking and divorce from the authoritative pronouncements of the established and dictatorial religions of France. The Pope is not infallible because the church pronounces the Pope to be infallible would not a syllogism make for Broca, even as it does not for many contemporaries. Sagan thought of these deeply troubling and philosophical issues as he stared at Broca.

HISTORY

These trips to Broca's apartments and paths became meaningful to me as well and steeped with the beverage of philosophical somberness. Here is where he labored, thought, matured, sneezed, and ate. The consciousness of history filtered through my thoughts as I pictured what went on here in the 19th century. History is more, so much more, than just a collection of hollow dates on a calendar and ambiguous artifacts in dusty cases. History is something very real and alive and evocative to all of us, and ironically encompasses the future as well as the past. It is, in fact, one of the vital things that helps to define us as a people, a society, even as individuals and as human beings—for what in due course separates us from the so-called lower forms is not just our language, our opposable thumbs, and our comprehension of death and hence the appalling apprehension of it, but *our sense of self and our collective sense of the past*. This preserved perception of the past and conserved identity may allow us to counter or dilute in some tealike fashion the apprehension of mortality. History and the value of it, in some strained sense, if it is not lost, can be the tisane of mortality. We will still get colds, until some future genius, who now may be playing Mortal Kombat 9 at the Games Workshop on Rue Serpente, finally comes up with a cure. We probably will still die, also. History has not been kind in that regard. But, in perhaps more than a metaphorical sense, history can be the brew of living forever. It can allow us to ruminate and give birth to thoughts, ideas, designs, values, and wisdom and permit these elements of the brain and mind to mutate and evolve. The ideas and work of Broca may stimulate Sagan and another young prodigy from Sainte-Foy-la-Grande who will take her place in the never-ending trudge of antiquity. History indeed is the tea of immortality.

CLINICAL EDUCATION

Just as in the present day in medicine and healthcare professions, clinical training and hands on experience is a large factor in the ascent to competence. Broca trudged through clinical experiences at many of the hospitals of Paris. Some of his clinical settings were up to date and associated with the brilliant mentors of the time. Some were pungent and staffed by professionals he regarded as less than clever. He was at least by one year the youngest of all the interns of the batch who were sent to the so-called "real world" for experience with the sick. The interns had their preferences and occasionally they would get an assignment that they thought was a living hell. Ironically, that is the impression Broca conveyed about his first visit to Bicêtre (Figure 8–5). This hospital in its history has been used succes-

Figure 8–5. *Bicetre Hospital.*

sively and simultaneously as an orphanage, a prison, an insane asylum, and a hospital. Its most notorious guest was the Marquis de Sade. The *Bicêtre* was most famous as the *Asylum de Bicêtre* where Superintendent Philippe Pinel is credited as being the first to introduce humane methods into the treatment of the mentally ill, in 1793. So when Broca arrived, it was more than just, in the jargon of the day, a "prison for lunatics." Pinel had first taken the chains off the insane at Bicêtre but it still had a prison within its walls and Broca was not amused by his assignment. Little did he realize that, years later, this institution would play a major role in his discovery of those special areas of the brain for speech. In the 1840s despite the foresight of Pinel, it was still bleak to the eyes of this young intern. As it turned out the chief of the service was Dr. Leuret, who did careful work on comparative anatomy of the brain, and Broca would benefit greatly from this assignment (Schiller, 1992). It still left a sour taste in his mouth. Wrote Broca, "Confronted with these indefinable and incomprehensible maladies I felt momentarily drained of all my strength; a visit to the insane is like a descent into hell of the ancient epic poets."

The youthful intern described his patients in quite eerie detail to his parents. Dr. Lauret apparently saw something in Broca that engendered trust and responsibility for he was assigned to minister to a wealthy duke. As Broca wrote,

> . . . of all the lunatics I have seen so far, our duke certainly is the most interesting from a scientific point of view. He is afflicted with intermittent religious mania. He goes into a rage, has to be tied, put in a straight jacket and shackled; in addition, my men have a tough job to prevent him from getting killed as he throws himself against the bed boards or tries to smother himself under his bed clothes. His delusions are most bizarre. He believes he is God, the devil, damned at one moment and chosen the next; today he thought he was dead . . . An hour ago I had to make him eat with an esophageal tube and a syringe. Needless to say I am taking meticulous notes. Goodbye poor liberty, not another moment of respite. My madman was much better for two weeks, now he has relapsed. We pour cold water on his naked body and are fully launched in our moral treatment . . . At present we are getting along fine with the family. There has been some bickering between them and us. Because of the cold affusions (Papa knows what they are) which are used to correct him, they got the revolting idea that we were punishing him, one of their own, a duke, and they naively tried to remonstrate with us. (Broca, 1886, 4/4/45, p. 281; 4/6/45, p. 287; 5/21/45, p. 292; Schiller, 1992)

Not all Broca's internships and studies went smoothly. Schiller, (1992) writes of a hiatus where he was suspended for some unspecified set of reasons from internship placements for a period of four months. We see in several of his biographies the seeds of some of his activism and political unrest and Schiller and others speculate that a group of interns banded and locked horns with some administrators at the hospitals and School of Medicine. There is a gap in his regular and predictable correspondence to his parents and there is no apparent evidence of the reasons for his suspension. At any rate, despite the intrigue, his correspondence resumes and he is back on track toward the end of 1846. Much to his satisfaction Broca became an intern with Pierre Nicolas Gerdy (1797–1856), anatomist, physiologist, and surgeon. In 1846 he was appointed Gerdy's assistant, and subsequently was permitted a fourth year of internship, with the surgeon Philippe-Frédéric Blandin (1798–1849) at the Hôtel-Dieu. As Broca writes, "Who could have told me six months ago that come January 1st I would have the finest surgical service in Paris?" (Broca, 1886, December, 1846, pp. 362–366).

FETID TONSILS AND INSURRECTION

By now Paul's *papa* and *maman* were beginning to realize that he was not destined to be a small town doctor and take over his father's practice. As he mentioned in letters he was not cut out for quiet happiness, but must have "those steeplechases" of academic and research pursuits. He also was to be in harm's way due to an infected pharynx during the swirling vortex of France's political scene. Broca's throat was sore and he complained of painful swallowing to his parents. His report of having a putrid tonsil excised by his mentor Dr. Blandin was nothing compared to what was developing outside his window. Clearly, the July Revolution of 1830 and the resultant compromise were not flourishing as the answer to the underlying problems with French society. The problems that had faced the government in 1848 were the same problems that had faced the government in 1830, except that in 1848 those problems had grown exponentially. On June 23, 1848, the people of Paris rose in insurrection. This uprising became known as June Days (Figure 8–6). The June Days were a bloody but unsuccessful rebellion by the Paris workers against a conservative twist in the Republic's course. On December 2, 1848, Louis Napoleon was elected President of the Second Republic, largely on peasant support. Three years later he suspended the elected assembly, establishing the Second French Empire, which lasted until 1871 (Rappaport, 2009). The events of 1848 and subsequently were precisely what some wag meant when he suggested history repeats itself: the first time as a tragedy, the second time as a farce.

Louis-Napoléon Bonaparte (April 20, 1808, to January 9, 1873) was the President of the French Second Republic and as Napoleon III, the ruler of the Second French Empire. He was the nephew and heir of the little tyrant with his hand in

Figure 8–6. *Outside Broca's windows. Prisoners from the "Days of June" 1848. Wikimedia Commons, public domain.*

his shirt, Napoleon I. The nephew was christened as *Charles Louis Napoléon Bonaparte*. Elected President by popular vote in 1848, he initiated a coup d'état in 1851, before ascending the throne as Napoleon III on December 2, 1852, the 48th anniversary of Napoleon I's coronation. He ruled as *Emperor of the French* until September 4, 1870. He embraces the strange distinction of being both the first president and the last monarch of France (Horne, 2004).

Paul Broca, medical student, was in the thick of it in February, 1848. He wrote to his parents,

> During the night the Municipal Guard opened fire on some workers in the Rue Transnonain of evil memory [an earlier massacre of working class people]. This morning the people are exasperated. In the streets the National Guard mix with the workers . . . they all shout in unison *Vive la reforme!* . . . But barricades are up . . . and some shooting has started. We are waiting for the casualties

to come in . . . I had to stay with three men all night; two of them have already died. This morning there were about thirty dead in Paris. In fact there must be many more. We do not get outside the colonnade of the hospital yard. Adieu, I embrace you on the run. (Broca, 1886, 2/28/43, p. 3; Schiller, 1992)

Against the backdrop of his tedious medical studies and duties during internships at hospitals, Broca realized that a larger societal transformation was playing out in France and for that matter in other parts of the world. Revolutions were not that far in the past or in the future in several lands. Corrupt autocratic monarchs were or were soon to be overthrown and executed; civil wars erupted; democratic parliaments were created and dissolved; military dictators seized power and created totalitarian states; factions bickered; political discussions and attempts at compromise dissolved into farce; and greater gaps were created between the haves and the have-nots, not unlike the contemporary Arab spring and summer of 2011.

History is a cruel teacher and societies have a tendency to ignore the lessons and not do their homework. This personal experience with societal unrest perhaps helped shape Broca's interest in politics. He would one day attempt to sculpt societal values as a member of the French Senate. As Schiller (1992) wrote, social conflagrations framed Broca's life and the lives of his parents, resulting in three republics, alternating with five monarchies, two Bonaparte emperors (each of whom started as the head of a republic and then apparently wine-sotted with clout and power, they transformed themselves into sovereign rulers).

Broca wrote of and marveled at the events of 1848. Even the French Revolution of 1789 with heads dropping everywhere thanks to Dr. Guillotin and in which both Broca's grandfathers had fought and suffered seemed not much more momentous than current times. Broca confessed that the face of the country changed as fast as the "decor on a stage," and he and his fiery friends were the actors. By the end of 1848 changes took place not only in the government of France, but within the structure of the École de Medicine. Bouillaud was replaced as Dean and Orfila, an administrator who suffered the wrath of Broca in many of his letters home, was charged and cleared, some say by falsified accounts, of embezzling. Broca even served in the National

Guard as casualty officer during the months of the insurrection of 1848. As one of his contemporaries noted he could be seen at the entrance of the Hôtel Dieu with his rifle in one hand a book in the other (Schiller, 1992). These wild days of 1848 left scar tissue and new growth on the skin of Broca's values and subsequently on his social conscience and his political undertakings.

Chapter 9

A Massive Thesis and Graduation

CULMINATION OF MEDICAL STUDIES

Paul Broca enrolled in the Faculty of Medicine at Paris in November, 1841, and passed successfully through the gauntlet of courses, competitive examinations, and bleak apartments until he became Anatomy Assistant of the Faculty in 1846, and then assumed the role of Prosector of the Faculty in 1848. A prosector is a person with the special task of preparing a dissection for demonstration in medical schools or hospitals. Many important anatomists and scientists began their careers as prosectors working for lecturers in anatomy and pathology. Paul Broca took his place in history alongside many famous scientists who worked as prosectors, including Korbinian Brodmann, who mapped the brain with numbered areas, Paul Langerhans, who described dendritic cells, and Sir William Bowman, whose work with microscopes must have inspired and piqued the curiosity of Broca. Prosectors for autopsies of diseased cadavers run a high risk of suffering from health problems as cadavers may harbor an array of diseases and microorganisms. Without strict precautions, preparing bodies for autopsy can expose the prosector or dissector to considerable hazard. Two diseases not uncommon in persons who must handle cadavers are named after prosectors:

- ◆ Prosector's paronychia: a primary injection of tuberculosis of the skin and nails;
- ◆ Prosector's wart, a skin lesion, also caused by contamination with tuberculous material.

Contracting infections caused by contaminated cadavers is a persistent danger among those who handle cadavers. If a skin puncture accident results from the sharp surgical instruments used in this kind of work there is high risk of suffering the ills of meddling with dead bodies. Thin surgical gloves are not enough to protect. There are many cases of pathologists who died of acute septicemia (blood poisoning) because of this. Another example, a famous historical case, is that of Dr. Ernst von Fleischl-Marxow, an Austrian physician, pathologist, and physiologist, who infected his finger during an autopsy and became dependent on morphine due to the pain, and, later, on cocaine, by instigation of his friend, Sigmund Freud (Hill & Anderson, 1988). In his writings to his parents, Broca mentions a few skin lesions that he contracted during his prosector days, but apparently he was able to avoid any catastrophic occupational hazards despite the somewhat less rigid preventative standards of his day.

FINALLY AND EFFICIENTLY, A DOCTOR

Broca became a Doctor of Medicine in 1849 and he presented many lectures on surgery and operative medicine in Paris during this time. He was not idle. He honed his skills and gained expertise as a surgeon and cultivated many paths for his curious mind by pursuing not only medical but political, social, and variegated scientific interests. Trained as a surgeon in Paris, Broca became a proficient microscopist and, in his doctoral thesis of 1849, demonstrated for the first time the spread of cancer by way of the veins (Figure 9–1). This was no small contribution for such a fledgling scientist.

His impressive thesis was not to be the last of Broca's writing. His fingerprints are all over the French National Library and

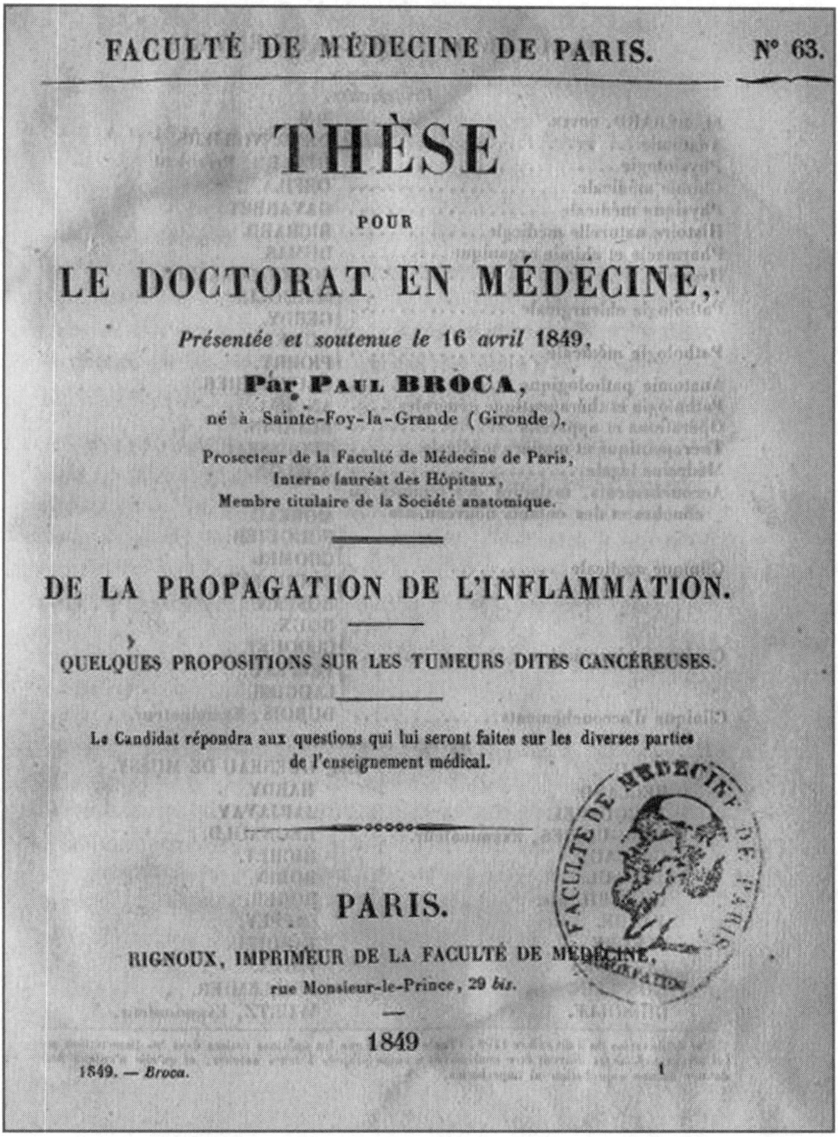

FACULTÉ DE MÉDECINE DE PARIS.   N° 63.

THÈSE

POUR

LE DOCTORAT EN MÉDECINE,

Présentée et soutenue le 16 avril 1849,

Par **PAUL BROCA**,

né à Sainte-Foy-la-Grande (Gironde),

Prosecteur de la Faculté de Médecine de Paris,
Interne lauréat des Hôpitaux,
Membre titulaire de la Société anatomique.

DE LA PROPAGATION DE L'INFLAMMATION.

QUELQUES PROPOSITIONS SUR LES TUMEURS DITES CANCÉREUSES.

Le Candidat répondra aux questions qui lui seront faites sur les diverses parties
de l'enseignement médical.

PARIS.

RIGNOUX, IMPRIMEUR DE LA FACULTÉ DE MÉDECINE,
rue Monsieur-le-Prince, 29 *bis*.

—

1849

1849. — *Broca.*

Figure 9–1. Title page of Broca's thesis. Reprinted with permission from Gallica, Bibliotique Nationale France.

he was just beginning his prolific writing calling. By the late 1850's he had written the definitive monograph on "aneurysms and their treatment," a mammoth work of close to 1,000 pages.

His countless interests mushroomed into full-fledged alleyways of inquiry and research. He apparently had few enemies, but his letters are sparkled with diatribes against colleagues whom he interpreted as stabbing him in the back or being disloyal. Though his letters catalogue a number of irritating, mosquitolike relationships, he developed close alliances and made many friends as the political mayhem in France unraveled.

As a Huguenot Christian, Broca was cognizant of the great loyalty his family and friends in Southwest France had to this minority religion. Despite his upbringing, he was not a strong believer himself and treaded lightly on these topics in letters to his mother. He was to take a great philosophical turn in a direction that questioned the authority and received wisdom of religion and the dominant Catholic church in France. As his nature and his experience had blossomed into that of an outright activist, he founded a society of freethinkers in 1848 and later supported Darwin's theory of natural selection. He questioned many of the fairy-tale-like religious and biblical stories of the talking snake, devils and demons, and immaculate conception. Most of humanity, even today, prays to invisible spirits and envisions mystical realms, and takes as the literal truth pronouncements passed down by gurus or prophets or authoritative books that are accepted without a questioning mind. To Broca's mind, all of these magical beliefs had a common denominator; they lacked tangible evidence. They were dependent on acceptance by blind faith and so many of the stories were the antithesis to physical and scientific laws that were understood at the time. One cannot test supernatural claims using the laws of science. They are supposed to be accepted by blind faith and those who do question superstitions may be condemned to a fiery place.

This was a time when traditional views of creation were being questioned vigorously and the European academies engaged in much discussion on these topics. Darwin's landmark publication in 1859 brought scientific credibility to the concept of evolution, but these discussions were going on even before this publication. Broca was rather inspired with the whole idea of evolution. He once declared, "I would rather be a transformed ape than a degenerate son of Adam" (Sagan 1979).

This was not a popular view in France at the time. The church still had a mighty hold on the dogma that should be taught in the universities and medical schools and swaying away from ecclesiastic views of creation and soul were dangerous and taboo. Eventually, he was denounced by authorities as a materialist and a corruptor of the youth. As will be learned, anthropology and Broca's role in popularizing it was interpreted as anti-government, anti-church, and anti-establishment. Anthropology was new and threatening and considered a suspect discipline at the time.

FREETHINKERS SOCIETY

If Broca was described as a Christian, he must have practiced it softly, because he founded a society for freethinkers in 1848. Indeed, he had little patience for superstition, saying, "Greedy for explanations, and rather than being satisfied with ignorance, the human mind treats itself to words devoid of meaning" (Sagan, 1979).

With only a modicum of irony intended, the conflict between science and religion was explored religiously by the members of Paul Broca's new Freethinkers Society. Of course this was much more dangerous in 19th century France than it is in today's freedom of speech and freedom of thought societies. The church ruled in France and ideas of dissidents filtered up to the powers and the controllers of purse strings. Broca put his professional career in jeopardy when he went public with his willingness to advance the views of skepticism and open discussion of the academy of free thought and ideas. His members debated and mulled all of the controversial and unpopular questions. Without doubt some of the scientists at the Freethinkers Society of Paris echoed the discussion and stance that is still alive and kicking today about the conflict between received authoritarian dogma of belief systems and science. As they might have argued, the major religions on the Earth contradict each other left and right. And most of them disavow any validity save their own. Most of them state that unless you believe like me you will not gain eternal reward. Broca and other freethinkers reasoned that they cannot all be correct. They must care about the truth, and what constitutes acceptable evidence. The way to winnow through all the differing contentions, as the members of Broca's Society discussed, is to be skeptical. Skeptics are not any more skeptical about religious beliefs than they are about every new scientific idea that is proposed. To the skeptic and the scientist, these are called hypotheses, not inspiration or revelation. In ordinary usage, skepticism (Greek: "σκέπτομαι" *skeptomai*, to think, to look about, to consider) refers to:

◆ an attitude of doubt or a disposition to incredulity either in general or toward a particular object;
◆ the doctrine that true knowledge or knowledge in a particular area is uncertain; or
◆ the method of suspended judgment, systematic doubt, or criticism that is characteristic of the scientific method (which holds that findings are the product of empirical research and findings and conclusions can be amended, fine-tuned or falsified by subsequent research).

Broca's establishment of a freethinker's society was only one example of his secular humanism. He loved, as one biographer said and was repeated by Sagan (1979), mainly serenity and tolerance. Broca was humanistic in that he was concerned with health care for the poor and was a major leader in the Assistance Publique. In the uproar of 1848, when Paris was conflagrated and in chaos, during the night, at the risk of his life, Broca smuggled out of Paris in a horse-drawn cart, seventy three million francs, stuffed into carpetbags and hidden under potatoes. This was the treasury of the Assistance Publique, which he believed he was saving from pillage and was at great peril. This would have jeopardized the continuation of medical treatment of the poor at this charity facility (Sagan, 1979). Broca took great personal risk to save these funds for medical care for the poor and even more risk from the church (and from his mother) by advocating free and scientific thinking.

LIFE IN PARIS

Paris in the 1850s and 60s was marked by unrelenting political and social turbulence. During this time of the Second Empire, the Emperor Napoléon III instigated sweeping changes on both the topographic and cultural landscape of the city. After firming up his empire, Louis Napoléon soon gained a title, Napoléon III. Once again France transitioned from a republic to an Empire with a supreme ruler, and a second supreme ruler named Napoléon. During his Second Empire Napoléon III promised order, reform, prosperity, and *"la gloire."*

Many of these promises remained unfulfilled and disenchantment with Napoléon III was rampant throughout the country by those who favored the more democratic system of the republic, including Paul Broca. Well seasoned across the letters he wrote to his parents, one can sense unhappiness with the government and particularly with Napoléon III. Since the Second Emperor was not a legitimate royal ruler of France, he could not risk much widespread unhappiness in his country. Perhaps he worried that he would meet the same fate as befell Louis Philippe in 1848, and the country would plunge once again into discontent and bloody revolution. When it came to gaining *"la gloire,"* Napoléon III did quite well for the first several years of his Empire. France emerged victorious in the Crimean War, he built the Suez Canal, hosted the glittering World's Fair which saw the construction of the "ugly" Eiffel Tower, and he modernized Paris to the beautiful city much like we recognize today (Plessis, 1989).

As the global stage unfolded, the Emperor occupied Mexico while the United States was engaged in its horrible Civil War. While Napoléon III was attempting to transform France, and Broca was transforming neuroscience, the United States was dealing with the aftermath of bloody battles such as the Battle of Shiloh where 13,000 out of 63,000 Union soldiers died, and 11,000 of 40,000 Confederate troops were killed. Surely, these domestic and global issues were in the conversations and debates of the great intellectual societies of Paris in the mid-1860s. During 1861 to 1862, Napoléon III positioned France to intervene in the American Civil War on the side of the Confederacy. The United States repeatedly warned that this meant war but the emperor inched steadily toward officially recognizing the Confederacy, especially after the crash of France's cotton textile industry and his successes in Mexico. Napoléon III, Emperor of the French, even went so far as to propose a "Grand Scheme for the Americas" that included recognition of the Confederate States of America and reintroducing a monarchy in Latin America. This "Grand Scheme" turned out to be not so grand and dissipated with subsequent political events in both Mexico and the United States.

By 1866, Louis Napoléon was looking pretty good. However, it was not to last and it would come crashing down in a sudden avalanche (Plessis, 1989).

PARIS MAKEOVER

An important legacy of Napoléon III's reign was the rebuilding of Paris. Design decisions were made to reduce the ability of future revolutionaries to challenge the government by capitalizing on the small, medieval streets of Paris to form barricades. This would be echoed a hundred years later in the 1960s when streets were paved to prevent angry students from throwing cobblestones at the police and authorities. Barricades, cobblestones, and angry students have played an abounding role in the political landscape of France. Broca and his like-minded peers juggled their studies and clinical responsibilities with a good deal of political engagement.

Napoléon III had a plan. This is where the aforementioned Georges-Eugène Haussmann came in as somewhat of a savior. The Emperor launched a great project to reform and reconstruct Paris. The architect Haussmann would transform the city. Downtown Paris was renovated by clearing out slums, widening streets, and constructing parks according to Baron Haussmann's plan. Haussmann accomplished all this by tearing up many of the old, twisting streets and dilapidated apartment houses, and replacing them with the wide, tree-lined boulevards and expansive gardens that Paris is famous for today. Broca and his contemporaries worked and lived through this significant era of constant construction during this chaotic Parisian facelift.

The Palais Garnier is an example of the great reconstruction of Paris. In 1858 the Emperor authorized Haussmann to clear the required 12,000 square meters of land on which to build a second theatre for the world-renowned Parisian Opera and Ballet companies (Figure 9–2).

During 1896, the falling of one of the counterweights for the grand chandelier resulted in the death of one person. This

Figure 9–2. *Opera Garnier, Paris.*

incident, as well as the underground lake, cellars, plus other elements of the Opera House (even the building itself) inspired Gaston Leroux to write his classic 1910 gothic novel, *The Phantom of the Opera* (Ayers, 2004). Napoléon III and Baron Haussmann's physical transformation of Paris was the most imitated work of city planning in modern history.

Haussmannization has infiltrated our language and it relates to the original 19th century plan that imprinted railroad stations, public libraries, transformed housing, lush parks, and wide, tree-lined boulevards onto the medieval map of the Paris.

Napoléon III has a historical reputation as a philanderer, yet he apparently thought of himself as irresistible and rationalized his behavior in the following manner: "It is usually the man who attacks. As for me, I defend myself, and I often capitulate." (Kelen, 1966) Apparently the Emperor was too attractive to resist and had great difficulty fighting off the actresses and celebrities of the day. Justine Marie Le Boeuf, also known as Marguerite Belenger, was an actress and acrobatic dancer, a skill that she found useful during her dates with the Emperor (Figure 9–3).

Figure 9–3. *Caricature of Marguerite Belenger: Mistress of the Emperor.* Wikimedia Commons, public domain.

Belenger was rumored to be the illegitimate daughter of a hang-man, and was the most universally loathed of the mistresses, although perhaps his favorite (Kelen, 1966).

He had a myriad assortment of women who courted the favors of the court. During his reign, it was the task of Count Felix Bacciochi, his social secretary, to arrange for trysts and to procure women for the emperor's favors. His affairs were not trivial sideshows: they distracted him from governing, affected his relationship with his wife, the empress, who allegedly found sleeping with him "disgusting" after they had secured an heir, and diminished him in the views of the other European courts (Plessis, 1989).

By his late forties, Napoléon started to suffer from a variety of medical ailments, including kidney disease, bladder stones, chronic bladder and prostate infections, arthritis, gout, obesity, and the effects of chronic smoking. The Emperor died during a multistage surgery under chloroform anesthesia in the attempt break up a bladder stone by British surgeons. The abuse visited on his nether regions had come to haunt him. It has been suspected and reported that the operation was botched due to the arrogance of his British surgeon Sir Henry Thompson, resulting in the Emperor's untimely death (Plessis, 1989). Napoléon III transformed Paris and created an ambiance of mistrust for Broca and his contemporaries. Broca raged against the Emperor in his writings and this backcloth of French history also seemed to color the doctrinal path of his future.

WIFE IN PARIS

In the foliage of history, Paul Broca does not come across as much of a romantic flower. There is little in his record that points to a series of amours or paramours. He was ambitious and a workaholic. As Schiller (1992) suggests, Broca had to listen to the chorus of his family and friends admonishing, cajoling, and suggesting to him that he find the girl of his dreams and get married. Broca had only a few recorded instances in his history of having ever been smitten, but he was a poet at heart and even his poetry is less than dripping with romance. His short lyrical pieces were more suggestive and somewhat mundane in that the ethereal subjects in a few of his poems were servants and scullery girls. Like some sophisticated romancers of this day who crave those below their socioeconomic level, perhaps he had a bit of the slumming urge. He certainly gave no indication of a fascination with raving French beauties, celebrities, or women of the arts, unlike the political leaders of the day or some of his peers. Broca was a bit curt with suggestions from home that he get with it and start organizing some suitable marriage contestants. He parried suggestions from home (most likely from his mother) that he get serious about finding a mate. "Is there no pity in your heart?" he wrote. "After my trials you want to plunge me into the tribulations of marriage?" He pleaded that they let him first catch his breath. He wrote that the sea is calm and there was no Parisian girl on the horizon. Broca was aware of his own luke warm romantic nature. He wrote that he was "not exactly a romantic" and his heart was not made of tinder (Schiller, 1992). Broca was somewhat of a cold fish when it came to the opposite sex. He went so far as to implicate marriage as being a hindrance to science. As Schiller reports, not only did Broca feel that science was the purview of young men, but grumpily characterized "private practice and marriage, [as the] two extinguishers of science."

He may not have succumbed completely to the dictates of his own emotional limbic lobe, which he was to describe subsequently in careful detail, but finally, he was ready to acquiesce to his relatives' pleadings and start looking for love in earnest. Perhaps it was not love he was looking for, but a compatible partner. But he set about the task with all the affection of a person setting out a job description or set of qualifications for employment. Romantic love did not play into it. But there were obstacles. His family would not allow him to marry a Catholic girl. That was out of the question, just as rigid religious requirement has inserted its ugly head into so many potential liaisons and happy pairings. He also would have difficulty with the selection of a very pious Protestant woman since his views on religion by now were well publicized and his association with free thinkers held no truck with acceptance of superstitious belief systems that were based on authoritarian dogma that relegated critical thinking to the dust bin.

ART, VIOLIN, AND IODINE

After a less than incendiary courtship, on July 6, 1857, Paul Broca married Adele-Augustine Lugol, daughter of the doctor who was most associated with the creation and therapeutic use of iodine. Broca was no doubt impressed by the credentials of Dr. Lugol and his family.

Dr. Jean Guillaume Lugol was born on August 18, 1788, in Montauban, France, another important city in the Huguenot heartland. The Protestant families of South Central and South-western France certainly formed a rich and thriving network of mutual support and intermarriage. The tragic wars of religion ensured a historic bond among its citizens for generations to come. The commercial importance of Montauban is and has been due to its trade in agricultural produce, horses, game and poultry, and earth-related crafts and industries including nursery-gardening, cloth-weaving, flour-milling, saw mills, and the manufacture of furniture, silk-gauze, and straw hats. This suited the earthy values of Broca and produced a degree of familiarity. The city is also the birthplace of the famous French painter Ingres, whose work still adorns the *Musée d'Orsay* with his remarkable contemporaries of the Impressionist movement. Ingres was cited by some as not only a great classical portraitist but also as the inspiration for abstract expressionism. He could also play a mean violin. Ingres's well-known passion for playing the violin gave to the French language a colloquialism, "*violon d'Ingres,*" meaning a second skill beyond the one by which a person is mainly known. So once again, South France is the spawning bed of great brains, both in art and science. During World War II, Leonardo da Vinci's Mona Lisa was briefly hidden in a secret vault behind a wine cellar at Montauban (Connor, 2002).

Dr. Lugol was raised in that regional hothouse of creativity. As the future father-in-law of Broca, Jean Guillaume Lugol would be appointed acting physician at Saint-Louis hospital of Paris in 1819, where Broca would tread the same halls 40 years later. Lugol was named head of a department at Saint-Louis, a post he held till he retired in 1851. Lugol was a French pioneer of iodine therapy, and is famous for his iodine-based solution, still registered in the French Codex, and present in most foreign

Pharmacopoeia. He produced four books on scrofulous (tuber-culosis) diseases and their treatment. These publications gather a wealth of the detailed observations of an excellent practitioner who consistently demonstrated a great independence of spirit towards some medical concepts of the day. He was very close to his patients and to his medical students, who admired the quality of his lessons, the efficiency of his therapeutic innovations, his intellectual uprightness as well as his success in private practice (Neuzil, 2002).

Eventually his rising star son-in-law gave a scientific nod to this iodine-popularizing father-in-law by authoring an article, according to Schiller (1992) on the treatment of a "vast abscess . . . of the groin and buttock, cured by a single iodine injection." Broca could be a pain in the buttock to his father-in-law, but apparently he also used the treatments of his wife's father to cure the same affliction.

MME. AUGUSTINE BROCA

Not much is laid down in Broca's writings about the courtship of Paul Broca and his wife Adele-Augustine Lugol (Figure 9–4) Schiller (1992) laments this fact. He characterizes the courtship as without detail and with only austere reflections from liv-ing relatives. As in keeping with expressed views on romance and dance, Broca was rather businesslike. He is not the type of party personality who would toss his head and cut out into an uninhibited personal dance rendition of "Wild Thing" or the muscial equivalent in the 1850s. He revealed little to his parents in his volumes of letters to them and Schiller (1992) appears to complain that perhaps if Augustine would have chosen to be a little more candid, his romantic life would not appear to be quite so cold-blooded. He focused on his wife's characteristics of intellectual, religious, and economic suitability and made little mention of her physical characteristics. This from a man who would later get deeply into the study of the limbic lobe and its connections with emotions, hormones, and sexuality. Even so, Schiller hints at Adele-Augustine's "severe beauty" and that she no doubt fulfilled Broca's criteria of "nubility." Additionally, some have speculated that Broca's contributions to the study of tumors

Figure 9–4. *Adele-Augustine Lugol Broca. From Schiller, 1992.*

and the heritability of cancers might have been triggered by his knowledge of his wife's familial association with these diseases. The Lugol family had an ancestry that was peppered with a history of carcinoma of the breast, stomach, and endometrium. This quite possibly piqued his interest in causes of cancer and may have led him to believe that in certain rare instances, cancer can be inherited (Krush, 1979).

The couple, Paul and Augustine, had three children, a daughter Pauline and two sons. The two boys Benjamin and

Elijah followed in the footprints of their father and became pro-fessors of the Faculty of Medicine of Paris. Benjamin, the older son, also served as an intern in Paris hospitals. The generations of Broca were firmly entrenched as Parisians and the days in Sainte-Foy-la-Grande were now a part of family history, although the citizens in the Gironde near Bordeaux would remember the family Broca fondly and name schools and art expositions after their village heroes.

Chapter 10

Landmark Cases:
M. Leborgne and M. Lelong

The *Musée Dupuytren* (Figure 10–1) is a treasure trove of weird and wonderful collections of anatomical and pathological objects (Figure 10–2). It is located at 15, Rue de l' École de Médecine, Les Cordeliers, in Paris. This is the Latin Quarter of Paris, so-named because many of the early classical scholars in the area could be heard conversing in Latin. Not so much today. This eclectic museum can be accessed off of the Boulevard St. Michel or by skipping down some steep steps from the Rue Monsieur le Prince. The charming little Hotel Saint Paul Rive Gauche was our temporary quarters for one of our early ventures to Paris and we soon discovered that our hotel almost backed up to the walls of the Dupuytren Museum. We slept within meters of the most famous French brains in history, for here was the longstanding home of the brains of Broca's two most celebrated patients.

The museum was established in 1835 by Dr. Mathieu Orfila, one of the leaders of the College of Medicine and a target of Broca's ire throughout his letters to his parents. It was established as the Museum of Pathological Anatomy of the Médecine Faculty of the University of Paris, with the bequest of Baron Guillaume Dupuytren, anatomist and a celebrated professor of surgery. The museum was installed in the old refectory of the

Figure 10–1. Dupuytren Museum courtyard.

Cordeliers Convent (Figure 10–3), gathering collections from throughout the university.

The building's origins date from 1221, when the third order of Saint Francis of Assisi was established. Its members, known as the Cordeliers, enjoyed special protection from King Charles V, who contributed to the creation of the convent. The Cordelier friars wore cords around their waists as do Franciscan monks and friars. This building was destined to become a place of great religious and historical importance. It became the meeting place of a political group, also known as the Cordeliers, who played an important role in the French Revolution. This Cordeliers district acquired the reputation as a famously radical area of Paris. The district, under the leadership of Georges Danton, played a significant role in the storming of the Bastille, and was home to several notable figures of the Revolution, including Danton himself (Hammersley, 2005).

As time passed the convent was gradually taken apart and demolished starting with the church and ending with the cloister in 1877. Today, only the 15th century refectory still stands and

Figure 10–2. *Statuary at the Dupuytren Museum.*

houses its amazing collection of oddities and pathologies. The term refectory refers to a dining room, especially in monasteries, and today this old edifice it hauntingly lit by vast windows that cast an eerie light in the room. It has housed praying friars,

Figure 10–3. *Cordeliers Convent.*

insurgents, and now keeps the pathological remnants of the University of Paris Medical School including the celebrated brains of Leborgne and Lelong. Guarding the entrance door of the Dupuytren is a noble bust of Broca (Figure 10–4).

Figure 10–4. Bust of Broca with medal at entrance to Dupuytren Museum.

The first catalog of this museum was compiled between 1836 and 1842, and listed about a thousand specimens (Figure 10–5). Skeletons, casts of wax and a veritable cornucopia of organs preserved in jars show malformations of the body that were considered for a long time as "monstrosities" and create the impression

Figure 10–5. *Collections in the Dupuytren Museum.*

of a Halloween House of Horrors to viewers who might not be accustomed to viewing medical pathologies (Figure 10–6).

Currently the museum contains about 6,000 objects, wax casts, bone pieces, and parts preserved in jars, as well as photos, paintings, prints and drawings, and some instruments for the practice of pathology. My guess is that somewhere in the deep recesses of the Dupuytren Museum is the overlooked brain of

Figure 10–6. *Medical anomalies of the Dupuytren Museum.*

Paul Broca as well. No one seems to know the whereabouts of Broca's own brain, although there is evidence from Sagan's work that at one time it was on display (LaPointe, 2010b, see Appendix C). Someone needs to search through the collection someday to see if this missing brain is indeed lost or just miscataloged or misplaced. Present day curators of the museum claim to have no knowledge of the whereabouts of Broca's brain and one went as far as to suggest that perhaps Sagan was incorrect and never in fact saw Broca's brain, but confused it with that of some of Broca's patient specimens. This is a mystery and still begs the question "Brother, wherefore art thou?"

The older waxes in the remarkable Dupuytren are from the end of the 18th century and are remnants of the collections of the Royal College of Surgery (Figure 10–7). There are thousands of pieces of bone, ranging from complete skeletons with skull or

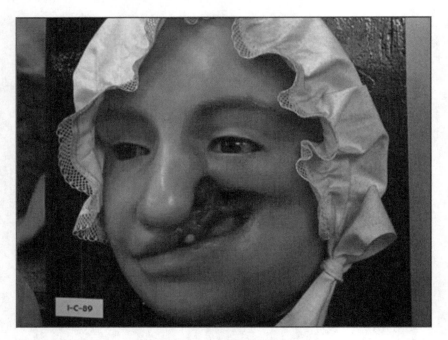

Figure 10–7. *Wax figure with craniofacial anomaly.*

bone fragments or bone and joint. These represent a variety of lesions, many of which have become very rare in the West but are unfortunately common in many developing countries. The third category of objects in the museum is a series of jars containing pieces immersed in a fixative.

Some sources suggest that the laboratory of the Dupuytren Museum generated its own secret recipes to be used as a fixative (Josette, 2012). The Dupuytren Museum also has a historical association with the Dejerine Foundation, which was established by another famous French neurologist Jules Dejerine (1849–1917). Dejerine was the famed professor of neurology at the medical faculty of Paris who practiced in the post-Broca era but who was reknowned in his own right for major and lasting contributions to brain-based disorders including research on acquired dyslexia. Dejerine was another of the pioneers in the study of localization of function in the brain, having first provided evidence that word blindness may occur as the result of lesions of the supramarginal and angular gyri in the dominant parietal lobe, regarded by many contemporary neuroscientists as the third major cortical area involved in language.

In 1888, eight years after the death of Broca, Dejerine married his student, Augusta Marie Klumpke, who had studied medicine in Paris and in 1887 was the first woman to become *interne des hôpitaux*, in the Paris hospitals. Dejerine died in 1917 at the age of 68 years, reportedly physically debilitated by the stress of work in a military hospital during World War I (Bassetti & Jagella, 2006). The influence of Dejerine on the collections in the Dupuytren Museum cannot be disregarded. He and his wife Augusta Marie, who sounded an early peal for the inclusion of women in science, just as had Broca some years before, contributed mightily to the Dupuytren collections including contributions to the library, microscopes, and instruments, as well as histological and clinical and neuropathological photographs from which he and his wife developed their tome on the "semiology of the nervous system."

The museum began a slow decline starting in the late 19th century, despite continued acquisition of new collections, and its upkeep became problematic. In 1937 Gustave Roussy ordered the museum shut, with many items subsequently lost or destroyed. However, in 1967 Jacques Delarue (1901–1971) brought the museum back to life with a general refurbishment. Today it still retains a superb collection, including specimens dating from the 17th century, as well as exquisite wax anatomical models, books, and photographs (Dupuytren, 2011).

THE LEGENDARY FRENCH BRAINS

Among many other notable items, the museum is the celebrated location of the brains of perhaps the two most historically significant persons with aphasia, preserved by the anatomist Pierre Paul Broca. These are the historic safeguarded brains that Broca observed, described in delicate detail, and conserved himself in the bottles of formalin that can to this day be examined. These artifacts transformed thought on the localization of function in the brain and specifically on critical areas for the localization of language, that most humanoid of all hominid acts.

Figure 10–8 shows the brain of Monsieur Leborgne, preserved in formalin, as it appeared in its jar in the Dupuytren Museum in 2011. On a previous visit in 2009 this preserved specimen was displayed with a label in front of it, but in 2011 it was on a shelf and the identification label was nowhere near it, but discovered by Dr. Charles Ouimet and me on a side shelf approximately three meters from the brain itself.

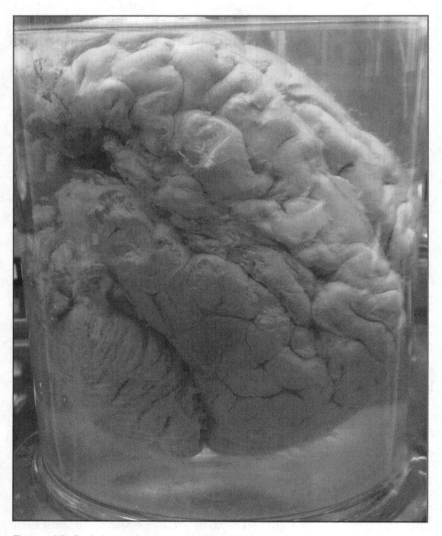

Figure 10–8. *Leborgne's preserved brain, 2011—Dupuytren Museum.*

LEBORGNE

Monsieur Leborgne, who was designated by his nickname "Tan" by Broca himself in his descriptions of the man, is somewhat of a mystery aside from the actual descriptions in Broca's classic presentations to the Anthropological Society and the Anatomy Society. The first hint of more extenive analysis to come was reported in the minutes of the April 18, 1861, meeting of the Society of Anthropology.

> Broca mentioned in a discussion on disturbances of speech an important observation, according to the notes: M. Broca presented the brain of a fifty-one-year-old man who had died [on the previous day] in his service at the hospital Bicêtre. For the last twenty-one years this man had lost the use of his speech. It is planned to deposit the specimen at the Musée Dupuytren and to publish the complete records in the Bulletin de la Société Anatomique.

In Green's remarkable translation (Green, 2000) we can appreciate most of what is known about Leborgne thanks to Broca's detailed history. Broca's words present most of the fragments that are known of Leborgne.

> On 11 April 1861, transported to the general infirmary of Bicêtre, surgery service, was a 50-year-old man, named Leborgne, suffering from a diffuse, gangrenous phlegmon of the entire right inferior limb, from the instep up to the buttock. To the questions that I addressed to him the next day on the origin of his malady, he responded only with the monosyllable "tan," repeated two times in sequence, and accompanied by a gesture of his left hand. I went for information on this man's history, who had been at Bicêtre for twenty-one years. I interrogated in turn his minders (surveillants), his fellows on the ward, and his parents, who came to see him, and here is what resulted from this inquest.
>
> He was subject, since his youth, to attacks of epilepsy; but he had been able to take up the trade of a hat-form maker [prendre l'état de formier] that he exercised up to the age of thirty. At this time, he lost the ability to speak, and it was for this reason that he was admitted as a patient to the hospice of Bicêtre. We did not know if the loss of speech came on slowly or rapidly, nor if any other symptoms had accompanied the onset of this affliction.

When he arrived at Bicêtre, it had already been two or three months that he had not been able to speak. He was then perfectly healthy and intelligent, and differed from a sane man only in the loss of articulated speech. He came and went in the hospice where he was known under the name of Tan. He understood all that was said to him; he even had very fine hearing; but, regardless of the question addressed to him, he always responded: "tan, tan," in conjunction with greatly varied gestures by means of which he succeeded in expressing most of his ideas. When his interlocutors did not comprehend his mime, he would easily become enraged, and then add to his [p. 344] vocabulary a great swearword, one only, and precisely the same that I indicated above, in speaking of a patient observed by Mr. Auburtin. Tan was regarded as being egotistical, vindictive, bad, and his comrades, who detested him, accused him even of being a thief. These faults could have been due in large part to the cerebral lesion; however, they were not pronounced enough to appear pathological, and, though this patient was at Bicêtre, one never thought of moving him to the division for the insane. He was considered, on the contrary, as a man perfectly responsible for his acts.

He had already been without speech for ten years when a new symptom appeared: the muscles of his right arm gradually weakened, and finally became entirely paralyzed. Tan continued to walk without difficulty, but the paralysis of movement won little by little the right inferior limb, and, after having dragged his leg for some time, the patient had to resign himself to keeping constantly to bed. It was about four years from the start of the paralysis of his arm up to the moment when that of his abdominal limb was advanced enough to render standing completely impossible. It was, therefore, close to seven years that Tan was in bed before he was brought to the infirmary. This last period of his life is that of which we have the least information. Having become incapable of doing harm, his comrades no longer occupied themselves with him, except for amusing themselves at his expense a few times (which gave him bitter fits of anger), and he had lost the little celebrity that the singularity of his illness had formerly given him in the hospice. It was noticed that his vision had declined notably over about the previous two years. This was the only complication noticed while he had been confined to his bed. Besides that, he had never been senile; his clothes were changed only once per week, with the result that the widespread phlegmon [gangrene] for which he was transported to the infirmary on 11 April 1861, was recognized by the nurses only when it had progressed considerably and had invaded the totality of his right abdominal limb, from the foot to the buttock.

The study of this unfortunate person, who could not speak and who, being paralyzed in the right hand, could not write, presented quite a few difficulties. He was moreover in such a generally grave state, [p. 345] that it would have been cruel to torment him with lengthy investigations.

I noted however that his general sensitivity was everywhere preserved, though it was uneven. The right half of his body was less sensitive than the other, and this doubtless contributed to the attenuation of the pain of the extensive phlegmon. The patient did not suffer much when not touched there, but palpation was painful, and a few incisions, that I was obliged to make, provoked agitation and cries.

The two right limbs were completely paralyzed of movement; the two other limbs were obedient to will, and, though weak, could, without any hesitation, execute all movements. The emission of urine and fecal matter was natural, but swallowing was done with some difficulty; mastication, on the contrary, was done very well. The face was not distorted; however, in the act of breathing, the left cheek seemed a little more swollen than the right, thus indicating that the muscles on this side of the face were a little weakened. There was no indication of strabismus. The tongue was perfectly free; it was not distorted; the patient could move it in all directions and stick it out of his mouth. The two halves of this organ were of equal thickness. The difficulty in swallowing that I mentioned above was due to a paralysis starting in the pharynx, and not to a paralysis of the tongue, for it was only the third time swallowing that was laborious. The muscles of the larynx seemed in no way altered, the quality of the voice was natural, and the sounds that the patient made in pronouncing his monosyllable were perfectly clear.

His hearing had kept its fineness: Tan heard well the tick of a watch; but his vision was weak; when he wanted to see the time, he was obliged to take the watch himself with his left hand and place it in a particular position, about 20 centimeters from his right eye, which seemed better than the left.

The state of intelligence could not be exactly determined. It is certain that Tan understood almost everything that was said to him; but, he could only express his ideas or his desires by the movement of his left hand, our dying person [moribond] could not make himself [p. 346] understood as well as he could understand others. Numerical responses were those that he could make the best, by opening or closing his fingers. I asked him many times how many days he had been sick? he [sic] responded sometimes five days, sometimes six days. For how many years had he been at Bicêtre? he [sic] opened his hand four times in sequence, and then pointed with a single finger; this would make twenty-one years, and one saw above that this information was perfectly exact. The next day, I repeated the same question, and I obtained the same response; but, when I wanted to return to this a third time, Tan understood that I was making him do an exercise; he became angry, and articulated the curse already named which I only heard from his mouth one time. I presented him with my watch two days in a row. The second hand was not moving; he could not, as a result, distinguish the three hands other than by their form or by their length; nevertheless, after having examined the watch for a few moments, he was able each time to indicate the time with exactitude. It is therefore incontestable that this man was intelligent, that he could reflect, and that he had preserved, in a certain measure, his memory for things past. He could even comprehend relatively complicated ideas: for instance, I asked him in what order his paralysis had progressed; he made first with the index finger of his left hand a little horizontal gesture that wanted to say: understand! then he pointed successively to his tongue, his right arm and his right leg. It was perfectly exact, apart from the fact that he attributed his loss of speech to paralysis of his tongue, which was very natural.

Nevertheless, various questions to which a man of ordinary intelligence would have found the means to respond to by gesture, even with a single hand, remained without response. Other times, one could not grasp the meaning of certain responses, which seemed to greatly annoy the patient; other times, at last, the response was clear, but false: thus, although he did not have children, he claimed to have them. It is not therefore doubtful that the intelligence of this man had undergone a profound change, being under the influence of his cerebral affliction, being under the influence of the fever that devoured him; but he was evidently much more intelligent than he had to be in order to speak.

It was seen clearly in the information obtained and in the present [p. 347] state of the patient that there existed a progressive cerebral lesion that, originally and during the first ten years of the sickness, was kept limited to a relatively circumscribed region, and which, in this first period, affected neither the organs of motility, nor the organs of sensitivity; that at the end of ten years, the lesion propagated to one or many organs of motility, but not yet [en respectant encore] the organs of sensitivity; and that, more recently finally, general sensitivity was blunted at the same time as vision, especially the vision of the left eye. With the complete paralysis of movement in the two limbs on the right side, and the sensitivity of these two limbs being moreover a little weak, the principle cerebral lesion had to occupy the left hemisphere, and what confirmed this opinion was the incomplete paralysis of the muscles of the left cheek and the retina of the same side, for it need not be repeated [inutile de rappeler] that paralyses of cerebral causes are crossed for the trunk and the limbs, and direct for the face.

It was a matter of determining more exactly, if possible, the seat of the original lesion, and, though the last discussion of the Anthropological Society left some doubt about the doctrine of Mr. Bouillaud, I wanted, in the upcoming autopsy, to proceed as if this doctrine were true; this was the best means of putting it to the test. Mr. Aubertin, having declared some days before that he would renounce it if one could show him a single case of aphemia, well-described, without a lesion to the anterior lobes, I invited him to come see my patient in order to know ahead of time what his diagnosis would be, and if this case was one of those in which he would accept the result as conclusive. Apart from the complications that had been observed for 11 years, my colleague found the current state and the antecedents sufficiently clear to affirm without hesitation that the lesion must have started in one of the anterior lobes.

Reasoning from this datum to complete the diagnosis, I considered that the striate body was the motor organ closest to the anterior lobes; it was without doubt in gradually spreading to this organ that the original lesion had produced the hemiplegia. The probable diagnosis was therefore: original lesion in the left anterior lobe, propagated to the striate body of the same side. As for the nature of this lesion, everything indicated that it was a matter [p. 348] of a progressive, chronic softening, but extremely slow, for the absence of all phenomena of compression excluded the idea of an intracranial tumor.

The patient died on 17 April, at eleven o'clock in the morning. The autopsy was done as soon as possible, that is to say, at the end of twenty-four hours. The temperature was slightly elevated. The cadaver showed no sign of putrefaction. The brain was shown a few hours later to the Anthropological Society, then placed immediately in alcohol. The organ was so altered that we had to take great precautions to conserve it. It was only after two months and after many changes of liquid that the specimen [pièce] began to firm up. Today it is in perfect condition, and it is deposited in the Dupuytren museum under no. 55a, of the nervous system.

> (Broca, 1861a; Green, 2000. This extensive translation of Broca's original article is presented with the kind permission of Christopher D. Green.)

CONCLUSIONS AFTER EXAMING "TAN" LEBORGNE'S BRAIN

The detailed preamble and discussion of Broca's examination of Leborgne's brain leaves little doubt that he (Broca) was only too aware of the chequered history and zealous debates about localization of function in the brain, and especially about precise localization of speech in selected cortical convolutions. The ghosts of the overgeneralization of phrenology and its questionable science were everpresent. The smell of Gall was in the hall. Even if Aubertin and Bouillaud were not strict phrenologists, they were still unconvinced that speech could not be localized in the "anterior" frontal lobes. Yet, only meager pathological evidence had been presented, except for the numerous cases of Bouillaud, which were still not widely accepted as evidence and certainly not deemed specific clinicopathological evidence of the whereabouts of speech in the brain. Broca was keen on finding prospective evidence of relatively circumscribed damage in patients who had been predetermined to exhibit disorders of speech and language. These were not the paralysis or paresis-based impairments of speech that could readily be attributed to disorders of underlying movement as in the dysarthrias. Broca searched for the more elusive, more greyzone disturbances that seemed to be indicative of an impaired "faculty" of language or "articulate speech." Tesak and Code (2008) trace some of this history on Broca, Broca's area, and the type of speech and/or language disorder presented by Broca's patients. It must be said that we still search that greyzone and frequently have difficulty determining whether the resultant speech disturbance is the result of activating, planning, sequencing, and memory of the motoric patterns of speech or of some related (and perhaps often comorbid) disruption of phonological, lexical, or semantic elements of verbal productions.

Broca grappled with these questions, along with the realization that mentation and the insidious "softening" of the cortical tissue around Leborgne's lesion could well play a role, and certainly would raise issues decades later about the circumscribed nature of the Tan lesion. Leborgne and Lelong both suffered from profound loss of speech. Today we are well aware of how severity of a disturbance can interact with conclusions about the quality or type of the disorder. Even the term "aphemia" was subsequently replaced by "aphasia" and this, too, contributed to loss of precision of meaning in the description of the disorders associated with the dominant cerebral hemisphere. He also was well aware of the impact of his presentation on the broader context of the ongoing debate on holistic versus localized functions in the brain. Listen to Broca mull these issues in his own words from that most detailed exposition of his classic 1861 paper (Broca, 1861a; Green, 2000).

> In placing ourselves, then, in this point view, we easily recognize that the pathological anatomy of aphemia can give something more than a solution to one particular question, and that it can throw a great deal of light on the general question of cerebral localization, by furnishing to cerebral physiology a point of departure, or rather a very precious point of comparison. If it were proven, for example, that aphemia can be the result of lesions affecting indifferently in any convolution and in any cerebral lobe, one would have the right to conclude not only that the faculty of articulated language is not localized, but also that very probably the other faculties of the same order are not localized either. If it were demonstrated on the contrary that the lesions that abolish speech consistently occupy one determinate convolution, one could hardly fail to admit that this convolution is the seat of the faculty of articulated language, and, that once the existence of a first localization was admitted, the principle of localization by convolutions would be established. Finally, between these two extreme alternatives, there is a third that could lead to a mixed doctrine. Let us suppose, in effect, that the lesions of aphemia consistently occupy the same cerebral lobe, but that, in this lobe, they do not consistently occupy the same convolution; it would result that the faculty of articulated language would have its

seat in a certain region, in a certain group of convolutions, but not in a particular convolution, and it would become very probable that the cerebral faculties are localized by regions, and not by convolutions.

Where Broca seems to hedge a bit in this discussion of regional versus precise localization of the definitive location of the damage that caused the aphemia in his patient, Leborgne, one can see throughtout his original paper and his method of argument, that he is a cautious and objective scientist and is well aware of alternate explanations that might arise from his findings. After his carefully detailed description of M. Leborgne's speech and language, particularly what was intact and what was impaired, coupled with his thorough examination and presentation of the pathology of the brain, Broca's conclusions were less equivocal. These are the conclusions that were persuasive and swayed the holistic-localization debate in the direction of much more widespread realization that, although not everything was localized, certain faculties and functions certainly were more likely to result from lesions in distinct areas of the cortex. Barely nine years after the landmark Broca year of 1861, Fritz and Hitzig (1870) would conduct their equally landmark research on dogs, observing what moved during electrical stimulation of the canine brains. This research solidified understanding of the localization of motor functions and their precise distribution to specific body parts. This underscored Broca's findings and the tide was turned away from the idea that "the brain is a bubble" and if you prick it anywhere you will cause holistic and tragic consequences. As we now are much more aware, the cerebral hemispheres contain elegant cortex and not so elegant cortex and some areas can be damaged without much corollary. Some of the elegant and eloquent cortex, however, when damaged can rob us of much of what makes us human, the power of human communication.

Broca's consummation to the footnoted and gracefully detailed presentation of his historic paper on Leborgne's brain ended with the following conclusions:

After having described these lesions, and researched their nature, seat, and anatomical progression, it is important to compare these results with those of clinical observation, to finally establish, if possible, a connection between the symptoms and the material disorders.

Anatomical inspection shows that the lesion was still in the act of propagating when the patient succumbed. The lesion had therefore been progressive, but it advanced very slowly, since it had taken twenty-one years to destroy a quite limited part of the cerebral mass. It is permissible to believe, as a consequence, that there was a long period during which it did not go beyond the limits of the organ in which it had started. Now, we saw that the original focus of the illness was situated in [p. 355] the frontal lobe, and quite probably in the third frontal convolution. This drives us to admit that from the point of view of pathological anatomy there had been two periods: one in which only one frontal convolution (probably the third) was altered; the other, in which the illness propagated itself little by little to the other convolutions, to the lobe of the insula or to the extra-ventricular nucleus of the striate body.

If now we examine the succession of symptoms, we find equally two periods: a first period which lasted ten years, during which the faculty of language was abolished, and when all the other functions of the encephalon were intact; and a second period of eleven years, during which a paralysis of movement, at first partial, then absolutely complete, successively invaded the superior limb and the inferior limb of the right side.

Having said this, it is impossible [not] to recognize that there had been a correspondence between the two anatomical periods and the two symptomological periods. Nor to ignore that the cerebral convolutions are not motor organs. The striate body of the left hemisphere is therefore of all the organs damaged [léssé] the only one in which one can find the cause of the paralysis of the two right limbs, and the second clinical period, that in which motility was altered, corresponds also to the second anatomical period, that is to say, to that in which the softening, overflowing the limits of the frontal lobe, reached the insula and the striate body.

Thus, the first period of ten years, characterized clinically by the unique symptom of aphemia, must correspond to the phase [*époque*] in which in the lesion was still limited to the frontal lobe.

Up to now, given the parallel between lesions and symptoms, I have mentioned neither troubles of intelligence, nor of their anatomical cause. We have seen that the intelligence of our patient, perfectly preserved for a long time, declined notably beginning at a time [*époque*] that cannot be determined, and that it was seriously weakened when we observed it for the first time. We found, in the autopsy, alterations more than sufficient to explain this state. Three frontal convolutions of four were profoundly damaged to a considerable extent, nearly the whole frontal lobe was more or less softened; finally all the mass [p. 356] of the convolutions of the two hemispheres were atrophied, sunken, and sensibly softer than in the normal state. One can scarcely understand that the patient was able to retain any intelligence at all, and it does not seem probable that one could live very long with this kind of brain. I think, for my part, that the general softening of the left frontal lobe, the general atrophy of the two hemispheres, and the general chronic meningitis, did not appear at a time much in the past [ne remontaient pas à une époque fort reculée]; I am disposed to believe that these lesions came about a long time after the softening of the striate body, of the sort that one could subdivide the second period into two secondary periods, and in doing so, summarize the history of the patient.

	LESIONS	**SYMPTOMS**
First Period (ten years)	*Softening of one frontal convolution (probably the third)*	*Simple aphemia*
Second Period (eleven years)	*a. Propagation to the left striate body*	*Crossed paralysis of movement*
	b. Softening of the whole left frontal lobe; general atrophy of the hemispheres	*Weakening of intelligence*

Facts that, like these ones, are attached to grand questions of doctrine, cannot be presented in too much detail, nor discussed with too much care. I need this excuse to pardon myself for the aridity of the description and the length of the discussion. I now only have but a few more words to add to bring out the consequences of this study.

1st Aphemia, that is to say the loss of speech, before all other intellectual trouble and before all paralysis, was the consequence of a lesion of one of the anterior lobes of the brain.

2nd Our observations therefore confirm the opinion of Mr. Bouillaud, who places in these lobes the seat of the faculty of articulated language.

3rd The observations assembled up to now, those at least that are accompanied by a clear and precise anatomical description, are not numerous enough that one can consider this localization of a particular faculty in a lobe to be determined [p. 357] like a definitive demonstration, but one can consider it at least extremely probable.

4th It is a much more difficult question to know whether the faculty of articulated language depends on the anterior lobe considered as a whole, or especially on one of the convolutions of this lobe; to know, in other terms, if the localization of the cerebral faculties is arranged one faculty per convolution, or only by groups of faculties and groups of convolutions. More observations should be collected with the goal of resolving this question. We must indicate exactly the name and the row of the ill convolutions, and, if the lesion is very extensive, to determine, as far as possible, by anatomical examination, the point in the convolution where the illness seems to have started.

5th In our patient, the original seat of the lesion was in the second or the third frontal convolution, more probably in the latter. It is therefore possible that the faculty of articulated language resides in one or the other of these two convolutions; but one still cannot know, considering that the previous observations are mute on the state of each convolution in particular, and one cannot even predict, since the principle of localization by convolution still rests on no certain basis.

6th In any case, it suffices to compare our observations with those that have preceded them to dismiss today the idea that the faculty of articulated language resides at a fixed point, circumscribed, and situated under any bump of the skull; the lesions of aphemia have been found most often in the most anterior part of the frontal lobe, not far from the eyebrow, and above the orbital arch; whereas in my patient, they exist mostly in front, and much more near the coronal suture than near the sourciliary arcade. This difference of seats is incompatible with the system of bumps; it would be perfectly coincident, by contrast, with the system of localizations by convolution, since each of the three great convolutions of the superior layer of the frontal lobe travel successively, in its antero-posterior trajectory, to all the regions in which have been found up to now the lesions of aphemia. (Broca, 1861a; pp. 355–357; Green 2000)

LELONG

Very little is known about the man Monsieur Lelong. In November 1861, some seven months after he made his historic presentation to the Society of Anthropology in Paris, Broca made another presentation, this time a series of details on what was to become his second classic case. (Pearce, 2009). On this November day, M. Lelong was the focus of attention and this report augmented the first case Broca had made with the presentation of M. Leborgne. In another interesting intersection of French history, it was during this month that the famous French politician and eventual Premier Georges Clemenceau arrived in the Latin Quarter of Paris to begin study of medicine. Clemenceau was a 20-year-old at the time who would eventually become statesman, a major player in the Allied victory in World War I, and author of the Treaty of Versailles (Monnerville, 2012). Broca may well have had the opportunity to rub elbows with the student Clemenceau. As has been observed, the Latin Quarter was an interesting mix of politics and medicine at this time in history and perhaps Clemenceau was influenced by debates and political discussions by some of the freethinkers on the Medical School faculty.

Pearce (2009) reports that with this presentation of Lelong (Broca, 1861b) Broca coined the term "aphemia" (a = without, *phème* = voice) but in a reading of Broca's presentation of his first patient, M. Leborgne, one can find a rather lengthy discussion of "aphemia," as noted in the previous discussion of Broca's report of Leborgne (Broca, 1861a; Green, (2000).

The case of Lelong is not nearly as well known as that of "Tan" Leborgne. Lelong was described as an 84-year-old man who, in April 1860, had suddenly become unconscious and, although he partly recovered, continued to demonstrate a severe aphasia. In October 1861, M. Lelong suffered a fracture of the femur in a fall and was transferred to the surgical service, at the Bicêtre Hospital where he died 12 days later. Broca reported that Lelong had a limited vocabulary and was capable of uttering only five words:

◆ *"oui"*
◆ *"non"*
◆ *"toi"*

◆ *"toujours" and*
◆ *"Lelo"*

These five words were reported in translations of Broca's work as meaning: "yes'; "no"; a mispronunciation of "trois," meaning "three," which Lelong used for any number; "always," and a mispronunciation of "Lelong," his own name).

At autopsy, Lelong was found to have a lesion in the same region of the lateral left cerebral frontal lobe as that seen in Leborgne (Figure 10–9). Broca reported his findings from Lelong to the Anatomical Society of Paris, solidifying the clinicopathological evidence on the localization of speech in the frontal lobe (Broca, 1861b). He wrote:

> The integrity of the third frontal convolution (and perhaps of the second) seems indispensable to the exercise of the faculty

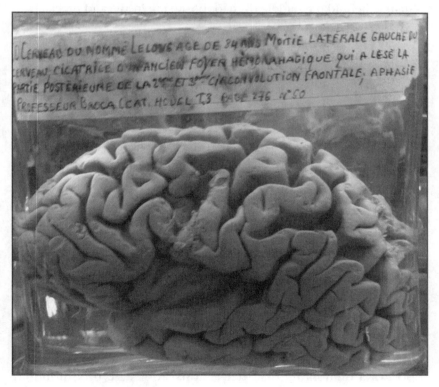

Figure 10–9. *Lelong's brain, Dupuytren Museum.*

of articulate language . . . I found that in my second patient, the lesion occupied exactly the same seat as with the first — immediately behind the middle third, opposite the insula and precisely on the same side.

Broca's somewhat tentative conclusions in his previous 1861 report on Leborgne were now not as tentative. He wrote:

I will not deny my surprise bordering on stupefaction when I found that in my second patient the lesion was rigorously occupying the same site as the first.

As in all the patients he examined, the right side of Lelong's brain was normal. At the meeting of the Anatomical Society, Broca stated:

The lesion occupied exactly the same seat as with the first — immediately behind the middle third, opposite the insula and precisely on the same side (Broca, 1861b).

After the presentation of these two cases in 1861 that set this historical year as a milestone in neuroscience, Broca continued to collect evidence and crystalized his views on the localization of speech in the brain in his brilliant review article of 1865. (Broca, 1865)

PICTURES AT AN EXHIBITION

Dronkers et al. (2007) conducted intriguing high resolution magnetic imaging of these two famous brains and presented interpretations particularly on the more extensive brain tissue that were damaged in these specimens. Lateral views of Lelong's brain are shown in figures below (panels C and D). The cortex is severely atrophied. The sylvian fissure has become so widened that the insula is, abnormally, almost completely exposed. Broca's writings indicate that Lelong had resided at the hospital for the 8 years previous to his stroke because of dementia. The report of a dementing disorder is consistent with the finding of atrophy in this brain of an 84-year-old.

Lelong's brain also shows evidence of a stroke that affected half of the pars opercularis in the posterior, inferior frontal gyrus, sparing the pars triangularis. Like Leborgne's lesion, Lelong's is also inconsistent with the location of Broca's area as it is defined today (Figure 10–10). In this case, the lesion actually spares the anterior portion of modern Broca's area. This is a significant finding as it implies that this second brain on which current theories of localization are based does not have a lesion encompassing the entire area we now call Broca's area. Thus, gross re-examination of these two important brains has revealed that the area defined by Broca as critical for articulation is not necessarily the same as the area currently described.

Dronker's et al. (2007), some 146 years after Broca's big year applied contemporary neuroimaging technology to these two famed brains of Leborgne and Lelong. As these authors stated, given the historical significance of Broca's original patients and the increasing reliance on Broca's area as a major speech center, it seemed important to re-inspect these brains to determine the precise location of their lesions as well as other possible areas of damage. They described the results of high resolution magnetic resonance imaging of the preserved brains of Broca's two patients in considerable detail. They reported that both patients' lesions extended significantly into medial regions of the brain, in addition to the surface damaged areas observed by Broca. Results also indicated inconsistencies between the area originally identified by Broca and what is now called Broca's area, a finding with significant ramifications for both lesion and functional neuroimaging studies of this well-known brain area (Dronkers et al., 2007). Others have used neuroimaging as well to explore these brains that have rested in the Dupuytren unmolested for all those years (Signoret, Castaigne, Lhermitte, Abelanet, & Lavorel, 1984). The findings of lesions that are a bit more extensive and deeper than Broca's early descriptions are not surprising.

Though this study applied some clarity to the role of Broca's area (or the convolution, as Broca was inclined to call it prior to its epononymous subsequesnt labeling), Dronker's et al. (2007) nor Signoret et al. (1984) did not denigrate the original findings of Broca. As they remarked, though the contemporary neuroimaging findings provided additional anatomical information, they by no means detract from Broca's extraordinary discovery.

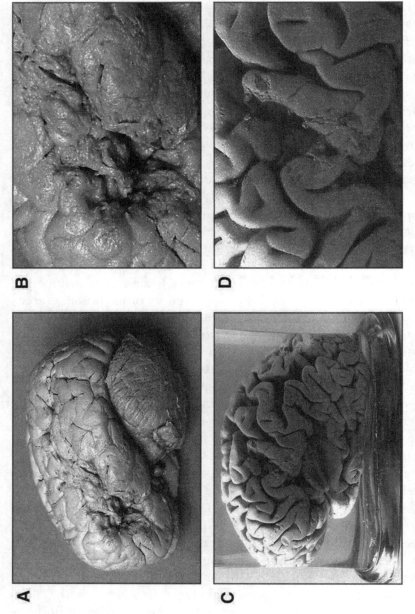

Figure 10–10. Leborgne's and Lelong's preserved brains. From Dronkers (2007). Used with permission.

Because Broca chose not to slice the brains, he could not have known the extent of underlying damage in his patients and the role it might play in their disorders of communication. Broca apparently understood the lesion extended subcortically in Leborgne, but could not determine how medially or posteriorly it stretched. Broca wrote that Leborgne's malady was progressive with the aphemia being the earliest and most permanent deficit. As the most apparent damage was in the inferior frontal convolution, Broca concluded that this area was the first affected and thus the cause of the disorder of aphemia or as Broca characterized it, disordered articulate speech. This conclusion (according to Dronkers et al., 2007) was consistent with neurological theory of his time, and Broca had little reason to consider other areas as the source of the speech and/or language disorder. Neuroimaging was quite a way down the historical path and still photography itself as just making its mark on the landscape.

In Broca's time, even still photography was a novelty. The American Civil War became a great milestone of photography and Mathew B. Brady secured permission from Lincoln to follow the Union troops in what was expected to be a short and glorious war (Metmuseum, 2012). A cadre of photographers took startling pictures of camp sites, troop assemblies, war commanders, and mud-covered grunts in the field (Figure 10–11). The public greedily devoured the published pictures, especially the images of the wounded with their stumps and missing eyes, much like the frenzy over today's tabloids, and helped popularize the emerging discipline of photography.

The war photographers worked with collodion-on-glass (wet-plate) negatives, which required brittle and laborious procedures even in the studio. When the shutterbug was ready for action, a sheet of glass was cleaned, coated with collodion, partially dried, dipped carefully into a bath containing silver nitrate, then exposed in the camera for several seconds and processed in the field darkroom tent—all before the silver collodion mixture had the time to dry. Given the danger of their situation and the technical difficulty of their task, front-line photographers rarely if ever attempted action scenes (Metmuseum, 2012).

French photography was evolving at the same time as the Civil War boost and perhaps at a faster clip. This allowed not

Figure 10–11. *Civil War photography. Wikimedia Commons, public domain. http:// www.radio1.si/strani/Oddaje.aspx?ID=10174&LNK=3*

only the historic portraits we now have of Broca and his contemporaries, but also the burgeoning contributions to medicine and the arts, including applications of neuroimaging such as that employed by Dronkers et al. (2007). Now these advances in photography and cinematography could revisit the deeper lesions of Leborgne and Lelong and clarify some of the observations made by Broca. Within a quarter-century of its birth and refinement in the mid-1800s, photography had established a ubiquitous presence in society and mushroomed into everyday society just as the internet has in contemporary times (Daniel, 2004)

Though it may not play as extensive a role as once thought, Broca's area or Broca's Convolution (as it was called in many post-1861 references) is certainly involved in the execution of articulatory movements. Perhaps other aspects of "articulated speech" are enfolded into Broca's early conceptualization of aphemia and the arguments persist to this day as to exactly what Broca meant by the term aphemia. Is it merely elements of motoric articulation? Is it schema and motoric planning of articulatory patterns? Is it phonological processing and incorporation of the grammar and rules of producing speech sounds? Is it a more linguistic manipulation of the grammar and rules of lexical-semantic and syntactic operations? Is it speech? Is it language? Is it both? Is it gray-zone cake batter with a mix of dry and wet ingredients that can never be accurately parsed once it is mixed? The arguments persist. Perhaps brilliant images will help us unravel these mysteries.

BROCA ON LANGUAGE, ARTICULATED SPEECH, AND APHEMIA

The disorders enfolded in the questions above have been in the vortex of 150 years of terminological and linguistic-vertiginous confusion. It was not much different in 1861. The debates have rolled on and nearly every conference, convention, or academy of neurologists, neurolinguists, or speech-language pathologists who gather over the delicate cubes of orange cheese on toothpicks are seemingly bound to introduce the deep and abiding questions on the nature and characteristics of apraxia of speech, phonological disruption in aphasia, or Broca's aphasia. This campfire was re-lighted in 1968 when Fred Darley, the eminent speech-language pathologist at the Mayo Clinic in Rochester, Minnesota, presented a paper alluding to 107 years of terminological confusion about the disorder (Darley, 1968). Darley presented his views on this, and introduced the new term "apraxia of speech" at this meeting and subsequent gatherings at the Academy of Aphasia and other meetings of clinical and scientific minds. Much confusion has arisen about exactly what Broca was describing in his detailed observations of Leborgne and Lelong. By today's standards and definitions, some agreement is reached that particularly Leborgne presented very little speech and language by which to judge the exact nature of his disorders. Perhaps "global aphasia" is a more accurate description by today's understanding of the disorders, but certainly by Broca's descriptions we can infer that M. Leborgne also presented a limited corpus of output that resembled what today we might describe as apraxia of speech. Broca was not unaware of these differences and subtleties of verbal output. In fact he discussed the nature of language, aphemia, and disrupted "articulated speech" at some length in the precursor to his presentation of Leborgne. Thanks to the excellent translations of Green (2000), and with his gracious permission, we are able to access the words of Broca and determine for ourselves what his views were on language, aphemia, articulate speech, and the other concepts that have entangled these discussions. Here is Broca's take on "terminological confusion" from his own article in 1861 (Broca, 1861c). Green's pagination in the extracted translation refers to the page number in Broca's original article (Appendix A).

There are, in effect, several species of language. Any system of signs permitting the expression of ideas in a manner more or less intelligible, more or less complete, more or less rapid, is a language in the most general sense of the word: thus speech, mimicry, typing [dactylologie], picture writing [l'écriture figurative], phonetic writing, etc., are all species of language.

There is a general faculty of language that presides over all these modes of the expression of thought, and it may be defined: the faculty of establishing a constant relation between an idea and a sign, whether this sign be a sound, a gesture, a figure, or any other trace. Moreover, each species of language necessitates the play of certain organs of emission and reception. The organs of reception are sometimes the ear, sometimes sight, sometimes even touch. As for the organs of emission, they are put in play by the voluntary muscles, like those of the larynx, or the tongue, of the soft palate [voile du palais], of the face, the upper limbs, etc. All regular language supposes therefore the integrity, (1) of a certain number of muscles, of the motor nerves that serve them, and the part of the central nervous system from which these nerves arise; (2) of a certain external sensory apparatus, of the sensory nerve that departs from these, and of the part of the central nervous system to which this nerve connects; (3) finally, the part of the brain that holds under its dependence the general faculty of language, such as we have come to define it.

The absence or abolition of this last faculty renders impossible all species of language. Congenital or accidental lesions of the organs of reception and the organs of emission can deprive us of the particular species of language that these organs contribute;

but if the general language faculty persists in us with a sufficient degree of intelligence, we can still compensate with another species of language for those we have lost. [p. 332]

The pathological causes that deprive us of a medium of communication ordinarily make us lose only half of it, because it is quite rare that the organs of emission and the organs of reception would be affected at the same time. For example, the adult who becomes deaf continues to express himself through speech, but for him to transmit an idea he uses a different language, such as gesture or writing. The inverse takes place when paralysis strikes the speech muscles; the ill person to whom we address ourselves in articulated language, responds to us then in another language. It is in this way that diverse systems of communication can be mutually compensatory.

This is only elementary physiology; but pathology permits us to push the analysis further on to that which concerns articulated language, which is the most important and probably the most complex of all.

There are cases where the general language faculty persists unaltered, where the auditory apparatus is intact, where all the muscles, not even excepting those of the voice and those of articulation, obey the will, and yet where a cerebral lesion abolishes articulated language. This abolition of speech, in individuals who are neither paralyzed nor idiots, constitutes a symptom so singular that it seems to me useful to designate it with a special name. I will give it, therefore, the name of aphemia (I speak, I pronounce); it is only the faculty of articulating words that these patients lack. They hear and comprehend all that one says to them; they all have their intelligence; they emit vocal sounds with ease; they execute with their tongue and their lips movements much more extensive and energetic than those required for the articulation of sounds, and yet the perfectly sensible response that they would want to make is reduced to a very small number of articulated sounds, always the same and always performed in the same manner; their vocabulary, if [one] can call it that, is composed of a short series of syllables, sometimes of a monosyllable that expresses everything, or rather that expresses nothing, for this unique word is most often a stranger to all vocabularies. Certain ill people have not even a vestige of articulate language; they make vain efforts without pronouncing a single syllable. Others have, in some sense, two degrees of articulation. In [p. 333] ordinary circumstances, they invariably pronounce their word of choice [prédilection]; but, when they have an angry outburst, they become able to articulate a second word, most often a coarse swearword, with which they were probably familiar before their sickness, then they stop after the latter effort. Mr. Auburtin has observed a patient who is still alive and who does not need to be excited to utter a stereotyped curse. All his responses start with a bizarre word of six syllables and invariably end with this supreme invocation: Sacred name of G . . .

Those who have for the first time studied these strange happenings have been able to believe, due to an [in-?]sufficient analysis, that the faculty of language, in similar cases, was abolished; but it obviously persists in its entirety, since these ill people perfectly comprehend articulated language and written language; since these who do not know how or are not able to write have enough intelligence (and it is mistaken in many similar cases) to find the means to communicate their thought, and since finally those who are literate, and who have the free use of their hands, clearly put their ideas on paper. They know therefore the sense and the value of words, in auditory form just as in graphic form. Articulated language that they could once speak is always familiar to them, but they cannot execute the series of methodical and coordinated movements that correspond to the searched-for syllable. This which has died in them [péri en eux], it is not therefore the faculty of language, it is not the memory for words, nor is it the action of the nerves and muscles corresponding to phonation [phonation] and to articulation, it is something else, it is a faculty particularly considered by Mr. Bouillaud as the faculty that coordinates the proper movements of articulated language, or more simply as the faculty of articulated language, since without it there is no articulation possible.

The nature of this faculty and the place that it must be assigned in the cerebral hierarchy can give rise to some hesitation. Is it only a species of memory, and the individuals who have lost it have lost only, not the memory of words, but memory for the procedure that must be followed to articulate words? Have they come to this by a condition comparable to that of a young child who already understands the language of those around him, who is sensitive to blame and praise, who points out with his fingers all the [p. 334] objects that he can name, who has acquired a crowd [foule] of simple ideas, and who, to express these, can do no more than stammer out a single syllable? Little by little, after innumerable efforts, he succeeds in articulating a few new syllables. Yet still he arrives so often at a mistake, saying, for example, papa when he wanted say mama, because at the moment of pronunciation of the latter word he no longer remembers the position that must be given to his tongue and to his lips. Soon he knows quite well the mechanism of some simple and easy syllables so that he can pronounce them at every attempt without error and without hesitation; but he hesitates and again makes mistakes on more complicated and more difficult syllables, and when finally he possesses much practical experience with [la practique de] many monosyllables, he needs to acquire new experience to learn to pronounce rapidly [passer tout à coup] one syllable after another, and to pronounce, in the place of the doubled monosyllables that constituted his first vocabulary, words composed of two or three different syllables. These gradual perfections of articulated language in children are due to the development of a particular species of memory that is not the memory for words, but that of the movements necessary to articulate words. And this particular memory is not related [en rapport] to other kinds of memory nor to the rest of intelligence. I knew a child of three years whose intelligence and will was above that of his age, who had a well-formed tongue, and who still did not know how to talk. I know another very intelligent child who, at the age of twenty-one months, perfectly understands two languages, who, as a consequence, possesses the highest degree of memory for words, and who up to this point, is not able to rise above the level of pronouncing monosyllables.

If adults who lose speech have only forgotten the art of articulation, if they have simply reverted [revenus] to the condition where they were before having learned to pronounce words, we must place [ranger] the faculty of which the illness has deprived them into the order of intellectual faculties. This hypothesis seems to me quite likely. It might be possible, however, that it is otherwise, and that aphemia is the result of a locomotor ataxia limited to the part of the central nervous apparatus that presides over movements governing the articulation of sounds. One objects, it is true, that these ill people can freely [p. 335] execute with their tongue and their lips all the movements other than those of articulation; that they can immediately move, when asked, the point of their tongue upwards, downwards, to the right, to the left, etc.; but these movements, precise as they may seem to us, are infinitely less so than the excessively delicate movements that are required for speech. In locomotor ataxia of the limbs, one observes that the patients voluntarily execute all the large movements: if one tells them to lift their hand, to open it, to close it, they do it almost always without hesitation; but when they want to execute more precise movements, to seize, for example, in a certain manner, an object of small volume, they go beyond or stay behind the goal; they do not know how to coordinate the contraction of their muscles in a manner to obtain a result of determined value, and they make mistakes much less in the direction of their movements than in the quantity of force that they have to deploy and in the order of succession of partial movements of which the grasping of objects is composed. One can therefore ask if aphemia is not one species of locomotor ataxia limited to the muscles for the articulation of sound, and, if it were so, the faculty that the ill people have lost would not be an intellectual faculty, that is to say a faculty belonging to the thinking part of the brain, it would be only a particular case of the general faculty of coordination of muscular action, a faculty that depends on the motor parts of the nerve centers.

One can therefore make at least two hypotheses about the nature of the special faculty of articulated language. In the first hypothesis, there would be a superior faculty, and aphemia would be an intellectual trouble; in the second hypothesis, it would be a faculty of a much less elevated order, and aphemia would be no more than a trouble of locomotion. Though the latter interpretation appears to me much less probable than the other, I would not yet dare to commit myself in a categorical manner if I were reduced to only the lights of clinical observation.

Whatever it might be, on the account of functional analysis, the existence of the special faculty of articulated language, such as that I have defined, cannot be placed in doubt, because a faculty that can perish alone, without those that are nearest to it being [p. 336] altered, is obviously a faculty independent of all the others, that is to say a special faculty.

If all the cerebral faculties were as distinct, as clearly circumscribed as this one, one would finally have a positive point of departure to enter upon the question so controversial as cerebral localization. It is unfortunate that this is not so, and that the greatest obstacle to progress in this part of physiology comes from the insufficiency and uncertainty of the functional analysis that must necessarily precede research on the organs related to each function.

Science is so little advanced on this point that it still has not even found its foundation, and what is in dispute today is not such-and-such phrenological system, but the very principle of localization, that is to say the prior question is knowing whether all parts of the brain that are concerned with thought have identical attributes or different attributes.

A communication of Mr. Gratiolet relevant to the cerebral and intellectual similarity of the human races, has, on several occasions, detained the Anthropological Society of Paris to examine this important question, and Mr. Auburtin, partisan of the principle of localization, has thought, with good reason, that the localization of a single faculty suffices to establish the truth of this principle; he has, therefore, sought to demonstrate, according to the doctrine of his teacher Mr. Bouillaud, that the faculty of articulated language resides in the frontal lobes of the brain.

For this, he first reviewed a series of cases in which a spontaneous cerebral event had abolished the faculty of articulated language without destroying the other cerebral faculties, and in which at autopsy a deep lesion was found in the frontal convolutions of the brain. The special nature of the symptom of aphemia did not depend on the nature of the illness, but only on its location [siège], since the lesion was sometimes a softening, sometimes apoplexy, sometimes an abscess or a tumor. To complete his demonstration, Mr. Auburtin invoked another series of cases where aphemia was the consequence of a traumatic lesion of the frontal lobes of the brain; these facts, following him, the equivalent of vivisections, and he ended by saying that to his knowledge no one has ever found the frontal lobes of the brain in a state of complete [p. 337] integrity, nor even in a state of relative integrity, at the autopsy of individuals who have lost the faculty of articulated language without losing the rest of their intelligence.

Some have opposed him with many remarkable facts relevant to individuals who had spoken right up to the last day, and yet in whom the frontal lobes of the brain had been the seat of deep spontaneous or traumatic lesions; but he responded that this proves nothing, that a lesion, even widespread, of the frontal lobes might not reach the part of the lobes where resides [siége] the faculty of articulated language, that the objection would only be valid if all the frontal convolutions had been destroyed on both sides to their full extent, that is to say up to the sulcus [sillon] of Rolando, and that, in the cases opposed to him, the destruction of the convolutions had been only partial. He therefore recognized that a lesion of the frontal lobes does not necessarily lead to a loss of speech, but he maintained that the latter is the certain sign of the former, that it permits such a diagnosis; that the diagnosis has been made many times during life, and has never been refuted [démenti] by autopsy; finally, after having cited the observation of a still-living individual who presents for many years in a most clean manner, the symptoms of aphemia, and who is actually at the hospice for Incurables, he declared that would renounce without reversion [retour] the doctrine of Mr. Bouillaud, if the autopsy of this ill person did not confirm the diagnosis of a cerebral lesion occupying exclusively or principally the frontal lobes. (see Bulletin de la Société d'anthropologie, 1. II, meeting of 4 April, 1861.)

I believe I should summarize in a few words this discussion to make salient the interest and the actuality of the observation that I am presenting today to the Anatomical Society. Without doubt, the value of facts is not limited [subordonnée] to the circumstances of the milieu in which we observe them; but the impression that they make on us depends on them in great part, and when, a few days after having heard the argument of Mr. Auburtin, I found one morning, in my care [service], a dying person who for twenty-one years had lost the faculty of articulated language, I collected with the greatest care observations from him, which seemed to come expressly to serve as a touch stone [pierre de touche] for the theory supported by my colleague. [p. 338]

Up to here, without rejecting the theory, and without ignoring as nothing the importance of the facts that are favorable to it, I had felt much hesitation in the presence of the contradictory facts that exist in science. Though a partisan of the principle of localization, I would ask myself, and I ask myself still, within what limits this principle is applicable. There is a point that appears to me to be pretty nearly established by comparative anatomy, by the anatomical and physiological parallel of the human races, and finally by the comparison of the varieties of normal individuals, abnormal or pathological men of the same race; to know that the highest cerebral faculties, those that constitute the understanding properly so-called, like judgment, reflection, the faculties of comparison and abstraction, have their seat in the frontal convolutions, while the convolutions of the temporal, parietal, and occipital lobes are involved with [affectées aux] the sentiments, the dispositions [penchants], and the passions. In other terms, there is in the mind [esprit] groups of faculties, and in the brain, groups of convolutions; and the facts acquired up to now by science permit us to accept, like I have said elsewhere, that the large regions of the mind [esprit] correspond to the large regions of the brain. It is in this sense that the principle of localization seems to me, if not [sinon] rigorously demonstrated, at least extremely probable. But to know with certainty whether each particular faculty has its own seat in a particular convolution, this is a question that seems to me all but insoluble in the current state of science.

The study of the facts relevant to the loss of the faculty of articulated language is one those that has the most chance of leading us to a positive or negative solution. The independence of this faculty is evinced by pathological observation, and though one can raise some doubts about its nature, though one can ask oneself, as has been seen above, if it is part of the intellectual functions or of the cerebral functions that are involved [en rapport] with muscular activity, it is allowable to place it, at least provisionally, in the purview of the first hypothesis, which already, at first glance, seems the most probable, and in favor of that which the pathological anatomy of aphemia establishes strong presumptions. In effect, in all the cases where up to now the autopsy has been able to be undertaken, one has found the substance of the convolutions [p. 339] profoundly altered to a notable extent; in a few subjects the lesion spread exclusively over the convolutions where it is permitted to conclude that the faculty of articulated language is one of the functions of the convoluted mass. Now, one admits generally that all the faculties we call intellectual have their seat in this part of the brain, and it seems from that strongly probable that reciprocally all the faculties that reside in the cerebral convolutions are faculties of the intellectual order.

In placing ourselves, then, in this point view, we easily recognize that the pathological anatomy of aphemia can give something more than a solution to one particular question, and that it can throw a great deal of light on the general question of cerebral localization, by furnishing to cerebral physiology a point of departure, or rather a very precious point of comparison. If it were proven, for example, that aphemia can be the result of lesions affecting indifferently in any convolution and in any cerebral lobe, one would have the right to conclude not only that the faculty of articulated language is not localized, but also that very probably the other faculties of the same order are not localized either. If it were demonstrated on the contrary that the lesions that abolish speech consistently occupy one determinate convolution, one could hardly fail to admit that this convolution is the seat of the faculty of articulated language, and, that once the existence of a first localization was admitted, the principle of localization by convolutions would be established. Finally, between these two extreme alternatives, there is a third that could lead to a mixed doctrine. Let us suppose, in effect, that the lesions of aphemia consistently occupy the same cerebral lobe, but that, in this lobe, they do not consistently occupy the same convolution; it would result that the faculty of articulated language would have its seat in a certain region, in a certain group of convolutions, but not in a particular convolution, and it would become very probable that the cerebral faculties are localized by regions, and not by convolutions.

It is important [importe], therefore, to study with the greatest care a special question that can have doctrinal consequences so general [p. 340] and so important. It is not only a matter of looking in which regions of the brain are located [siégent] the lesions of aphemia; one must as well designate by name and by row the affected [malades] convolutions and the degree of alteration of each. This is not how we have proceeded up to now. We have confined ourselves, in the most complete observations, to saying that the lesion began and finished so many centimeters from the frontal extremity of the hemisphere, so many centimeters from the great central fissure [scissure] or from the Sylvian fissure. But that is completely insufficient, because, given these indications, meticulous as they are, the reader cannot guess which is the affected convolution. Thus, there are cases where the illness is situated in the most frontal part of the hemisphere; others where it is situated 5 or even 8 centimeters behind this point, and it seems, given this, that the seat of the lesion might be very variable; but if one imagines [songe] that the three antero-posterior convolutions of the convexity of the frontal lobe begin at the level of the sourciliary arcade and run side by side, front to back, all three flowing into the frontal transverse convolution that forms the anterior side of the sulcus [sillon] of Rolando; if one imagines that this sulcus is situated more than 4 centimeters behind the coronal suture[1], and [p. 341] that the three frontal antero-posterior convolutions occupy more than two-fifths of the total length of the brain,—one will understand that the same convolution is able to be reached by lesions situated in points very different and very distant from each other. It is therefore, much less important to indicate the level of damage [mal] than to say which convolutions are ill.

Broca's words are testament to the idea that he had given considerable thought to these neverlands of speech production. Others continue to grapple with these concepts to this day. In a cogent Letter-to-the-Editor in the journal *Brain*, Bonilha and Fridriksson (2009) comment on the persisting debate about the role of Broca's area in nonfluent speech production. They interpret some of the conclusions of the work by Dronkers (1996) and Dronkers et al. (2007) and state:

> This timely examination by Dronkers et al. combines a historical perspective and the current debate regarding the critical lesion location associated with non-fluent speech. In an earlier study employing lesion mapping in chronic stroke patients, Dronkers (1996) suggested that damage to the left anterior insula, but not to Broca's area, is the crucial lesion location associated with non-fluent speech. Until then, Broca's initial findings were largely undisputed by tangible evidence. These observations, however, were contrasted in a controlled study by Hillis and colleagues (2004) which investigated acute patients and observed that, indeed, Broca's area, as opposed to left anterior insular damage, is strongly associated with non-fluent speech. In support of these findings, numerous studies utilizing functional MRI in normal participants have demonstrated a strong relationship between Broca's area activity and speech production (Bonilha et al.,2006; Ozdemir et al., 2006; Guenther et al., 2006).
>
> In conclusion, in accordance with Dronkers et al. findings, we suggest that Broca's area is crucial for speech production, while its disconnection (e.g. at the level of the anterior insula) from the posterior language areas may also result in non-fluent speech. The integrity of the insular white matter and of the connections between the superior temporal cortex and the inferior frontal area is crucial for speech production. (Bonilha & Fridriksson, 2009, pp. 1–2)

Fridriksson and colleagues continue their pursuit of refined understanding of Broca's famous convolution with the remarkable advances in technology and neuroimaging. When these tools are used cautiously and appropriately, and when sampling is substantiated to represent the whole, we can expect value-added clarity and focus to our understanding of the cortical localization of communication, just as the photographers of the 1860s preserved images for enriched forward movement in science and art. The use of neuroimaging in human communication is summarized in a chapter by Fridriksson entitled "Neuroimaging and Brain-Based Communication Disorders" (2011). Prior to the advent of the CT scan and its following refinements of seeing the brain in vivo, Broca's autopsy observation was the method of choice for determining localization of behavioral functions in the brain. The methods continue to be refined and the next decade may hold strategies for determining the location of speech in the brain that we cannot even imagine in this second decade of the 21st century.

Neuroimaging has created tunnels of light in our understanding, but it too is evolving. One cannot assign too much blame to understanding or practices that were common before clinical and scientific breakthroughs turned into preferred practice. One only has to view the old time photographs and paintings of surgeons in less than sterile conditions to appreciate how changes can affect the clinical science. Lister came along as the "father of surgical antisepsis" and dramatic changes were made in surgical and infectious outcomes. Prior to Lister the state of medical science was comfortable with surgeons conducting procedures with bare, unwashed hands, sandwiches, and dangling cigars.

Although neither the conception of a faculty of articulate language nor even the notion of its localization in the anterior portion of the brain were especially novel in 1861, what Broca provided was a research finding and a research method (clinico-pathological inference) that galvanized scientific opinion on the localization hypothesis. Controversy would follow the celebrity of Broca's reports and arguments about the role of the third frontal convolution and even the name of the disorder would bubble for years to follow (Marie, 1906). The detail of Broca's account, the fact that he had gone specifically in search of evidence for the patients' speech loss rather than employing cases post hoc as support for localization, his use of the pathological rather than the phrenology craniological method, his focus on the convolutional topography of the cerebral hemispheres, and, perhaps most importantly, the fact that the time was ripe for such a demonstration, all contributed to the instantaneous sensation created by Broca's findings (Pearce, 2009). The march of science and the sophistication of scientific toys proceeds as it has and as it will. Milestones will be marked as science marches, however, and Broca's cogent descriptions of the man who could only say "tan" will retain its historic luster and its place in the chronological account of the past.

PRECEDENCE AND THE PAIR A DAX

Marc Dax was another French neurologist (1771–1837) whose work has created somewhat of a tempest in a teapot about precedence of who first noted that loss of speech was associated with the left hemisphere of the cerebral cortex. His paper is associated with a presentation in the year 1836, some 25 years before Broca's 1861 paper. The year, 1836, also marks the death of another notable personality. On July 10, 1836, exactly 104 years before the birth of Rosenbek and Arlo Guthrie, the papers of Paris carried the news of the death of another of France's savants or great scientists, André-Marie Ampère. This is the year that Marc Dax was alleged to have gathered in a paper, his thoughts on cortical localization of language and the brain. Ampère was a famed mathemetician and physicist who discovered and amplified theories of electromagnetism. The measurement of electrical current, the ampere, of course, is named after him. His name, and the name of Broca and 70 other eminent French savants (including Coulomb, Daguerre, and Fourier) is engraved in cast iron on the Eiffel Tower. This bit of perhaps not so trivial French history is a morsel that most tourists who gaze at the Tower overlook. Few of the estimated 175 couples per day who engage wedding proposals at the foot of the Tower are likely to look up and notice the names of the famous. Broca's name is among the 72, but much to the dismay of a few historians, the name Dax is missing.

Marc Dax (1771–1837) is sometimes attributed to discovering the link between neurological damage to the left hemisphere, right-sided hemiplegia, and a loss of the ability to produce and comprehend speech and language (aphasia). His contributions have engendered a good deal of speculation and some outright frustration about his place in history. Dax is reported to have submitted his discovery, based on the observations of three patients in Montpellier, to the French Academy of Sciences and two previous notes were allegedly published in 1836, a quarter of a century before Paul Broca's more recognized description. Montpellier actually was the seat of considerable medical science and research. Its importance can be traced throughout publications of the National Biblioteque in France and also has been called to my attention by my friend and fellow historian Hugh Buckingham. He forwarded a citation of a work by Williams (1996) that tracks some of the important contributions of this medical university town in the far south of France. In addition to the Dax clan, Montpellier was the one-time location of students Rabelais and Nostradamus, so has enjoyed its share of controversial personalities. This is not the only time Buckingham has unearthed previously unrecognized contributors to neuroscience. He pointed me to one W. Moxon's 1866 writing "On the connection between loss of speech and paralysis of the right side" as exemplified in an essay entitled "Moxon and the Flying Trapeze," originally published in the *Journal of Medical Speech-Language Pathology* and reprinted in a collection of essays (LaPointe, 2010b).

The papers of Dax were titled, *"Observations Tending to Prove the Constant Coincidence of Disturbances of Speech with a Lesion of the Left Hemisphere of the Brain,"* and *"Lesions of the Left Half of the Encephalon Coincident with the Forgetting of Signs of Thinking"* (Dax, M. 1863; Dax, G. 1863). Marc Dax died one year later in 1837 and was not around for all of the debate and excitement of 1861 but his son was to exhume his paper perhaps from under the socks and underwear in his bedroom bureau. His attributed discovery remained obscure until Dax, *fils* came along.

In 1863, Gustave Dax, the proud son of Marc Dax, revivified and published his father's work on the subject. This was after the considerable flurry of attention caused by the pioneering presentations of Paul Broca's patients Leborgne and Lelong two years earlier to the *Société d'Anthropologie*. This new Dax publication included the 1836 memoir of Marc Dax, his deceased father, and additional clinical annotations of his own on 140 patients. His contributions are reported to have received a negative appraisal by the Academy, however, and Gustave Dax was overlooked by the scientific establishment of the time. The medical historians Cubelli and Montagna (1984), H. Buckingham (1981, 2006), S. Finger (2000, 2009), Finger and Roe (1996, 1999), M. Critchley (1964), and A. L. Benton (1984) were responsible for bringing to light the role and importance of the Daxes for neuroscience in a number of papers. Some continue to argue for recognition of the Daxes, or at least further investigation of it. As Buckingham

(2006) reports, it was not until 1865 that Broca clearly, non-hesitatingly, and unambiguously claimed that the faculty was in the *left* hemisphere as opposed to vague and bi-hemispheric assumptions earlier. Buckingham (2006), detailed some of the activities of Gustave Dax, who claimed that six weeks before Broca's paper appeared, he had published the paper he claimed his father had written in 1836. In 1863, in fact, Gustave (Buckingham may be on a first name basis with the Daxes) had submitted his (Gustave's) long monograph on aphemia, integrating what he claimed to be his father's 1836 pronouncement along with some of his own data. G. Dax sent this communication to the French Academy of Sciences and to the French Academy of Medicine and heard nothing back from either academy. After waiting two years, he managed to publish his material. Gustave's valiant move to promote his father's priority for one of the most significant conclusions in the history of the neurosciences is a lesson in frustration. Buckingham suggests that Broca's attitude towards Gustave's case was disarmingly nonchalant and that the issue deserves further historical inquiry (Buckingham, 2006). If it wasn't published, it didn't exist is the attitude that some historians have taken about the Dax manuscript that laid inactive for all those years.

Despite the postclimactic ejaculation of the Daxes, Broca continues to be recognized as the one force that carried the world's attention to speech and brain. As historians continue to dig from the archives of history even earlier vague and imprecise references to hemispheric specialization and cortical localization will no doubt surface. These revelations of priority and precedence can only amplify the detail and regard of Broca's work.

MUCH EARLIER PRECEDENCE ON HEMISPHERIC SPECIALIZATION AND LOCALIZATION

Assiduous historical reading has uncovered several much earlier sources of discussion on the nature of hemispheric specialization. Lokhorst (1996) has written about these cloudy days of historical precedence and purports to unveil references to pre-19th century insinuations to the role of the hemispheres, though not necessarily regarding lateralization of speech functions. Nevertheless, assertions and documentation by Lokhorst reveal considerable discussion, much of it speculative and inaccurate relative to present day knowledge of anatomy and physiology. Some of these early conceptualizations about the human body are curious and absurd by today's standards, but once again, we must be tolerant with practices that preceeded the advance and evolution of science.

Lokhorst has uncovered a medieval codex that speaks to the issue. The codex was the predecessor to the modern day book and was a collection of pages bound together and usually graced with a protective cover of some sort. The codex took the place of scrolls in the evolution of the book (Roberts & Skeat, 1983). Ancient and pre-Gutenburg codices were hand-written by scribes. The codex held significant hands-on advantages (literally) over other book formats. A codex was compact, sturdy, and allowed random access, as opposed to a scroll, which necessitated sequential access. Modern books have many similarities to the codex, but the evolution of the book from stone tablets, papyrus, vellum (calfskin), scrolls, and eventually the post printing press codex marks a significant path of the transmission of understanding and knowledge. We are at another historic milestone in the evolution of the book as electronic tablets and other forms are generating the nooks and kindles of ever encroaching change in our reading habits. The scholarly study of codex manuscripts from the point of view of the bookbinding craft is called codicology (Roberts & Skeat, 1983).

Lokhorst (1996) has scoured scrolls and codices and has modified some of his earlier ideas about ancient and medieval references to brains and lobes and special functions. As he reports, "Until recently, histories of hemispheric specialization invariably asserted that there are no publications in this field from before 1800. However, in 1981 I happened to notice a much older theory. It is preserved in a codex from about 1100 and it probably dates from classical antiquity. Some classical philologists already knew about this theory, but they had largely kept this knowledge to themselves. I published some articles about the theory and it has by now reached the standard literature about the history of hemispheric specialization.

"The reason that I want to discuss it again is that I have come to drastically different conclusions regarding the authorship, the dating, and the interpretation of the theory than I have put forward before" (Lokhorst, 1996, p. 295).

The text that I discuss is still the only pre-1800 text about hemispheric specialization which has come to light. The only other passage which comes anywhere close is to be found on a drawing from about 1410. It reads as follows:

> The forthyr parte of the brayn is hoot ande drye, the medyl parte hoot ande moyste, the hyndyr parte colde ande moyste, the rygth syde hoot ande dry, the leyfte syde colde ande dry. (Lokhorst, 1996, p. 296)

The reanalyzed medieval codex according to Lokhorst (1996) adds a few rays of light on the problem of precedence of hemispheric specialization. As Lokhorst reports:

> The theory in question [of pre-19th century hemispheric specialization] is to be found in an anonymous medical treatise which nowadays bears the title *De semine* (On sperm). This treatise has only been preserved in manuscript no. 1342-50 of the Royal Library at Brussels (folio 48r-52v). This codex probably dates from the end of the eleventh century or the beginning of the twelfth century. (Lokhorst, 1996, p. 297)

The unknown author of this medieval codex places considerable emphasis on *pneuma* or the transfer of spirits or air throughout the body. The codex author writes that these spirits and air are taken not only by the lungs but by the pores on the skin. As this codex author states, "these pores vary with the senses, which accounts for the differences between the senses. If the pores of the skin had the same diameter as those of the eyes, we would see with our whole body. The finest channels are the best conveyors of the perceptive faculty because they allow the least admixture of air; this explains why the eye is the most acute sensory organ. Sensation arises not only in the heart but also in the brain." (Lokhorst, 1996, p. 301).

Next is the part of the medieval codex that Lokhorst interprets as referring to specialization of hemispheric functions.

He says that phrenitis is caused by an inflammation of the heart and a suffocation of the innate heat, on the basis of which the brain provides sensation and intellect. That with which we understand is namely different from that with which we perceive. There are accordingly two brains in the head. The one gives us our intellect, the other provides the faculty of perception. That is to say: the brain on the right side is the one that perceives, whereas the left brain is the one which understands. As a result of this, this is also being done by the heart, which lies under the latter organ, and which is also continually vigilant, hearing and understanding, because it too has ears to hear. (Lockhorst, 1996 p. 302)

The medieval codex references to precedence of hemispheric specialization have not achieved a consenual following among historians. As Lokhorst himself has remarked,

Much can be said to detract from the value of the theory about hemispheric specialization in the *De semine*: it is false when taken literally, it does not seem to be based on cogent arguments or acute observations, and it did not have any influence as far as we know. All this does not, however, make it any less remarkable. Many centuries were to pass before the concept of functional cerebral asymmetry was again brought up. The theory described in the Brussels codex is therefore still a striking instance of being (more or less) right for the wrong reasons. (Lokhorst, 1996, p. 312)

Despite the seemingly never-ending arguments of precedence and priority, from the pair of Dax to the medieval codex, today the discovery of the primary link between clinicopathological methods of evidence for the left hemisphere and human communication is characteristically credited to Pierre Paul Broca and the remarkable expositions of 1861.

Chapter 11

Broca's Auxiliary Contributions

As a person, his contemporaries described Paul Broca as a "generous, compassionate, and kind, with unbreakable fortitude and honesty, venerated by all " (Sabbatini, 2000). So his many contributions were fashioned against the backdrop of a personality that was appreciated by those who knew him and worked with him. And these contributions were numerous.

Many contemporary scientists and writers have remarked and lauded the spectrum of contributions of Paul Broca. Clower, and the prolific neurohistorian Stanley Finger have noted (2001), Paul Broca published more than 500 scientific articles, and above all, he was respected for his ardent intellect and ability to scrutinize things from many perspectives. Many facets of the gems of new knowledge became visible with his inspection. His talent was as broad as it was deep. The wide array of disciplines to which Broca applied his talents is genuinely mindboggling. These include neurology, neuroanatomy, comparative anatomy, human evolution and diversity, pathology, oncology, and therapeutics. Perhaps one of his greatest gifts was that he had the forethought to be instrumental in merging laboratory science with medicine and clinical findings. His revolution in thinking regarding the cerebral cortex and localization of cerebral function was only one of his myriad contributions, including the founding of modern anthropology (Clower & Finger, 2001). One wonders when he slept.

PRIORITY AND PRECEDENCE WITH A MODICUM OF APPRECIATION

Some sources have intriguing documentation of Broca's priority in medical and scientific areas for which he was not best known (Priority, 2012). He is reported to have described muscular dystrophy as a primary affection of muscle before Guillaume Duchenne (1806–1875). He also described rickets as a nutritional disease before Rudolf Virchow (1821–1902), and speculated about the venous spread of cancer well before future research by Karl von Rokitansky (1804–1878) confirmed it.

Broca also conducted the first experiments on the continent using hypnotism for surgical anesthesia. His beguilement with hypnotism did not last long, but he was considerably ahead of his time and for a while was "mesmerized" by this incredible interplay of mind and body. Broca also liked instruments as will be seen in telling of his inventive side in cephalometrics. His fascination with the newly developed microscope ensured that it was part of his wish list for graduation presents (Schiller, 1992). He helped popularize the use of the microscope in the diagnosis of cancer but saw it as a breakthrough innovation in many emergent medical specialties, including genetics.

LIMBIC SYSTEM

Paul Broca's contributions to science were so much broader than his most reknowned celebrity as the eponymous contributor to brain location and human communication. His early scientific works dealt with the histology of cartilage and bone, but he also made extensive and significant contributions to the pathology of cancer, the treatment of aneurysms, and infant mortality.

As a neuroanatomist, he had an important role in the understanding of the limbic system (Figure 11–1) and rhinencephalon.

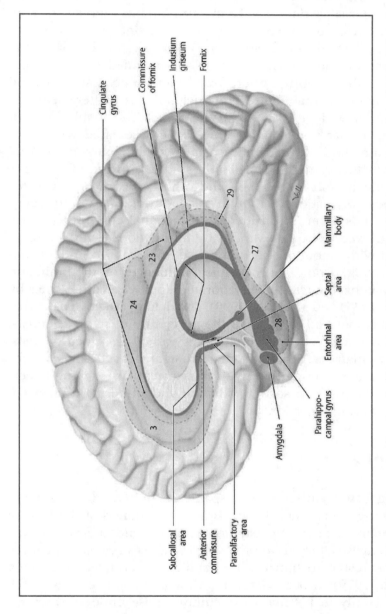

Figure 11–1. *Limbic system. Reprinted with permission. Thieme Medical Publishers. LaPointe, L. L. (2011). Atlas of Neuroanatomy for Communication Science and Disorders.*

Broca coined the term limbic lobe (Broca, 1878) and wrote an extensive treatise on it. The Latin word "limbus" implies the concept of circle, ring, surrounding, or hem), since it forms a kind of border around the brainstem. Broca called attention to the fact that, on the medial surface of the mammalian brain, right underneath the cortex, there exist some special small neural communities, containing several nuclei of gray matter (neurons) that he labeled *"le grand lobe limbique."* The limbic lobe, of course, is that system that came to be associated with emotions and the base and more primal human pursuits and all that is Saturday night. The limbic system consists of the phylogenetically old limbic lobe and other subcortical structures and their connections. Although still enduring some controversy, the limbic system is considered a functional concept that may be employed to explain various brain functions richly interconnected with emotion. This system, so important to understanding physiologic and neurochemical influences on the brain and human behavior, was to be elaborated upon years after Broca by Papez (1937) and Maclean (1990). The field of affective neuroscience has matured to become the prefecture of neuroscientists, neuropsychologists, speech-language pathologists, neurologists, and psychiatrists. Broca was there first, and set the tabletop for future understanding that was to have such far-reaching effects on everything from sexual addiction and stuttering to altruism and nurturing behavior.

CANCER

As suggested earlier in the sparse section on Broca's wife, Adele-Augustine Lugol Broca, Broca's awareness of the history of carcinoma of the breast, stomach, and endometrium in his wife's ancestry may have piqued his interest in causes of cancer and suggested to him the heritability of certain rare cancers (Krush, 1979). Broca related his thoughts about cancer in his his two-volume treatise entitled *Trait des Tumeurs* (1866). In this comprehensive tome, Broca revealed once again what a historian and scholar he had truly become. He reviewed the history of medical ideas about tumors and cancer as follows:

During the Renaissance (seventeenth and eighteenth centuries) tumors were separated into three large groups:

(1) Tumores secundam naturam, tumors that produce something in a natural physiological way such as pregnancy and milk in mammary glands;

(2) Tumores supra naturam, in which the natural parts are displaced, such as in a fracture; and

(3) Tumores praeter naturam, or those produced by unnatural parts, such as new tissues, accumulation of "humors" etc. (Krush, 1979, p. 126)

Broca's writing on tumors and cancer are all the more remarkable given the state of clinical science on this disease in the 1880s. These contributions may well have as much impact on current medicine as did his scholarly work on brain localization of function. Broca meticulously traced the pedigree of a "Mrs. Z" and arrived at startling conclusions for the time on cancer's heridability. As Krush (1979 has noted, Broca took note that another notable fact was that the four daughters of Mrs. Z, all of whom later died of cancer, were born at least 15 years, and one of them 30 years, before cancer overtook their mother. Broca felt that the answer may be that the disease was dormant and not revealed until a given moment. He wrote that it was not the disease itself that was dormant, but that a cause of the disease remained inactive in the body for an indefinite time in an undefined state, a predisposition toward the disease. Predisposition to diseases is now recognized as a potent familial influence. Finally, Broca wondered why or how a dormant condition could last from 50 to 60 years and then "explode" and kill the person within 1 to 2 years. He felt that this was an impossible phenomenon to explain. In 2012 there are still many questions that are clouded in the mist of unanswered puzzles concerning the etiology of polyps, tumors, and cancer, but Broca was way ahead of his time in speculating about the genetic nature of cancer and disease in general. Androutsos and Diamantis (2007) publishing in the rather obscure *Journal of the Balkan Union of Oncology* laud Broca's contributions across disciplines. They state, "Paul Broca was an eminent surgeon, neurologist and anthropologist. He wrote many articles on brain anatomy, pathology of bones and joints, aneurysms, craniometry and physical anthropology, and he invented measuring instruments which are used even today . . . Thanks to his works on cancer and on tumors in general, he is considered as precursor of oncology" (Androutsos & Diamantis, 2007).

BROCA AND HANDEDNESS

Controversy has arisen over exactly what Broca believed regarding the relationship of handedness to language dominance in the brain (Harris, 1991). Several historical accounts, report that Broca (1865) stated that left-handers are the mirror-reverse of right-handers for cerebral control of speech, with the right hemisphere being dominant in left-handers, and the left hemisphere dominant in right-handers. This has been articulated by some, mostly over the clam dip at neuroscience and academy receptions, as Broca's Folly. Accounts note that Broca's error in light of current evidence that the majority of left-handers are left-dominant for speech just as are nearly all right-handers, and that Broca was tripped up by sampling bias and a hasty generalization about where language was located in left-handers. Eling (1984) has called such statements misrepresentations of Broca's position and has argued that Broca's analysis actually was more compatible with the current view that there is a disjunction, meaning an absence of an intimate anatomical relationship, between cerebral control for handedness and speech. Harris (1991) reviews Broca's work, describes the context in which his views were first articulated, and traces the development of the mirror-reversal principle. The conclusion is reached that, judged by a narrow reading of the 1865 paper, Broca's views could indeed be construed as an anticipation of the modern disjunction principle. However, judged by a broader reading, by consideration of his other writing, and in the context of the philosophical and scientific tradition that shaped his work, it is suggested that it was the mirror-reversal principle to which Broca was actually disposed (Harris, 1991).

ANTHROPOLOGY

Broca wrote a significant amount on Darwinism (known as *"transformism"* in France), and took a great interest in physical anthropology. Broca undeniably was a pioneer in the field of physical anthropology and is credited by some as the founder of the science. He founded the Anthropological Society of Paris, the *Revue d'Anthropologie*, and with his friend, Mortillet, the School of Anthropology. Broca had a difficult time establishing the society of anthropology in France at this time. The Minister of Public Instruction and the Prefect of Police believed that discussing knowledge about human beings was against the state in some way. The Prefect of Police held Broca responsible for anything said in meetings that may be "against society, religion, or the government" (Sagan, 1979).

The Anthropological Society gathered for the first time on May 19, 1859, the same year that Darwin's *On the Origin of Species* was published. Every branch of science was discussed at these meetings as well as many other topics. In 1876 the Roman Catholic political party organized a major campaign against the teaching of the subject at the Anthropological Institute of Paris, which was founded by Broca. This new science and its societies struggled against the beliefs and values of the church and state and these pioneers were courageous in their defiance and their rights to interpret science objectively and without repression.

Broca also took extensive measurements of the human body, particularly the head, to determine its other functions. Broca believed that brain size was a good general reference to intelligence. This conclusion was based on two sets of data. The first was the results of the autopsies that he had taken in four Paris hospitals. He collected 292 brains of men and 140 brains of women. The average weight of the males' brains was 1,325 grams, and the average weight of the womens' brains was 1,144 grams with a difference of 181 grams. He also measured the brain capacities of prehistoric skulls. In those skulls he found a difference of 99.5 cubic centimeters, and with contemporary brains, there was a difference from 130 to 221 cubic centimeters (Hothersall, 1995). He concluded from these data that the brains of primitive people were smaller than the brains of modern people, but that sex differences in brain volume were increasing over time. He assumed that mature adults are more intelligent than the elderly, and that men are more intelligent than women. These gender-based beliefs on the relationship of intelligence to cranial and brain size would come under fire, however, as will be seen, Broca considered other social implications and interpretations of these differences. Pineau (1980) is another French writer who has focused on Broca's contributions to anthropology. His writings are in French, but available from the Biblioteque Nationale France and available for translation. He chronicles Broca's works in anthropology. Pineau has an interesting bibiolography himself, including an intriguing article entitled "The Need for Follow-up Following a Death."

THE FRENCH ANTHROPOLOGY SOCIETY: A VENUE FOR PIONEERING PRESENTATIONS AND DEBATE

After 1859, Broca pursued a double purpose. Without neglecting any of his combinations of medical duties, he undertook the considerable task of founding a new society, and perhaps a new science. The incidents which led to this began in 1847, when Broca, as medical assistant, was appointed for the study of the bones, upon a special commission charged with making a report on the excavations, in the Church of the Celestins. In preparing to draw up his report, he was led to read the works in which craniology was discussed; and from then on, although his interests and abiding curiosity drew him to different studies, he continued to read with interest the books, then rare, which focused on the more macro issues of man and the human races. The ethnology of the day tended to concentrate its theories around the then overshadowing question of monogeny (the idea that all human races have a common origin) or polygeny (theories of multiple origin of human races), and the Ethnological Society of Paris had so exhausted itself with the reiteration of its narrow debates that it had stopped meeting in 1848. Ten years afterward, Broca, having reported research and conclusions about hybridity, desired to communicate them to the Society of Biology. He had not foreseen the reluctance and timidity of some of his colleagues. Some of Broca's positions, well seasoned with iconoclasm and freethinking concepts that grated the church-bound establishment, were contradictory to the doctrine of the monogenists. This raised flags of alarm to the president of the Ethnological Society, and he scurried away from controversy at the views contained in it, and asked Broca to withhold his communications on the subject (Schiller, 1992). Broca apparently had no choice but to seek another venue for the publication of his ideas. This imposed censorship apparently was not Broca's idea of free and open thinking.

This incident suggested the inevitability of founding a new society, in which questions relating to mankind could be given free scope. This motivation formed the genesis and embryology of the Anthropology Society. The project was embarked on no gentle stream and had class five rapids to negotiate. To meet requirements for forming a new society, Broca wanted to obtain 20 members, but after a whole year of paddling, he had to begin with nineteen. Rocks and obstacles in getting authorization for the meeting of the society were both apparent and submerged. The Government officers were spooked by its name, perceiving that the strange word "anthropology" might cover some political or social scheme and rouse the ire of the haloed heads of the church and government administration. Finally, the prefect of the police, judging that a meeting of one short of twenty persons did not require extraordinary authorization, gave Broca permission to meet with his friends, on the condition that he should be personally responsible for all that might be said against society, religion, or the Government. Just to be on the safe side, he also decreed that an agent of police should always be present in citizen's dress to see that no harm was done by the discussion or generation of abrasive ideas. Broca, said M. E. W. Brabrock, of the Anthropological Institute, "liked to tell an amusing anecdote on the subject of this supervision: The police officer acquitted himself of his mission with so great regularity, and had got so much the habit of sitting among the members, that he seemed soon to have forgotten that he was there in a special capacity. Wishing one day to be able to take a holiday with a clear conscience, he approached the officers with an amiable smile, and addressed Broca: 'There will be nothing interesting today, I suppose? May I go?' 'No, no, my friend,' Broca immediately replied, 'You must not go for a walk; sit down and earn your pay.' He returned to his place very unwillingly, and never after ventured to ask a holiday from those he was set to look after" (Pozzi, 1888).

The society held its first meeting May 19, 1859. When it was seen at work, adhesions came fast; and after it had published the first volume of its *Bulletins,* and shown the exclusively scientific character of its labors, the suspicions which it had provoked before its birth began to subside. The Minister of Public Instruction deigned at last to authorize it in 1861, and three years afterward it was recognized as a society of public utility. M. Broca, all agreed, was the nucleus of the group and was anointed by his former intern and biographer Pozzi, as the "soul of this society."

SCHOOL OF ANTHROPOLOGY

In 1876 Broca along with Louis Laurent Gabriel de Mortillet founded the École d'Anthropologie with private funds, having collected one or more subscriptions of 1,000 francs from each of its thirty-four founders. Mortillet was an anthropologist friend and colleague of Broca and had interesting concurrence and harmony with his scientific and political interests. Both were embryonic in the development of the new and risky field of anthropology and both were political and active in the uprisings of 1848. Mortillet was implicated in the Revolution of 1848 and sentenced to two years' imprisonment. He fled the country and during the next 15 years lived abroad, primarily in Italy, but spent considerable effort in Switzerland where he established his anthropological reputation by studying Swiss lake-dwellings. Mortillet returned to Paris in 1864, and soon afterward was appointed curator of the museum at St. Germaine (Hecht, 2005).

Today a statue in honor of Mortillet still stands in the ancient Arénes de Lutéce in the 5th arrondisement of Paris. The Arènes de Lutèce is among the most significant remains from the Gallo-Roman era in Paris (formerly known as Lutèce in French or Lutetia in Latin), together with the Thermes de Cluny, the remains of baths at the site of the present day Museum of the Middle Ages which houses the famous tapestries of the Lady and the

Unicorn. Lying in what is now the Latin Quarter, this ancient Roman amphitheater, just a stone's throw from our haunts along Rue Mouffetard in the summer of 2011, could once seat 15,000 people and was used to present gladiatorial combats. Heads rolled. Arms were scratched. The score for many an afternoon's match was Lions 14, Christians 0.

The lovely statue pictured below is dedicated to the French anthropologist Louis Laurent Gabriel de Mortillet (1821–1898) and serves as one of the few monuments of this freethinker, anthropologist, friend of Broca, and cofounder of the French School of Anthropology (Figure 11–2).

Joined by Eugene Dally and Paul Topinard, Mortillet and Broca served as the French School of Anthropology's first professors. The school and its freethinking anthropologists embraced Darwinian ideas and endured the suspicion and wrath of the church and government, but the school and the society thrived despite these intrusive molestations. By 1880 (the year of Broca's death), the school was receiving 20,000 francs per year from the French state. The Insitut Anthropologique received a yearly 6,000 francs from the Department of the Seine, and the laboratory was awarded another 6,000 yearly. These funds, along with the substantial gifts and donations, allowed the school to pay an annual salary of 3,000 francs to each of its seven professors (Hecht, 2005). Broca's contributions to anthropology, despite controversy set against the context of the times, were equally as prolific as his contribution to neuroscience (Figure 11–3).

CORNFLOWERS AND HYBRIDS

In the same year as his momentous reports on the seat of articulate language in the brain, Broca was at work on another slow-moving aspect of research. Inspired by the work of Darwin, he divided his attention to the burgeoning field of genetics. A contemporary of Gregor Mendel, Broca was attempting to breed cornflowers from wild seed collected in the fields. He supervised and helped tend a small garden on the grounds of the Bicêtre Hospital. He also dabbled in breeding generations of corn after his farmer in Sainte-Foy-la-Grande showed him a seemingly mutant dark cob from his field of blond maize (Schiller, 1992).

Figure 11–2. Statue honoring Gabirel Mortillet at Arénes de Lutéce, Paris.

Figure 11–3. *Philippe Mennecier, Director of Collections of National Museum of Natural History, displays a relief plaque of Paul Broca.*

This is not the first of his curiosity about genetics and hybrids and Schiller has a lengthy review of his writings in a chapter entitled "Flaws of Evolution." Broca was by no means a creationist and his gentle release of the traditional Christian dogma he had absorbed from his youth had long given way to free-thinking and scientific questioning. He did, however, discuss some of the issues that were in need of further research about the permanence and transformation of species. In his little garden at the Bicêtre Hospital he proceeded to sow plots of the deviant dark cobs of maize and reported the results of these special seedlings across several generations of maize from 1866 to 1868.

GENETIC INTERRUPTION

Broca's work on hybrids of cornflowers and dark maize were interrupted once again by the dark clouds of war and unrest in France. This time it was the terrible Franco-Prussian War of

1870 (Wawro, 2003). This was a ravaging conflict that raged for much of 1870 and 1871 and marked the downfall of the Second French Empire (Napoléon III) and the beginning of the Third French Republic. Times were tough. Over a 5-month campaign, the Prussian army (joined by the other German states) defeated the newly recruited French armies in a series of battles fought across northern France. Paris was under a prolonged siege and fell on January 28, 1871. The siege of Paris was notable on several fronts. It marked the first use of anti-aircraft artillery, a German piece built specifically to shoot down the hot air balloons being used by the French as couriers and observers.

This was no balloon joy ride. In Paris, Broca was enlisted to take charge of an ambulance and a dozen sheds that lined the Jardin des Plantes where the wounded were kept and treated. Broca had a hard time recruiting medical personnel to help him mind the sheds of wounded in the garden. Four interns from his former Hopital Pitié were recruited to help him tend the wounded (Schiller, 1992). Ironically, the temporary home of the Musee de l'Homme in July of 2011, where I accessed material on the life and times of Broca is the same Jardin des Plantes with it's beautiful tree-lined aisles and gardens of botanical specimens. The Pitié hospital was located across the rue from the Jardin where today there is a mosque with its wonderful café where one can enjoy brass glasses of mint tea (Figures 11–4 and 11–5).

The Franco-Prussian War of 1870 ravaged the people of Paris. The weather was freezing and food supplies were cut off from the city. Paris suffered badly during the Prussian blockade of the city. Food was in such short supply that people would eat anything that moved including dogs, cats, rats, goldfish, and even zoo animals. The menagerie of the Jardin des Plantes was fair game (no pun premeditated) and many of the animals at this beautiful zoological garden were sacrificed to feed the starving people of Paris. The Parisians were again in the vanguard of haute cuisine as witnessed by the incredible Christmas Day menu of delicate zoo animal preparations. Among the delectibles on a restaurant menu were stuffed donkey's head, elephant consommé, roast camel, kangaroo stew, antelope terrine, bear ribs, cat stuffed with rat, and wolf haunch in deer sauce. The full menu is available at Wikimedia Commons at: http://upload.wikimedia.org/wikipedia/commons/5/59/Menu-siegedeparis.jpg

Figure 11–4. *Jardin des Plantes and Mosque Café.*

Figure 11–5. *Jardin des Plantes and Mosque Café.*

Even Victor Hugo, who knew all about *Les Miserables*, got on the zoo animal bandwagon and is reported to have said, "Rats are made into *pâté*. Quite good, I'm told." Hugo, in his seventies, is whispered to have penned the following to one of his young paramours,

> Ah, had you come and listened to my wooing,
> I would have served you an unheard of course:
> Of Pegasus, by killing him and stewing,
> I'd given you delicious wing of horse.

(Schiller, 1992, p. 237)

This was was a bloody walk through for the Prussians. Bismarck is quoted as saying, "A week without cafe au lait will break the Parisians" (Franco-Prussian War, 2012).

It was a bristly time for all of Paris and for Paul Broca with no exception. His biographer, former student, and lifelong friend Samuel Pozzi stated in Broca's eulogy and biography how the war of 1870 to 1871 interrupted his work. In fact it almost destroyed much of his previous work. In the words of Pozzi,

> The house he lived is located just off the Rue de Lille, where the fire [wreaked such] great havoc. That . . . intellectual wealth long and painfully amassed [was nearly] devoured by flames. [We can] understand the emotion of Broca [thinking his books and journals were destroyed]. The danger past, he found intact his books and manuscripts. The tears that poured over [himself was] indicative of a [grateful] heart; those [tears] produced by [one who had] high interest [in] the nation [and] humanity. [This] belongs [to] only great souls. (Pozzi, 1880b, p. 12)

After the fall of Napoléon III a treaty was finally exacted. The Treaty of Frankfurt was signed May 10, 1871, marking the end of the Franco-Prussian War. The war had lasted 5 months and cost 88,488 German and around 150,000 French lives. France was able to repay the huge indemnity demanded by the treaty in two years, thanks in part into the boom in wine exports after the development of the pasteurization of wine by Louis Pasteur (Franco-Prussian War, 2012). Through frozen toes, bloody battles, massive casualties, and more domestic social unrest, France was somehow to retain its style. Broca again was part of the tapestry of the politcal and social maelstrom and his work on genetics in his quaint hospital garden of cornflowers and dark maize was outside of the windows of the rooms that may have housed Leborgne and Lelong a few years earlier had to be disrupted. Still, his writings on the topic are impressive and testament to his careful study of the implications of Darwin's and Mendel's work.

ANTHROPOMETRY AND CEPHALAMETRICS

Broca also contributed to the science of cranial anthropometry by creating new types of measuring devices and numerical indices. He is known for describing for the first time trephined skulls from the Neolithic period in his studies of comparative anatomy of primates. Apes and monkeys were not outside Broca's research interest.

The measurement of the human body, its parts and relative dimensions, such as body weight, height, length of limb bones, pelvic bones, skull, and penis is known as anthropometry. The word anthropometry comes from the Greek *anthropos*, meaning man, plus the word *metron*, which means measure. Anthropometry is a scientific tool presently used in several disciplines including medicine, anthropology, archeology, and forensic science to study and compare relative body proportions among human groups and between genders. For example, by measuring and interpreting relative body and bone proportions between two groups of children of the same age, under normal and abnormal conditions, physicians can determine the influence of malnourishment on physical development during childhood. Broca's definition and founding of the budding field of anthropology has allowed scientists to compare cranial and body proportions to identify sets of characteristics common to individuals of a given race and the morphological differences among races (Lerner & Lerner, 2006).

Anthropology is the discipline that has developed anthropometrical comparison studies into a set of reliable standardized data and mathematical formulae, which are now useful for both modern forensic science and archeology. The popular American CSI television series based on forensic science principles and myths regularly popularize methods of anthropometirical comparisons. Broca invented or contributed to the refinement of a number of instruments used in the field.

In addition to Broca's convolution or Broca's area, he has a plane of measurement named after him. Broca's plane is a measurment that includes the tip of the interalveolar septum between the upper central incisors and the lowest point of the left and right occipital condyles. Presently, anthropometry is a well-established forensic technique, which uses anthropological databanks to calculate computational ratios of specific bones and skull features associated with differences between genders and specific races. When a complete skeleton is available, the level of reliability in establishing sex, age, and race through anthropometrics is almost 100%. Pelvic bones alone offer a 95% reliability, whereas pelvic bones plus the skull result in an accurate estimation 98% of the time. Gender can be determined by studying the size and shape of some skull bones and by comparing them with the well-established dimorphisms (differences in shape) between human male and female skulls. For instance, the mastoid process, a conic protuberance forming the posterior part of the right and left temporal bones, is large enough in males for the skull to rest on it on the surface of a table. In the female skull, however, the mastoid process will tilt backward to rest on the occipital area or other portions of the skull. This happens because the mastoid process in the female skull is not large enough to keep it in a balanced position on a flat surface. Gender dimorphisms are also found in many other human bones (Lerner & Lerner, 2006).

In the two manuals that Broca published as guides to the studies of general anthropology and craniology, he condensed in a few pages the work of several years. He insisted especially on the importance of accurate measurements, and of having conclusions supported by the averages of a large number of experimental cases (Broca, 1868). For these purposes he invented more than thirty simple, accurate, and convenient instruments of measurement (Figures 11–6 and 11–7). His anthropological memoirs are numerous, and pertain to all branches of the science, prehistorical, historical, ethnographical, and linguistic, and repeatedly illustrate the activity and encyclopedic comprehension of his intellect.

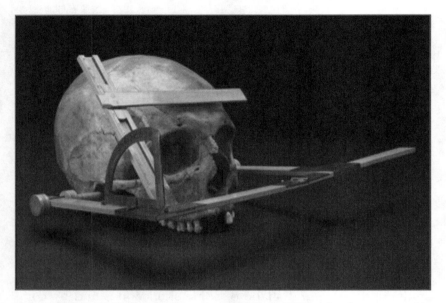

Figure 11–6. *Cephalametric instruments of Broca. Wikimedia Commons, public domain.*

CONTROVERSY AND RACISM

Broca took extensive measurements of the human body, particularly the head, to determine its possible relationship to behavior and characteristics of intellect and personality. Broca wrote in several publications in anthropology that brain size might be a good general reference to intelligence. This conclusion was based on two sets of data. The first was the results of the autopsies that he had taken in four Paris hospitals. He collected 292 brains of men and 140 brains of women. The average weight of the males' brains was 1,325 grams, and the average weight of the women's brains was 1,144 grams with a difference of 181 grams. He also measured the brain capacities of prehistoric skulls in an extensive project he undertook that resulted in measuring the crania of skeletons from cemeteries around France. In those skulls he found a difference of 99.5 cubic centimeters, and with contemporary brains, there was a difference from 130 to 221 cubic centimeters (Hothersall, 1995). He reported from these data that the brains of primitive people were on average smaller

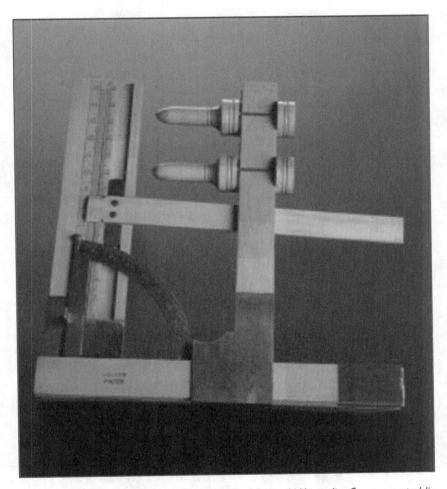

Figure 11–7. Cephalametric instruments of Broca. Wikimedia Commons, public domain.

than the brains of modern people, but that gender differences in brain volume appeared to be increasing over time. He assumed that mature adults are more intelligent than the elderly, and that men might be more intelligent than women. Subsequent writings indicated that social opportunity might account for these differences, and body size was also a factor that should be factored into any discussion of the relationship between skull size, brain size, and intellegence (Hothersall, 1995). Some of these reservations have been lost in subsequent writings about Broca's views. The skulls that Broca studied became a part of the Broca Museum, which later merged with the Museum of Man in Paris and constituted many of the 83 or so cabinets in the Broca collection that I had access to in the summer of 2011. This collection was truly impressive and spoke well of his anthropological efforts. Many cabinets of Gall's and Spurzheim's work are held in this museum as well (Figure 11–8).

Broca and other scientists practicing anthropometric measurement in the 1800s believed the skull's shape and size showed Europeans were superior. Broca was called to task for some of his writings of the day that suggested that, based on some of his craniometric and brain weight studies, black skin and wooly hair, especially of the Australian aboriginal people and Hotentots, were associated with lower intelligence whereas white skin and straight hair were "equipment of the higher groups" (Feagin, 2010).

Broca's practices have been branded as racist and sexist by some (Gould, 1980), and in fact his work has been used

Figure 11–8. Cabinets in the Broca, Gall, and Spurzheim Collection Musee de l'Homme, Paris.

by some to promote scientific racism, but Broca's politics were complicated. His political and social views are well seasoned with irony and some contridiction. He was regarded as a supporter of progressive social causes and though he wrote about differences in skull size across races, he argued against African enslavement. Unlike many of his contemporaries, Broca did not oppose the mixing of different racial or ethnic groups. However, his interpretations about the relationship between physical difference and ability helped foster racist and sexist theories. Many of these ideas were not rejected until after the Second World War (Hecht, 2005). Broca presented his numbers of measured differences in skulls and brains and infered differences in intellect but he does not appear to be the racist that some have painted and in fact was a supporter of social equity causes throughout his career (Figure 11–9).

As Finger (1994, p. 301) has remarked, in his later years, Broca began retreating from his earlier pronouncements that larger brains equaled higher intelligence. He recognized that many other variables, including societal advantages, were related to measured differences in intellect and achievement. But his objectivity and scientific mind, despite swimming among 19th century scientists whose predominant belief was that racial and gender differences were a truism, guided him to attempt to explain differences by social disadvantage. As Johnson (2012) formerly of the Centre for Human Biology from the University of Leeds suggests, Broca wasn't completely successful in detracting those who would use his data as arguments for scientific racism. Broca's memorial in anthropology was his work on brain size and civilization, which could grow into the social tumor of misrepresentation by those who would misuse it. Johnson (2012) suggests that Broca's modifications of his interpretations are a good example of hope shaping subsequent conclusions. Broca considered himself a liberal. He speculated that women's brains were small because of socially enforced underuse. Given a changed society they might grow. Primitive tribes had small brains because of lack of intellectual challenge. But in Europe brain size had naturally increased with the march of civilization. Given what we now understand in neuroscience as the effect of experience on neuroplasticity and especially on connectivity and neural pruning, these interpretations of Broca do not

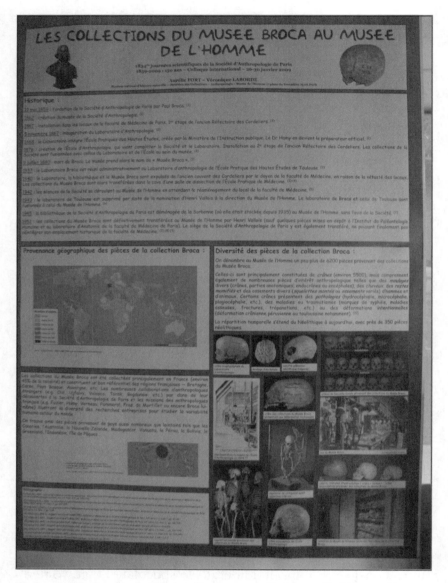

Figure 11–9. Poster of old Broca Mussee assembled by staff of National Natural History Museum.

appear too far fetched. It was not too many years ago that the predominant belief was that one central nervous system neurons die, there is no resurrection. Neurons had no Easter, according to many diehard neurologists and neuroscientists even through the 1960s and 1970s. Current research on changes in neuroarchitecture and neuroconnectivity have weakened that early chestnut about dead neurons. Broca's ideas on richness of experiences and societally imposed impoverishment of advantage might be *au current* (Doidge, 2007).

The Full Moon, Interpretation, and Refutability

Broca's earlier works in anthropology persist as examples of scientific racism but as with many of us, he changed his views as he aged, and retained a healthy dose of skepticism about the maleability of earlier scientific interpretations. One more requirement is added to what a curriculum for science literacy needs to deliver: and that is a recognition that science professionals in disagreement about the interpretation of data can be a legitimate feature of science. The process of scientific inquiry must contain the potential for refutability. Dogma and superstition are characterized mostly by irrefutability. What is said is right and it is supported by authority and tradition. This is not as true in appropriate scientific inquiry and application of the scientific method. Science is vulnerable to all that resides in our Broca-named limbic systems. This marvelous community of neural structures and connections that are infused with emotions and evolutionary self-preservation make our scientific objectivity difficult to say the least. Much research has demonstrated confirmatory bias not only in the collection of data but in interpretation of results. We are prone to selectively generate or recall that which confirms our crusty beliefs. Experimenter and confirmatory bias must be guarded against and rigorously controlled in the design of experiments. So must illusionary correlations.

Illusionary correlations are rampid in our belief systems. One is hard-pressed to extract the confidently held belief, even by educated professionals, that emergency rooms and community jails are not overrun during full moons. Despite many studies to the contrary, illusionary correlation rears its little snake head every time there is a full moon. "We were swamped," reports the emergency room physician or nurse. "The full moon effect strikes again."

The moon holds a mystical place in the history of human culture, so it is no wonder that many myths: from werewolves to induced lunacy to epileptic seizures, have proliferated regarding its supposed effects on us.

"It must be a full moon," is a phrase heard frequently when strange things happen and is documented by researchers to be burbled commonly by late-night cops, psychiatry staff, and emergency room personnel. Reliable studies comparing the lunar phases to births, heart attacks, deaths, suicides, violence, psychiatric hospital admissions, and epileptic seizures, among other things, have over and over again found little or no connection. Yet, illusionary correlation is marvelously robust and contributes a bit to the scientific illiteracy of not only the general public but the educated public. One piece of evidence may convince those who feel comfortable in the persistence of lunar madness and illness. To evaluate this, Thompson and Adams (1996) studied if there is any effect of the full moon on emergency department (ED) patient volume, ambulance runs, admissions, or admissions to a monitored unit, a retrospective analysis of the hospital electronic records of all patients seen in an ED during a 4-year period was conducted in an ED of a suburban community hospital in the United States. A full moon occurred 49 times during the study period. There were 150,999 patient visits to the ED during the study period, of which 34,649 patients arrived by ambulance. A total of 35,087 patients was admitted to the hospital and 11,278 patients were admitted to a monitored unit. *No significant differences* were found in total patient visits, ambulance runs, admissions to the hospital, or admissions to a monitored unit on days of the full moon. The occurrence of a full moon has *no effect* on ED patient volume, ambulance runs, admissions, or admissions to a monitored unit (Thompson & Adams, 1996).

Similar results have been found for crimes (including murder, robberies, and assults), admissions to veterinary clinics, and arthritis pain and rainy days. Illusionary correlations and confirmatory bias have plagued scientific interpretation since well before Broca's day, and no doubt will continue as a contaminent of genuine scientific literacy and understanding.

Despite ever present threats to scientific objectivity, careful empirical study design, control of independent variables that are threats to both internal and external validity of research, and reining in the amphetemine-crazed Clydsdale horses of confirmatory bias and illusionary correlations can struggle to keep our science relatively objective and out of the camp grounds of superstition and dogma.

Broca's changing views on brain size and intellect are a good example of how early interpretations can be called into question, modified, or discarded. Would that all science were as easily tempered.

NEUROIMAGING AND BROCA'S THERMOMETRIC CROWN

Another area of scientific contribution by Paul Broca is his pioneering interest in in vivo inferences about brain condition. He used measures of scalp temperature for the early diagnosis of brain lesions, as well as for drawing conclusions about brain function in normal subjects. Cohen, Smith, and Loroux-Hugon (2004), researchers from the Brain Stimulation Unit at the National Institutes of Health in the United States and the Hôpital de la Salpêtrière in Paris, have called attention to Broca's use of scalp and skin temperature to construct inferences about conditions of the arterial system below the surface. Today these strategies can be seen as early precursers to contemporary techniques such as magnetic resonance imaging. Broca's imaging ideas were inspired from studies at the time that measured skin temperature to infer the localization and mechanism of arterial lesions of the limbs, and to guide amputation whenever necessary.

Broca took this approach of skin temperature measurement and attempted to apply it to the field of neurology. Always his inventive and technical self, Broca devised a "thermometric crown, allowing the simultaneous application of six thermometers around the head. It is made of a series of small identical cotton pockets, tied together with a circular band of elastic material, with thermometers placed inside the pockets" (Broca, 1879, p. 1332).

He later improved this apparatus by means of two additional thermometers critically located over the inferior frontal gyrus "which is assigned to language."

Broca tried to infer underlying pathophysiological mechanisms, and surmised that progressive thrombosis, contrary to embolism, leads to increased rather than to reduced temperatures. In fact, Broca applied this technique to a patient who had suffered speech loss (Cohen et al., 2004). Broca reports:

> One of the first patients in which I made this exploration was a doctor from the provinces who was introduced to me by his son, himself a doctor. Speech was not abolished, but it was already severely impaired; there was no disorder of sensation or motility. I easily recognized with my hand that the temperature of the left temporal region was notably increased, and I observed, using two thermometers applied on the temporal regions, that this increase was of 3 degrees, an excessive figure which I never observed again. (Broca, 1879, p. 1334)

He predicted that the condition should worsen as a consequence of an extension of a "congestive softening" to the whole hemisphere. Indeed, the patient's son soon informed Broca that "speech was entirely abolished, that intelligence was deeply impaired, that the patient was bed-ridden," and three months later that his father eventually died.

In these days of measuring electrophysiological correlates of cognitive effort such as the use of eye-tracking, pupilometry, galvanic skin response, and others, it is surprising to see how far ahead of the curve was Broca's early work on skull temperature measurement. He wrote that mental effort might indeed be revealed by these thermal changes. He hypothesized that brain temperature should increase with the execution of mental or intellectual tasks by normal subjects. Importantly, according to Cohen et al. (2004), he thought that thermal variations should be local, mostly affecting frontal regions dedicated to higher brain functions. He observed that, "following intellectual work, the frontal temperature increases more than the temporal temperature, and the latter more than the occipital temperature. One may confirm this by placing the thermometric crown on a resting subject. After about 20 minutes, when all thermometers have reached equilibrium, one asks the subject to perform a mental task. If he is only half-literate, if he does not read very fluently, one asks him to read a text aloud, and after a few minutes, one sees the thermometers rise, mainly the frontal ones" (Broca,

1879, p. 1337). Stressing the influence of cultural acquisitions on brain function, Broca noted that "the result is nil or extremely minuscule if the subject can read without difficulty. To make the cerebral temperature rise [in medical students], I had to give them a more arduous work, generally consisting in adding thirty five digit numbers. Then the thermometers, mainly the frontal ones, rose substantially."

These attempts to correlate somatic measurements with cognitive-linguisitc effort are eerily similar to some of our contemporary attempts to determine heart-rate and respiratory variation with increasing cognitive-linguistic loads (Chih, Stierwalt, LaPointe, Kashak, & Lasker, 2011). Again, Broca was there first. His creativity and inventiveness was 150 years ahead of his time. As Cohen et al. (2004) remarked, "we deemed it justified to acknowledge his open mindedness and curiosity." Broca perhaps would have felt both perfectly comfortable and infinitely excited with the present abundance of brain imaging techniques.

TREPANATION AND SURGERY

In the mid 1870s, and nearing the end of his illustrious journey into observing and writing about all things related to the brain and other medical mysteries, Broca continued his fascination with the boney helmet that encases the brain. The *crane* or skull drew his anthropological attention increasingly and led him to explore historical theories about trepanation, that ancient art of burrowing and cutting through the skull for a variety of superstitious, magical, and medical reasons (Broca, 1876a, 1876b, 1876c).

Trepanation is the practice of making a hole in the skull intentionally. Many crania are scattered throughout the battlefields and graveyards of history with skull holes inflicted by everything from saber-tooth tiger claws to stone axes and shrapnel generated by pilotless drone planes. Since the stone age, however, healers have inflicted the art of burrowing into the skull to release spirits, pressure, and seemingly establish a bit of homeostasis in people who shreaked, thrashed, or spewed. What has probably been perpetrated however, is an ancient trail of death and holey skulls. An instrument called a trepan is used to make the hole. Throughout history, the trepanning tool has developed dramatically, evolving from a crude hunk of sharpened flint in prehistoric times to a hand-cranked auger, not unlike those used to make a hole and ice-fish in a frozen lake to, in contemporary times, an electric drill. Brain surgery by Black and Decker. Trepanation was practiced on every continent through every time period and by every race of mankind until and including the advent of brain surgery in this century.

Even today, under the aegis of the remarkable umbrella of "alternative and complementary medicine" one can find websites railing against contemporary medicine, current "doctors" and lauding the so-called benefits of improving "brain pulsations" by proper trepanation (Trepanation Guide, 2012).

Magical thinking knows no specific century. Bart Huges (b. 1934), a medical school graduate who has never practiced medicine except for a bit of self-surgery, believes that trepanation is the way to higher consciousness. He says that he wanted to be a psychiatrist but failed the obstetrics exam and so never went into practice. In 1965, after years of experimentation with LSD, cannabis, and other drugs, Dr. Huges realized that the way to enlightenment was by boring a hole in his skull. He used an electric drill, a scalpel, and a hypodermic needle (to administer a local anesthetic). The operation took him 45 minutes. How does it feel to be enlightened? "I feel like I did when I was 14," says Huges. This report from the skeptics dictionary website, devoted to debunking pseudoscience and medical quackery, illustrates that magical thinking is alive and well (Skeptics Dictionary, 2012).

Broca's strong interest in anthropology led him into deep discussion and speculation as to the reasons for the ancient practice of trepanation. In a penetrating review of trepanation and Broca's contributions to the study of this practice, Clower and Finger (2001) burrow into the depths of the motivations and practice of it. They report Broca's fascination with this ancient practice and his application of some of its principles to explain possible underlying conditions manifest in clinical reports from the past and the contemporary 1870s. As Clower and Finger (2001) report, Broca threw himself into his skull study with characteristic intensity. Broca immersed himself in analyzing the ancient skulls found in France during the 1870s.

Although he found few skulls himself, he studied the findings made by many others, especially those unearthed by P. Barthélemy Prunières, his friend and associate.

In the central and southwest regions of France, not far from where Broca was raised in Sainte-Foy-le-Grande, Prunières explored and excavated the megalithic granite dolmens (from the Breton language, meaning stone tables). In the dolmens of Lozère, he discovered some skulls with large openings (more than 200 skulls would eventually come from these sites). He also found rounded, polished, and beveled pieces of cranial bones nearby and even within some of these skulls. From some of these findings grew the belief that portions of skulls that were extracted during the process of trepanation were polished and used as amulets in ancient times to ward off evil spirits and perhaps the vampires and walking dead zombies of yesteryear. Speculation has been around the halls of neuromythology for years about the origins of the word *skoal* during triumphant toasts. Clower and Finger (2001) suggest that Prunières pondered the significance of the cut-out regions of the ossified helmet and concluded that skulls once served as a celebratory goblet. The word *skoal*, meaning skull, has long been used in Scandinavian countries as a toast to one's health before drinking. The word also means bowl in Norse languages. Some suggest its origins of reference to drinking aquavit or some suitable other adult beverage from the conquered half-skull of an enemy smacks of urban legend. It is not hard to imagine the etymology of the celebratory toast arising from a Viking party of conquering drinkers who lift the boney bowl of a half skull and cheerily say "Skoal!"

Broca published several articles and, as prolific and loquacious as he was at oral presentation, gave many lectures on trepanation after his interest was piqued in the 1870s. He now sought to do two things. First, he wanted to convince more people that some of the holes observed in these skulls were not caused by infectious processes, congenital defects, tumors, gnawing animals, accidents, or battle wounds. Second, he wanted to incorporate all of the facts into a single theory that could readily account for the reason trepanation was performed in the Neolithic period. He also fostered the belief that many trepanations were performed on infants and children (Clower & Finger, 2001). From

Broca's perspective, Neolithic people used trepanation (Figure 11–10) to provide an exit for the demons that caused childhood convulsions. It was easy, in the days of rampant superstition, to believe that the thrashing convulsions of a seizure disorder were the result of wild spirits trying to get out. Perhaps trepanation facilitated the escape. Exorcism perhaps seemed eminently rationale to Neolithic people. If exorcism didn't work perhaps a nice burr-hole in the skull would do it.

Broca, depite his conviction that trepanation was born of superstition, used it to help make surgical decisions. He even published an article on his own experience with trepanation of a sort. Stone (1991) chronicled Broca's contributions to surgery and detailed one of Broca's many published clinical studies. In this particular case study, Broca details a craniotomy conducted on a patient that was guided by his previous discovery

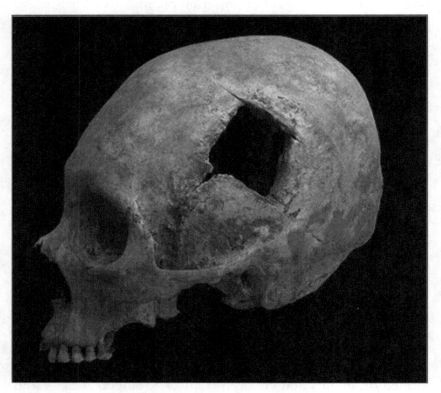

Figure 11–10. *Trepanated skull. Wikimedia Commons, public domain.*

of the cerebral localization of disrupted speech. According to Stone (1991) in 1871, Broca treated a man who had sustained a scalp laceration from a blow to the head without loss of consciousness or skull fracture (Broca, 1876d). The patient exhibited what Stone has characterized as a "nonfluent aphasia" about one month after injury and became progressively dull, unresponsive, and eventually comatose. Suspecting an intracranial abscess, Broca conducted a craniotomy (earlier called trepanation) at the region of the left third frontal convolution and drained an epidural abscess. The patient improved transiently but died a few days later. Autopsy showed a left-sided, predominantly frontal purulent meningoencephalitis. Broca's other neurosurgical contributions included details of a variety of surgical cases, methods for scalp localization of the cerebral convolutions, and extensive studies of skull and brain abnormalities (Stone, 1991).

Early renditions of trepanation are even captured in classic medieval paintings. Hieronymus Bosch painted an all-time classic capture of early medical practices that both elucidates and puzzles. In this public domain exquisite painting of what appears to be an early atttempt at trepanation and has been labeled in some historic sources as an attempt to remove the "stone of madness" (Figure 11–11) or the "stone of folly" from a fortuitous patient, we see illustrated the attempt to trepanate the skull. Surgical attendants are represented in the painting as well, but some questions may be raised about the medical rationale of the woman attendant's balancing of a book on her head. In fact, the patient perhaps generated his own doubts upon seeing the surgeon come to the procedure with what appears to be a funnel on his head. Times change. Surgical procedures evolved into more aseptic surroundings and some perhaps with as many bewilderments in the mind of the patient.

THE FRENCH SENATE

An interesting aspect of Broca's charisma and value system is that he took a committed and unrelenting interest in public health and public education. He published several works in areas related to social causes, including infant mortality, the population development in France, and the medical service in the

Figure 11–11. *The Extraction of the Stone of Madness* by Hieronymus Bosch. *Wikimedia Commons, public domain.*

French army. He was concerned with health care for the poor and perhaps his personal experience with public and worker unrest during the turbulent political years during which he lived caused him to become an important figure in the *Assistance Publique*. When he was elected a member of the French Senate for life in 1880 his record, though it would turn out to be short, was marked by promotion of public health and education issues. The fairly recent Hôpital Broca (Figure 11–12) commemorates Broca's public assistance work and the bronze bust of him in the lobby welcomes visitors to the Geriatric Center (Figure 11–13).

Broca advocated that the education of women should be independent of the church, opposing bishop Félix-Antoine-Philibert Dupanloup's (1802–1878) claim that the education of women should take place *sur les genoux de l'église*. Dupanloup, Roman Catholic bishop of Orléans, was a clerical spokesman for the liberal wing of French Catholicism during the mid-19th century and did not take kindly to the ideas of the free-thinking Paul Broca (Priority, 2012).

Figure 11–12. *Hôpital Broca.*

Figure 11–13. *Bronze bust of Broca with one of his biographers in lobby of Hôpital Broca.*

M. Broca was elected Senator for life in early 1880 and his tenure was to be short-lived. After his election, he wrote in reply to the congratulations of an English academy over his new advancement: "In choosing their candidate for the first time from outside the political world, the 'Left' of the Senate have wished to manifest their good disposition toward the sciences; and, if I am happy in having been chosen on that ground, I am especially happy that anthropology should have acquired so much importance in public opinion as to be called to have its representative in the Senate."

Broca's election to the Senate was duly noted by his contemporaries in other countries and especially by his medical friends in England. In the British Medical Journal of February 14, 1880 a "special correspondent" mentioned his appointment:

As I anticipated in my last, Professor Broca has been elected Senator. His election took place on Thursday, the 5th instant, and the favourable result of the ballot of that day in the French Senate was communicated to him while he was at his post at the bimonthly meeting of the Anthropological Society of Paris, of which he is the general secretary. The news was immediately proclaimed to the members present, and was received with great applause. Some of them at once constituted themselves into a committee for the purpose of getting up a banquet to celebrate the event. It is to come off on Thursday, the 19th instant.

Professor Broca's election brings up the number of members of the different academies in the Senate to nineteen, and to three of the Academy of Medicine, the other two being Professor Robin and Dr. Theophile Roussel. I shall say nothing of the political significance of the new election; but its importance to the profession cannot be over-estimated, as it will not only raise the status of its members, but we can count upon one more who, if he use his influence aright, will be able to render immense service to them. M. Broca has been long known to the profession, and though comparatively a young man, he being in his fifty-sixth year, his career has been a very brilliant one. (Special Correspondence, *British Medical Journal*, 1880, p. 263)

Le Temps, an influential Paris newspaper noted Broca's election to the Senate and reported the banquet initiated by his colleagues in the Anthropological Society. According to *Le Temps*, "Colleagues, friends, students of Dr. Broca met yesterday evening at the Continental Hotel to offer a banquet to the newly elected member of the Senate. Over 300 [were] in attendance" (Le Temps, 1880).

At the February banquet, given him by his friends in honor of his nomination, he made some ominous comments which had a strange bearing in view of his sudden death just a few months hence:

"My friends, I am too happy . . . Yes, I am too happy. If I was superstitious, I should regard my nomination to the Senate as the presage of some great misfortune, perhaps as the presage of death."

Chapter 12

Broca's Legacy

BROCA'S DEATH

Broca was described as strongly built, with an expansive forehead and lustrous brown eyes. Fiery, righteous, benevolent, and an excellent storyteller, he was adored by his associates, and described by many, especially his students, as generous and compassionate. Broca the man was as much as Broca the scientist according to those who knew him and sanctified him. His photographs today exhibit through his 56 years a gradually receding hairline, a somewhat chubby face, and fashionable colossal mutton-chops.

The exact circumstances of the death of Pierre Paul Broca are not consistent in the literature. First among these inconsistencies is the exact date. Some sources list July 8 as his death date and others list July 9, 1880. Part of the confusion arises from the fact that he expired around midnight on July 8. Several sources cite that he was sticken for the second time, after his spell of unconsiousness in the French Senate on July 6, 1880. One popular source is representative of several accounts of his passing.

> On the 6th of July, 1880, he was seized with a fainting-fit at his place in the Senate. He resumed his work on the two following days, but was attacked again at midnight on the 8th, and died in ten minutes. His organs were found to be all sound, and his death was attributed to cerebral exhaustion arising from overwork. (M. Paul Broca, 1881, p. 265)

In an account published in the British medical journal, *Lancet,* his British colleagues presented this narrative of his death.

> On Tuesday, the 6th inst. (July), he fainted in the Senate House; on the ensuing Wednesday he felt sufficiently recovered to resume his labours; but towards midnight on Thursday he was suddenly seized with a fit of dyspnoea, rose from his bed, and expired in ten minutes. Strange to say, the post-mortem examination gave no clue to the mystery of his unexpected death, all the organs being apparently sound. We shall probably not be far from the truth in attributing the catastrophe to cerebral exhaustion, arising from too protracted a course of severe intellectual exertion. (Ball, 1880)

Broca's passing was noted as well in the upstart country of the United States of America. In its prestigious journal *Science*, his death was noted among those of several other French scientists.

> His sudden death is supposed to have been due to a cerebral hemorrhage, induced perhaps, by excess of labor and fatigue. Thus in the vigor of life and in the midst of his work, has died a scholar, philosopher and statesman, whose illustrious example will continue to enlighten the path of those who follow his imperishable footprints. (Science, 1880)

In 1982 Huard and his associates published an article in the French *Journal of Radiology* that detailed their views on aspects of Broca's death. This historical study briefly recalls circumstances of Broca's death, and reports some new data concerning his autopsy, and an analysis of macroscopic, microscopic, and computed tomography appearances of his brain following its discovery by Huard. The authenticity of the origin of the brain was established, and the hypothesis that Broca's death was due to rupture of a vascular malformation or a cerebrovascular accident was confirmed (Huard, Aaron, Askienazy, Corlieu, Fredy, & Vedrenne, 1982).

EULOGIES AND BIOGRAPHIES

Among the most personal narratives of the life of Paul Broca is that written by his great grandson, Phillippe Munod-Broca, himself a French physician. He included the life of his renowned relative among the French savants of Louis Pasteur and Claude

Bernard (Munod-Broca, 2005) and characterized them as 19th century "giants." The book remarked that Broca's contributions to contemporary neuroscience and our understanding of the brain as "immense."

Munod-Broca also presented a more personal glimpse of the humanity of Broca in his publication entitled, "Broca: The surgeon, the man" (Munod-Broca, 1980). Paul Broca had three children, two boys who eventually followed their father's footsteps into medicine, and a daughter, Pauline, who is buried beside him in the Paris cemetary of his final resting place.

His sons both achieved prominence in their specialties. The death of Broca's son, Auguste was noted in an American medical publication. The historic archives of the *Journal of the American Medical Society (JAMA)* note the passing of Paul's son in 1924, 100 years after Paul was born. In somewhat antiquated and non-person-first language the JAMA notes:

> Auguste Broca was the son of the anthropologist and surgeon Paul Broca, whose centenary was recently celebrated (*The Journal*, Aug. 16, 1924, p. 545). He was appointed surgeon to the hospitals of Paris in 1890, four years after becoming doctor of medicine. In 1895, he became agrégé professor. He was called to occupy the chair of operations and appliances at the *Faculté de Médecine* of Paris, and later to that of clinical surgery for children. From the beginning of his career, Broca devoted himself more particularly to pediatric surgery and achieved a great reputation in this field. He published works on harelip, cleft palate, the treatment of tuberculous ostearthritis in children, surgery of the middle ear and the mastoid process. (Auguste Broca, 1924)

Interestingly, homage to Paul Broca was codified at a 21st century conference of remembrance primarily by a group of anthropologists. This "homage to Paul Broca, Father of Anthropology" was held in Sainte-Foy-la-Grande amid the very streets where Broca followed his village physician father on his rounds in the 1830s (Broca Conference, 2001).

Pierre Paul Broca has had several prominent eulogists and biographers. Samuel Pozzi's tribute to his friend and colleague is among the most precious. The Pozzis and Brocas grew up in the Dordogne river region and the sons of both families moved to Paris and became prominent in each of their medical specialties.

Today the region of the Gironde and its tributary the Dordogne are idyllic with country villages, such as Sainte-Foy-la-Grande, and is peppered with limestone caves, ancient castles, and attractive hills. Escapists these days are likely to hire canoes or kayaks and float down these serene rivers, perhaps with foie gras, truffles, walnuts, or other specialties of the region. The entire district is almost literally covered in walnut trees growing in rows, neatly delineating fields, and sprinkled with irrigation systems that wait for the walnuts to achieve maturity in early autumn and then are harvested through the use of shaking machines. Foie gras is a regional (and international) lip-smacking foodstuff that, when coupled with a torn crust of perfect baguette is treated as a major delicacy. One sees signs everywhere for farm sales and shop sales, all accompanied by a variety of visual treatments depicting a happy goose and appearing beside the roads and outside of shops. Anything to do with geese or ducks is on sale in shops and supermarkets and is always somewhere on the menu in all classes of restaurants. The Dordogne is colored with fields of sunflowers that stretch as far as the eye can see, truffle-hiding oak trees, meandering riverside lanes, and astonishing spots that were made for leisurely picnics.

Perhaps these early visions and memory scraps of years gone by were troubling Pozzi as he struggled to find words to eulogize his countryman and colleague, Paul Broca. These families of long-ago Italian heritage enjoyed the fruits of the Dordogne and the fruits of their famous sons.

Samuel Pozzi strained to eulogize Broca. He lamented, "It is too early to write on Broca. Like the great monuments, the great men can [only] be well seen from afar. After three months, we are not yet in [the] point of view needed to wrap our [thoughts around] all aspects of this imposing figure and to judge [his] value" (Pozzi, 1888, p. 1)

In several sections of his eulogy, Pozzi illuminated the critical thinking and fine mind of Broca. "[He] was able to excite the zeal of some, dampen the ardor of others, [and] exercise authority over all [areas] that were unknown, testable and unquestioned" (Pozzi, 1880b, p. 9).

Pozzi also alludes to a major work by Broca that was in process when he died. "Broca was working on a comprehensive book on brain morphology that brilliantly summarized the result of his studies. Although unfinished, the precious manuscript will not be lost to science; pious hands have met its scattered leaves, and [try] to publish the complete [work] with notes taken during anatomical anthropology" (Pozzi, 1880b, p. 16).

Pozzi grappled with his eulogistic words, but he succeeded in characterizing the man and the scientist with reverence and dignity.

> Alas! The extent of the void that the death of our dear colleague [is immeasurable]. We [can] measure the position he occupied, and, what will be missed, [and] [what] we think that [he] brought us. But how many months or years will it take to forget this incredible [encountering] of merit, skill, and intellectual qualities. Broca's moral [fortitude] was truly exceptional. [It will take a] long-time to match [his traits]: [enthusiasm], perseverance, honesty, kindness, justice, intelligence, wit, [elegance]. His brain accumulated a sum so unprecedented [of] literary and scientific knowledge that [we] remain [mystified] by this living encyclopedia. Goodbye. We will cherish [your] memory up to our last hour. [You] leave [a] noble example to those who survive! (Pozzi, 1880b, p. 59)

Two boys from the petite village of Sainte-Foy-la-Grande along the walnut tree-lined banks of the Dordogne. One tearfully acknowledging and realizing the contributions of a mind that would take its place among the grandest in history.

The French brains of the roiling 19th century contributed much to our contemporary culture and societies. French impressionism broke with tradition to form an everlasting influence on art. The invention of collapsible metal tubes in the 1840s allowed long-term storage and transport of oil paints, making extended outdoor oil-painting trips much more feasible. Until then, oil paints were stored in little pouches made from pigs' bladders that the painter pierced with a tack to squeeze out the paint. Artists had sketched in the open air before and it was not new to art in the 19th century. But what was new was the method of completing many works directly in the open air, and the unfinished and "impressionistic" look of these compositions. Impressionists rejected the highly finished surfaces of academic painting of the time to create a visual language of bright, rapidly applied color to capture light and atmosphere. Impressionist painters developed a way of applying pigment that has been called "broken color" or "broken brushstrokes." The paint is applied in mosaiclike patches which creates a rough irregular surface texture. Though not immediately the darling of critics, impressionism has taken its place as a lasting influence that continues to amaze and inspire both neophytes and old pros in the art world (Rewald, 1973).

So too did Pierre Paul Broca face critics of his work in anthropology, cephalametrics, intellect and skull size, and free-thinking. He had to struggle against the dictates and theoso-phy of the church and prevailing ideas of holism versus cortical localization of function. He did this against a demanding milieu of tides of social unrest. Two French brains of patients with pro-found communication impairment came to epitomize his impact, though it can be argued that his deep work and thinking, late into the night in those small Parisian flats and in his laboratories and clinics and classrooms, were so broad that it is unrepresen-tative to only remember him for a solitary aspect of his work.

Amid the patisseries and bistros of the Latin Quarter with its students and touristes sipping espresso and enjoying the salted caramel flavored dessert of the week, reside Leborgne and Lelong, whose brains still float in the formaldehyde of his-tory in the *Musée Dupuytren*. These French brains symbolize the largesse of the Master French brain. Broca's most profound contributions were to be that of the final intellectual frontier, the human brain. His work has provided foundation and principled theoretic rationale for modern and surely forthcoming advances in what we know about our brain, our *cerveau*, and our most human trait, the ability to communicate. Our brain is the origin of our being and our identity. It is you. It is me. It is us.

Broca realized that and marked a profound boulevard that has allowed us to continue our trek and perhaps better under-stand ourselves.

Broca's final resting place is among his family members and friends in the Montparnasse Cemetery in Paris (Figure 12–1).

We wandered through these winding lanes of Montparnasse cooled by the plane trees in July of 2011. Students, who would gather in the area, named it "Montparnasse," derived from the ancient Greek "Mount Parnassus," the home of Apollo, the god of poetry, music and beauty. Montparnasse is the cemetery of poets, artists, musicians, philosophers, mathemeticians, scientists, and

Figure 12–1. *Montparnasse Cemetery—Broca's final resting place.*

many luminaries of French society. This peaceful place is now the everlasting home of Pierre Paul Broca, whom some might regard as the Apollo of the brain.

We strolled with nostalgia and a degree of wistfulness amid the mossy gravestones and dappled lanes of Montparnasse. Pierre Paul Broca was there and seemed to be there. The words of Emily seemed to capture much of what his life was about:

> *The Brain is wider than the Sky*
> *For put them side by side*
> *The one the other will contain*
> *With ease and You beside*
> *Emily Dickinson* (1924)

Appendix A

Green Translation of Broca's 1861 Paper on the Faculty of Articulated Language

(Reprinted with permission of Christopher D. Green)

Green, C. Classics in the history of psychology: Remarks on the seat of the faculty of articulated language, following an observation of aphemia (loss of speech) by Mr. Paul Broca (1861) First published in *Bulletin de la Société Anatomique*, 6, 330–357.

Retrieved January 23, 2012 from http://psychclassics. yorku.ca/Broca/aphemie-e.htm

Classics in the History of Psychology

An Internet resource developed by

Christopher D. Green

York University, Toronto, Ontario

Remarks on the Seat of the Faculty of Articulated
Language, Following an Observation of Aphemia
(Loss of Speech)

by Mr. Paul Broca (1861)

Surgeon of the Bicêtre Hosptial

First published in *Bulletin de la Société
Anatomique*, 6, 330–357.

Translation by Christopher D. Green

[*Translator's Note:* I have made an explicit attempt to keep this translation as literal as possible, which accounts for some of its clumsiness in English. For instance, I have rendered "langage articulé" as "articulated language" throughout, rather than as the perhaps more felicitous "spoken language," in order to maintain the technical style, and to distinguish it from the more colloquial "langage parlé." I have also refrained from using the seemingly more felicitous, but less precise, "articulate language." In addition, I have often used "ill people" for "malades" rather than "patients," especially in the first half of the article, because it emphasizes their condition rather than their relationship to the physician. I have also tried to retain the archaic vocabulary as much as possible. Special thanks to Classics Editorial Assistant, Daniel Denis, whose recommendations improved the translation immeasurably. —cdg—]

The paper and remarks that I am presenting to the Anatomical Society comes to the defense of the ideas professed by Mr. Bouillaud concerning the seat of the faculty of language. This question, both physiological and pathological, merits more attention than most doctors have accorded it up to now, and the matter is delicate enough, the subject obscure enough, and complex enough, that it seems useful to begin with some remarks relating the facts that I have observed.

I.

We know that the phrenological school placed at the front part of the brain, in one of the convolutions that lie on the orbital arch, the seat of the faculty of language. This opinion, which had been accepted, like so many others, without sufficient evidence, and which besides rested only on a very imperfect analysis of language phenomena, would have without doubt disappeared with the rest of the system, if Mr. Bouillaud had not saved it from foundering by making some important modifications to it, and by surrounding it with a parade of evidence borrowed above all from pathology. Without considering language as a simple faculty dependent on a single cerebral organ, and without looking to hem into an area of a few millimeters the location of this organ, as had been done by Gall's school, this professor was led by the analysis of a great number of clinical facts, followed by autopsies, to concede that certain lesions of the hemispheres abolish speech without destroying intelligence, and that the lesions always [p. 331] have their seat in the frontal lobes of the brain. He concluded that somewhere in these lobes, one or several convolutions holds under their dependence one of the elements essential to the complex phenomenon of speech, and thus, less restricted than in Gall's school, placed in the frontal lobes, without specifying further, the seat of the faculty of articulated language, which must not be confused with the general faculty of language.

There are, in effect, several species of language. Any system of signs permitting the expression of ideas in a manner more or less intelligible, more or less complete, more or less rapid, is a language in the most general sense of the word: thus speech, mimicry, typing [dactylologie], picture writing [l'écriture figurative], phonetic writing, etc., are all species of language.

There is a general faculty of language that presides over all these modes of the expression of thought, and it may be defined: the faculty of establishing a constant relation between an idea and a sign, whether this sign be a sound, a gesture, a figure, or any other trace. Moreover, each species of language necessitates the play of certain organs of emission and reception. The organs of reception are sometimes the ear, sometimes sight, sometimes even touch. As for the organs of emission, they are put in play by the voluntary muscles, like those of the larynx, or the tongue, of the soft palate [voile du palais], of the face, the upper limbs, etc. All regular language supposes therefore the integrity, (1) of a certain number of muscles, of the motor nerves that serve them, and the part of the central nervous system from which these nerves arise; (2) of a certain external sensory apparatus, of the sensory nerve that departs from these, and of the part of the central nervous system to which this nerve connects; (3) finally, the part of the brain that holds under its dependence the general faculty of language, such as we have come to define it.

The absence or abolition of this last faculty renders impossible all species of language. Congenital or accidental lesions of the organs of reception and the organs of emission can deprive us of the particular species of language that these organs contribute; but if the general language faculty persists in us with a sufficient degree of intelligence, we can still compensate with another species of language for those we have lost. [p. 332]

The pathological causes that deprive us of a medium of communication ordinarily make us lose only half of it, because it is quite rare that the organs of emission and the organs of reception would be affected at the same time. For example, the adult who becomes deaf continues to express himself through speech, but for him to transmit an idea he uses a different language, such as gesture or writing. The inverse takes place when paralysis strikes the speech muscles; the ill person to whom we address ourselves in articulated language, responds to us then in another language. It is in this way that diverse systems of communication can be mutually compensatory.

This is only elementary physiology; but pathology permits us to push the analysis further on to that which concerns articulated language, which is the most important and probably the most complex of all.

There are cases where the general language faculty persists unaltered, where the auditory apparatus is intact, where all the muscles, not even excepting those of the voice and those of articulation, obey the will, and yet where a cerebral lesion abolishes articulated language. This abolition of speech, in individuals who are neither paralyzed nor idiots, constitutes a symptom so singular that it seems to me useful to designate it with a special name. I will give it, therefore, the name of aphemia (deprive, I speak, I pronounce); it is only the faculty of articulating words that these patients lack. They hear and comprehend all that one says to them; they all have their intelligence; they emit vocal sounds with ease; they execute with their tongue and their lips movements much more extensive and energetic than those required for the articulation of sounds, and yet the perfectly sensible response that they would want to make is reduced to a very small number of articulated sounds, always the same and always performed in the same manner; their vocabulary, if can call it that, is composed of a short series of syllables, sometimes of a monosyllable that expresses everything, or rather that expresses nothing, for this unique word is most often a stranger to all vocabularies. Certain ill people have not even a vestige of articulate language; they make vain efforts without pronouncing a single syllable. Others have, in some sense, two degrees of articulation. In [p. 333] ordinary circumstances, they invariably pronounce their word of choice [prédilection]; but, when they have an angry outburst, they become able to articulate a second word, most often a coarse swearword, with which they were probably familiar before their sickness, then they stop after the latter effort. Mr. Auburtin has observed a patient who is still alive and who does not need to be excited to utter a stereotyped curse. All his responses start with a bizarre word of six syllables and invariably end with this supreme invocation: Sacred name of G . . .

Those who have for the first time studied these strange happenings have been able to believe, due to an [in-?]sufficient analysis, that the faculty of language, in similar cases, was abolished; but it obviously persists in its entirety, since these ill people perfectly comprehend articulated language and written language; since these who do not know how or are not able to write have enough intelligence (and it is mistaken in many similar cases) to find the means to communicate their thought, and since finally those who are literate, and who have the free use of their hands, clearly put their ideas on paper. They know therefore the sense and the value of words, in auditory form just as in graphic form. Articulated language that they could once speak is always familiar to them, but they cannot execute the series of methodical and coordinated movements that correspond to the searched-for syllable. This which has died in them [péri en eux], it is not therefore the faculty of language, it is not the memory for

words, nor is it the action of the nerves and muscles corresponding to phonation [phonation] and to articulation, it is something
else, it is a faculty particularly considered by Mr. Bouillaud as
the faculty that coordinates the proper movements of articulated
language, or more simply as the faculty of articulated language,
since without it there is no articulation possible.

The nature of this faculty and the place that it must be
assigned in the cerebral hierarchy can give rise to some hesitation. Is it only a species of memory, and the individuals who have
lost it have lost only, not the memory of words, but memory for
the procedure that must be followed to articulate words? Have
they come to this by a condition comparable to that of a young
child who already understands the language of those around
him, who is sensitive to blame and praise, who points out with
his fingers all the [p. 334] objects that he can name, who has
acquired a crowd [foule] of simple ideas, and who, to express
these, can do no more than stammer out a single syllable? Little
by little, after innumerable efforts, he succeeds in articulating
a few new syllables. Yet still he arrives so often at a mistake,
saying, for example, papa when he wanted say mama, because
at the moment of pronunciation of the latter word he no longer
remembers the position that must be given to his tongue and
to his lips. Soon he knows quite well the mechanism of some
simple and easy syllables so that he can pronounce them at every
attempt without error and without hesitation; but he hesitates
and again makes mistakes on more complicated and more difficult syllables, and when finally he possesses much practical
experience with [la practique de] many monosyllables, he needs
to acquire new experience to learn to pronounce rapidly [passer
tout à coup] one syllable after another, and to pronounce, in
the place of the doubled monosyllables that constituted his first
vocabulary, words composed of two or three different syllables.
These gradual perfections of articulated language in children are
due to the development of a particular species of memory that is
not the memory for words, but that of the movements necessary
to articulate words. And this particular memory is not related [en
rapport] to other kinds of memory nor to the rest of intelligence.
I knew a child of three years whose intelligence and will was
above that of his age, who had a well-formed tongue, and who
still did not know how to talk. I know another very intelligent

child who, at the age of twenty-one months, perfectly understands two languages, who, as a consequence, possesses the highest degree of memory for words, and who up to this point, is not able to rise above the level of pronouncing monosyllables.

If adults who lose speech have only forgotten the art of articulation, if they have simply reverted [revenus] to the condition where they were before having learned to pronounce words, we must place [ranger] the faculty of which the illness has deprived them into the order of intellectual faculties. This hypothesis seems to me quite likely. It might be possible, however, that it is otherwise, and that aphemia is the result of a locomotor ataxia limited to the part of the central nervous apparatus that presides over movements governing the articulation of sounds. One objects, it is true, that these ill people can freely [p. 335] execute with their tongue and their lips all the movements other than those of articulation; that they can immediately move, when asked, the point of their tongue upwards, downwards, to the right, to the left, etc.; but these movements, precise as they may seem to us, are infinitely less so than the excessively delicate movements that are required for speech. In locomotor ataxia of the limbs, one observes that the patients voluntarily execute all the large movements: if one tells them to lift their hand, to open it, to close it, they do it almost always without hesitation; but when they want to execute more precise movements, to seize, for example, in a certain manner, an object of small volume, they go beyond or stay behind the goal; they do not know how to coordinate the contraction of their muscles in a manner to obtain a result of determined value, and they make mistakes much less in the direction of their movements than in the quantity of force that they have to deploy and in the order of succession of partial movements of which the grasping of objects is composed. One can therefore ask if aphemia is not one species of locomotor ataxia limited to the muscles for the articulation of sound, and, if it were so, the faculty that the ill people have lost would not be an intellectual faculty, that is to say a faculty belonging to the thinking part of the brain, it would be only a particular case of the general faculty of coordination of muscular action, a faculty that depends on the motor parts of the nerve centers.

One can therefore make at least two hypotheses about the nature of the special faculty of articulated language. In the first hypothesis, there would be a superior faculty, and aphemia would be an intellectual trouble; in the second hypothesis, it would be a faculty of a much less elevated order, and aphemia would be no more than a trouble of locomotion. Though the latter interpretation appears to me much less probable than the other, I would not yet dare to commit myself in a categorical manner if I were reduced to only the lights of clinical observation.

Whatever it might be, on the account of functional analysis, the existence of the special faculty of articulated language, such as that I have defined, cannot be placed in doubt, because a faculty that can perish alone, without those that are nearest to it being [p. 336] altered, is obviously a faculty independent of all the others, that is to say a special faculty.

If all the cerebral faculties were as distinct, as clearly circumscribed as this one, one would finally have a positive point of departure to enter upon the question so controversial as cerebral localization. It is unfortunate that this is not so, and that the greatest obstacle to progress in this part of physiology comes from the insufficiency and uncertainty of the functional analysis that must necessarily precede research on the organs related to each function.

Science is so little advanced on this point that it still has not even found its foundation, and what is in dispute today is not such-and-such phrenological system, but the very principle of localization, that is to say the prior question is knowing whether all parts of the brain that are concerned with thought have identical attributes or different attributes.

A communication of Mr. Gratiolet relevant to the cerebral and intellectual similarity of the human races, has, on several occasions, detained the Anthropological Society of Paris to examine this important question, and Mr. Auburtin, partisan of the principle of localization, has thought, with good reason, that the localization of a single faculty suffices to establish the truth of this principle; he has, therefore, sought to demonstrate, according to the doctrine of his teacher Mr. Bouillaud, that the faculty of articulated language resides in the frontal lobes of the brain.

For this, he first reviewed a series of cases in which a spontaneous cerebral event had abolished the faculty of articulated language without destroying the other cerebral faculties, and in which at autopsy a deep lesion was found in the frontal convolutions of the brain. The special nature of the symptom of aphemia did not depend on the nature of the illness, but only on its location [siège], since the lesion was sometimes a softening, sometimes apoplexy, sometimes an abscess or a tumor. To complete his demonstration, Mr. Auburtin invoked another series of cases where aphemia was the consequence of a traumatic lesion of the frontal lobes of the brain; these facts, following him, the equivalent of vivisections, and he ended by saying that to his knowledge no one has ever found the frontal lobes of the brain in a state of complete [p. 337] integrity, nor even in a state of relative integrity, at the autopsy of individuals who have lost the faculty of articulated language without losing the rest of their intelligence.

Some have opposed him with many remarkable facts relevant to individuals who had spoken right up to the last day, and yet in whom the frontal lobes of the brain had been the seat of deep spontaneous or traumatic lesions; but he responded that this proves nothing, that a lesion, even widespread, of the frontal lobes might not reach the part of the lobes where resides [siége] the faculty of articulated language, that the objection would only be valid if all the frontal convolutions had been destroyed on both sides to their full extent, that is to say up to the sulcus [sillon] of Rolando, and that, in the cases opposed to him, the destruction of the convolutions had been only partial. He therefore recognized that a lesion of the frontal lobes does not necessarily lead to a loss of speech, but he maintained that the latter is the certain sign of the former, that it permits such a diagnosis; that the diagnosis has been made many times during life, and has never been refuted [démenti] by autopsy; finally, after having cited the observation of a still-living individual who presents for many years in a most clean manner, the symptoms of aphemia, and who is actually at the hospice for Incurables, he declared that would renounce without reversion [retour] the doctrine of Mr. Bouillaud, if the autopsy of this ill person did not confirm the diagnosis of a cerebral lesion occupying exclusively or principally the frontal lobes. (see Bulletin de la Société d'anthropologie, 1. II, meeting of 4 April, 1861.)

I believe I should summarize in a few words this discussion to make salient the interest and the actuality of the observation that I am presenting today to the Anatomical Society. Without doubt, the value of facts is not limited [subordonnée] to the circumstances of the milieu in which we observe them; but the impression that they make on us depends on them in great part, and when, a few days after having heard the argument of Mr. Auburtin, I found one morning, in my care [service], a dying person who for twenty-one years had lost the faculty of articulated language, I collected with the greatest care observations from him, which seemed to come expressly to serve as a touch stone [pierre de touche] for the theory supported by my colleague. [p. 338]

Up to here, without rejecting the theory, and without ignoring as nothing the importance of the facts that are favorable to it, I had felt much hesitation in the presence of the contradictory facts that exist in science. Though a partisan of the principle of localization, I would ask myself, and I ask myself still, within what limits this principle is applicable. There is a point that appears to me to be pretty nearly established by comparative anatomy, by the anatomical and physiological parallel of the human races, and finally by the comparison of the varieties of normal individuals, abnormal or pathological men of the same race; to know that the highest cerebral faculties, those that constitute the understanding properly so-called, like judgment, reflection, the faculties of comparison and abstraction, have their seat in the frontal convolutions, while the convolutions of the temporal, parietal, and occipital lobes are involved with [affectées aux] the sentiments, the dispositions [penchants], and the passions. In other terms, there is in the mind [esprit] groups of faculties, and in the brain, groups of convolutions; and the facts acquired up to now by science permit us to accept, like I have said elsewhere, that the large regions of the mind [esprit] correspond to the large regions of the brain. It is in this sense that the principle of localization seems to me, if not [sinon] rigorously demonstrated, at least extremely probable. But to know with certainty whether each particular faculty has its own seat in a particular convolution, this is a question that seems to me all but insoluble in the current state of science.

The study of the facts relevant to the loss of the faculty of articulated language is one those that has the most chance of leading us to a positive or negative solution. The independence of this faculty is evinced by pathological observation, and though one can raise some doubts about its nature, though one can ask oneself, as has been seen above, if it is part of the intellectual functions or of the cerebral functions that are involved [en rapport] with muscular activity, it is allowable to place it, at least provisionally, in the purview of the first hypothesis, which already, at first glance, seems the most probable, and in favor of that which the pathological anatomy of aphemia establishes strong presumptions. In effect, in all the cases where up to now the autopsy has been able to be undertaken, one has found the substance of the convolutions [p. 339] profoundly altered to a notable extent; in a few subjects the lesion spread exclusively over the convolutions where it is permitted to conclude that the faculty of articulated language is one of the functions of the convoluted mass. Now, one admits generally that all the faculties we call intellectual have their seat in this part of the brain, and it seems from that strongly probable that reciprocally all the faculties that reside in the cerebral convolutions are faculties of the intellectual order.

In placing ourselves, then, in this point view, we easily recognize that the pathological anatomy of aphemia can give something more than a solution to one particular question, and that it can throw a great deal of light on the general question of cerebral localization, by furnishing to cerebral physiology a point of departure, or rather a very precious point of comparison. If it were proven, for example, that aphemia can be the result of lesions affecting indifferently in any convolution and in any cerebral lobe, one would have the right to conclude not only that the faculty of articulated language is not localized, but also that very probably the other faculties of the same order are not localized either. If it were demonstrated on the contrary that the lesions that abolish speech consistantly occupy one determinate convolution, one could hardly fail to admit that this convolution is the seat of the faculty of articulated language, and, that once the existence of a first localization was admitted, the principle of localization by convolutions would be established. Finally, between these two extreme alternatives, there is a third that could lead to a mixed doctrine. Let us suppose, in effect, that the lesions of aphemia consistently occupy the same cerebral lobe, but that, in this lobe, they do not consistently occupy the same convolution; it would result that the faculty of articulated language would have its seat in a certain region, in a certain group of convolutions, but not in a particular convolution, and it would become very probable that the cerebral faculties are localized by regions, and not by convolutions.

It is important [importe], therefore, to study with the greatest care a special question that can have doctrinal consequences so general [p. 340] and so important. It is not only a matter of looking in which regions of the brain are located [siégent] the lesions of aphemia; one must as well designate by name and by row the affected [malades] convolutions and the degree of alteration of each. This is not how we have proceeded up to now. We have confined ourselves, in the most complete observations, to saying that the lesion began and finished so many centimeters from the frontal extremity of the hemisphere, so many centimeters from the great central fissure [scissure] or from the Sylvian fissure. But that is completely insufficient, because, given these indications, meticulous as they are, the reader cannot guess which is the affected convolution. Thus, there are cases where the illness is situated in the most frontal part of the hemisphere; others where it is situated 5 or even 8 centimeters behind this point, and it seems, given this, that the seat of the lesion might be very variable; but if one imagines [songe] that the three antero-posterior convolutions of the convexity of the frontal lobe begin at the level of the sourciliary arcade and run side by side, front to back, all three flowing into the frontal transverse convolution that forms the anterior side of the sulcus [sillon] of Rolando; if one imagines that this sulcus is situated more than 4 centimeters behind the coronal suture[1], and [p. 341] that the three frontal antero-posterior convolutions occupy more than two-fifths of the total length of the brain,—one will understand that the same convolution is able to be reached by lesions situated in points very different and very distant from each other. It is therefore, much less important to indicate the level of damage [mal] than to say which convolutions are ill.

This kind of description is without doubt less convenient than the other, for the classical anatomy treatises have not vulgarized up to now the study of cerebral convolutions that the phrenologists themselves had made the great mistake of neglecting. One is left to be dominated by the old prejudice that the cerebral convolutions have nothing fixed about them, that they are simple folds made haphazardly, comparable to the disordered bendings [flexuosités] of the intestinal loops, and what has accredited this idea, is that the secondary folds, which depend on the degree of development of the fundamental convolutions, vary not only from individual to individual, but often even within the same individual, from one hemisphere to the other. It is no less true that these fundamental convolutions are fixed and constant in all animals of the same species, and that, considered in the animal hierarchy, they behave much like perfectly distinct organs. The description and enumeration of the fundamental convolutions, of their connections and of their associations [rapports], would find no place here. One will find them in the special works of MM. Gratiolet and Rudolphe Wanger.[2] [p. 342]

And since I have expressed regrets over the lack of precision in the relevant descriptions of lesions of the cerebral hemispheres, I will point out an annoying confusion that has induced error in many observers. Many people, who are in the habit of studying the brain mainly by its inferior face, imagine that the anterior lobes include only the part of the hemispheres that is situated in front of the chiasm of the optic nerves and of the anterior extremity of the temporal-sphenoidal lobe. This is almost, in effect, like stopping at the inferior face of the anterior lobes; but, looking at the convex sides of the hemispheres, these lobes have a length at least double that above, and extend below the fissure of Sylvius, of which they form the superior edge, up to the sulcus of Rolando, which separates them from the parietal lobes. When one reads, in certain observations, that ill people who have had the two anterior lobes entirely destroyed continued to speak up to the moment of their death, it is permitted to believe, in the absence of any other indication, that the author wanted to speak mainly of the lobes that cover the orbital arch. It is said, for example, in the most celebrated of these observations, that a man, injured in the forehead by a mine explosion, had his two anterior lobes entirely crushed and reduced to pulp. But it is clear that no traumatic action can pound immediately, completely and in the same blow the totality of the two anterior lobes without crushing at the same time the whole front half of the brain, including the insula, the striate body, the corpus callosum, the arch to three pillars, etc., and this kind of lesion is not admissible in a man who had been able to walk to his bed, who had retained all his intelligence, and who had survived twenty-four hours without having presented either contracture or paralysis. Similarly, when I exhibited for the first time, at a meeting of physicians, the brain of the man of which I today publish my observations, many people cried out that this work was in contradiction with the ideas of Mr. Bouillaud, that the anterior lobes were very nearly healthy, that the lesion was almost entirely behind these lobes. One will see nevertheless that the frontal (or anterior) convolutions were destroyed to a very considerable extent.

But I have to excuse myself for having developed too far [p. 343] these preliminary remarks. It is time to pass to the relation of my observation of aphemia.

II.

Aphemia dating to twenty-one years, produced by the chronic and progressive softening of the second and third convolutions of the upper level of the left frontal lobe.

On 11 April 1861, transported to the general infirmary of Bicêtre, surgery service, was a 50-year-old man, named Leborgne, suffering from a diffuse, gangrenous phlegmon of the entire right inferior limb, from the instep up to the buttock. To the questions that I addressed to him the next day on the origin of his malady, he responded only with the monosyllable tan, repeated two times in sequence, and accompanied by a gesture of his left hand. I went for information on this man's history, who had been at Bicêtre for twenty-one years. I interrogated in turn his minders (surveillants), his fellows on the ward, and his parents, who came to see him, and here is what resulted from this inquest.

He was subject, since his youth, to attacks of epilepsy; but he had been able to take up the trade of a hat-form maker [prendre l'état de formier] that he exercised up to the age of thirty. At this time, he lost the ability to speak, and it was for this reason that he was admitted as a patient to the hospice of Bicêtre. We did not know if the loss of speech came on slowly or rapidly, nor if any other symptoms had accompanied the onset of this affliction.

When he arrived at Bicêtre, it had already been two or three months that he had not been able to speak. He was then perfectly healthy and intelligent, and differed from a sane man only in the loss of articulated speech. He came and went in the hospice where he was known under the name of Tan. He understood all that was said to him; he even had very fine hearing; but, regardless of the question addressed to him, he always responded: tan, tan, in conjunction with greatly varied gestures by means of which he succeeded in expressing most of his ideas. When his interlocutors did not comprehend his mime, he would easily become enraged, and then add to his [p. 344] vocabulary a great swearword, one only, and precisely the same that I indicated above, in speaking of a patient observed by Mr. Auburtin. Tan was regarded as being egotistical, vindictive, bad, and his comrades, who detested him, accused him even of being a thief. These faults could have been due in large part to the cerebral lesion; however, they were not pronounced enough to appear pathological, and, though this patient was at Bicêtre, one never thought of moving him to the division for the insane. He was considered, on the contrary, as a man perfectly responsible for his acts.

He had already been without speech for ten years when a new symptom appeared: the muscles of his right arm gradually weakened, and finally became entirely paralyzed. Tan continued to walk without difficulty, but the paralysis of movement won little by little the right inferior limb, and, after having dragged his leg for some time, the patient had to resign himself to keeping constantly to bed. It was about four years from the start of the paralysis of his arm up to the moment when that of his abdominal limb was advanced enough to render standing completely impossible. It was, therefore, close to seven years that Tan was in bed before he was brought to the infirmary. This last period of his life is that of which we have the least information. Having become incapable of doing harm, his comrades no longer occupied themselves with him, except for amusing themselves at his expense a few times (which gave him bitter fits of anger), and he had lost the little celebrity that the singularity of his illness had formerly given him in the hospice. It was noticed that his vision had declined notably over about the previous two years. This was the only complication noticed while he had been confined to his bed. Besides that, he had never been senile; his clothes were changed only once per week, with the result that the widespread phlegmon, for which he was transported to the infirmary on 11 April 1861, was recognized by the nurses only when it had progressed considerably and had invaded the totality of his right abdominal limb, from the foot to the buttock.

The study of this unfortunate person, who could not speak and who, being paralyzed in the right hand, could not write, presented quite a few difficulties. He was moreover in such a generally grave state, [p. 345] that it would have been cruel to torment him with lengthy investigations.

I noted however that his general sensitivity was everywhere preserved, though it was uneven. The right half of his body was less sensitive than the other, and this doubtless contributed to the attenuation of the pain of the extensive phlegmon. The patient did not suffer much when not touched there, but palpation was painful, and a few incisions, that I was obliged to make, provoked agitation and cries.

The two right limbs were completely paralyzed of movement; the two other limbs were obedient to will, and, though weak, could, without any hesitation, execute all movements. The emission of urine and fecal matter was natural, but swallowing was done with some difficulty; mastication, on the contrary, was done very well. The face was not distorted; however, in the act of breathing, the left cheek seemed a little more swollen than the right, thus indicating that the muscles on this side of the face were a little weakened. There was no indication of strabismus. The tongue was perfectly free; it was not distorted; the patient could move it in all directions and stick it out of his mouth. The two halves of this organ were of equal thickness. The difficulty in swallowing that I mentioned above was due to a paralysis starting in the pharynx, and not to a paralysis of the tongue, for it was only the third time swallowing that was laborious. The muscles of the larynx seemed in no way altered, the quality of the voice was natural, and the sounds that the patient made in pronouncing his monosyllable were perfectly clear.

His hearing had kept it fineness: Tan heard well the tick of a watch; but his vision was weak; when he wanted to see the time, he was obliged to take the watch himself with his left hand and place it in a particular position, about 20 centimeters from his right eye, which seemed better than the left.

The state of intelligence could not be exactly determined. It is certain that Tan understood almost everything that was said to him; but, he could only express his ideas or his desires by the movement of his left hand, our dying person [moribond] could not make himself [p. 346] understood as well as he could understand others. Numerical responses were those that he could make the best, by opening or closing his fingers. I asked him many times how many days he had been sick? he [sic] responded sometimes five days, sometimes six days. For how many years had he been at Bicêtre? he [sic] opened his hand four times in sequence, and then pointed with a single finger; this would make twenty-one years, and one saw above that this information was perfectly exact. The next day, I repeated the same question, and I obtained the same response; but, when I wanted to return to this a third time, Tan understood that I was making him do an exercise; he became angry, and articulated the curse already named which I only heard from his mouth one time. I presented him with my watch two days in a row. The second hand was not moving; he could not, as a result, distinguish the three hands other than by their form or by their length; nevertheless, after having examined the watch for a few moments, he was able each time to indicate the time with exactitude. It is therefore incontestable that this man was intelligent, that he could reflect, and that he had preserved, in a certain measure, his memory for things past. He could even comprehend relatively complicated ideas: for instance, I asked him in what order his paralysis had progressed; he made first with the index finger of his left hand a little horizontal gesture that wanted to say: understand! then he pointed successively to his tongue, his right arm and his right leg. It was perfectly exact, apart from the fact that he attributed his loss of speech to paralysis of his tongue, which was very natural.

Nevertheless, various questions to which a man of ordinary intelligence would have found the means to respond to by gesture, even with a single hand, remained without response. Other times, one could not grasp the meaning of certain responses, which seemed to greatly annoy the patient; other times, at last, the response was clear, but false: thus, although he did not have children, he claimed to have them. It is not therefore doubtful that the intelligence of this man had undergone a profound change, being under the influence of his cerebral affliction, being under the influence of the fever that devoured him; but he was evidently much more intelligent than he had to be in order to speak.

It was seen clearly in the information obtained and in the present [p. 347] state of the patient that there existed a progressive cerebral lesion that, originally and during the first ten years of the sickness, was kept limited to a relatively circumscribed region, and which, in this first period, affected neither the organs of motility, nor the organs of sensitivity; that at the end of ten years, the lesion propagated to one or many organs of motility, but not yet [en respectant encore] the organs of sensitivity; and that, more recently finally, general sensitivity was blunted at the same time as vision, especially the vision of the left eye. With the complete paralysis of movement in the two limbs on the right side, and the sensitivity of these two limbs being moreover a little weak, the principle cerebral lesion had to occupy the left hemisphere, and what confirmed this opinion was the incomplete paralysis of the muscles of the left cheek and the retina of the same side, for it need not be repeated [inutile de rappeler] that paralyses of cerebral causes are crossed for the trunk and the limbs, and direct for the face.

It was a matter of determining more exactly, if possible, the seat of the original lesion, and, though the last discussion of the Anthropological Society left some doubt about the doctrine of Mr. Bouillaud, I wanted, in the upcoming autopsy, to proceed as if this doctrine were true; this was the best means of putting it to the test. Mr. Aubertin, having declared some days before that he would renounce it if one could show him a single case of aphemia, well-described, without a lesion to the anterior lobes, I invited him to come see my patient in order to know ahead of time what his diagnosis would be, and if this case was one of those in which he would accept the result as conclusive. Apart from the complications that had been observed for 11 years, my colleague found the current state and the antecedents sufficiently clear to affirm without hesitation that the lesion must have started in one of the anterior lobes.

Reasoning from this datum to complete the diagnosis, I considered that the striate body was the motor organ closest to the anterior lobes; it was without doubt in gradually spreading to this organ that the original lesion had produced the hemiplegia. The probable diagnosis was therefore: original lesion in the left anterior lobe, propagated to the striate body of the same side. As for the nature of this lesion, everything indicated that it was a matter [p. 348] of a progressive, chronic softening, but extremely slow, for the absence of all phenomena of compression excluded the idea of an intracranial tumor.

The patient died on 17 April, at eleven o'clock in the morning. The autopsy was done as soon as possible, that is to say, at the end of twenty-four hours. The temperature was slightly elevated. The cadaver showed no sign of putrefaction. The brain was shown a few hours later to the Anthropological Society, then placed immediately in alcohol. The organ was so altered that we had to take great precautions to conserve it. It was only after two months and after many changes of liquid that the specimen [pièce] began to firm up. Today it is in perfect condition, and it is deposited in the Dupuytren museum under no. 55a, of the nervous system.

I will not relate [passe sous silence] the details relevant to the diffuse phlegmon. The muscles of the two right limbs were entirely fatty and reduced to a small volume. All the viscera were healthy, except the brain.

The skull was opened with a saw with a great deal of care. All the sutures were knit together; the thickness of bone was a little increased; the diploe was replaced by compact tissue. The internal surface of the cranial vault presented in all its extent an appearance of fine wormholes [vermoulure], a certain indication of chronic osteitis (no. 55b).

The external face of the dura mater was red or very vascularized; the membrane was very thick, very vascularized, almost fleshy, and internally covered with a pseudo-membranous film infiltrated with serous fluid, and the appearance of grease [lardacée]. The dura mater and the false membrane together had an average thickness of 5 millimeters (minimum, 3 millimeters; maximum, 8); from which it necessarily follows that the brain must have lost a notable portion of its original volume.

Lifting the dura mater, the pia mater appeared very perforated [injectée] at certain points, thick throughout, and, in places, opaque, infiltrated with a plastic yellowish material that had the color of puss, but that was solid, and that, when examined through a microscope, did not contain purulent globules.

On the lateral part of the left hemisphere, at the level of the Sylvian fissure, the pia mater was raised by an amount of [p. 349] transparent serous fluid, that was lodged in a large and deep depression of the cerebral substance. This liquid was evacuated by puncturing it, collapsing the pia mater, pushing it down deeply, and resulting in the opening of a long cavity of capacity equivalent to the volume of a chicken egg, connected to the Sylvian fissure, and separating thereby the frontal lobe from the temporal lobe. It extended at the rear up to the level of the sulcus of Rolando, which separates, as we know, the anterior or frontal convolutions from the parietal convolutions. The lesion was therefore situated throughout the entire region in front of this sulcus, and the parietal lobe was healthy, at least relatively speaking [d'une manière relative], for no part of the hemispheres was in a state of absolute integrity.

In cutting and peeling back [écartant] the pia mater at the level of the cavity I have here described, one recognized at first glance that this corresponded not to a depression, but to a loss of substance of the cerebral mass; the liquid that filled it had been produced continuously to fill the space as it formed, as took the place of the chronic softening of the superficial layers of the brain or the cerebellum [cervelet]. The study of the convolutions that formed the edges of the cavity effectively demonstrates that they were the seat of one of these chronic softenings of which the progress was slow enough that the cerebral molecules, dissociated in some way one from another, were able to be absorbed [résorber] and be replaced by an emission of serous fluid.[3] A notable part of the left hemisphere had thus been destroyed gradually; but the softening extended well beyond the limits of the cavity; this was by no means circumscribed, and cannot under any circumstances be described as a cyst. Its inner faces [parois], irregular and with crevices almost everywhere, were constituted of the cerebral substance itself, which was extremely soft at this level, and which the most internal surface, in direct [p. 350] contact with the secreted serous fluid, was on its way to slow and gradual dissolution when the patient succumbed. The inferior face alone was smooth and had a quite firm consistency.

It is clear, consequently, that the original home of the softening was where today is found the loss of substance, that the illness thereafter expanded to further and further through the continuity of tissue, and that the point where it started is to be found not within the organs now softened, or on their way to softening, but among those which are more or less completely destroyed. We will therefore, based on inspection of the parts that limit the loss of substance, draw up the list of those that have disappeared.

The cavity that we will describe is situated, as we have already seen, at the level of the Sylvian fissure; it consequently lies between the frontal lobe and the temporal-sphenoidal lobe, and if the organs that surround it were only interfered with [refoulés] without being destroyed, one should find on its inferior or temporal side the marginal inferior convolution, on its superior or frontal side the third frontal convolution[4], and finally, on its inner face, [p. 351] the lobe of the insula. Now, this is not without significance [il n'en est rien]. 1) The inferior face of the cavity is limited by the second temporo-sphenoidal [p. 352] convolution, which was moreover entirely intact, and which possessed a quite firm consistency. The entire thickness of the marginal inferior convolution had therefore been destroyed, that is to say, up to the parallel fissure. 2) The deep wall of the cavity no longer presents traces of the lobe of the insula; this lobe is entirely destroyed, as well as the inner half of the extra-ventricular nucleus of the striate body; finally, the loss of substance is extended from this side up to the anterior part of the ventricular nucleus of the striate body, of such a sort that our cavity connects [communique], by a long opening of half a centimeter and with irregular edges, with the lateral ventricle of the brain. 3) Finally, the superior edge, or rather, the superior wall of the cavity, encroaches considerably on the frontal lobe, which presents at this level a large and deep indentation. The posterior half of the third frontal convolution is completely destroyed throughout all its thickness; the second frontal convolution is a little less altered. At least its two external layers have disappeared, and the external layer, which is still in place [retrouve], is extremely softened. Behind, the inferior layer of the frontal transversal convolution is destroyed, throughout its thickness, up to the Rolandic sulcus.

In summary, as a consequence, the destroyed organs are the following:

The small inferior marginal convolution (temporo-sphenoidal lobe); the small convolutions of the lobe of the insula, and the part subjacent to the striate body; finally, on the frontal lobe, the inferior part of the transversal convolution, and the posterior half of the two great convolutions designated by the name of second and third frontal convolutions. Of the four convolutions that form the superior layer of the frontal lobe, one alone, the first and the most internal, did not preserve its integrity, for it is softened and atrophied, but did preserve its continuity; and if one imaginatively restores [rétablit par la pensée] all the parts that have been destroyed, one finds that at least three-quarters of the cavity that has been hollowed out comes from the frontal lobe.

It now remains to be determined the location at which the lesion must have begun. Now, examination of the cavity left by the loss of substance shows first of all that the center of its focus [foyer] corresponds to the frontal lobe. As a consequence, if the softening had spread [p. 353] uniformly in all directions, this lobe would have been the point of departure for the illness. But it is not only the study of the cavity that should guide us, we should also take account of the state of the parts that surround it. These parts are very unequally softened, they are affected to a highly variable extent. Thus, the second temporal convolution, that forms the inferior limit of the focus, presents a smooth surface and relatively firm consistency; it is softened, without doubt, but is not much so, and it is softened only in its uppermost layer. On the opposing side, on the frontal lobe, the softening is, by contrast, almost fluid in the neighborhood of the focus; as one increases one's distance from it, the cerebral substance gradually becomes firmer, but the softening extends, in reality, up to a considerable distance, and reaches almost all of the frontal lobe. It is therefore primarily in this lobe that the softening was propagated, and it is almost certain that the other parts were invaded subsequently.

If one were looking to be more precise, one might remark that the third frontal convolution is that which presents the most extensive loss of substance, that it is not only cut across the level of the anterior extremity of the Sylvian fissure, but still is entirely destroyed throughout its posterior half, that it alone has suffered a loss of substance equal to about half of the total loss of substance; that the second convolution, or middle convolution, although very profoundly damaged, still preserves the continuity of its most internal part, and that as a consequence, according to all probabilities, it is in the third frontal convolution that the disease began.

The other parts of the hemispheres are relatively healthy; they are, it is true, a little less firm than is typical, and one can say that all the exterior parts of the encephalon have suffered notable atrophy, but they have preserved their form, their continuity, their normal aspect. As for the deep parts, I abstained [renoncé] from studying them, so as not to destroy the specimen, which it seemed important to me to deposit in the Museum. However, the opening that connects the exterior to the anterior part of the left lateral ventricle was, despite my efforts, enlarged during the dissection of the pia mater so that I was able to examine half the internal surface of this ventricle, and I saw that all of the striate body was [p. 354] more or less softened, but that the optic stratum maintained [avait] its color, its volume, and its normal consistency.

The whole encephalon, weighed with the pia mater, after evacuation of the liquid that filled the focus, was not greater than 987 grams. It is therefore almost 400 grams lighter than the average weight of the brains of 50-year-old men. This considerable loss was carried almost entirely by the cerebral hemispheres. One knows, in effect, that the rest of the encephalon in a normal state, never reaches the weight of 200 grams, and stays almost constantly below 180. Now, the cerebellum, the protuberance and the bulb, although not voluminous in our subject, are certainly not much below the average, and in supposing, impossibly, that they had lost a quarter of their weight, this would account only for a minimal part of the total loss.

The destruction of the organs that surround the Sylvian fissure of the left hemisphere contributes, no doubt, much to the diminution of the brain weight; but I have taken from a healthy brain the same amount of substance, and the mass that I lifted weighed no more than 50 grams. It is therefore infinitely probable that the cerebral hemispheres have suffered, throughout their extent, a quite considerable atrophy, and this probability is changed to certitude if one considers the relative thickness of the meninges and of the distorted [fausse] arachnoid membrane, that reaches a thickness at certain points of 5 or 6 millimeters.

After having described these lesions, and researched their nature, seat, and anatomical progression, it is important to compare these results with those of clinical observation, to finally establish, if possible, a connection between the symptoms and the material disorders.

Anatomical inspection shows that the lesion was still in the act of propagating when the patient succumbed. The lesion had therefore been progressive, but it advanced very slowly, since it had taken twenty-one years to destroy a quite limited part of the cerebral mass. It is permissible to believe, as a consequence, that there was a long period during which it did not go beyond the limits of the organ in which it had started. Now, we saw that the original focus of the illness was situated in [p. 355] the frontal lobe, and quite probably in the third frontal convolution. This drives us to admit that from the point of view of pathological anatomy there had been two periods: one in which only one frontal convolution (probably the third) was altered; the other, in which the illness propagated itself little by little to the other convolutions, to the lobe of the insula or to the extra-ventricular nucleus of the striate body.

If now we examine the succession of symptoms, we find equally two periods: a first period which lasted ten years, during which the faculty of language was abolished, and when all the other functions of the encephalon were intact; and a second period of eleven years, during which a paralysis of movement, at first partial, then absolutely complete, successively invaded the superior limb and the inferior limb of the right side.

Having said this, it is impossible [not] to recognize that there had been a correspondence between the two anatomical periods and the two symptomological periods. Nor to ignore that the cerebral convolutions are not motor organs. The striate body of the left hemisphere is therefore of all the organs damaged [léssé] the only one in which one can find the cause of the paralysis of the two right limbs, and the second clinical period, that in which motility was altered, corresponds also to the second anatomical period, that is to say, to that in which the softening, overflowing the limits of the frontal lobe, reached the insula and the striate body.

Thus, the first period of ten years, characterized clinically by the unique symptom of aphemia, must correspond to the phase [époque] in which in the lesion was still limited to the frontal lobe.

Up to now, given the parallel between lesions and symptoms, I have mentioned neither troubles of intelligence, nor of their anatomical cause. We have seen that the intelligence of our patient, perfectly preserved for a long time, declined notably beginning at a time [époque] that cannot be determined, and that it was seriously weakened when we observed it for the first time. We found, in the autopsy, alterations more than sufficient to explain this state. Three frontal convolutions of four were profoundly damaged to a considerable extent, nearly the whole frontal lobe was more or less softened; finally all the mass [p. 356] of the convolutions of the two hemispheres were atrophied, sunken, and sensibly softer than in the normal state. One can scarcely understand that the patient was able to retain any intelligence at all, and it does not seem probable that one could live very long with this kind of brain. I think, for my part, that the general softening of the left frontal lobe, the general atrophy of the two hemispheres, and the general chronic meningitis, did not appear at a time much in the past [ne remontaient pas à une époque fort reculée]; I am disposed to believe that these lesions came about a long time after the softening of the striate body, of the sort that one could subdivide the second period into two secondary periods, and in doing so, summarize the history of the patient.

Facts that, like these ones, are attached to grand questions of doctrine, cannot be presented in too much detail, nor discussed with too much care. I need this excuse to pardon myself for the aridity of the description and the length of the discussion. I now only have but a few more words to add to bring out the consequences of this study.

1st Aphemia, that is to say the loss of speech, before all other intellectual trouble and before all paralysis, was the consequence of a lesion of one of the anterior lobes of the brain.

2nd Our observations therefore confirm the opinion of Mr. Bouillaud, who places in these lobes the seat of the faculty of articulated language.

3rd The observations assembled up to now, those at least that are accompanied by a clear and precise anatomical description, are not numerous enough that one can consider this localization of a particular faculty in a lobe to be determined [p. 357] like a definitive demonstration, but one can consider it at least extremely probable.

4th It is a much more difficult question to know whether the faculty of articulated language depends on the anterior lobe considered as a whole, or especially on one of the convolutions of this lobe; to know, in other terms, if the localization of the cerebral faculties is arranged one faculty per convolution, or only by groups of faculties and groups of convolutions. More observations should be collected with the goal of resolving this question. We must indicate exactly the name and the row of the ill convolutions, and, if the lesion is very extensive, to determine, as far as possible, by anatomical examination, the point in the convolution where the illness seems to have started.

5th In our patient, the original seat of the lesion was in the second or the third frontal convolution, more probably in the latter. It is therefore possible that the faculty of articulated language resides in one or the other of these two convolutions; but one still cannot know, considering that the previous observations are mute on the state of each convolution in particular, and one cannot even predict, since the principle of localization by convolution still rests on no certain basis.

6th In any case, it suffices to compare our observations with those that have preceded them to dismiss today the idea that the faculty of articulated language resides at a fixed point, circumscribed, and situated under any bump of the skull; the lesions of aphemia have been found most often in the most anterior part of the frontal lobe, not far from the eyebrow, and above the orbital arch; whereas in my patient, they exist mostly in front, and much more near the coronal suture than near the sourciliary arcade. This difference of seats is incompatible with the system of bumps; it would be perfectly coincident, by contrast, with the system of localizations by convolution, since each of the three great convolutions of the superior layer of the frontal lobe travel successively, in its antero-posterior trajectory, to all the regions in which have been found up to now the lesions of aphemia.

Footnotes

[1] It is generally believed that the sulcus of Rolando is situated directly beneath the coronal suture, and Mr. Gratiolet, following this, accords very particular importance to the study of this suture, which would permit the establishment of a very precise relation between the frontal region of the skull and the anterior lobes of the brain. This would be an infinitely precious datum [donnée] in the comparison of the human races. Unfortunately, this datum is completely inaccurate: the brain, taken out of the skull and placed on a table, is slack [s'étale] and stretched, and if one measures the length of the anterior lobe of the hemisphere, one finds that it is nearly equal to that of the frontal bone. But, in examining the organs in place, I have arrived at a completely different result. Here is how I proceed. After having lifted the integument and the pericranium, I sink gimlets [vrilles] at various points of the coronal suture, and I push through the gimlet holes little wooden pins [chevilles] into the cerebral substance. The skull is then opened with a saw; the brain is lifted and stripped of its membranes, and I study the situation of the pins with respect to [par rapport au] the sulcus of Rolando. I have done this research on eleven subjects of the masculine sex, having reached or surpassed the age of adulthood, and I have found consistently that the sulcus of Rolando begins, on the median line, at least 4 centimeters behind the coronal suture, (minimum 40 millimeters; maximum 63 millimeters). At its external part, this sulcus, which is oblique and not transverse, is brought together with the coronal suture; at 4 centimeters from the median line, it is situated only 2 centimeters at least, 3 at most, behind this suture. The same procedure has permitted me to verify that there is to the contrary a quite constant relation between the lambdoid suture and the occipital transverse sulcus that separates the parietal lobe from the occipital lobe of the hemisphere. The pins sunk into the lambdoid suture ordinarily penetrate the occipital sulcus or very near to it. I have never found them more than 15 millimeters from this sulcus, and the deviation [écart] is rarely more than 5 millimeters.

[2] Gratiolet et Leuret, Anatomie comparée du système nerveux, 1. II, p. 110, Paris, 1857, in-8. The second volume is exclusively the

work of Mr. Gratiolet.—Gratiolet, Mémoire sur les plis cérébraux de l'homme et des primates, Paris, 1854, in-4, with atlas in-folio.— Rudolphe Wagner, Abhandlung über die typischen Verschieden-heiten der Windungen der Hemisphæren, etc., Gottingen, 1860, in-4, with atlas, p. 13 to 25. One will find further on, in another note, an abridged description of the anterior or frontal convolutions.

[3] It is thus not that these things happened in the softening that started in the medullary layer of the convolutions: it is only when the lesion has its point of departure under the pia mater, that is in the cortical layer of the convolutions, that the softened and slowly-absorbed substance is replaced by the serous fluid. I observed the diverse phases of this mechanism on the cerebellum as well as the on the cerebrum [cerveau]. The first work [pièce] that I reported [recueillie] (and that I presented in January 1861 to the Anatomical Society) first confused me; but since then many others have relieved [levé] my doubts.

[4] It seemed to me necessary, for understanding that which follows, to recall here, in summary form, the disposition of and relations among the cerebral organs that I should mention.

The anterior lobe of the brain includes the whole part of the hemisphere situated above the Sylvian fissure, which separates it from the temporo-sphenoidal lobe, and in front of the Rolandic sulcus, which separates it from the parietal lobe. The location of the latter sulcus has been made precise in a previous note (p. 340). Its direction is nearly transverse; starting at the median line, it goes almost in a straight line, having hardly any bends, to end at its lower and outside point at [décrivant à peine de légères flexuosités, aboutir en bas et en dehors à] the Sylvian fissure, which it meets almost at a right angle, behind the posterior edge of the lobe of the insula.

The anterior lobe of the brain is composed of two layers, the inferior or orbital one, formed of many convolutions known as orbital, that lie on the vault [vôute] of the orbit, and of which I will have nothing to say; the other superior, located under the shell [écaille] of the frontal bone and under the most forward part of the parietal.

This superior layer is composed of four fundamental convolutions, that are known as the frontal convolutions, properly called: one is posterior, the others are anterior. The posterior, not very flexuous [peu flexeuse], forms the anterior edge of the

Rolandic sulcus; it is therefore almost transversal, and it turns back from outside to inside, from the Sylvian fissure to the great median fissure that receives the falx of the brain: this is why one designates it indifferently by the names of frontal posterior convolution, transversal or ascendant. The three other convolutions of the superior layer are very flexuous, very complicated, and one must have a certain knack [habitude] for distinguishing them along their full length, in order to avoid confusing the fundamental sulci that separate them, with the secondary sulci that separate the second-order layers, and that vary, following the individual ones, according to the degree of complication, that is to say according to the degree of development of the fundamental convolutions. These three anterior convolutions are antero-posterior, and, run side by side, covering from front to back the full length of the frontal lobe. They start at the level of the sourciliary arcade, from which they bend back and continue [se réfléchissent pour se continuer] along the convolutions of the inferior layer, and end, in the back, at the frontal transversal convolution, into which all three empty. They carry the names of first, second, and third frontal convolutions. One can also call them internal, middle [moyenne], and external; but the ordinary terms are more prevalent.

The first goes along with the great fissure of the brain; it consistently presents, in the human species, a more or less complete antero-posterior sulcus that divides into two folds of the second-order. It is therefore divided into two convolutions; but the comparative anatomy shows that these two folds form only a single fundamental convolution.

The second frontal convolution offers nothing in particular; it is not the same as the third, which is the most external. This one presents a superior or internal edge contiguous with the fluxuous edge of the middle convolution, and an inferior or external edge the connections [rapports] of which differ depending on whether one examines them at the front or back. In its anterior half, this edge is in contact with the external edge of the most external orbital convolution. In its posterior half, it is free, by contrast, and separated from the temporo-sphenoidal lobe by the Sylvian fissure, of which it forms the superior edge. It is because of this last connection that the third frontal convolution is sometimes designated by the name of marginal superior convolution.

We add that the inferior edge of the Sylvian fissure is formed by the superior convolution of the temporo-sphenoidal lobe, which is for this reason called the marginal inferior convolution. It is an antero-posterior fold, thin and almost rectilinear, which is separated from the second temporo-sphenoidal convolution by a sulcus parallel to the Sylvian fissure. This sulcus is designated by the name of parallel fissure (insinuated into the Sylvian fissure).

Finally, when one spreads apart the two marginal convolutions, superior and inferior, of the Sylvian fissure, one perceives a large hill [éminence] and a small bulge [saillante] the summit of which gives birth to five small simple convolutions, or rather to five rectilinear folds radiating in the shape of a fan: this is the lobe of the insula which covers the extra-ventricular nucleus [noyau] of the striate body, and which, rising from the base of the Sylvian fissure, is found to be a continuous substance, via its cortical layer, with the deepest part of the two marginal convolutions, by its medullary layer with the extra-ventricular nucleus of the striate body. It follows from this connection that a lesion that is spread, by way of this continuity, from the frontal lobe to the temporo-sphenoidal lobe, or reciprocally, passes almost necessarily by the lobe of the insula, and that from there it is likely to spread to the extra-ventricular nucleus of the striate body, given [attendu] that the substance of the insula proper, which separates this nucleus from the surface of the brain, forms only a very thin layer.

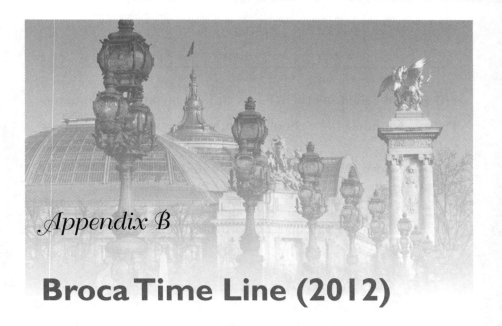

Appendix B

Broca Time Line (2012)

1824 — Broca was born in Sainte-Foy-la-Grande in the Dordogne region of France on June 28.

1841 — Entered medical school at just the age of 17.

1844 — Graduated from medical school at Hotel Dieu in Paris at the age of 20.

1848 — Founded the society of freethinkers, although he was a Christian. Supported Darwin's theory of natural selection.

1853 — Appointed surgeon in Paris, France.

1856 — Published _Aneurysms and Their Treatment_.

1859 — Founded the Anthropological Society of Paris and published _The Ethnology of France_.

1861 — Present classic papers on cortical localization of speech by clinicopathological studies of his two famous patients, M. Leborgne and M. Lelong.

1865 — Published _General Instructions on Anthropological Research_.

1868 — Became the Paris Medical School professor of surgical pathology and inducted into member of the Legion of Honour.

1872 — Founded the _Anthropological Review_.

1875—Published Instructions on Craniology and Craniometry.

1876—Founded the School of Anthropology at University of Paris.

1880—Near the end of his life, appointed a lifetime member in Science of the French Senate and the French Academy.

1880—Broca died on July 9 at age 56, presumably and ironically from a brain vascular malformation or a cerebrovascular accident (stroke).

Appendix C

Editorial
Broca's Brain: Brother, Wherefore Art Thou?*

"I washed your brain, but I had trouble getting the think stains out."

Cindy (character in *The Adventures of Jimmy Neutron: Boy Genius*, 2002)

Leonard L. LaPointe, PhD

Editor-in-Chief

Journal of Medical Speech-Language Pathology

The *Musée de l'Homme* (Museum of Man) was created in 1937 by Paul Rivet, for the splendiferous event of the World's Fair in Paris. Amid the lavishness of the Fair exhibits was Pablo Picasso's Guernica, commissioned for the Spanish Pavilion and hailed by many as modern art's most dramatic antiwar statement. The

---

*Reprinted with permission from L. L. LaPointe, (2010). *Voices: Collected Essays on Language, Laughter, and Life.* Clifton Park, NY: Delmar Cengage Publishing, 2010, pp. 33–37.)

Museum of Man is the descendant of the Musée d'Ethnographie du Trocadéro founded in 1918, and occupies most of the Passy wing of the Palais de Chaillot in the 16th arrondissement. In 1937 the world was boiling with social unrest with the continuing tragedies of the Spanish Civil War (the inspiration for Picasso's mural) as well as the architectural posturing of the Soviet and Nazi Germany architects and edifices. The mounting social turmoil did not prevent 32 million visitors from enjoying boat races on the Seine, grand boxing championships, horse racing, and a wine harvesting festival. Ice cream, hamburgers, and fairy floss, reincarnated as cotton candy, were already around and popular thanks to the 1904 St. Louis World's Fair, and the visitors on the banks of the Seine marveled at the Trocadero and Chaillot palace as a perfect repository for a museum dedicated to the natural history of humankind.

Carl Sagan, the Harvard and Cornell researcher and professor of astrophysics who became famous for his popularization of astronomy and debunking of junk science, wrote an influential book in 1979 entitled *Broca's Brain: Reflections on the Romance of Science* (Sagan, 1979). I remember reading that collection of essays in the early 1980s and being enthralled by Sagan's intellect and the breadth of his interests. In fact, one comes across the observation by Isaac Asimov on various internet sites that Sagan was one of only two people he had ever met who were clearly smarter than Asimov himself. The other was computer and artificial intelligence wizard, Marvin Minsky. I also had the impression that Sagan was a profound intellect and was amazed at his appearances on the American late night television show with Johnny Carson by his ability to pique interest in remarkably highbrow and philosophical subject matter. *Broca's Brain* was an immensely popular crossover best seller in the 1980s that set Sagan up for further writing that earned him a Pulitzer Prize as well as a sojourn to Hollywood to work on the adaptation of his book *Contact* for a film with Jody Foster. Although his manner of speech (particularly his pronunciation of "billions and billions") became fodder for many standup comedians, those in the scientific community never doubted or tarnished Sagan's remarkable contributions.

So it came to pass that Carl Sagan rhapsodized in *Broca's Brain* about the exquisite experience of standing in the Musée de l'Homme as he contemplated and gazed upon the preserved brain of Pierre Paul Broca (June 28, 1824–July 9, 1880) the scientific giant of the 19th century who contributed so much of what we know about the localization of articulate speech in the brain of humans. Broca was a French physician, anthropologist, and eventually a senator who believed that by studying the brains of cadavers and correlating the known experiences and behaviors of the former possessor of the organs, human behavior could be revealed, associated with brain function, and better understood. For that purpose he collected hundreds of human brains in jars of the preservative formalin. Upon his death in 1880 with exquisite irony, his own brain is preserved in formalin and added to the collection in the museum, along with hundreds of skulls that Broca had used in his comparative cephalametric studies. When Sagan happened upon Broca's brain in the museum, along with that of Broca's milestone patient "Tan" Leborgne, he was awestruck by the irony of it all. Here was Broca, for whom the region of the frontal lobe of the cortex that he had described was subsequently named, with his own Broca's area discernible. Sagan was mesmerized by the incongruity of all of this. In *Broca's Brain* he used that visit to the Museum of Man to launch philosophical questions that challenge some core ideas of human existence and consciousness such as "How much of that man known as Paul Broca can still be found in this jar?"

Because of this recollection of Sagan's fascination with Broca's and Leborgne's brains and consistent with a professional mild case of celebrity worship (so I have a personalized license plate that says Broca; doesn't everyone?), I was eager on a recent professional visit to Paris to visit the Musée de l'Homme and reflect as Sagan did, upon Broca's area in Broca's very brain. It was not to be. Brother Broca, wherefore art thou?

As it happened, I was visiting Paris with two friends and colleagues, Dr. Mike Theodoros, a renowned Australian psychiatrist, and his wife Dr. Deborah Theodoros, a renowned Australian speech-language pathologist at the University of Queensland. My wife Corinne, a renowned wife and gerontology healthcare professional accompanied us. All were keen to join me on my visit to the shadows of the Eiffel Tower to search for the brain of Broca in the Museum of Man. Our first visit had to be aborted. The museum was closed (Monday closing), but an employee graciously informed us that "all neurologique material including brains has been transferred to the newly opened Quai Branly museum." We were informed, "cross the river, turn left at the Eiffel Tower, go a couple of blocks, you can't miss it."

We set out again, and after a walk along the Seine enjoyed the modern architecture of the very recently opened Branly museum, along with its most unique "living wall" (200 m long by 12 m tall) on part of the exterior of the museum. This botanic wall was designed and planted by Patrick Blanc. Seeing the exotic plants and vines covering the walls of the new museum was as unique as the exhibits of indigenous art, cultures and civilizations from Africa, Asia, Oceania, and the Americas. With barely contained enthusiasm we purchased tickets and inquired at the information desk as to where we would find the neurological exhibits and Broca's brain in particular. We were met with a response that clearly indicated that we might as well have asked to see the corpse of Edith Piaf. After more inquiry and the assurance by a museum administrator that there were absolutely no exhibits or holdings on topics European, we were informed that no registration of "Broca" was currently encrypted on the Branly master computer list. A kindly employee suggested that we had been misinformed and that Broca certainly was still housed at the Museum of Man.

The hour was late and the brasseries were calling, so we redirected our efforts and vowed to continue the next day on this now rather mystifying search for the missing Broca's brain. Upon our re-visit to the Musée de l'Homme, we went directly to an information desk and explained that we were in search of Broca's brain and had been misdirected to the new Branly museum whose administrators insisted that the collection had not been moved and indeed resided in its original home. After referral to two levels of supervisory inquiry we were met with very helpful staff who invited us to their private coffee break room behind the scenes and informed us that they would attempt to contact one of the principal curators at the museum, who currently was on his day off work. They indeed contacted the curator who in fact promised to come in on his day off and help us search for Broca's brain. In less than 30 minutes, Dr. Philippe Mennecier, a linguist and researcher on Inuit dialects and languages of Greenland was at our service, and kindly asking how he could help.

He informed us that they indeed had an extensive collection of Broca's work, in fact 83 cabinets of skulls, death masks, and cephalametric artifacts, but he was unaware of the museum's holding of either Broca's or Leborgne's brain. He kindly took us to his most unique office however, and offered to search his data bases more thoroughly. As he searched, he invited us to step outside his office through an office window that led to a remarkable arched terrace with an absolutely astonishing view of the Eiffel Tower. After a bit, he invited us back into his office and said that in all likelihood the brains of Broca and Leborgne were now in the Dupuytren Museum at the College of Medicine of the University of Paris.

Dr. Philippe Mennecier proceeded then to invite us to a behind the scenes tour of the collections of Broca as well as those of Franz Josef Gall, the infamous neurologist and phrenologist who advocated that character of people could be discerned by reading their cranial configuration and bumps on the head. We spend a fascinating two hours in the company of Dr. Mennecier as he opened cabinet after cabinet to display the skull casts and death masks of hundreds of individuals who had been measured and studied by Broca or by Gall. Casts of criminals, famous composers (Franz Liszt et al), intellectuals and an assortment of saints and sinners were revealed as Dr. Mennecier unlocked the cabinets of cranial history. Our guide was most helpful and gracious and we are indebted to him for a remarkable journey into the 19th Century and the starch-colored world of Broca and Gall. We did not find the preserved brains of Broca or Leborgne this time, but further detective work has all but convinced us that on the next trip to Paris we will head straight to the Dupuytren Museum and gaze upon the wonders that so fascinated Carl Sagan as he contemplated Broca's brain and all of its ramifications to neuroscience and that greatest gift of all, human language.

REFERENCES

Amunts, K. (2006). Broca's region. International Brain Research Organization Retrieved from http://www.ibro.org/Pub_Main_Display.asp?Main_ID=15

Broca, P. (1861a). Perte de la parole, ramollissement chronique et des-struction partielle du lob antérieur gauche de cerveau. *Bulletins de la Société d'Antrhopologie, 62*, 235–238.

Broca, P. (1861b). Remarques sur le siége de la faculté du langage articulé, suivies d'une observation d'aphemie (Perte de la Parole). *Bulletins et memoires de la Societe Anatomique de Paris, 36*, 330–357.

Broca, P. (1863). Localisation des fonctions cérébrales.—Siege du langage articulé. *Bulletins de la Société d'Anthropologie Séance*, 2 Avril 1863, pp. 200–204.

Broca, P. (1865). Sur la siege de la faculté langage articulé. *Bulletin of the Society of Anthropology, 6*, 377–396.

Exposition Internationale des Arts et Techniques dans la Vie Moderne. (2006). Retrieved from http://en.wikipedia.org/wiki/Exposition_Internationale_des_Arts_et_Techniques_dans_la_Vie_Moderne_(1937)#Festivals_of_the_Exposition

Sagan, C. (1979). *Broca's brain: Reflections on the romance of science.* New York, NY: Random House.

Appendix D

Permission to Access the Collections of the Musee de l'Homme, Paris

See following page.

Ministère de l'Enseignement Supérieur et de la Recherche
Ministère de l'Ecologie, de l'Energie, du Développement durable et de la Mer

MUSEUM NATIONAL D'HISTOIRE NATURELLE

Direction des Collections

CP 43 - 57 rue Cuvier - 75005 PARIS tel 33(0)1 40793971 courriel dircol@mnhn.fr

Unité de Gestion des Collections d'anthropologie biologique
Le Chargé de conservation
Dr Philippe Mennecier

À QUI DE DROIT

Nous avons l'honneur d'inviter Monsieur Leonard L. LaPointe de juin à juillet 2011 au Musée de l'Homme (Muséum national d'histoire naturelle) afin qu'il puisse effectuer ses recherches sur les cerveaux conservés dans les collections anthropologiques.

À Paris, le 13 septembre 2010.

TO WHOM IT MAY CONCERN

It is a great privilege for us to welcome Mr Leonard L. LaPointe in the Musée de l'Homme (National museum of natural history) from June to July 2011, so that he can study the brains kept in the anthropological collections.

Paris, 13 September 2010.

Muséum national d'histoire naturelle – CP 140 (Musée de l'Homme) – 57 rue Cuvier – 75231 PARIS Cedex 05
Téléphone : +33 – (0)1 40 79 57 58 – Courriel : phm@mnhn.fr

328

References

Allen, J. P. (2005). *The art of medicine in ancient Egypt*. New York, NY: The Metropolitan Museum of Art.

Amunts, K. (2007). *History of neuroscience: Broca's region*, IBRO History of Neuroscience. Retrieved from http://www.ibro.info/Pub/Pub_Main_Display.asp?LC_Docs_ID=3489

Anderson, J. (1824). Transactions of the phrenological society, instituted 22nd February 1820, (pp. 89–130). Edinburgh, Great Britain, xvi, 448 pp. A view of some of Dr. Spurzheim's lectures, as delivered at Edinburgh, in the Winter of 1816. Transactions of the phrenological society, instituted 22nd February 1820. (PsycINFO Database Record (c) 2010 APA, all rights reserved)

Andral, G. (1834). Aphasie and the lobes anterior. *Clinique Medicale*, 5, 382.

Androutsos, G., & Diamantis, A. (2007). Paul Broca (1824–1880): Founder of anthropology, pioneer of neurology and oncology. *Journal of Balkan Union of Oncology*, 12(4), 557–564.

Auburtin, E. (1861). Reprise de la discussion sur la forme et le volume du cerveau. *Bulletin Society of Anthropology*, 2, 209–220.

Auguste Broca. (1924). Obituary of Auguste Broca, Retrieved from http://jama.ama-assn.org/content/83/18/1444.full.pdf

Ayers, A. (2004). *The architecture of Paris*. London, UK: Edition Axel Menges.

Ball, P. (1880). P. Broca, *Lancet*, 115, 24.

Bassetti, C. L., & Jagella, E. C. (2006). Joseph Jules Dejerine (1849–1917). *Journal of Neurology*, 253(6), 823–824.

Bateman, (2011). On aphasia. Bateman, F. (1890). On aphasia or loss of speech and the localisation of the faculty of articulate speech Retrieved from http://www.archive.org/details/onaphasiaorlosso00bateuoft

Bechtel, W. (2001). Linking cognition and brain: The cognitive neuroscience of language. In W. Bechtel, P. Mandik, J. Mundale, & R. S. Stufflebeam (Eds.), *Philosophy and the neurosciences: A reader.* Oxford, UK: Basil Blackwell.

Bechtel, W. (in press). The epistemology of evidence in cognitive science. In R. Skipper Jr., C. Allen, R. A. Ankeny, C. F. Craver, L. Darden, G. Mikkelson, & R. Richardson (Eds.), *Philosophy and the life sciences: A reader* (pp. 1–25). Cambridge, MA: MIT Press.

Bellis, M. (2011) History of the guillotine. Retrieved from http://inventors.about.com/od/gstartinventions/a/Guillotine.htm

Benedict, P. (2002). *Christ's churches purely reformed: A social history of Calvinism.* New Haven, CT: Yale University Press.

Benton, A. (1984). Hemispheric dominance before Broca. *Neuropsychologia, 22*(6), 807–811.

Benton, A. L., & Joynt, R. J. (1960). Early descriptions of aphasia. *Archives of Neurology, 3*(2), 205–222.

Benjamin, L. T., & Baker, D. B. (2004). The beginnings of psychological practice: Having your head examined: Phrenology. *From séance to science: A history of the profession of psychology in America.* Belmont, CA: Wadsworth/Thomson Learning.

Berker, E. A., Berker, A. H., & Smith, A. (1986). Translation of Broca's 1865 report: Localization of speech in the third left frontal convolution. *Archives of Neurology, 43*, 1065–1072.

Blainville, H. (1858). *American Journal of the Medical Sciences,* 152. Retrieved from http://www.todayinsci.com/B/Blainville_Henri/BlainvilleHenri-Quotations.htm

Bogousslavsky, J., & Assal, G. (2010). Stendhal's aphasic spells: The first report of transient ischemic attacks followed by stroke. *Frontiers of Neurology and Neuroscience, 27,* 130–142.

Bonilha, L., & Fridriksson, J. (2009). Subcortical damage and white matter disconnection associated with non-fluent speech. *Brain, 132,* 1–2.

Bonilha L., Moser, D., Rorden, C., Baylin G. C., & Fridriksson J. (2006). Speech apraxia without oral apraxia: Can normal brain function explain the physiopathology? *NeuroReport, 17,* 1027–1031.

Boston Medical and Surgical Journal. (1832). Retrieved from https://www.countway.harvard.edu/chm/rarebooks/exhibits/talking_heads/spurzheimobit.html

Bouillaud, J. (1825). Recherches clinique propres a démontrer que la perte de la parole correspond à la lésion del lobules antèrieurs du cerveau. *Archives Générale del a Médicine, 8,* 25–45.

Bouillaud, J. (1830). *Recherches expérimentales sur les fonctions du cerveau en général, et sur celles de sa partie antérieure en particulier; lues à l'Institut, en septembre 1827.* Paris, France: Baillière.

Bouillaud, J. (1864–1865). Discussion sur la faculte "du langage articule," *Bulletin de l'Academie Imperiale de Medecine, 30,* 575–638.

Bouillaud, J. (2011). Retrieved from http://www.medarus.org/Medecins/MedecinsTextes/bouillaud_jb.html

Brais, B. (1992). The third left frontal convolution plays no role in language: Pierre Marie and the Paris debate on aphasia (1906–1908). *Neurology, 42,* 690–695.

Broca, P. (1861a). Perte de la parole, ramollissement chronique et destruction partielle du lobe antérieur gauche du cerveau. *Bulletin Société Anthropologique, 2,* 235–238.

Broca, P. (1861b). Nouvelle observation d'aphémie produite par une lésion de la moitié postérieure des deuxième et troisième circonvolution frontales gauches. *Bulletin Society of Anatomy (Paris), 36,* 398–407.

Broca, P. (1861c). Remarques sur le sie`ge de la faculte´ du langage articule´: Suivies d'une observation d'aphemie. *Bulletin Society of Anatomy (Paris), 6,* 330–357.

Broca, P. (1863). Localisation des fonctions cerebrales: Sie "e du langage articule." *Bulletin Society of Anthropology (Paris), 4,* 200–203.

Broca, P. (1865). Sur le sie`ge de la faculte´ du langage articule *Bulletin Society of Anthropology (Paris), 6,* 337–393.

Broca, P. P. (1866). *Traite des tumeurs.* Paris, France: P. Asselin.

Broca, P. (1868). On the stéréographe, a novel instrument of craniography [in French]. *Bulletin Society of Anthropology, 3,* 99–126.

Broca, P. (1876a). On the prehistoric trepanations [in French]. *Bullein Society of Anthropol, 11,* 431–440.

Broca, P. (1876b). Prehistoric trepanation: Crania trepanned with the aid of a shard of glass [in French]. *Bulletin Society of Anthropology, 11,* 512–513.

Broca, P. (1876c). The so-called cranial amulets [in French]. *Bulletin Society of Anthropology, 11,* 461–463.

Broca, P. (1876d). Diagnosis of an abscess situated at the level of the region of language: Trepanation of the abscess [in French]. *Review of Anthropology, 5,* 244–248.

Broca, P. (1878). Anatomie comparée des circonvolutions cérébrales: le grand lobe limbique. *Annual Review of Anthropology, 1,* 385–498.

Broca, P. (1879). Sur les températures morbides locales. *Bulletin de l'Académie de Medecine, 8,* 1331–1347.

Broca, P. (1886). *Paul Broca: Correspondence: 1841–1857* (2 Vols.). Paris, France: Schmidt.

Broca Conference. (2001). Proceedings of the Conference "Homage to Paul Broca, founder of anthropology," Sainte Foy la Grande, 2 & 3 February 2001, *Biometrics Human and Anthropology, 19*, 3–4.

Broca Timeline (2012). Retrieved from http://www.muskingum.edu/~psych/psycweb/history/broca.htm

Buckingham, H. W. (1981). A pre-history of the problem of Broca's aphasia. In *Clinical Aphasiology Conference: 1981* (11th), Kerrville, TX, May 10–14, 1981. BRK Publishers, pp. 3–16.

Buckingham, H. W. (2006). The Marc Dax (1770–1837)/Paul Broca (1824–1880) controversy over priority in science: Left hemisphere specificity for seat of articulate language and for lesions that cause aphemia. *Clinical Linguistics and Phonetics, 20*(7–8), 613–619.

Butler, R. O. (2007). *Severance*. San Francisco, CA: Chronicle Books.

Bynum, W. F. (1970). Wernicke, Carl. In C. C. Gillispie (Ed.), *Dictionary of scientific biography*, New York, NY: Charles Scribner.

Cambier, J. (1980). Paul Broca cent ans après sa mort (1880–1980). *La Nouvelle Presse Médicale, 9*, 29.

Cantor, D. (2002). *Reinventing Hippocrates*. Burlington, VT: Ashgate.

Caplan, D. (1987). The discoveries of Paul Broca: Localization of the faculty for articulate language and classical connectionist models. *Neurolinguistics and linguistic aphasiology*. Cambridge, UK: Cambridge University Press.

Caryle, T. (1839). *The French Revolution In three volumes, Volume 3: The Guillotine*. New York, NY: Charles C. Little and James Brown (Little Brown).

Castaigne, P., Lhermitte, F., Signore, J. L., & Abelanet, R (1980). Description et étude scannographique du cerveau de Leborgne: la découverte de Broca. *Revue neurologique, 136*, 563–583.

Chadwick, O. (1977). *The Reformation*. London, UK: Penguin Books.

Chih, Y., Stierwalt, J. A. G., LaPointe, L. L., Kashak, M., & Lasker, J. (2011). *Physiological correlates of word retrieval: Individuals with and without aphasia*. Paper presented to the Annual Convention of the American Speech-Language-Hearing Association, San Diego, CA.

Clarke, D. M. (1999). *Discourse on method and related writings*, translated by Desmond M. Clarke. (London, UK: Penguin Books, 1999).

Cohen, L., Smith, M. J., & Leroux-Hugon, V. (2004). Paul Broca's thermometric crown. *Journal of Neurology, Neurosurgery, and Psychiatry, 75*, 32.

Clower, W. T., & Finger, S. (2001). Discovering trepanation: The contributions of Paul Broca. *Neurosurgery, 49*(6), 1417–1425.

Combe, G. (1853). *A system of phrenology* (5th ed.). Edinburgh, UK: Maclachlan.

Connor, P. (2002). *Huguenot Heartland: Montauban and Southern French Calvinism during the Wars of Religion*. London, UK: Aldershot.

Critchley, M. (1962). Dr. S. Johnson's aphasia. *Medical History, 6*, 27–44.

Critchley, M. (1964). La controverse de Dax et Broca. *Revue neurologique, 110*, 553–557. [English translation in Critchley, (1979). *The divine banquet of the brain and other essays* (pp. 72–82). New York, NY: Raven Press.]

Cubelli, R., & De Bastiani, P. (2011). 150 Years after Leborgne: Why is Paul Broca so important in the history of neuropsychology? *Cortex, 47*(2), 146–147.

Cubelli, R., & Montagna, C. G. (1994). A reappraisal of the controversy of Dax and Broca. *Journal of the History of Neuroscience, 3*(4), 215–226.

Curtis, G. (2006). *The cave painters: Probing the mysteries of the world's first artists*. New York, NY: Knopf.

Damasio, A. (1994). *Descartes' error: Emotion, reason, and the human brain*. New York, NY: Avon.

Daniel, M. (2004). The industrialization of French photography after 1860. In Heilbrunn *Timeline of art history*. New York, NY: The Metropolitan Museum of Art. Retrieved from http://www.metmuseum.org/toah/hd/infp/hd_infp.htm

Darley F. L. (1968) *Apraxia of speech: 107 years of terminological confusion*. Paper presented at the Annual Convention of the American Speech and Hearing Association, Denver, CO.

Darley, F. L. (1969). *The classification of output disturbances in neurogenic communication disorders*. Paper presented at the American Speech and Hearing Association Annual Convention, Chicago IL.

Dax, G. (1865). Notes sur la me`me sujet. *Gaz hbd Me´d Chir (Paris), 2*, 262.

Dax, M. (1865). Lesions de la moitie´ gauche de l'ence´phale coincident avec l'oublie des signes de la pensee. *Gaz hbd Me´d Chir (Paris), 2*, 259–262.

DeCosta, C., & Miller, F. (2006). Dr. Samuel-Jean Pozzi: Portrait of a ladies' man. *History Today, 56*, 3.

DeCosta, C., & Miller, F. (2007). Sarah Bernhardt's "Doctor God": Jean-Samuel Pozzi (1846–1918). *Australian and New Zealand Journal of Obstetrics and Gynaecology, 47*, 352–356.

DeCosta, C., & Miller, F. (2010). *The diva and Dr. God: Letters from Sarah Bernhardt to Dr. Samuel Pozzi*. Retrieved from http://www.Xlibris.com

Descartes, R. (1637). *Discourse on the method of rightly conducting one's reason and of seeking truth in the sciences. The Harvard Classics* (Vol. XXXIV, Part 1). New York, NY: P. F. Collier & Son.

Descartes, (2011). Descartes. Retrieved from http://library.thinkquest .org/18775/descartes/biod.htm

Dickinson, E. (1924). *The complete poems of Emily Dickinson*. Boston, MA: Little, Brown.

Doidge, N. (2007). *The brain that changes itself: Stories of personal triumph from the frontiers of brain science*. New York, NY: Viking.

Dronkers N. F. (1996). A new brain region for coordinating speech articulation. *Nature, 384*, 159–161.

Dronkers, N. F., Plaisant, O., Iba-Zizen, M. T., & Cabanis, E. A. (2007). Paul Broca's historic cases: High resolution MR imaging of the brains of Leborgne and Lelong. *Brain, 130*, 1432–1441.

Duffy, J. R., & Wertz, R. T. (2001). Remembering Frederic L. Darley: Special Issue (A Special Issue of the Journal *Aphasiology*), C. Code (Ed.), March, 2001. London, UK: Taylor & Francis.

Dupuytren. (2011). History of the Musée Dupuytren. Retrieved from http://www.upmc.fr/fr/culture/patrimoine/patrimoine_scientifique/ musee_dupuytren.htm

Ebert, T. (2009). *The mysterious death of René Descartes*. Berlin, Germany: Alibri Verlag.

Eling, P. (1984). Broca on the relation between handedness and cerebral speech dominance. *Brain and Language, 22*, 158–159.

Eling, P. (1994) *Reader in the History of Aphasia: From Franz Gall to Norman Geschwind*. Amsterdam, The Netherlands: John Benjamin.

Fancher, R. (1996.) *Pioneers of psychology* (3rd ed.) New York, NY: W. W. Norton.

Farrell, S., & Sutherland, J. (1986). *Madame Guillotine: The French Revolution*. London, UK: Armada Books.

Feagin, J. R. (2010). *Racist America: Roots, current realities, and future reparations* (2nd ed.). New York, NY: Routledge.

Feinberg, T. E., & Farah, M. J. (Eds.). (1997). *Behavioral neurology and neuropsychology*. New York, NY: McGraw-Hill.

Finger, S. (1994). *Origins of neuroscience: A history of explorations into brain function*. New York, NY: Oxford University Press.

Finger, S. (2000). *Minds behind the brain: A history of the pioneers and their discoveries*. New York, NY: Oxford University Press.

Finger, S. (2009). The birth of localization theory, In S. Finger, F. Boller, & K. Taylor (Eds.) *Handbook of clinical neurology: History of neurology* (Vol. 95, pp. 117–128). Amsterdam, The Netherlands: Elsevier.

Finger, S., & Roe, D. (1996). Gustave Dax and the early history of cerebral dominance. *Archives of Neurology, 53*(8), 806–813.

Finger S., & Roe, D. (1999). Does Gustave Dax deserve to be forgotten? The temporal lobe theory and other contributions of an overlooked figure in the history of language and cerebral dominance. *Brain and Language*, 69(1), 16–30.

Flourens, P. (1824) *Recherches expérimentales sur les propriétés et les fonctions du systeme nerveux dans les animaux vertébrés*. Paris, France: Bailliére.

Flourens, P. (1842). *Recherches expérimentales sur les propriétés et les fonctions du systeme nerveux dans les animaux vertébrés* (Deuxième ed.). Paris, France: Bailliére.

Flourens, P. (1851). *Examen de la Phrénologie*. Paris [uncorrected rtf] and English translation: *Phrenology examined*. trans. by C. de Lucena Meigs, Philadelphia, PA.

Franco Prussian War. (2012). Retrieved from http://francoprussianwar .com/war.htm

Fridriksson, J. (2011). Neuroimaging and brain-based communication disorders. In L. L. LaPointe (Ed.), *Aphasia and related neurogenic language disorders* (4th ed., pp. 59–68). New York, NY: Thieme Medical.

Fritz, G. T., & Hitzig, E. (1870). On the electrical excitability of the cerebrum InG. Von Bonin(1960) trans., *Some papers on the cerebral cortex*. Springfield IL: Charles C. Thomas.

Fuchs, R. E., (1969). Academic freedom—Its basic philosophy, function and history. In L. Joughin (Ed.), *Academic freedom and tenure: A handbook of the American Association of University Professors*. Madison, WI: University of Wisconsin Press.

Gall, F. J., & Spurzheim, J. G., (1810). *Anatomie et physionomie du système nerveux en général et du cerveau en particulier. Premier volume. Anatomie et physiologie du système nerveux en général et anatomie du cerveau en particulier*. Paris, France: F. Schoell.

Gall, F. J., & Spurzheim, J. G. (1811). *Des dispositions innées de l'âme et de l'esprit: du matérialisme, du fatalisme et de la liberté morale, avec des réflexions sur l'éducation et sur la législation criminelle*. Paris, France: F. Schoell.

Gall, Franz Joseph. (2011). Retrieved from http://www.nndb.com/ people/604/000104292/

Gall, New World Encyclopedia. (2011). Retrieved from http://www .newworldencyclopedia.org/entry/Franz_Joseph_Gall

Gaukroger, S. (1995). *Descartes: An intellectual biography*. New York, NY: Oxford University Press.

Goldenberg, G. (2003). Apraxia and beyond: Life and work of Hugo Liepmann. *Cortex*. 39(3), 509–524.

Goodglass, H. (2011). The Harold Goodglass Aphasia Research Center. Retrieved from http://www.bu.edu/aphasia/

Goodwin, C. J. (1999). The neurophysiology context: Localization of brain function. *A history of modern psychology* (pp. 66–70). New York, NY: John Wiley & Sons.

Gordon, J. (1815, June). The doctrines of Gall and Spurzheim. *Edinburgh Review, 25,* 227–268.

Gorst-Williams, J. (1977). *Elizabeth, the Winter Queen.* London, UK: Abelard.

Gould, S. J. (1980). *The panda's thumb* (pp. 145–148). New York, NY: W. W. Norton.

Green, C. (2000). Classics in the history of psychology: Remarks on the seat of the faculty of articulated language, following an observation of aphemia (loss of speech) by Mr. Paul Broca (1861). First published in *Bulletin de la Société Anatomique, 6,* 330–357. Retrieved from http://psychclassics.yorku.ca/Broca/aphemie-e.htm

Greenblatt, S. H., (1995). Phrenology in the science and culture of the 19th century. *Neurosurgery, 37,* 790–805.

Guenther, F. H., Ghosh, S. S., & Tourville, J. A. (2006). Neural modeling and imaging of the cortical interactions underlying syllable production. *Brain and Language, 96*(3), 280–301.

Hall, S. (2006). *Size matters.* New York, NY: Houghton Mifflin Harcourt.

Hammersley, R. (2005). *French Revolutionaries and English Republicans: The Cordeliers Club 1790–1794.* Rochester, NY: Boydell & Brewer.

Harris, L. J. (1991). Broca and mirror reversal of language in right and left handers. *Brain and Language, 40*(1), 1–50.

Head, H. (1926). *Aphasia and kindred disorders of speech* (Vol. 1, p. 16). Cambridge, UK: Cambridge University Press.

Hecaen, H., & Dubois, J. (1969). *La naissance de la neuropsychologie du langage 1825–1865 (textes et documents).* Paris, France: Flammarion.

Hecht, J. M. (2005). *The end of the soul: Scientific modernity, atheism, and anthropology in France.* New York, NY: Columbia University Press.

Hill, R. B., & Anderson, R. F. (1988). *The autopsy—medical practice and public policy.* Boston, MA: Butterworth.

Hillis, A. E., Work, M., Barker, P. B., Jacobs, M. A., Breese, E. L., & Maurer, K. (2004). Re-examining the brain regions crucial for orchestrating speech articulation. *Brain, 127*(Pt. 7), 1479–1487.

History. (1824). Retrieved from http://www.brainyhistory.com/years/1824.html

History. (1861). Retrieved from http://kansas150slk.blogspot.com/2011/01/world-in-1861.html

Horne, A. (2004). *Seven ages of Paris.* New York, NY: Vintage Books (Random House).

Hothersall, D. (1995). *History of psychology*. New York, NY: McGraw-Hill.

Huard, P. (1961). Paul Broca (1824–1880) avec une bibliographie des travaux de Broca, par Samuel Pozzi (1846–1918). *Revue d'histoire des sciences et de leurs applications, 14*, 47–86.

Huard, P. (1964). Le Gaurichon (Jean): Contribution à la bio-bibliographie de Paul Broca. *Revue d'histoire des sciences et de leurs applications, 17*(1), 80.

Huard, P., Aaron, C., Askienazy, S., Corlieu, P., Fredy, D., & Vedrenne, C. (1982). [The brain of Paul Broca (1824–1880). Correlation of pathological and computed tomography findings.] *Journal De Radiologie, 63*(3), 175–180.

Huguenot Society. (2011). Huguenot history. Retrieved from http://www.huguenotsociety.org.uk/history.html

Jacyna, L. S. (1999). The 1874 aphasia debate in the Berliner Gesselschaft für Anthropologie. *Brain and Language, 69*(1), 5–15.

Jacyna, L. S. (2000). *Lost words: Narratives of language and the brain 1825–1926*. Princeton, NJ: Princeton University Press.

Jefferson, A. (1988). *Reading realism in Stendhal* (Cambridge Studies in French). Cambridge, UK: Cambridge University Press.

Jellinek, E. H., (2002). An unlikely aphasiologist: D. J. Larrey (1766–1842). *Journal of the Royal Society of Medicine, 95*(7), 368–370.

Johnson, D. R. (2012). Measuring heads. Retrieved from http://www.leeds.ac.uk/chb/lectures/anthl_05.html

Johnson, P. (2002). *Napoleon: Penguin lives*. London, UK: Viking Press.

Joynt, R. J. (1961).Centenary of patient "Tan": His contribution to the problem of aphasia. *Archives of International Medicine, 108*(6), 953–956.

Josette, P. (2012). Dupuytren museum. Retrieved from: http://www.upmc.fr/fr/culture/patrimoine/patrimoine_scientifique/musee_dupuytren.html

Katz, R. C., LaPointe, L. L., & Markel, N. N. (2005). Coverbal behavior and aphasic speakers. *Aphasiology, 18*(12), 1213–1220.

Katz, R. C., LaPointe, L. L., Markel, N. N., & Silkes, J. (2005). Coverbal behavior and aphasic speakers: Revised. *Aphasiology, 18*(12), 1221–1225.

Kaufman, M. H., & Basden, N. (1996). Items relating to Dr. Johann Gaspar Spurzheim (1776–1832) in The Henderson Trust collection, formerly the museum collection of the Phrenological Society of Edinburgh: With an abbreviated iconography. *Journal of Neurolinguistics, 9*(4), 301–325.

Kelen, B. (1966). *The mistresses: Domestic scandals of the 19th-century monarchs*. New York, NY: Random House.

Krush, A. J. (1979). Contributions of Pierre Paul Broca to cancer genetics. *Transactions of the Nebraska Academy of Sciences and Affiliated*

Societies, Paper 316. Retrieved from http://digitalcommons.unl.edu/tnas/316

La Berge, A. E. F. (2004). Debate as scientific practice in nineteenth-century Paris: The controversy over the microscope. *Perspectives on Science, 12*(4), 424–453.

LaPointe, L. L. (1996). On being a patient. *Journal of Medical Speech-Language Pathology, 4*, 1.

LaPointe, L. L. (2001). Darley and the psychosocial side. In J. R. Duffy & R. T. Wertz (Eds.), *Remembering Frederic L. Darley: Special Issue (A Special Issue of the Journal Aphasiology). 15*(3), 249–260.

LaPointe, L. L. (2010a). *Aphasia and related neurogenic language disorders* (4th ed.). New York, NY: Thieme.

LaPointe, L. L. (2010b). Broca's brain: Brother, wherefore art thou? *Voices: Collected essays on language, laughter, and life* (pp. 33–37). Clifton Park, NY: Delmar Cengage.

LaPointe, L. L. (2011). Pathography of love. *Journal of Medical Speech-Language Pathology, 19*, 3, iv.

LaPointe, L., Murdoch, B. E., & Stierwalt, J. A. G. (2010). *Brain-based communication disorders.* San Diego, CA: Plural.

Larrey, D. J. (1817). *Mémoires de Chirurgie Militaire et Campagnes* (4 Vols.). Paris, France: J. Smith.

Larson, B. (2009). Mapping the body and the brain: Neurology and localization theory in the work of Rodin. *Canadian Art Review, 34*, 1.

Lazar, R. M., & Mohr, J. P. (2011). Revisiting the contributions of Paul Broca to the study of aphasia. *Neuropsychology Review, 21*(3), 236–239.

Lee, D. A. (1981). Paul Broca and the early history of aphasia. *Neurology, 31*(5), 600.

Le Figaro. April 4, 1861, pp. 6–7. Retrieved from http://gallica.bnf.fr/ark:/12148/bpt6k269984c/f1

Lerner, K., & Lerner, B. (2006). *World of forensic science.* Independence, KY: Gale-Cengage.

Le Temps. (1861). Retrieved from http://gallica.bnf.fr/ark:/12148/bpt6k220905j/f1

Le Temps. (1880). Broca elected to the senate. *Le Temps*, 1880/02/21 (Numéro 6881).

Leuret, F., & Gratiolet L. P. (1839). *Anatomie compare du système nerveux considéré dans ses rapports avec l'intelligence* (Vol. 1). Paris, France: Ballière.

Lichtheim, L. (1885). On aphasia. *Brain, 7*, 433–484.

Lichtheim, L. (1885). Über Aphasie. *Deutsches Archiv für klinische Medicin, 36*, 204–268.

Liepmann, H. (1900). Das Krankheitsbild der Apraxie ('motorischen Asymbolie') auf Grund eines Falles von einseitiger Apraxie. (The syndrome of apraxia (motor asymbolia) based on a case of unilateral apraxia). Translated by Bohne W., Liepmann K., Rottenberg, D. A. from *Monatsschrift für Psychiatrie und Neurologie, 8*, 15–44. In D. A. Rottenberg & F. H. Hochberg (Eds.), *Neurological classics in modern translation* (1977). New York, NY: Hafner Press.

Liepmann, H. (1905). Der weitere Krankheitsverlauf bei dem einseitig Apraktischen und der Gehirnbefund auf Grund von Serienschnitten. *Monatschrift fur Psychiatrie und Neurologie, 17*, 289–311; *19*, 217–243.

Liepmann, H. (1908). *Drei Aufsätze aus dem Apraxiegebiet.* Berlin, Germany: Karger.

Lokhorst, G. J. C. (1996). The first theory about hemispheric specialization: Fresh light on an old codex. *Journal of the History of Medicine and Allied Sciences, 51*, 293–312.

Long, B. (2004). Lordat's aphasia. Retrieved from http://www.drbilllong .com/MoreWords/Aphasia.html

Lorch, M. P. (2008). The merest logomachy: The 1868 Norwich discussion of aphasia by Hughlings Jackson and Broca. *Brain, 131*(6), 1658–1670.

Luzzatti, C., & Whitaker, H. (2001). Jean-Baptiste Bouillaud, Claude-Francois Lallemand, and the role of the frontal lobe—Location and mislocation of language in the early 19th century. *Archives of Neurology, 58*(7), 1157–1162.

Mackey. (1997). Phrenological Whitman. Retrieved from http://www .conjunctions.com/archives/c29-nm.htm

Maclean, P. D. (1990). *The triune brain in evolution: Role in paleocerebral functions.* New York, NY: Plenum Press.

Macmillan, M. (1986). A wonderful journey through skull and brains: The travels of Mr. Gage's tamping iron. *Brain and Cognition, 5*(1), 67–107.

Macmillan, M. (2000). *An odd kind of fame: Stories of Phineas Gage.* Cambridge, MA: MIT Press.

Macmillan, M., & Lena, M. L. (2010). Rehabilitating Phineas Gage. *Neuropsychological Rehabilitation, 20*, 1–18.

Marie, P. (1906). La troisième circonvolution frontale gauche ne joue aucun rôle spécial dans la function du langage. *La Semana Médica, 26*, 241–247.

Marshall, R., Golper, L., Boysen, A., & Katz, R. (2009). Contributions of the Department of Veterans Affairs to clinical aphasiology. *Aphasiology, 23*(9), 1079–1085.

McNeil, M. R., & Copland, D. (2011). Models of aphasia. In L. L. LaPointe (Ed.), *Aphasia and related neurogenic language disorders* (4th ed.). New York, NY: Thieme Medical.

McNeil, M. R., Pratt, S. R., & Fossett, T. R. D. (2004). The differential diagnosis of apraxia of speech. In B. Maassen (Ed.), *Speech motor control in normal and disordered speech* (pp. 389–412). New York, NY: Oxford University Press.

Metmuseum. (2012). Retrieved from http://www.metmuseum.org/toah/hd/phcw/hd_phcw.htm

Minagar, A., Ragheb, J., & Kelley, R. E. (2003). The Edwin Smith surgical papyrus: Description and analysis of the earliest case of aphasia. *Journal of Medical Biography, 11*(2), 114–117.

Mooney, C. (2005). *The Republican war on science, revised and updated.* New York, NY: Basic Books.

Monnerville, G. (2012). Georges Clemenceau. Retrieved from http://www.britannica.com/EBchecked/topic/120962/Georges-Clemenceau#toc1351

Munod-Broca, P. (1980). Paul Broca (1824–1880). The surgeon, the man [Paul Broca (1824–1880). The surgeon, the man] [in French]. *Bulletin de l'Académie Nationale de Médecine, 164*(6), 536–544.

Munod-Broca, P. (2005). *Paul Broca, a giant of the 19th century.* Paris, France: Vuibert.

Murdoch, B. E. (2010). *Acquired speech and language disorders: A neuroanatomical and functional neurological approach* (2nd ed.). London, UK: Wiley & Sons.

Nadeau, S., Gonzalez Rothi, L., & Crosson, B. (2000). *Aphasia and language: Theory to practice.* New York, NY: Guilford Press.

Nestor, P. (2003). Baron Dominique Jean Larrey 1766–1842. *Journal of Emergency Primary Health Care, 1*(3–4), 1–7.

Neuzil, E. (2002). Jean Guillaume Auguste Lugol (1788–1851): His life and his works: A brief encounter, 150 years after his death. *History of Science, Techology, and Medicine, 36*(4), 451–464.

Neurophilosophy. (2011). Retrieved from http://neurophilosophy.wordpress.com/2007/04/26/old-brains-new-ideas/

Nieder, C. (2000). *The autobiography of Mark Twain.* New York, NY: Harper Collins.

Ogar, J., Slama, H., Dronkers, N., Amici, S., & Gorno-Tempini, M. L. (2005). Apraxia of speech: An overview. *Neurocase, 11*, 427–432.

Ouimet, C. (2011). Broca and Monet. Personal communication.

Ozdemir, E., Norton, A., & Schlaug, G. Shared and distinct neural correlates of singing and speaking. *NeuroImage, 33*, 628–635.

Papez, J. W. (1937). A proposed mechanism of emotion. *Archives of Neurology and Psychiatry, 38*, 725–743.

Pearce, J. M. S. (2006). Louis Pierre Gratiolet (1815–1865). The cerebral lobes and fissures. *European Neurology, 56*, 262–264.

Pearce, J. M. S. (2009). Broca's aphasiacs. *European Neurology, 61*, 183–189.

Pineau, H. (1980). Paul Broca and anthropology. *Bulletin de l Academie Nationale de Medecine (Paris), 164*(6), 557–562.

Plessis, A. (1989). *The rise and fall of the Second Empire 1852–1871*. Paris, France: Cambridge University Press.

Poe, E. A. (2011). *Edgar Allen Poe and life sciences*. Retrieved from http://poe4life.weebly.com/phrenology-and-physiognomy.html

Popular Science Monthly. (1881). M. Paul Broca, Vol. 20, p. 265.

Poynter, F. (1958). *The history and philosophy of knowledge of the brain and its functions: An Anglo-American Symposium,* London, July, 1957. Springfield, IL: Charles C Thomas.

Pozzi, S. (1880a). Paul Broca. *Revue d'Anthropologie 2e*(2), 577–608.

Pozzi, S. (1880b). *Paul Broca, biographie, bibliographie*. Paris, France: G. Masson.

Prins, R., & Bastiaanse, R. (2006). The early history of aphasiology: From the Egyptian surgeons (c. 1700 BC) to Broca (1861). *Aphasiology, 20*(8), 762–791.

Priority. (2012). Pierre Paul Broca. Retrieved from http://www.whonamedit.com/doctor.cfm/1982.html

Provain, R. (2011). Sainte-Foy-la-Grande Retrieved from http://www.saintefoylagrande.net/

Rapport, M. (2009). *1848: Year of revolution*. New York, NY: Basic Books.

Reclus, P. (1880). Paul Broca. *Rev. mens. de méd et chir, 4*, 45–764.

Rewald, J. (1973). *The history of impressionism* (4th, rev. ed.). New York, NY: The Museum of Modern Art.

Richardson, R. G. (1974). *Larrey: Surgeon to Napoleon's imperial guard*. London, UK: John Murray.

Riese, W. (1947). The early history of aphasia. *Bulletin of the History of Medicine, 6*, 322–334.

Roberts, C. H., & Skeat, T. C. (1983). *The birth of the codex*. London, UK: Oxford University Press.

Roch Lecours, A. (1999). Aphasia debates [in French]. *Revue neurologique, 155*(10), 833–847.

Rodin, A. (2009). *Rodin on art and artists*. London, UK: Dover Press.

Rolleston, J. D. (1937). Jean Baptiste Bouillaud. *Proceedings of the Royal Society of Medicine, 24*, 1253–1262.

Rosenblum, R. (1989). *Paintings in the Musée d'Orsay*. New York, NY: Stewart, Tabori & Chang.

Ross, I. (1956). *Angel of the battlefield: The Life of Clara Barton*. New York, NY: Harper and Brothers.

Sacks, O. (1984). *A leg to stand on*. New York, NY: Harper and Row.

Schiller, F. (1979). *Paul Broca: Explorer of the brain*. New York, NY: Oxford University Press.

Schiller, F. (1992). *Paul Broca: Explorer of the brain*. New York, NY: Oxford University Press.

Science. (1880). Dr. Paul Broca. 21 August 1880, 93.

Shorto, R. (2009). *Descartes' bones: A skeletal history of the conflict between faith and reason*. New York, NY: Doubleday.

Signoret, J. L., Castaigne, P., Lhermitte, F., Abelanet, R., & Lavorel, P. (1984). Rediscovery of Leborgne's brain: Anatomical description with CT scan. *Brain and Language, 22*, 303–319.

Silverman, B. (1996). Jean-Baptiste Bouillaud. *Clinical Cardiology, 19*, 836–837.

Skeptics Dictionary. (2012). Retrieved from http://www.skepdic.com/trepanation.html

Special Correspondence, *British Medical Journal*. (1880). Paris [FROM OUR OWN CORRESPONDENT.] M. Broca in the French Senate.-Police Help in Accidents.-Creches.-The Weather-and the Public Health, p. 263.

Spencer, C. (1861). Retrieved from http://gazette.unc.edu/archives/01may23/file.3.html

Spencer, H. (1855). *Principles of psychology*. London, UK: Longman, Brown, Green, and Longmans.

Spoerl, H. D. (1934). *The problem of faculties in the psychology of character during the nineteenth century*. Unpublished doctoral dissertation. Harvard University, Cambridge, MA.

Stone, J. L. (1991). Paul Broca and the first craniotomy based on cerebral localization. *Journal of Neurosurgery, 75*, 1, 154–159.

Stone, J. L. (2003). Mark Twain and phrenology. *Neurosurgery, 53*(6), 1414–1417.

Stookey, B. (1963). Jean-Baptiste Bouillaud and Ernest Aubertin: Early studies on cerebral localization and the speech center. *Journal of the American Medical Association, 184*(13), 1024–1029.

Sutton, W., & Sutton, J. (2007) Fortean times. Retrieved from http://www.forteantimes.com/features/articles/73/animal_spirits.html

Tartakovsky, M. (2011). Phrenology. Retrieved from http://psychcentral.com/blog/archives/2011/01/27/phrenology-examining-the-bumps-of-your-brain/

Tesak, J., & Code, C. (2008). *Milestones in the history of aphasia: Theories and protagonists*. London, UK: Psychology Press.

Thompson, D. A., & Adams, S. L. (1996). The full moon and ED patient volumes: Unearthing a myth. *American Journal of Emergency Medicine, 14*(2), 161–164.

Trepanation Guide. (2012). Retrieved from http://www.trepanationguide.com/

Trousseau, A. (1864). De l'aphasie, maladie décrite récemment sous le nom impropre d'aphemie. *Gazette des Hôpitaux Civil et Militaires*, pp. 13–14.

Tsapkini, K., Vivas, A. B., & Triarhou, L. C. (2008). "Does Broca's area exist?" Christofredo Jakob's 1906 response to Pierre Marie's holistic stance. *Brain and Language, 105*(3), 211–219.

Twain, M. (2010). *Autobiography of Mark Twain* (Vol. 1). Berkeley, CA: University of California Press.

Van Wyhe, J. (2002). "George Combe." *The dictionary of nineteenth century British philosophers.* Bristol, UK: Thoemmes Press.

Van Wyhe, J. (2004). *Phrenology and the origins of Victorian scientific naturalism.* London, UK: Ashgate.

Van Wyhe, J. (2007). The diffusion of phrenology through public lecturing. In A. Fyfe & B. Lightman (Eds.), *Science in the marketplace: Nineteenth-century sites and experiences* (pp. 60–96). Chicago, IL: University Press.

Van Wyhe, J. (2011). History of phrenology on the Web. Retrieved from http://www.historyofphrenology.org.uk/

Verghese, A. (2009). *Cutting for stone.* New York, NY: Knopf.

Walsh, A., (1974). *Johann Christoph Spurzheim and the rise and fall of scientific phrenology in Boston: 1832–1842.* Unpublished doctoral thesis. University of New Hampshire, Durham.

Warrack, J., & West, E. (1979). *The Oxford dictionary of opera.* New York, NY: Oxford University Press.

Wawro, G. (2003). *The Franco-Prussian War: The German conquest of France in 1870–1871.* Cambridge, UK: Cambridge University Press.

Wertz, R. T., LaPointe, L. L., & Rosenbek, J. C. (1984). *Apraxia of speech: The disorder and its management.* New York, NY: Grune and Stratton.

Whitaker, H. (1998). History of neurolinguistics. In B. Stemmer & H. Whitaker (Eds.), *Handbook of neurolinguistics* (pp. 27–54). San Diego, CA: Academic Press.

Wilkins, R. H. (1964, March). Neurosurgical classic-XVII. Edwin Smith surgical papyrus. *Journal of Neurosurgery,* pp. 240–244.

Williams, E. (1996). Medicine in the civic life of eighteenth-century Montpellier. *Bulletin of the History of Medicine, 70,* 2.

Wozniak, R. H. (1995). Mind and body: René Déscartes to William James. Retrieved June 29, 2011, from http://serendip.brynmawr.edu/Mind/; Originally published in 1992 at Bethesda, MD & Washington, DC by the National Library of Medicine and the American Psychological Association.

York, G. (2005). The great aphasia debates. *Neurology Today, 5*(7), 18–19.

Zago, S., & Berkovic, S. F. (2006). Antonio Berti and the early history of aphasia. *Italian Journal of the Neurological Sciences, 27*(6), 449–452.

Index

A

Aberdeen Phrenological Society, established, 29
Academic freedom, 101–103
Académie de Médecine, 67
  Bouillaud's paper read at, 121
  translation of Broca's 1861 paper, 289–318
Academy of Aphasia, 69, 225
Academy of Medicine, 86
Academy of Sciences, Gall denied membership in, 64
Acquired dyslexia, 71
Acquisitiveness, 42
Adhesiveness, 36
Agnel, Georges, 145
Alvarenga Prize Essay, 86
Amativeness, 36
  sex and, 52–54
American Journal of Medicine, 96
American Phrenological Journal
  ceased publication, 31
  established, 29

Anatomie et physiologie du système nerveux en général, et du cerveau en particulier, Avec des observations sur las possibilité de reconnoître plusieurs dispositions intellectuelles et morales de l'homme et des animaux, par la configuration de leurs têtes, published, 27–28
Anatomy Society, 207
  translation of Broca's 1861 paper, 289–318
Anima, 14
Anthropological Society of Paris, 131, 207, 230
  translation of Broca's 1861 paper, 289–318
Anthropometry, 260–261
Aphasia
  early reports of, 67
  post world wars and, 76
  sensory, 71

Aphasia *(continued)*
   treating with leeches, 87–88,
      90 94
   Wernicke's, 71
Aphemia, 73, 120, 225–236, 292,
      295, 299–315
Apraxia
   defined, 72–73
   ideational, 72
   ideomotor, 72
   Liepmann and, 72–74
"Apraxia of speech," 225
Arc de Triomphe, 112–113
Archives generales de medecine,
      118
Arènes de Lutèce, 252
Articulated language, 225–236
Assistance Publique, 186, 277
Asylum de Bicêtre, 173–174
Aubertin, Simon Alexandre
      Ernest, 5, 6, 117
   catalytic spatula case, 127–129
   Société de Anthropologie
      debates and, 140–144
Auburtin, M., 228, 230–231, 293,
      296–297
   1861 presentation, 137
   localization and, 231, 296
   Tan and, 208, 303
*The Autobiography of Mark
   Twain*, 60

B

Bacciochi, Felix, 191
Bain, Alexander, 131–132, 134
Balzac, 116
Barton, Clarissa Harlowe (Clara),
      59
Barton, Sarah, 59
Barton, Stephen, 59
Bastille, Georges Danton and,
      198

Bateman, Frederic, 86–88, 90–99
Battle of Shanghai, 138
Battle of Shiloh, 187
Belenger, Marguerite, 189–191
Benevolence, 43
Bergerac, 156
Bernard, Claude, 282
Bernhardt, Sarah, 156–157
Berti, Antonio, 71
Beyle, Marie-Henri, 134
Bicêtre Hospital, 173–174, 253
Bigelow, Henry Jacob, 97–98
Birmingham Phrenological
      Society, established, 29
Bizet, Georges, 157
Blandin, Philippe-Frédéric, 176
Bleeding bowls, 125
Bloodletting, as a cure, 125
Boleyn, Anne, 105
Bonaparte, Charles
         Louis-Napoléon
   death of, 191
   rebuilding of Paris, 188–191
Bonaparte, Louis-Napoléon, 113,
      153, 176–177, 187–188
*Boston Medical and Surgical
   Journal*, 54–57
Boston Phrenological Society,
      established, 29
Bouillaud, Jean-Baptiste, 5, 6, 64,
      116–127
   alleged folly, 123–127
   death of, 124
   Gall and, 113, 118
   on Gall's theory of speech and
      frontal lobes, 124
   replaced as Dean and Orfila,
      178
Bouillon Racine, 4
Bourbon, Henri de, 147
Bowls, bleeding, 125
Bowman, William, 181
Boxer rebellion, 138

Brain
  first use of the word, 12
  Flourens research and, 51
  functional localization in, 26
  legendary French, 205–212
  as separate from mind, 14–15
Brain [journal], 74
Brain Stimulation Unit, 269
British Association for the
    Advancement of Science,
    29
British Medical Journal,
    278–279
British Phrenological Association
  established, 29
  schism within, 30
British Phrenological Society, 31
Broca, Adele-Augustine, 194–196,
    246
Broca, Annette, 153–154
Broca, Aubertin, 64
Broca, Auguste, 283
Broca, Benjamin, 153
Broca, Léotine, 159
Broca, Pauline, 283
Broca, Pierre Paul, 3–6, 64, 101
  1861 paper translation by
      Green, 289–318
  anthropology and, 248
  anthropometry and, 260–261
  aphasia and, 67, 71
  aphemia and, 73
  auxiliary contributions,
      243–279
  becomes a doctor of medicine,
      182–185
  clinical education, 173–176
  culmination of medical studies,
      181–182
  death of, 281–282
  doctoral thesis, 182–183
  editorial about, 321–325
  eulogies/biographies, 282–287

  Freethinkers Society and,
      185–186
  French Senate and, 275–280
  genetics research by, 253–260
  handedness and, 248
  June Days revolution and,
      176–179
  Lancet obituary, 282
  language, articulated speech
      and aphemia, 225–236
  leaves home, 160
  life in Paris, 186–188
  limbic system, 244–246
  lineage, 151–152
  marriage of, 193
  medical student, 165–179
  neuroimaging and, 269–271
  in Paris, 170
  prodigy, 158–160
  racism/sexism and, 262–267
  romance and, 191–192
  Société de Anthropologie
      debates and, 142–144
  studies of genetics, 253–260
  thermometric crown and,
      269–271
  time line of, 319–320
  trepanation/surgery and,
      271–275
  writings on cancer and,
      246–248
  year of his birth, 152–154
Broca Museum, 264
Broca's area, 6
Broca's Brain, 171–172
Broca's family
  ancestral village, 148–149
  historians, 149–151
  history of, 145–164
  Huguenot persecution and,
      146–148
  lineage, 151–152
Broca's Folly, 248

Broca's Society, 185–186
Brodmann, Korbinian, 181
Brooklyn Museum, 13
Brownlee, James, 28
Bulletin de la Société
    Anatomique, translation
    of Broca's 1861 paper,
    289–318
Burke, Robert O'Hara, 138
Butler, Robert Olen, 105, 106

C

Cadavers, inflections from,
    181–182
Calvin, Jean, 147
Cartesian philosophy, 14
Catalytic spatula case, 127
Causality, 45
Cautiousness, 43
Cave, paleolithic paintings in,
    145
Cephalametrics, 260–261
Cerebral hemispheres, results of
    removal of, 50
Cerebral localization, 64, 118,
    122, 230, 233, 296
  aphemia anatomy and, 299
  Aubertin on, 129
  Bateman and, 86
  Bouillaud and, 118
  Broca and, 71, 213
  of disrupted speech, 275
  Gall and, 25, 33, 99
  of language, 163
  M. Leborgne and, 4
  negative response to, 126
  Spencer and, 133
Cerebrum, Flourens research
    and, 50–51
Chambers, Robert, *Vestiges of
    the Natural History of
    Creation*, published, 30

Chapel of the Val de Grace, 81
Charité, 117
Charles V, 198
"Charterhouse," 135
Cheffer, Marie, 161
Christian Phrenological Society,
    established, 30
Church of Genevieve-du-Mont,
    18
Church of the Celestins, 250
Clairin, Georges, 156
Claudel, Camille, 161
Clemens, Samuel L., 60–63
Clinical Aphasiology Conference,
    68–69
  Web site, 69
Cluny, Thermes de, 252
Code, Christopher, *Milestones in
    the History of Aphasia*, 69
Coencas, Simon, 145
Collège de Sainte-Barbe, 160,
    165, 168
  Broca tutors at, 167
College of Medicine at Florida
    State University, 3
Coloring, 45
Combativeness, 42
Combe, Andrew, 28, 57–66
Combe, George, 28–29, 57–66
  on Amativeness, 52
  death of, 30
  differentiate the sizes of,
    45–46
  lectures in Germany, 30
  published Constitution of Man,
    29
Communal College of Sainte-Foy,
    159
Comparison, 45
Concentrativeness, 36
Conscientiousness, 43
Constitution of Man, published,
    29

Constructiveness, 42
Coober Pedy, 86
Cordeliers, 198
Cordeliers Convent, 198
Corn, Broca's research, 253
Cornflowers, Broca's research,
    253–260
Cortical localization, 135–137,
    235, 239
  British expansions on, 131–134
  Marc Dax and, 237
Cranial anthropometry, 260–261
Crapper, Thomas, 137
Crichton, Alexander, 67, 90–92
Crimean War, 187
Cutting the Stone, 85

ⅅ

Dally, Eugene, 253
Damasio, António, 14–16
Danton, Georges, 198
Darley, Frederic L., 70, 225
Darwin, Charles, 126, 184, 249
Darwin, Etty, treated at Lane's
    hydropathic establishment,
    30
Dax, Gustave, 238–239
Dax, Marc, 237–238
De Medici, Catherine, 147
Debates
  at *Société de Anthropologie*,
    140–142
  1861, 135–137
  Broca and, 142–144
Degas, Edgar, 161
Dejerine, Joseph Jules, 204–205
Delarue, Jacques, 205
Democritus, 9
Department of the Seine, 253
Descartes, René, 11, 14–24
  admired by Flourens, 47
  death of, 18

early life of, 17
photo of skull, 23–24
Descartes' Bones, 18
Destructiveness, 42
Deux Magots, 14
DeVille, J., 29
Dewey, James, 133
Dewey, John, 133
Diabetes, 9
Dickens, Charles, 138
Diogenes, 9
Discourse on the Method, 16
Dôme des Invalides, 81
Donkin, B., 29
Dordogne River, 145
Dreyfus affair, 157
Dualism, 14
Dublin Phrenological Society,
    published, 29
Dublin Quarterly Journal, 93, 94
Dumfries Phrenological Society,
    established, 30
Dupanloup, Félix-Antoine-
    Philibert, 277
Dupuytren, Guillaume, 197
Dupuytren Museum, 6, 161
Dyslexia, acquired, 71

ℰ

Eastern Counties Asylum for
    Idiots, 86
Eau des Melisse des Carmes, 144
Ebert, Theodor, on Descartes
    death, 18
École d'Anthropologie, 252
École de Medicine, 161, 163, 178
École Polytechnique, 159
Edict of Nantes, 108, 147
Edinburgh Phrenological Society
  established, 28
  last meeting of, 31
  schism within, 29

Edinburgh Review
  publishes Jeffrey's attack on
    phrenology, 29
  Spurzheim criticized in, 28
Eiffel Tower, 187
Elements of Phrenology,
    published, 29
Elliotson, John, 29
Ellis, William, 29
Emancipation Proclamation, 137
Endocarditis, Bouillaud's
    identification of, 118
Endocardium, Bouillaud's
    identification of, 118
Engeldue, W., declares
    phrenology proves
    materialism correct, 30
Epilepsy, Hippocrates on, 11
Epps, John, 30
Ethnological Society of Paris,
    250–251
Eventuality, 45
Executions, 18th century France,
    103
Exeter Phrenological Society,
    established, 30
External senses, 44

F

Faculté de Médecine, 49
Faculties, 36–45
Faculty of Medicine, Broca
    enrolls in, 181
Falret, Jules, analysis of aphasia,
    67
Father Charlet, 17
Finger, Stanley, 17
Firmness, 43
First Taranaki War, 138
Fischof, Sedelmeyer, 157
Fitzsimons Army Hospital, 76
"Flaws of Evolution," 255

Fleischl-Marxow, Ernst von, 182
Flourens, Jean-Pierre, 47–52
Form, 44
Forster, Thomas, 28
Fosdick, W. W., 138
Fowler Institute, established, 31
Fowler, Lorenzo Niles, 29
  establishes the Fowler
    Institute, 31
  travels to Britain, 30
Fowler, Orson Squire, 29
  travels to Britain, 30
France
  18th century executions in,
    103
  Calvinism and, 147
  freedom of religion in, 108
Francis II, forbids Gall to lecture
    or publish, 27
Franciscan monks, 198
Franco-Prussian War, 113, 256
Frankfurt, treaty of, 259
Freedom of religion, French law
    and, 108
Freethinkers Society, Broca and,
    185–186
French Anthropology Society,
    250–252
French brains, legendary,
    205–212
French Codex, 193
French National Biblioteque, 129
French Senate, Broca, Pierre Paul
    and, 275–280
Full moon effect, 267–269

G

Gage, Phineas, 97
Galen, 9
Gall, Franz Josef, 5, 25
  American tour, 54–57
  birth of, 26–27

Bouillaud and, 116, 118, 124
cerebral localization concepts
  and, 99
death of, 29, 64
denied membership in
  Academy of Sciences, 64
eyes and speech and, 33–34
life of, 31
localized language and,
  119–120
method used by, 31–32
phrenology time line and, 27
visits London, 65
Games Workshop on Rue
  Serpente, 173
Gerdy, Nicholas, 175–176
Gesner, Johann, aphasia and, 67
"Global aphasia," 225
Goodglass, Harold, 70
Goodglass Aphasia Research
  Center, 76
Gordon, John, 28, 57
"Grand Scheme for the
  Americas," 187–188
Gratiolet, Louis Pierre, 129–131,
  230–231
  Société de Anthropologie
    debates and, 140–144
Great Comet of 1861, 138
Great Expectations, 138
The Great Hall of the Bulls, 145
Green, Christopher D.,
  translation of Broca's 1861
  paper, 289–318
Guillotin, Joseph Ignace, 103–105
  death of, 107
Gulliver's Travels, 77

H

Halley's Comet, Gall's birth and,
  26
Hamilton, Sir William, 29

"Hammer Palsy," 98
Handbuch der Phrenologie, 30
Harlow, John, 97
Harvard Medical School,
  Spurzheim's skull on
  display at, 56
Haussmann, Georges-Eugène,
  188–191
Hawkins, J., 30
Head bumps, 36–45
Health Restored to the Sick, 156
Heart
  Bouillaud's weighing/
    measuring of, 118
  Pascal on, 16
Henderson Trust, 56
Henry IV, 147
  issues Edict of Nates, 108
Hephsestic Hemiplegia, 98–99
Hippocrates, 9, 65
  on epilepsy, 11
Hirschfeld, E., *Handbuch der
  Phrenologie*, 30
Hope, 43–44
Hôpital de la Salpêtrière, 269
Hospital Broca, 154
Hôtel-Dieu, 167
Huges, Bart, 272
Hugo, Victor, 259
Huguenots
  Edict of Nantes and, 108
  exodus from France, 148
  persecution of, 146–148
Hun, Thomas, 95–97
Hundred Days (1815), 116

I

Ideality, 43–44
Ideational apraxia, 72
Ideomotor apraxia, 72
Impressionism, 1
Index of Forbidden Books, 21

Individuality, 44
Infections, from contaminated
    cadavers, 181–182
Ingres, Jean Auguste Dominique,
    193
Inhabitiveness, 36
Inner ear, function of
    semicircular canals, 50
Institut Anthropologique, 253
Institutional Review Board (IRB),
    105
Intellectual faculties, 44–45
Invalides gardens, 81
Iodine therapy, 193–194
IRB (Institutional Review Board),
    105

J

Jackson, John Hughlings, 92–93,
    133–134
Jackson, S., 94–95
*JAMA (Journal of the American
    Medical Society)*, 283
Jardin des Plantes, 165, 256
    Gall's skull housed in, 65–66
Jeffreys, Francis, attacks
    phrenology, 29
Johnson, Samuel, on his own
    aphasia, 77–78
Journal of Radiology, 282
*Journal of the American Medical
    Society (JAMA)*, 283
*Journal of the Balkan Union of
    Oncology*, 247
*Journal of the Society of Medical
    Practice of Montpellier*, 83
June Days revolution, 176–179

K

Karr, Jean-Baptiste, 76
Kinetic apraxia, 72

"King of the Urban Forest," 165
Klumpke, Augusta Marie, 205
Knowing faculties, 44–45
Kussmaul, Adolph, 90

L

*La Bibliothèque nationale de
    France*, 83
La Chartreuse de Parme, 135
La Haye-Descartes, 17
Lady and the Unicon, 252–253
Lancaster Phrenological Society,
    established, 30
Lancet, on Broca's death, 282
Langerhans, Paul, 181
Language, 45
    localized, Gall and, 119
Large Clenched Left Hand, 161
Larrey, D. J., 78–81, 86
Lascaux II, 145
Lauret, François, 174–175
Le Boeuf, Justine Marie, 189–191
Le Figaro, 140–144
Le Flore, 14
"Le grand lobe limbique," 246
Le Pere Goriot, 116
Le Rouge et le Noir, 134
Le Temps, 127, 279
Leaves of Grass, 60
Leblanc, Georgette, 157
Leborgne, M., 4, 6, 73, 129,
    225–226
    preserved brain, 206–217
        conclusions after examining,
        212–217
    imaging and, 220–225
Leeches, 59
    treating aphasia with, 87–88,
    90, 94
Lelong, M., 4, 6
    preserved brain, 218–220
        imaging and, 220–225

Leroux, Gaston, 189
Les Miserables, 259
"Lesions of the Left Half of the Encephalon Coincident with the Forgetting of Signs of Thinking," 238
Lichtheim, Ludwig, 74–76
Lie-detectors, 26
Liepmann, Hugo Karl, 71
  apraxia and, 72–74
Limbic lobe, 158, 244–246
Limbic system, 244–246
"Limbus," 246
Locality, 45
Localization, cerebral, 64, 118, 122, 230, 233, 296
  aphemia anatomy and, 299
  Aubertin on, 129
  Bateman and, 86
  Bouillaud and, 118
  Broca and, 71, 213
  of disrupted speech, 275
  Gall and, 25, 33, 99
  of language, 163
  M. Leborgne and, 4
  negative response to, 126
  Spencer and, 133
Localized language, Gall and, 119
Lokhorst, Gert-Jan, 240
London Christian Phrenological Society, established, 30
London Phrenological Society, established, 29
London plane tree, 165
London Science Museum, 125
Longfellow, Henry Wadsworth, 138
Lordat, Jacques, 83–86
Lost Worlds: Narratives of Language and the Brain, 83
Loth-Cazalis, Therese, 157

Louis XIV, 107–111
  Huguenots and, 147
Louis XVI, 107
"Love Me Tender," 138
Lugol, Augustine, 193, 194–196
Lugol, Jean Guillaume, 193–194
Luther, Martin, 147

M

Machu, Maurice, 157–158
Mackenzie, Sir George Steuart, 28
Mackersey, Lindsey, 28
Macmillan, Malcolm, 97
"Madame Guillotine," 107
Maitland, Gerald, 50
Manchester Phrenological Society, established, 29
Manez, Louis, 78–79
Mansfield, Jayne, 105
Marie Antoinette, 107
Marjolin, Jean-Nicolas, 166
Marsal, Jacques, 145
Mayo Clinic, 157, 225
Mazarin, Jules, Louis XIV and, 108–109
McNeil, Malcolm, aphasia and, 68–69
"Median claw hand," 161
Meditation, Descartes advocates, 17
Medulla oblongata, results of removal of, 50
Medusa, 105
Melville, Herman, 64
Mendel, Gregor, 253
Mennecier, Philippe, 18, 66, 138
Michelangelo, 161
Milestones in the History of Aphasia, 69
Mind, as separate from brain, 14–15

Moby Dick, 64
Monet, Claude, 1, 161
Monsieur Grat, 17
Montauban, 193
Montparnasse Cemetery, 286
Mortillet, Louis Laurent Gabriel,
    252–253
Mount Auburn cemetery,
    Spurzheim buried at, 56
Moxon, W., 238
"Moxon and the Flying Trapeze,"
    238
Munod-Broca, Phillippe, 282–283
Musée d' Assistance-Publique,
    156
Musée de d'Histoire Naturelle,
    130
Musée de l'Homme, 256
    Gall's skull housed in, 65–66
Musée d'Orsay, 4, 193
Musée Dupuytren, 4, 197–205,
    286
Museum of Man, 264
Museum of Middle Ages, 252
Museum of Pathological
    Anatomy, 197
Mustafa Agha, 13
*Mysterious Death of René
    Descartes*, 18

N

Napoleon Bonaparte, 111–113
Napoleon III, 113, 153, 176–177,
    187–188
    death of, 191
    rebuilding of Paris, 188–191
National Institutes of Health, 269
"National razor," 107
National University of Singapore,
    27
National Veterans Aphasia
    Centers, 76

Neue Teutsche Merkur, 27
New York Academy of Medicine,
    13
New York Historical Society, 13
Noel, Robert, lectures in
    Germany, 30
Norfolk and Norwich Hospital, 86
Number, 45

O

"Observations Tending to Prove
    the Constant Coincidence
    of Disturbances of Speech
    with a Lesion of the Left
    Hemisphere of the Brain,"
    238
*An Odd Kind of Fame: Stories of
    Phineas Gage*, 97
Odéon Theatre, 156
Order, 45
Orfila, Mathieu Joseph
    Bonaventure, 119, 197
Organs, differentiate the sizes of,
    45–46
On the Origin of Species, 249
Ouimet, Charles, 3–4, 206
Outlines of Phrenology, 35

P

Palais Garnier, 188
Paleolithic cave paintings, 145
Palsy, hammer, 98
Pantheon, 18–22
Paris, Napoléon III's rebuilding
    of, 188–191
Paris Academy of Medicine, 127
Paris Museum of Natural History,
    21
Paris Phrenological Society, 29
Park Street Church, Spurzheim's
    funeral at, 56

Pascal, Blaise, 15
on the heart, 16
Pasteur, Louis, 259, 282
"Pathography of Love," 85
Paul, Pierre, 163
Paul Broca: Explorer of the Brain, 149–151
Pearce, J. M. S., 130
Petite Chronique des Theatres, 144
The Phantom of the Opera, 189
Philippe, Louis, 187
Philoprogenitiveness, 36, 53–54
Phrenological Cabinet, 60
"Phrenological Fowlers," 30
Phrenological Journal (of Edinburgh), founded, 29
Phrenological Society of Edinburgh
founded, 57
inherited Spurzheim's materials, 56
Phrenologist, described, 26
Phrenology
early history of, 25–27
faculties and head bumps, 36–45
misuses of, 65
principles of, 35
time line of, 27–31
The Physiognomical System of Drs. Gall and Spurzheim, 28
Pinel, Philippe, 173–174
Pioneers of Psychology, 77
"*Platane à feuille d'érable*," 165
Plato, 9
Pliny the Elder, aphasia and, 68
Pliny the Younger, 68
Pneumatic physiologists, 11
Poe, Edgar Allan, 60
Polygraphs, 26
Porch, Bruce, aphasia and, 68

Poulton, George R., 138
Pozzi, Catherine, 157
Pozzi, Jacques, 157
Pozzi, Jean, 157
Pozzi, Samuel-Jean, 154–158, 259, 284–285
Presley, Elvis, 138
Princess Elisabeth of Bohemia, 17
Principles of Psychology, 133
"Prison for lunatics," 173–174
Propensities, 36, 42
Prosector's paronychia, 182
Prosector's wart, 182
Protestant Reformation, 147
Protestants, exodus from France, 148
Proust, Marcel, 156
Provain, 148
Prunier, Theotime, 105
Pythagoras, 9

Q

Quarterly Review, Spurzheim criticized in, 28
Queen Christina, Descartes and, 17

R

Racism, 262–267
Raleigh, Sir Walter, 105
Ravidat, Marcel, 145
"*Recherches cliniques propres d' demontrer que la perte de la parole correspond d la lésion des lobules anterieurs dit cerveau, et á confirmer l'opinion de M. Gall sur le siegede l'orga'ne du langage articulé*," 118

Recherches expérimentales sur les propriétés et les fonctions du système nerveux, 49
The Red and the Black, 134
Reflecting faculties, 45
Reign of Terror, 107
Remembrance of Things Past, 156
Renoir, Pierre-Auguste, 163
Revolt in the Vendée, 107
Revue d'Anthropologie, 249
Robespierre, Maximillien, 26
Rodin, François-Auguste-René, 161–163
Rodin, Jean-Baptiste, 161
Roi Soleil, 107–111
Rolandic fissure, 71
"Rousing the Dormant Faculty of Language," 99
Roussy, Gustave, 205
Royal College of Physicians, 86

S

Sacks, Oliver, 85
Sagan, Carl, 170–172
Saint Francis of Assisi, 198
Sainte-Foy-la-Grande, 148–149
Saint-Hilaire, E. Geoffroy, 64
Scheve, Gustav, lectures in Germany, 30
Schiller, Francis, 149
Schmidt, Tobias, 105
School of Anthropology, 252
Science, on Broca's death, 282
Second French Empire, fall of, 256
Secretiveness, 42
Self-esteem, 42
Sensory aphasia, 71
Sentiments
    common with lower animals, 42–43

proper to man, 43–44
Severance, 105
Sex, amativeness and, 52–54
Sexism, 262–267
Shanghai, battle of, 138
Sheffield Phrenological Society, established, 30
Shiloh, battle of, 187
Shorto, Russell, 18
Sisley, Alfred, 161
Size, 44
Skeptomai, 185
Smith, Edwin, 11, 13
Société de Anthropologie, 121, 126–127, 129, 140, 238
    debates at, 140–142
    1861, 135–137
    Broca and, 142–144
Société Phrénologique, 116
Society of Anthropology, 4, 5
    translation of Broca's 1861 paper, 289–318
Society of Biology, 250
Sorbonne, 167
Souche, M., 144
Spencer, Cornelia Phillips, 137
Spencer, Herbert, 132–134
Spirit, 14
Spurzheim, J. G.
    American tour, 54–57
    begins publishing on the new system, 28
    death of, 29, 54–56
    defends views in Edinburgh, 57
    Gall and, 27–28
    lecture tour, 46–47
St. Germaine des Prés, 20–21
Stendhal, 134
Struve, Gustav von, 30
Suez Canal, 187
Sun King, 107–111
    Huguenots and, 147

Surgical Papers of the Egyptians, 67
Surgical Papyrus, 11–13
Swift, Jonathan, 14, 77

T

Taiping Rebellion, 138
Tan (Leborgne, M.), 4, 6, 73, 129
  conclusions after examining, 212–217
  preserved brain, 206–217
Tannhauser, 138
Taranaki War, 138
Tesak, Jürgen, *Milestones in the History of Aphasia*, 69
"The Terror," 107
Theophrastus, 9
Third French Republic, 256
Thompson, Henry, 191
"Three Glorious Days," 159
TIAs (Transient ischemic attacks), 135
Time, 45
Topinard, Paul, 253
Trait des Tumeurs, 246
Transient ischemic attacks (TIAs), 135
A Treatise on Gynaecology, 154
Treaty of Frankfurt, 259
Trepanation, 271–275
Trousseau, Armand, aphasia and, 67
Tune, 45
Twain, Mark, on phrenology, 60–63

U

University of Paris School of Medicine, 3

University of Pittsburgh, Clinical Aphasiology Conference and, 67

V

Van Wyhe, John van, 27
  criticizes Gall and Spurzheim, 34, 42–43
Veneration, 43
Verghese, Abraham, 85
Vestiges of the Natural History of Creation, published, 30
Veterans Administration Hospital in Albuquerque, Clinical Aphasiology Conference and, 68
"Violon d'Ingres," 193
Von Fleischl-Marxow, Ernst, 182

W

Waddell, William, 28
Wagner, Richard, 138
Wakefield Phrenological Society, established, 29
Warren Museum, Spurzheim's skull on display at, 56
Wars of Religion, 147
Watson, Hewett, abandons phrenology, 30
Weight, 45
Welsh, David, 28
Wernicke, Carl, 71
  Liepmann and, 72
Wernicke's aphasia, 71
Wernicke's area, 71
Whitman, Walt, 60
Wills, William John, 138
Wit, 43–44
Wivenhoe Pocket, 70
Wizard of Oz, 11
Wonder, 44

Zeitschrift für Phrenologie,
      established, 30
Zola, Emile, 157